Seashore Animals of the Southeast

SEASHORE ANIMALS

OF THE

SOUTHEAST

A GUIDE TO COMMON SHALLOW-WATER
INVERTEBRATES OF THE
SOUTHEASTERN ATLANTIC COAST

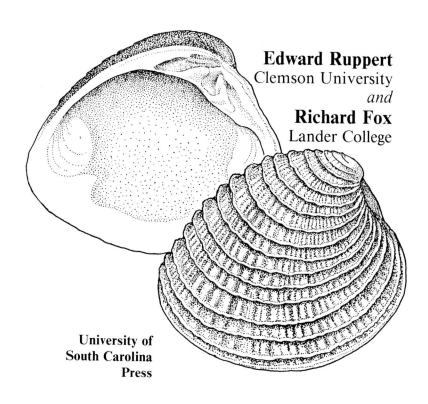

Edward Ruppert
Clemson University
and
Richard Fox
Lander College

University of
South Carolina
Press

© 1988 University of South Carolina

Published in Columbia, South Carolina,
by the University of South Carolina Press

Manufactured in the United States of America

18 17 16 15 14 13 12 11 10 09   9 8 7 6 5

Library of Congress Cataloging-in-Publication Data

Ruppert, Edward E.
    Seashore animals of the Southeast : a guide to common shallow-water
invertebrates of the southeastern Atlantic Coast / Edward Ruppert and Richard Fox.
    p.   cm.
    Bibliography: p.
    Includes index.
    ISBN 0-87249-534-5. ISBN 0-87249-535-3 (pbk).
    1. Marine invertebrates—Southeastern States—Identification. 2. Marine
invertebrates—Atlantic Coast (U.S.)—Identification. 3. Seashore biology—
Southern States. 4. Seashore biology—Atlantic Coast (U.S.) I. Fox, Richard S.
II. Title.
    QL 135.R87 1988   87-27349
    592.0975—dc 19

ISBN 13: 978-0-87249-535-7 (pbk)

To Ette

CONTENTS

Seashore Animals of the Southeast

INTRODUCTION

Seashore Animals of the Southeast is a field guide for the identification of shallow-water invertebrate animals of the Atlantic coast of the southeastern United States. It is designed for use by the public but also contains information that will make it valuable to classes at the high school and college level and to graduate students in marine biology.

Until now, the Southeast has been without a field guide for the identification of its marine animals. Several very good guides for the Northeast, the Florida Keys, and the Pacific coast are available but they include few of the southeastern species. *Seashore Animals of the Southeast* covers the area from Cape Hatteras, North Carolina to Cape Canaveral, Florida (Fig. 1). It will also be useful in the Gulf of Mexico, and, to a limited extent, in south Florida and the middle Atlantic states. Of the approximately 1000 species of coastal marine invertebrate animals in the Southeast, 740 of the most common or conspicuous are discussed and 360 are illustrated. The animals included are those species inhabiting waters of wading depth or less that are large enough to be observed without special equipment. Only invertebrate animals are covered as there are other guides to fishes and birds of the region. Students and professional biologists should find it to be a useful introduction to the fauna of the area.

3

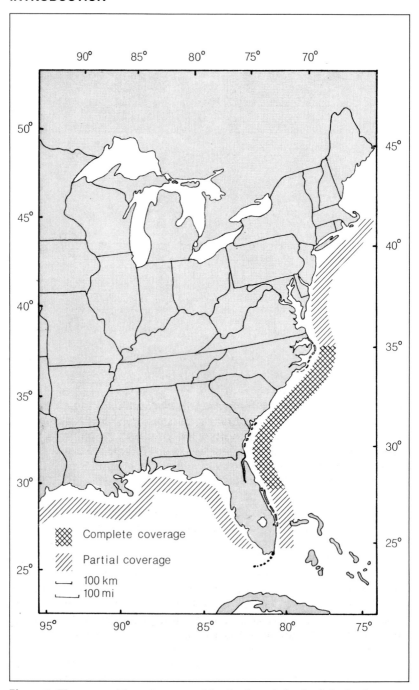

Figure 1 The geographic region covered by *Seashore Animals of the Southeast*

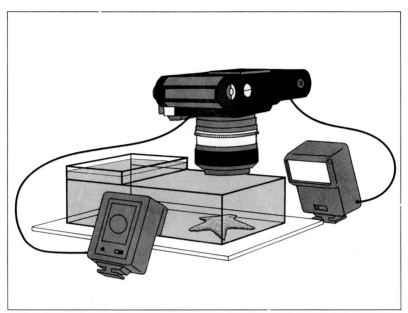

Figure 2 Photographic apparatus used to make most of the photographs of aquatic invertebrates.

Seashore Animals of the Southeast includes 100 color photographs, 75 black and white photographs, and 200 line drawings. All photographs and drawings are new. The color photographs were made by the authors during six years of field work on the southeastern coast. The photographs were all made from living specimens using a single lens reflex camera with a flash arrangement as shown in Figure 2.The black and white photographs were made from the color photographs and the line drawings were made by John Norton, also from the color photographs. The information in the text is based on the authors' field work and on the literature.

One of the reasons for publishing this guide is to popularize our coastal invertebrates and stimulate an interest in them. This desired interest is a two-edged sword however that could manifest itself either as increased support for safeguarding the environment or as increased pressure on already threatened marine ecosystems. We must all realize that the sea is not an inexhaustible resource that can withstand unlimited exploitation. Coastal ecosystems are fragile, vulnerable, and accessible to thoughtless collectors, professional scientists and laypersons alike. They cannot withstand indiscriminate and unnecessary collecting and continue to remain the fascinating natural systems they are. Whenever possible, the animals and plants in these habitats should be enjoyed and studied in their habitat without removing them to home or laboratory. This is an observer's, not a collector's, guide and it is

5

INTRODUCTION

designed to be used in the field to enhance your enjoyment and understanding of living animals in the context of their natural ecological communities. It is not necessary or desirable to collect and kill the animals to enjoy them. On excursions into these habitats make an effort to leave behind no reminder of your visit and be careful to return stones, boards, and oyster clumps to their original positions after you look beneath them. Citizens of the Florida Keys and the Pacific Coast have learned to their sorrow that collectors can have an undesirable impact on coastal communities and we hope to avoid the habitat destruction and the depauperation of faunas that has occurred in those areas.

The heart of this guide is the species identification chapter with its photographs and drawings. This section illustrates and discusses all of the species that are likely to be found by casual observers. Many other species are discussed in the text and are compared with the illustrated species. Preceding the identification section is a short illustrated key to the major groups of animals. This key will give you some idea of the group to which an unknown animal belongs. It is organized around the general appearance of the animals.

For more serious beachcombers and students, the identification chapter is followed by chapters on the biology of our marine animals and on simple physical and biological oceanography. A glossary is included to help you understand the technical terms in the text. A chapter on classification gives the complete biological classification of all southeastern species mentioned in the book. It includes important synonyms and the author and date of publication of most scientific names. A short bibliography will be useful to those who desire more information or who want to identify species not included in this guide.

During the six years this book was in preparation the authors have enjoyed the indispensable assistance of numerous individuals and institutions. We received financial support for the project from the Lander Foundation, the Lander College Faculty Development Fund, the Belle W. Baruch Institute of the University of South Carolina, and the Southern Regional Educational Board. The field and laboratory work essential to the publication of this guide would not have been possible without this support.

Laboratory space, boat time, and living accommodations have been provided by the Belle W. Baruch Laboratory of the University of South Carolina, the University of North Carolina Institute of Marine Sciences, the University of North Carolina at Wilmington Department of Marine Sciences, the South Carolina Marine Resources Research Institute, the Grice Laboratory of the College of Charleston, the University of South Carolina at Beaufort Department of Marine Science, the Marine Institute of the University of Georgia, and the Whitney Laboratory of the University of Florida. We are grateful to their directors and resident scientists, Dr. Dennis Allen, Dr. F. John Vernberg, Dr. Dirk

Frankenberg, Dr. Charles Peterson, Dr. Anne McCrary, Dr. Victor Burrell, Dr. Robert Van Dolah, Dr. Charles Biernbaum, Dr. Edsel Caine, Dr. Ronald Kneib, and Dr. Michael Greenberg. Without their help the field work could not have been accomplished. We appreciate their hospitality and cooperation.

While at these laboratories we have enjoyed and profited from the enthusiastic cooperation of the resident staff and students. We appreciate the help of Wendy Allen, Lynn Barker, Mark Caldwell, Kathy Heinsohn, Kathy Klemanowicz, David Knott, Roberta McCutchen, Gino Olmi, Carolina O'Rourke, Beth Roland, and Hal Summerlin. In the field we have often benefited from the companionship and expertise of Drs. Charles Jenner, Ron Kneib, Anne McCrary, Thomas Fox, and Edsel Caine.

The manuscript has been read by many biologists and their criticism has increased the accuracy, completeness, and readability of the text. We are deeply grateful for the time they have devoted to this tedious task. Dr. Stephen Stancyk (University of South Carolina) and Mr. Rudy Mancke (South Carolina Educational Television) read the entire manuscript and made several important suggestions. Dr. Charles Jenner (University of North Carolina) and Dr. W. Herbert Wilson (University of Washington) read the complete species identification section. Mr. Hugh Porter (University of North Carolina) and Mr. Richard Petit read the mollusc identification section. Dr. Austin Williams (National Marine Fisheries Systematics Laboratory), Dr. Richard Heard (Gulf Research Laboratory), and Dr. Anne McCrary (University of North Carolina at Wilmington), reviewed the arthropod section. The chapter on sponges was examined by Dr. Klaus Rützler (Smithsonian Institution) and that on Hydrozoa and Scyphozoa by Dr. Dale Calder (Royal Ontario Museum). Dr. Daphne Fautin (California Academy of Sciences) and Dr. Kenneth Sebens (Northeastern University) read the Anthozoa section. The phoronid, brachiopod, and bryozoan sections were reviewed by Dr. Judith Winston (American Museum of Natural History). Dr. Stephen Stancyk (University of South Carolina) and Mr. Tom Vandergon (Clemson University) read the phoronid descriptions. The tunicate section was reviewed by Dr. Françoise Monniot and Dr. Claude Monniot (Museum National d'Histoire Naturelle) and by Dr. Craig Young (Harbor Branch Oceanographic Institution). The echinoderm section was read by Dr. Stephen Stancyk (University of South Carolina, Dr. Gordon Hendler (Los Angeles County Natural History Museum), Mr. John Miller (Harbor Branch Oceanographic Institution), and Dr. David Pawson (Smithsonian Institution). Dr. Mary Rice (Smithsonian Institution) read the sipunculan pages. Dr. W. Herbert Wilson (University of Washington) and Mr. Peter Smith (Clemson University) read the annelid chapter. The nemertean section was re-

INTRODUCTION

viewed by Dr. James Turbeville (Clemson University). The arthropod and mollusc chapters were read by Ms. Ellen Damalas, Ms. Inga Hunt, and Ms. Betty Williams, all of Lander College.

We have encountered many species identification problems as we prepared this guide and have relied on the assistance of numerous specialists who gave freely of their time and knowledge. Dr. Dale Calder (Royal Ontario Museum) and Dr. Kenneth Sebens (Northeastern University) identified some troublesome cnidarians for us. With the molluscs we had the help of Mr. Hugh Porter (University of North Carolina), Mr. Richard Petit, Dr. Kenneth Boss (Harvard University), Dr. Thomas Fox (North Georgia College), Dr. Paul Mikkelson (Harbor Branch Oceanographic Institution), Dr. Malcolm Edmunds (Lancashire Polytechnic), Dr. Donald Moore (University of Miami), Dr. Robert Robertson (Academy of Natural Sciences of Philadelphia), and Dr. Eric Powell (Texas A & M University). Dr. Judith Winston (American Museum of Natural History) and Dr. Frank Maturo (University of Florida) assisted with the bryozoans. Dr. Stephen Stancyk (University of South Carolina), Dr. David Pawson (Smithsonian Institution), Mr. John Miller (Harbor Branch Oceanographic Institution), and Dr. Gordon Hendler (Los Angeles County Natural History Museum) helped with the brittle stars and sea cucumbers. Dr. James Turbeville (Clemson University) identified several nemerteans and Dr. Klaus Rützler (Smithsonian Institution) helped with the sponges. Ms. Elizabeth Balser (Clemson University) identified the hemichordate, *Ptychodera jamaicensis,* for us. Dr. Richard Heard (Gulf Research Laboratory), Dr. Austin Williams (National Marine Fisheries Systematics Laboratory), Dr. Allan Child (Smithsonian Institution), Dr. Larry Harris (University of New Hampshire), and Dr. Willis Wirth (United States Department of Agriculture) assisted with difficult arthropods. Dr. Françoise Monniot and Dr. Claude Monniot (Museum National d'Histoire Naturelle) provided valuable assistance with the tunicates. Dr. Christer Erséus (University of Göteborg) helped with the oligochaetes. We had assistance with the polychaetes from Dr. Marian Pettibone (Smithsonian Institution), Dr. Meredith Jones (Smithsonian Institution), Dr. Kristian Fauchald (Smithsonian Institution), Dr. Stephen Gardiner (Bryn Mawr College), and Dr. Thomas Perkins (Florida Department of Natural Resources). Dr. Larry Dyck (Clemson University) identified seaweeds for us. We are grateful to Dr. Frank Schwartz (University of North Carolina Institute of Marine Sciences) for assistance with the fishes.

Mr. Tom Smoyer and Mr. John Miller, both of the Harbor Branch Oceanographic Institution, generously provided advice on photographic technique. We extend special thanks to John Norton of Clemson University for his careful and faithful rendering of the line drawings in this guide.

ILLUSTRATED KEY TO SEASHORE ANIMALS

Most of us have little difficulty recognizing the major groups of terrestrial organisms. As land-dwelling animals ourselves, we are familiar with and distinguish between similar but unrelated organisms, such as hawkmoths and hummingbirds, earthworms and snakes, and mushrooms and flowers. On the other hand, the sea is foreign to us, many of its animals are unfamiliar and are not represented on land. Like animals on land, unrelated marine organisms may resemble each other, function similarly, and occupy similar habitats. Consequently, there is often a conflict between the appearance of an animal and its true identity. The following key has been designed to help beginners classify animals correctly. Unlike the other chapters in this book, this one groups animals according to their overall appearance rather than to genealogical, or evolutionary, relationship. To use this key, choose the best match between the animal in hand and one of the illustrations. Then follow the reference accompanying each illustration to the appropriate section in the animal identification chapter. If a specimen resembles more than one illustration then all the references should be checked.

SLENDER, ERECT, BUSHY OR PLANTLIKE

Fig. 3
Hydroids 0.2–4″
Cnidaria (p. 26)

Fig. 4
Moss Animals 0.5–6″+ (1.3–15+ cm)
Bryozoa (p. 82)

Fig. 5
Hydroids 1–4″ (2.5–10 cm)
Cnidaria (p. 26)

Fig. 6
Sea Squirts 0.1–3″+ (0.3–8 cm)
Chordata (p. 59)

THICK BRANCHES OR LOBES

Fig. 7
Sponges 1–4″ (2.5–10 cm)
Porifera (p. 17)

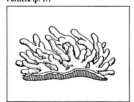

Fig. 8
Sponges 1–8″+ (2.5–20+ cm)
Porifera (p. 17)

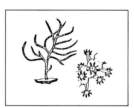

Fig. 9
Sea Whips 2–20″+ (5–51+ cm)
Cnidaria (p. 26)

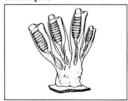

Fig. 10
Tunicates 1–2″ (2.5–5 cm)
Chordata (p. 59)

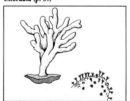

Fig. 11
Moss Animals 1–6″+ (2.5–15 cm)
Bryozoa (p. 82)

ILLUSTRATED KEY TO SEASHORE ANIMALS

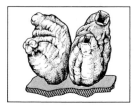

Fig. 12
Sea Squirts 2–4″ (5–10 cm)
Chordata (p. 59)

LOW BUMPS, PITS, CUSHIONS

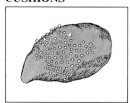

Fig. 13
Boring Sponges 0.1–8″+ (0.2–20cm)
Porifera (p. 17)

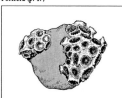

Fig. 14
Corals 2″ (5 cm)
Cnidaria (p. 26)

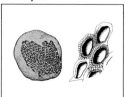

Fig. 15
Moss Animals 1″+ (2.5+ cm)
Bryozoa (p. 82)

Fig. 16
Sea Pansies 2″ (5 cm)
Cnidaria (p. 26)

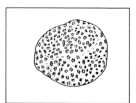

Fig. 17
Sea Pork 1–4″ (2.5–10 cm)
Chordata (p. 59)

Fig. 18
Sponges 5–10″ (13–25 cm)
Porifera (p. 17)

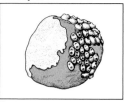

Fig. 19
Tunicates 4–8″ (10–20 cm)
Chordata (p. 59)

FLOWERLIKE

Fig. 20
Anemones 0.25–4″ (0.6–10 cm)
Cnidaria (p. 26)

Fig. 21
Phoronids 6″ (15 cm)
Phoronida (p. 80)

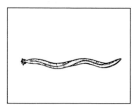

Fig. 22
Sea Cucumbers 6″ (15 cm)
Echinodermata (p. 69)

Fig. 23
Peanut Worms 1–8″ (2.5–20 cm)
Sipuncula (p. 89)

Fig. 24
Fanworms 1″ (2.5 cm)
Annelida (p. 185)

Fig. 25
Sponges 0.5″ (1.3 cm)
Porifera (p. 17)

Fig. 26
Nodders 0.5–1″ (1.3–2.5 cm)
Kamptozoa (p. 87)

10

ILLUSTRATED KEY TO SEASHORE ANIMALS

FLAT AND SOFT

Fig. 27
Flatworms 0.5-2″ (1.3-5 cm)
Platyhelminthes (p. 180)

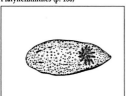

Fig. 28
Sea Slugs 1.5″ (3.8 cm)
Mollusca (p. 92)

Fig. 29
Sea Slugs 1.5″ (3.8 cm)
Mollusca (p. 92)

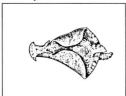

Fig. 30
Sea Hares 8″ (20 cm)
Mollusca (p. 92)

OCTOPUS OR SQUIDLIKE

Fig. 31
Octopus 8-24″ (20-61 cm)
Mollusca (p. 92)

JELLYFISHLIKE

Fig. 32
Man-o'-War 12 ″ (30 cm)
Cnidaria (p. 26)

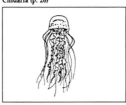

Fig. 33
Jellyfishes 6-8″ (15-20 cm)
Cnidaria (p. 26)

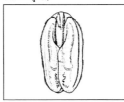

Fig. 34
Comb Jellies 4″ (10 cm)
Ctenophora (p. 55)

Fig. 35
Egg Capsules 1″ (2.5 cm)
Annelida (p. 185)

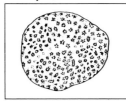

Fig. 36
Sea Pork 1-4″ (2.5-10 cm)
Chordata (p. 59)

SAUSAGE-SHAPED, UNSEGMENTED

Fig. 37
Sea Cucumbers 4″ (10 cm)
Echinodermata (p. 69)

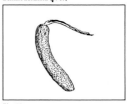

Fig. 38
Spoon Worms 3-6″ (7.5-15 cm)
Echiura (p. 183)

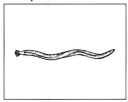

Fig. 39
Sea Cucumbers 6″ (15 cm)
Echinodermata (p. 69)

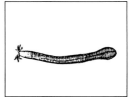

Fig. 40
Burrowing Anemones 1-4″ (2.5-10 cm)
Cnidaria (p. 26)

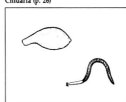

Figs. 41, 42
Peanut Worms 1-12″ (2.5-30 cm)
Sipuncula (p. 89)

11

ILLUSTRATED KEY TO SEASHORE ANIMALS

UNSEGMENTED WORMS

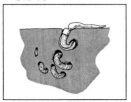

Fig. 43
Acorn Worms 3–12″ (8–30 cm)
Hemichordata (p. 57)

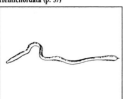

Fig. 44
Ribbon Worms 2–20″ (5–51 cm)
Nemertea (p. 175)

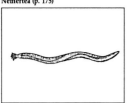

Fig. 45
Sea Cucumbers 6″ (15 cm)
Echinodermata (p. 69)

Fig. 46
Burrowing Anemones 1–4″ (2.5–10 cm)
Cnidaria (p. 26)

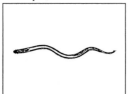

Fig. 47
Roundworms 0.2–2″+ (0.5–5+ cm)
Nematoda (p. 295)

SEGMENTED WORMS

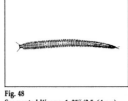

Fig. 48
Segmented Worms, 1–25″ (2.5–64 cm)
Annelida (p. 185)

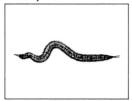

Fig. 49
Segmented Worms 1–25″ (2.5–64 cm)
Annelida (p. 185)

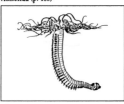

Fig. 50
Segmented Worms 6″ (15 cm)
Annelida (p. 185)

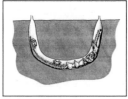

Fig. 51
Segmented Worms 10″ (25 cm)
Annelida (p. 185)

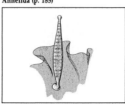

Fig. 52
Leeches 1″ (2.5 cm)
Annelida (p. 185)

FISH-SHAPED

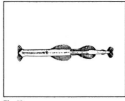

Fig. 53
Arrow Worms 0.25–1″ (0.6–2.5 cm)
Chaetognatha (p. 289)

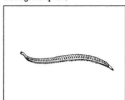

Fig. 54
Segmented Worms 1″ (2.5 cm)
Annelida (p. 185)

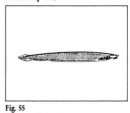

Fig. 55
Lancelets 2″ (5 cm)
Chordata (p. 59)

STARFISH OR URCHINLIKE

Fig. 56
Sea Stars 6″+ (15+ cm)
Echinodermata (p. 69)

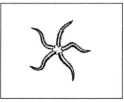

Fig. 57
Brittle Stars 1–16″ (2.5–41 cm)
Echinodermata (p. 69)

12

ILLUSTRATED KEY TO SEASHORE ANIMALS

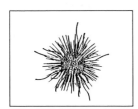

Fig. 58
Sea Urchins 3″ (7.6 cm)
Echinodermata (p. 69)

Fig. 59
Sand Dollars 3–5″ (7.6–13 cm)
Echinodermata (p. 69)

SNAIL-LIKE

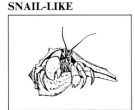

Fig. 60
Hermit Crabs 1–7″ (2.5–18 cm)
Arthropoda (p. 223)

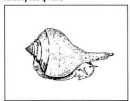

Fig. 61
Snails 0.5–24″ (1.3–61 cm)
Mollusca (p. 92)

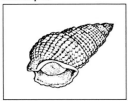

Fig. 62
Snails 0.1–4″ (0.3–10 cm)
Mollusca (p. 92)

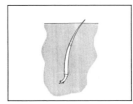

Fig. 63
Tusks 2″ (5 cm)
Mollusca (p. 92)

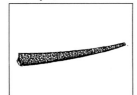

Fig. 64
Ice Cream Cone Worms 2″ (5 cm)
Annelida (p. 185)

Fig. 65
Segmented Worms 2″ (5 cm)
Annelida (p. 185)

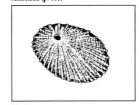

Fig. 66
Keyhole Limpets 1″ (2.5 cm)
Mollusca (p. 92)

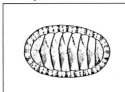

Fig. 67
Chitons 1″ (2.5 cm)
Mollusca (p. 92)

CLAMLIKE

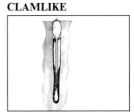

Fig. 68
Lamp Shells 4″ (10 cm)
Brachiopoda (p. 81)

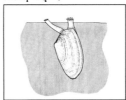

Fig. 69
Clams 0.5–5″ (1.3–13 cm)
Mollusca (p. 92)

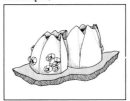

Fig. 70
Barnacles 0.4–1.6″ (1–4 cm)
Arthropoda (p. 223)

Fig. 71
Goose Barnacles 1.5″ (4 cm)
Arthropoda (p. 223)

SPIDERLIKE

Fig. 72
Spider Crabs 4″ (10 cm)
Arthropoda (p. 223)

13

ILLUSTRATED KEY TO SEASHORE ANIMALS

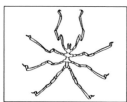

Fig. 73
Sea Spiders 0.2-1.5″ (0.5-4 cm)
Arthropoda (p. 223)

SHRIMPLIKE OR LOBSTERLIKE

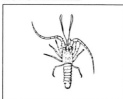

Fig. 74
Spiny Lobster 1′ (2.5 cm)
Arthropoda (p. 223)

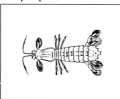

Fig. 75
Mantis Shrimps 2.5-6″ (6.4-15 cm)
Arthropoda (p. 223)

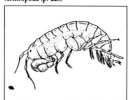

Fig. 76
Amphipods 0.5″ (1.3 cm)
Arthropoda (p. 223)

Fig. 77
Shrimps 6″ (15 cm)
Arthropoda (p. 223)

CRABLIKE

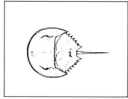

Fig. 78
Horseshoe Crab 24″ (61 cm)
Arthropoda (p. 223)

Fig. 79
Mole Crabs 1.5″ (4 cm)
Arthropoda (p. 223)

Fig. 80
Crabs 3-8″ (7.6-20 cm)
Arthropoda (p. 223)

INSECTLIKE

Fig. 81
Roly-Polies 0.2-1″ (0.5-2.5 cm)
Arthropoda (p. 223)

Fig. 82
Skeleton Shrimps 0.8″ (2 cm)
Arthropoda (p. 223)

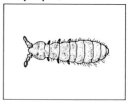

Fig. 83
Springtails 0.1″ (0.3 cm)
Arthropoda (p. 223)

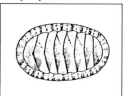

Fig. 84
Chitons 1″ (2.5 cm)
Mollusca (p. 92)

14

IDENTIFICATION

PORIFERA

Sponges

Felt Sponge *Craniella laminaris*

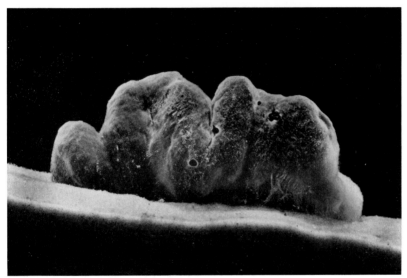

Figure 85

A characteristic but uncommon species of tidal creek bottoms, the felt sponge, *Craniella laminaris,* has the appearance and texture of a thick strap of brown or yellow wool felt. The face of the individual shown in the photograph is pockmarked with a few large exhalent openings, the oscules. Rootlike projections composed of elongated siliceous spicules anchor the sponge in the silty bottom. A few of these long spicules are seen extending from the lower right part of the sponge shown above. The individual in the photograph is approximately 5″ (12 cm) in length and 0.8″ (2 cm) in thickness, although *Craniella* can reach 12″ (30 cm) or more in length and exceed 1.2″ (3 cm) in thickness. *Craniella* is eaten by a green doridid sea slug, *Doris verrucosa,* which nestles in pockets in the sponge.

Sponges

Yellow Boring Sponge *Cliona celata*

There are several common boring sponges in our region, but *Cliona celata* is by far the most common and conspicuous. All sponges of the family Clionidae bore into limestone. The most frequently attacked

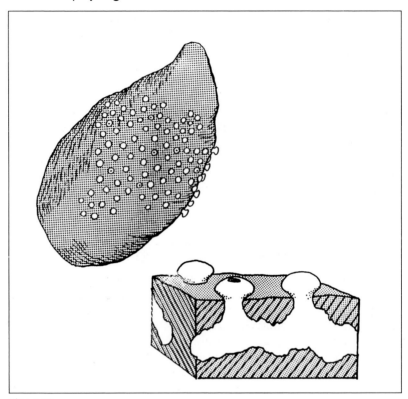

Figure 86

surfaces in our area are the shells of living or dead oysters although any calcareous object is suitable. Boring sponges damage oyster shells and are a pest to the oyster industry. *Cliona* excavates its galleries by chemically etching away tiny chips of shell. These chips enter the water stream which flows through the sponge and are expelled from exhalent openings. These openings (oscules) are located on small yellow bumps (papillae) which project above the surface of the attacked shell. Some of these papillae have exhalent while others have inhalent openings. Underwater, one can observe the sponge ejecting tiny chips of shell. Shell collectors are familiar with the effects of *Cliona celata* on their objects of interest: the shells are perforated with 0.04–0.1″ (1–3 mm) diameter round holes, as if shot with birdshot.

The several other species of *Cliona* in our area leave a similar record on shells but the perforations are 0.04″ (1 mm) or less in diameter and resemble pinholes. Usually *Cliona* destroys its substratum completely and must spread to adjacent shells or perish. Sometimes however, it becomes free-living, massive, and independent of calcareous substrata. Such specimens develop into a bright yellow lumpy cushion reaching 8″

(20 cm) or more in diameter and 1″ or more in thickness. The drawings show *Cliona* attacking an oyster shell and an enlarged cutaway view of galleries eroded by *Cliona* within the shell. *Cliona* is shown with its major predator, the yellow sea slug, *Doriopsilla pharpa,* on Plate B12.

When in its massive growth form, *Cliona* may be confused with another massive sponge, probably an undescribed species of *Amorphinopsis,* which has been called *Xestospongia halichondrioides* in the local literature. *Amorphinopsis* is firm and dense, but tears easily. It is probably restricted to open waters on rock jetties where it forms a thick orange, not yellow, cushion with its smooth surface broken into low gently rounded mounds each bearing an exhalent opening. The sponge may be 1″ (3 cm) or more in thickness and 12″ (30 cm) or more in diameter.

Sponges   *Color Plate A1*

Sulfur Sponge *Aplysilla longispina*

This encrusting sponge is soft and slick and bears numerous soft pointed projections on its upper surface. The surface of *Aplysilla longispina* has a glossy lacquered appearance. The sulfur yellow pigmentation of healthy individuals changes to purple when the sponge is injured or dead. Sulfur sponges occur infrequently on floating docks, rock jetties, seawalls, and other hard surfaces where they may exceed 6″ (15 cm) in diameter and 0.8″ (2 cm) in thickness. *Aplysilla* belongs to a group of sponges that lacks skeletal parts of silica or calcium carbonate. These sponges support themselves solely with thick tough fibers of the protein spongin. Because spongin fibers are soft and flexible, several similar tropical species are harvested commercially, dried, and marketed as bath sponges. The sponge industry flourished in the Tarpon Springs area of Florida as well as in Cuba during the first half of this century. It has now been largely superseded by the production of inexpensive synthetic sponges, although natural sponges remain available in speciality markets. Spongin fibers are visible below the surface of *Aplysilla* where they form complex patterns and project into and support the characteristic surface projections.

A sponge lacking both spicules and spongin skeleton occurs in North Carolina. It is a species of *Halisarca,* probably *H. purpura,* that forms slippery reddish, yellowish, or purplish-brown films on seaweeds and on rock rubble.

Sponges

Pink Tubular Sponge *Adocia tubifera*

Some sponges in the order Haplosclerida, which includes *Haliclona permollis* and *Adocia tubifera,* have skeletons composed of a latticework

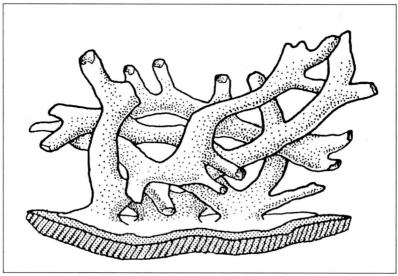

Figure 87

of needles (spicules) joined at their tips by a spot of spongin glue. These latticeworks resemble the repeated polygonal patterns of geodesic domes and in sponges are called an isodictyal pattern. In these two species, the isodictyal pattern is confined to the skin of the sponge. The deeper internal skeleton consists of networks of bundled spicules in tracts. *Adocia tubifera* is a common inhabitant of firm stable surfaces in shallow water including seawalls, rock jetties, and floating docks. It is soft, somewhat crisp, and can be torn or broken very easily. Although usually pink, *Adocia* may also be more deeply pigmented and sometimes appears reddish-purple or even brown. The tubes are thin, transparent, and about 0.1–0.2″ (3-5 mm) in width. The sponge is commonly 2-4″ (5-10 cm) in diameter but can grow larger under favorable conditions.

A similar species, *Haliclona permollis,* the volcano sponge, is reported from our area. It is similar to *Adocia* in size, shape, and color. The two species reportedly can be distinguished by microscopic examination of the spicular skeleton. In both sponges the superficial skeleton is composed of straight or slightly curved glass spicules pointed at both ends and cemented together at their tips into a triangular isodictyal pattern. In *Adocia,* there are similar spicules bound together in parallel to form conspicuous longitudinal fibers below the outer surface of the sponge. These fibers are absent in *Haliclona.*

Sponges   *Color Plate A2*

Eroded Sponge *Haliclona loosanoffi*

This purple or tan species may form thin crusts with short, rough, upright tubes terminating in large exhalent openings, or when fully developed may form large massive mounds 8″ (20 cm) or more in diameter with an open spongy texture. The sponge shown in the photograph is a small specimen. Regardless of its degree of development, the surface of *Haliclona* appears rough and eroded in sharp contrast to the similarly colored pink tubular sponge, *Adocia tubifera,* or the volcano sponge, *Haliclona permollis. Haliclona loosanoffi* is often tan and, even when lavender or purple, it may be dusted with a veneer of silt which obscures its natural color. Its spicules resemble those of *Adocia* but are never arranged in an isodictyal pattern.

The open texture of *Haliclona* is inviting to symbiotic animals seeking shelter, food, or access to the sponge's ventilating water flow. Two tiny amphipod crustaceans, *Colomastix halichondriae* and *Leucothoe spinicarpa,* may be found inhabiting the exhalent apertures of this sponge. A filter-feeding polychaete with two long palps, *Polydora colonia,* builds silty tubes in the pores of *Haliclona* and perhaps takes advantage of the water flow provided by the sponge to gather food. A predatory polychaete, *Syllis spongicola,* also lives within the sponge and probably specializes on the easy availability of sponge tissue for a convenient meal. The sea slug, *Doris verrucosa,* feeds on this sponge.

Sponges   *Color Plate A3*

Flabby Sponge *Mycale americana*

This red or orange-red sponge is easily confused with the red beard sponge, *Microciona prolifera* (Pl. A4), particularly because both sponges often occur in the same habitat. *Mycale americana* grows on oyster reefs, floating docks, pilings, and on shell rubble in tide creeks. Although it is similar to *Microciona* in growth form, size, and color, it is fragile and has a soft texture whereas *Microciona* is very tough and difficult to tear. The spicules of the two species are totally dissimilar. An easy test to distinguish these two species is to place the sponge in a dish of seawater and leave it overnight. By the next morning, if the sponge has disintegrated, it is *Mycale.* If the sponge remained intact, it is not *Mycale* and is probably *Microciona.* The specimen in Plate A3 was collected from a muddy tide creek where it was growing attached to dead oyster shells in the shallow subtidal zone. *Mycale americana* is usually red but is reported to be yellow, olive, tan, or lavender as well. The appendages emerging from the sponge are arms of the spiny brittle star, *Ophiothrix angulata,* an echinoderm often found on sponges.

21

Sponges

Garlic Sponge *Lissodendoryx isodictyalis*

Figure 88

This yellowish or translucent grey sponge is given the common name garlic sponge because when broken its strong spicy odor resembles freshly crushed garlic. The garlic sponge, *Lissodendoryx isodictyalis* (Pl. B13), is firm and brittle and almost always has a dirty appearance. The surface characteristically bears numerous small projections (papillae), as shown in the photograph, and these are useful for field identification of *Lissodendoryx*. The papillae are strongly contractile, however, and are not reliable for identification of preserved or recently disturbed specimens. Garlic sponges grow to a large size particularly in subtidal areas where adequate surface is available for attachment. Individual specimens often reach 8″ (20 cm) in diameter.

The sea slug, *Doris verrucosa*, preys on *Lissodendoryx* and other sponges. Garlic sponges also host a number of symbionts in common with the bread sponge, *Halichondria bowerbanki*, including the small predatory polychaete, *Syllis spongicola*.

Sponges   *Color Plate A4*

Red Beard Sponge *Microciona prolifera*

The red beard sponge, *Microciona prolifera*, is the most common red shallow-water sponge in our area. When young, the sponge grows as a

22

thin red crust on surfaces such as shells, pilings, and rocks. As the sponge grows older it develops upright, crooked, irregular lobes which elongate and divide to produce an erect intricately branched sponge. *Microciona* can be 8″ (20 cm) or more in height, is tough and stiff in texture, and its surface appears smooth to the unaided eye. *Microciona* occurs throughout the year but slows its growth during the summer months. The doridid sea slug, *Doris verrucosa,* feeds on *Microciona.*

Microciona prolifera was studied experimentally by the famous sponge biologist, H. V. Wilson, during the early part of this century. Wilson squeezed *Microciona* through fine, silk, bolting cloth to separate it into individual cells. He found that the isolated cells would migrate and join together in small clumps, each of which would then regenerate a small sponge.

Two other red sponges occur in habitats where *Microciona* is found, the flabby sponge, *Mycale americana* (Pl. A3), and the bristly red sponge, *Cyamon vickersi. Cyamon* forms thin reddish crusts that resemble early stages in the development of *Microciona* and the two are easily confused if casually observed. *Cyamon,* however, is always a very thin crust less than 0.1″ (3 mm) in thickness, never develops erect lobes, and its surface is distinctly bristly because of the long, thin, skeletal spicules that project vertically above its surface. *Mycale* also forms thin crusts when young but later it develops into an erect sponge up to 8″ (20 cm) in diameter. *Mycale* is distinguished from *Microciona* by its very soft texture, its fragile easily torn body, and its propensity to disintegrate in a dish of seawater within hours after being collected.

Sponges   *Color Plate A5*

Bread Sponge *Halichondria bowerbanki*

The bread sponge, *Halichondria bowerbanki,* is easily confused with another yellow sponge, the sun sponge, *Hymeniacidon heliophila* (Pl. A6), because of its similar color, texture, shape, and habitat. Unlike the sun sponge, however, it does not occur where it will be exposed to air or in areas receiving direct sunlight. To be certain of identifying this sponge correctly it is necessary to examine its skeletal spicules with a microscope. This is accomplished by dissolving a small chunk of sponge in a dish filled with household bleach which digests everything but the glassy spicules. The spicules sink to the bottom and can be removed to a microscope slide with an eyedropper. The spicules should be observed with moderate magnification (200–400×) under the microscope. If the spicules are needles with points on both ends (oxeas), then the sponge is *Halichondria bowerbanki.* If the spicules are needles with a point on one end and rounded on the other (styles), then the sponge is

Hymeniacidon heliophila. Halichondria is very soft, tears easily, has a very irregular shape, and its quite open in texture. It is typically light yellow but can be light orange or even beige in moribund specimens.

The open texture of the body of *Halichondria,* like *Hymeniacidon,* encourages colonization by numerous small invertebrates. These include the amphipods, *Colomastix halichondriae* and *Leucothoe spinicarpa,* living in the exhalent openings, a kamptozoan, *Loxosomella cricketae,* attached to the sponge surface, a hydroid, *Turritopsis nutricula,* partly embedded in the surface (lower right of sponge in photograph), and the syllid polychaete, *Syllis spongicola,* which lives within the sponge by the hundreds and probably preys on sponge tissues. The numerous small animals seen clinging to the surface of the sponge in the photograph are caprellid amphipods known as skeleton shrimp.

Sponges   *Color Plate A6*

Sun Sponge *Hymeniacidon heliophila*

Few sponges can tolerate exposure to air and direct sunlight. In fact, one function of the brightly colored pigments of many sponges is to protect them from sunburn. The sun sponge, *Hymeniacidon heliophila,* is exceptional among our sponges because healthy specimens can be found growing in full sunlight near low tide level where they are periodically exposed to air as the tide ebbs. Sun sponges occur intertidally attached to exposed clumps of oysters, in sand where they anchor to buried shells, on concrete bridge pilings, and on the boulders of rock jetties. Sun sponges achieve their greatest sizes in the latter two habitats where, growing in partial shade, they may exceed 16″ (40 cm) in diameter. Specimens have the appearance of encrusting sheets with numerous erect, rough, fingerlike projections. In older specimens, these projections fuse along their sides to form a substantial sponge body which is roughly furrowed and has an irregular open texture. In sunny locations, *Hymeniacidon* is usually light yellow with olive green tints whereas, in shady locations, it can be deep orange or reddish-orange.

Because of the loose and open organization of this sponge, it is host to many smaller animals that live within its interstices. Most of these are small and require a microscope for proper appreciation but others, such as the spiny brittle star, *Ophiothrix angulata,* can occasionally be found here too. Large specimens of *Hymeniacidon* are soft and easily torn whereas smaller individuals are stiffly spongy and fleshy in texture.

Sponges

Purse Sponge *Scypha barbadensis*

This vase-shaped diminutive sponge, approximately 0.4″ (1 cm) in height, is a member of a group of sponges that has calcareous instead of siliceous skeletal spicules. *Scypha* occurs commonly on floating docks in higher salinity areas and on inlet jetties. The body organization of purse sponges exemplifies the simple syconoid pattern discussed in the general discussion of the sponges.

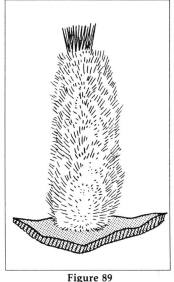

Figure 89

The simplest body organization in sponges, the circular cylinder, or asconoid pattern, is encountered in another calcareous sponge found in the Southeast, the doily sponge, *Clathrina coriacea.* It occurs infrequently in habitats with *Scypha barbadensis.* Small *Clathrina* colonies are minute, open, white, vertical tubes which arise from a creeping, rootlike, tubular base. Later the colony develops into a tangle of tiny, white, hollow tubes resembling a latticework or lace doily. Calcareous sponges may also have a complex internal organization (leuconoid pattern) like that of the siliceous sponges. One species in our waters, *Leucetta imberbis,* or dead man's fingers, exhibits this pattern. *Leucetta* is brittle, white, beige or pale pink, and may cover areas 10″ (25 cm) or more in diameter. It forms low, meandering, upright lobes each of which bears an exhalent opening near its tip, 0.8–0.2″ (2–5 mm) in diameter. It is found in shaded crevices on rock jetties in high salinity water.

CNIDARIA

Jellyfishes *Color Plate A7*

Lion's Mane Jelly *Cyanea capillata*

This jelly starred in Sir Arthur Conan Doyle's story, "Adventures of the Lion's Mane," as the cause of a mysterious death. *Cyanea capillata* can indeed sting and should be handled carefully. *Cyanea* is also known as the "winter jelly," because it typically appears during the colder months in the Southeast. *Cyanea* is at home in colder water north of our region. Under such conditions, it is said to grow to 7' (2 m) in diameter with tentacles 98' (30 m) in length and is the largest jelly known. The largest individuals in our waters reach 6–8" (15–20 cm) across the bell. As in *Aurelia* and *Chrysaora,* the relaxed bell is rather flat and saucer-shaped but is cup-shaped when contracted. *Cyanea* is recognized by the presence of numerous long tentacles in eight distinct clusters arising from the underside of the bell. The reddish-brown oral arms flanking the central mouth hang downward like lace curtains when the animal is afloat. *Cyanea* fishes for plankton such as tiny crustaceans, larvae, and small fishes by stinging them with the tentacles as it swims. The trapped animals are moved to the oral arms and conveyed into the mouth. *Cyanea* is also reported to feed on the moon jelly, *Aurelia aurita.* Reproduction of *Cyanea* is similar to that of *Aurelia.*

Two small fish are occasionally associated with *Cyanea* and with sea nettles, *Chrysaora quinquecirrha.* These are the harvestfish, *Peprilus alepidotus,* and the Gulf butterfish, *Poronotus burti.* Both nibble on the jellies for at least the early part of their lives and, like *Nomeus gronovii,* which lives among man-o'-war tentacles, are resistant but not immune to the stings of their hosts.

Jellyfishes reproduce sexually and each individual is either male or female. Males release sperm into the sea where they find their way to, and enter the mouth of, a female jelly. Fertilization and early embryonic development occur in the female. Small swimming planula larvae eventually leave the mouth, crawl about the oral arms, and them swim away, soon to settle on the bottom of the sea and become sedentary polyps.

Jellyfishes

Sea Nettles *Chrysaora quinquecirrha*

This stinging jelly should be avoided in the water and handled carefully when washed ashore. The 6–8" (20 cm) disk is flattened and saucerlike when relaxed and has long marginal tentacles (up to 16'; 5 m in length) and 4 long oral arms. Sea nettles are found along the eastern

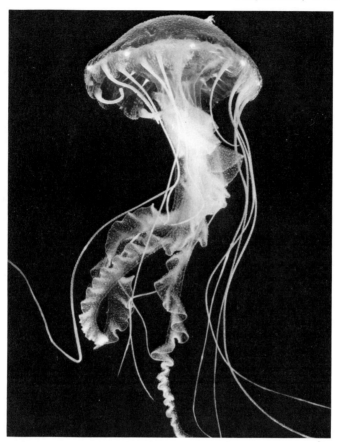

Figure 90

coast of the United States from Cape Cod to the Gulf of Mexico. They can be abundant in nearshore habitats during summer months and are sometimes called the "summer jellyfish." In Chesapeake Bay, their numbers may become so great that they clog the nets of fishermen and block water intakes. Swimming under these conditions becomes unpleasant at best.

Chrysaora quinquecirrha feeds on the comb jelly, *Mnemiopsis,* and also on small fishes and zooplankton. Its reproductive cycle is similar to that of the moon jelly, *Aurelia aurita.* The southern harvestfish, *Peprilus alepidotus,* a small, laterally flattened, silvery fish, often swims rapidly among the tentacles of *Chrysaora.* The young of the *Peprilus* are commensals, but as they grow they become ectoparasites or predators feeding on the jelly. Eventually the harvestfish lives independently of jelly but continues to prey actively on this and other species of jellies.

27

The blue crab, *Callinectes sapidus,* has been observed riding on the upper surface of the bell of *Chrysaora* in much the same way as the larvae of spiny lobsters hitchhike on jellyfish. The small crab on the bell of the jellyfish in the photograph is a juvenile spider crab, *Libinia dubia.* A single jelly may support several small spider crabs which probably feed on mucus and jelly tissue.

Pelagia noctiluca, the oceanic jelly, is a similar stinging species that washes ashore occasionally. It is smaller (up to 3″; 8 cm) than *Chrysaora,* has only 8 tentacles on the margin of the bell, and is strongly bioluminescent.

Jellyfishes

Moon Jelly *Aurelia aurita*

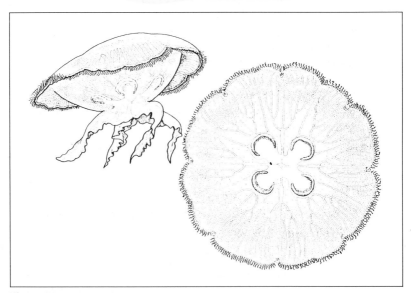

Figure 91

This harmless, distinctive, saucer-shaped jelly is found along all coasts of the United States in spring, summer, and fall. Transparent whitish moon jellies are typically 6–8″ (15–20 cm) in diameter but can exceed 20″ (50 cm). The margin of the flattened bell, which becomes hemispherical during swimming contractions, bears hundreds of short tentacles. In open water, the tentacles are extended and hang down like a veil. The swimming movements of the bell force water outward through this gossamer net, trapping zooplankton on the tentacles. Food is also collected on the upper and lower surfaces of the bell where cilia carry it, entrapped in mucus, to the margin. Here it collects in eight small pockets. The food is removed from the pockets by the tips of four long, fleshy, oral arms flanking the mouth. A ciliated groove in the wall of each of these oral arms transfers food to the mouth. The fine lines radiating outward from the stomach to the margin are the circulatory canals of the gastrovascular system.

The four gonads are distinctive and horseshoe-shaped, one in each pocket of the stomach. They are pink in males and white in females. When males spawn, the sperm enters the mouth of females and fertilizes eggs within the stomach. The fertilized eggs are released through the mouth and enter special brood pouches on the oral arms. Here they develop into planula larvae. The swimming larvae escape, seek shaded surfaces for attachment, and metamorphose to small polyps. Polyps rarely exceed 0.2″ (5 mm) in height, have long threadlike tentacles, and turn pinkish when they divide asexually to form tiny immature medusae.

The amphipod, *Hyperia galba,* lives with the jellies, *Aurelia, Chrysaora,* and *Cyanea* in northern waters. It has not been reported south of Cape Lookout, North Carolina.

Jellyfishes   *Color Plate A8*

Cannonball Jellyfish *Stomolophus meleagris*

During the summer and fall these large jellies (8″; 20 cm in diameter) are a common sight along the coast. *Stomolophus meleagris* is the most common jelly in our area and fortunately is not a virulent stinger although mild stings have been reported by some people who have handled the animals. It is considered to be a pest by commercial fishermen because, when present in large numbers, it clogs their nets. The hemispherical white bell is handsomely decorated with a rich chocolate brown band around the free edge. Below the bell hangs a firm, gristlelike, feeding apparatus used to remove plankton from the water. The bell also has eight equally spaced sensory capsules (rhopalia) around its margin. Each rhopalium appears in the photograph as a bright white spot. The rhopalia sense light, odor, and position, and may be responsible for the cyclic vertical migrations of this animal consisting of upward movement during the day and downward movement at night. The rhopalia are also pacemakers which control the rate of contraction of the swimming muscles. Pulsations of the bell margin provide thrust for swimming but also push water over the feeding apparatus where the planktonic animals are trapped in mucus and passed through thousands of tiny mouths into the gut. These jellies consume tremendous amounts of zooplankton and are an important part of nearshore food webs. A cannonball jellyfish, which is also called a jellyball or cabbagehead, has no tentacles.

A similar species, *Rhopilema verrilli,* the mushroom jelly, is less common but may also be found washed ashore on our beaches. *Rhopilema,* which reaches 20″ (50 cm) in bell diameter, is much larger than *Stomolophus,* lacks the brown band, and has long, fingerlike, gelatinous appendages hanging below the feeding apparatus.

Several animals, including some fishes, associate with *Stomolophus* but perhaps the most interesting symbiont is the spider crab, *Libinia dubia,* shown in the photograph clinging to the feeding apparatus. Juvenile crabs ride under the bell and as many as 70% of these jellies may carry at least one crab. The crabs presumably eat the zooplankton captured in the mucus of the jelly and themselves must arrive as planktonic larvae which settle and remain. Damage to the feeding apparatus of jellies carrying crabs is common and apparently hungry crabs graze on their hosts. *Stomolophus* is prey to the spadefish, *Chaetodipterus faber.*

Jellyfishes

Sea Wasp *Chiropsalmus quadrumanus*

The sea wasp, *Chiropsalmus quadrumanus,* and other jellyfishes in the order Cubomedusae, are mostly tropical jellyfishes that are square when viewed from above, hence the prefix "cubo." They are also known as "box jellies." Box jellies feed on small fish that are caught on the trailing tentacles as the jelly swims. Fish are subdued quickly by powerful stinging capsules on the tentacles and are then transferred to the mouth which hangs below the bell. Box jellies are strong swimmers with potent stings that justify the common name, sea wasp. These animals should be treated with respect; severe dermatitis and a few human fatalities have been attributed to the stings of Pacific species, and *Chiropsalmus* stings have hospitalized a few swimmers. Contact with the tentacles of any of our box jellies should be avoided. Some of the pain of jellyfish and anemone stings can be alleviated by applying a paste of powdered meat tenderizer to the affected area of skin. This treatment is most effective if used soon after being stung.

A mature specimen of *Chiropsalmus quadrumanus* can be 5–6″ (12–15 cm) in bell diameter and 4–6″ (10–15 cm) in height. Each lower corner of the square bell bears a lobe with several long tentacles. *Chiropsalmus* can be common in inshore waters in the late summer months.

A similar species, *Tamoya haplonema,* also occurs along our coast. Mature specimens of *Tamoya* (4″; 10 cm) resemble the size and shape of *Chiropsalmus* but can be recognized by the single long tentacle from each of the four lobes of the bell.

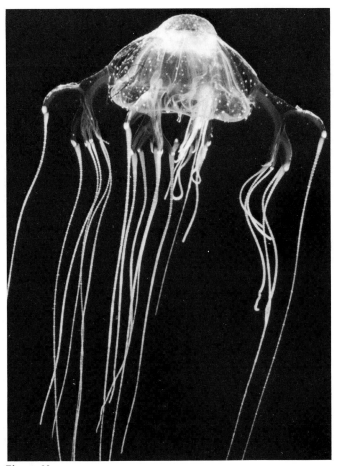

Figure 92

Hydroids   *Color Plate A9*

Eudendrium carneum
Bougainvillia rugosa

Colonies of *Eudendrium carneum* (Pls. A9, C9), one of our most colorful hydroids, reach 5″ (12 cm) in diameter and are composed of irregularly arranged branched stems which bear polyps. The polyps sport a trumpet-shaped hypostome, a characteristic of the family, surrounded by up to 26 filamentous tentacles in one whorl. Colonies are male or female. Female colonies bear specialized reproductive structures, called sporosacs, on the polyps. Each sporosac looks like a minute orange surrounded by a bifurcated branch (spadix) of the colonial

31

digestive tract which forms a tiny placenta. The single egg within the sporosac develops directly into the characteristic cnidarian larva (planula) and is released from the colony. The sporosac, in reality, is the medusa generation reduced to a single egg cell. Male colonies bear grapelike clusters of orange sacs filled with sperm and are known simply as male gonophores.

Two other species of *Eudendrium* are common in our area, *E. ramosum* and *E. tenellum*. Both species produce female sporosacs and male gonophores at the base of unmodified polyps whereas, in *E. carneum,* the polyps are reduced and do not have tentacles or hypostomes. *Eudendrium tenellum* forms networks of irregular low colonies less than 0.8″ (2 cm) high with annulated stems, branches, and pedicels.

Eudendrium is preyed on by our largest shallow-water sea spider, *Anoplodactylus lentus* (Pl. C9, Fig. 293), a clinging animal with a long suctorial proboscis, and by the sea slugs, *Doto chica* and *Dondice occidentalis.* The small sea spider to the left of the colony is *Tanystylum orbiculare.*

The bushy grey or white colonies of *Bougainvillia* (4″; 10 cm) are common in the warm months of the year. The main stems are thick and each is a composite of slender individual stems bound together like wires in a cable. *Bougainvillia,* unlike *Eudendrium,* produces free-swimming sexual medusae that are released into the water in summer.

Hydroids

Feather Hydroid *Halocordyle disticha*

These graceful featherlike hydroids are conspicuous members of high salinity epifaunal communities where there is moderate to strong bidirectional water flow, as on rock jetties or in tidal channels. The pinnate arrangement of branches and the flattened shape of the colony are adaptations to life in areas of uni- or bidirectional water flow. The animals orient themselves with their flat surfaces perpendicular to the water current. This orientation not only places all the polyps in unobstructed contact with incoming food and oxygen but also reduces twisting of the main stem and abrasion between the branches. Occasionally specimens of *Halocordyle disticha* are not bilateral with pinnate branches. Instead, the branching is irregular and occurs in all planes. It is not certain whether this form is a response to local environmental conditions or a separate species.

Halocordyle disticha is common in the summer and fall of the year. It reaches 8″ (20 cm) in height and has black stems and pinkish-white polyps. The polyps of *Halocordyle* have a conical hypostome with a whorl of long filamentous tentacles at its base and short club-shaped tentacles, in several whorls, at its apex (upper figure, inset). *Halocordyle* releases minute swimming medusae during the summer months and

Figure 93

one of these, which is corncob-shaped, is shown in Figure 93 (inset). Bathers who swim in waters where *Halocordyle* is abundant may experience mild stings from these microscopic jellyfish. At least two sea slugs prey on *Halocordyle.* These are an undescribed species of *Doto* (0.6″; 1.5 cm) and *Cratena pilata* (0.8″; 2 cm), the latter and its white loosely coiled egg mass are shown in the photograph on the hydroid.

Hydroids

Snail Fur *Hydractinia echinata*

Hermit crab shells that appear fuzzy with a tan covering about 0.08″ (2 mm) thick probably support a colony of this interesting hydrozoan. The colony in the photograph is growing on the shell of the mud snail, *Ilyanassa obsoleta,* currently being occupied by the hermit, *Pagurus*

33

Figure 94

longicarpus. Both species make excellent aquarium animals. Colonies also occur on shells inhabited by the flat-clawed hermit, *Pagurus pollicaris* and are also found independently of hermit crabs. Other hermits tend to avoid colonizing shells overgrown with *Hydractinia.* Snail fur, *Hydractinia echinata,* is unusual among hydroids because the basal portion of the colony is a continuous sheet of tissue, rather than a rootlike network, from which the various polyps arise. When more than one colony grows on a shell, a distinct polyp-free no-man's-land is maintained between them. There is also an exoskeleton of short stiff spines which project upward between polyps from the surface of the colony.

Three kinds of polyps are present. Feeding polyps (gastrozooids) having numerous tentacles with rounded ends occur over the surface of the colony (inset). Short, male and female, reproductive polyps (gonozooids) bear spherical bulges of gonophores at their bases and rudimentary tentacles at their tips. At the aperture of the snail shell, there are a few very long polyps, the spiralzooids, with only rudimentary tentacles, each bearing batteries of stinging capsules. One of the spiralzooids, coiled like a spring, is visible in the photograph below the crab's right eye. *Hydractinia* colonies are either male or female (dioecious) and spawn gametes when exposed to light after several hours of darkness.

34

The interaction between the hydroid and its hermit host has been the subject of some research and much speculation. The larvae of the hydroid preferentially settle on shells in response to specific bacteria associated with the hermit. It has been suggested that the hydroid steals tidbits of food and even eggs from the hermit using the long spiralzooids. *Hydractinia* is intolerant of exposure to air and would not survive if its shell was appropriated by an intertidal hermit, such as *Clibanarius vittatus,* the striped hermit. Conveniently, *Clibanarius* is sensitive to stings and is discouraged from colonizing empty *Hydractinia*-covered shells. On the other hand, subtidal hermits avoid desiccation, are not bothered by stings, and are not discouraged by *Hydractinia.* The presence of *Hydractinia* on hermit crab shells discourages attacks by *Octopus* and stone crabs.

Hydroids   *Color Plate A10*

Tubularia crocea

Each naked, pink polyp of *Tubularia crocea* extends from its own tubelike stem which reaches 6″ (15 cm) in length. Under low magnification, clusters of these large polyps resemble clumps of tiny wildflowers. The polyps have numerous club-shaped medusa buds between two whorls of about 20 tentacles each. *Tubularia* can be common or abundant on rock jetties, floating docks, pilings, and other hard surfaces throughout the year, but it does not occur in water below about ⅔ the salinity of seawater. It is preyed on by a white sea slug, *Cratena pilata,* which also eats the feather hydroid, *Halocordyle disticha.*

A similar species, *Ectopleura dumortieri,* occurs in low salinity water to about ⅓ the strength of seawater and coexists with *Tubularia* in higher salinity areas. *Ectopleura* is similar in shape and color to *Tubularia* but it is smaller, rarely exceeding 2″ (5 cm) in height, and when reproducing, liberates swimming medusae that resemble tiny jellyfish and have four short tentacles. *Tubularia,* on the other hand, releases a larva, called an actinula. The ovoid actinula has several long polypoid tentacles in addition to four low, rudimentary, medusoid tentacles. The polypoid tentacles radiate stiffly outward giving the actinula the appearance of a child's jack. Those interested in distinguishing *Tubularia* and *Ectopleura* should maintain the polyps in dishes of seawater and examine them periodically with a hand lens or microscope for the appearance of their characteristic young. Both species can cast off their flowerlike hydranths under stress and regenerate them when conditions improve.

Pelagic Hydroids   *Color Plate A11*

Blue Button *Porpita porpita*

Large numbers of these harmless animals blow ashore from the warm Gulf Stream on winds produced by offshore storms. The blue button,

Porpita porpita, is a polyp, 1–2″ (3–5 cm) in diameter, that floats on the surface of the sea with its marginal tentacles radiating outward like petals on a daisy. Blue buttons, Portuguese man-o'-war (*Physalia physalis*), janthina snails (*Janthina janthina*), and by-the-wind sailors (*Velella velella*) are a few of the specialized animals that are characteristic of the neuston, the community of animals that float at the surface of the sea. Flotation in blue buttons is provided by the whitish, central, chitinous disk which encloses up to 100 concentrically arranged air chambers. The disk has the texture and buoyancy of a styrofoam chip. The skin of the animal secretes a water repellent mucus, like swimmer's grease, that may also aid in flotation. *Porpita* does not have a sail like its close relative, *Velella velella,* the by-the-wind sailor. A central feeding mouth hangs down into the water below the disk and is surrounded by many smaller feeding and reproductive organs. These produce small cup-shaped medusae that swim free of the adults, mature, and undergo sexual reproduction. The tissues of *Porpita* and *Velella* possess large numbers of algae (zooxanthellae) belonging to the species, *Amphidinium chattoni.* It is possible that, as with the brown anemone, *Aiptasia pallida,* a proportion of their food requirements is met by the photosynthetic activity of these plant cells.

Pelagic Hydroids

By-The-Wind Sailor *Velella velella*

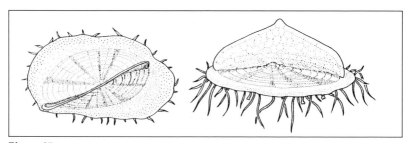

Figure 95

Velella velella (3″; 8 cm) is a giant, deep blue, pelagic, solitary polyp that is a miniature raft with a triangular sail set diagonally across it. The float, like that of *Porpita,* consists of a chitinous disk with gas-filled flotation chambers. It corresponds to the exoskeleton of typical attached polyps, such as the long-stemmed hydroid, *Tubularia crocea.* The skeleton is internalized, however, and the ancestral stalk is now a float. This allows the polyps to colonize a previously unexploited habitat, the surface of the open sea. The underside of the raft bears a large central mouth and long marginal tentacles. Numerous medusa buds, or medusoids, are situated between the mouth and the tentacles. The medusa buds produce small thimble-shaped medusae which sink into the deep sea and undergo sexual reproduction. Each resulting juvenile secretes a gas-filled float and rises to the surface of the sea. The appendages that hang down into the water function as rudders and enable *Velella* to sail at 45° or more to the wind direction and even to tack against the wind. The edge of the raft can fold over into the water to provide additional steering control. *Velella* is distributed worldwide in warm offshore waters. It is sometimes cast ashore in great numbers by storms, especially in south Florida.

Porpita and *Velella* are eaten by the beautiful blue and white sea slug, *Glaucus atlanticus* (blue glaucus), and by the purple and white snail, *Janthina janthina. Velella* is preyed upon by another sea slug, *Fiona pinnata,* which also feeds on the goose barnacle, *Lepas anatifera.* Perhaps the most devastating predator on *Velella* is the giant ocean sunfish, *Mola mola,* which can weigh more than a ton and fills its stomach with *Velella.*

Hydroids

Obelia dichotoma

This species is present throughout the year on firm surfaces where it grows in delicate, bushy, brown tufts branching in all directions and extending to 6″ (15 cm). Each tiny polyp produces approximately 20 simple tentacles in a single whorl (inset). The polyps are enclosed in a microscopic, wine glass-shaped, transparent, skeletal cup (theca) with a smooth rim (inset). Large, specialized, reproductive polyps, which are enclosed in cylindrical skeletal cups (gonotheca), occur in the older parts of mature colonies. Tiny medusae are formed within the gonotheca and are released through a terminal opening as they become fully developed, usually in summer. Several investigations of growth in *Obelia* indicate that the rate of growth is related directly to temperature. In one day at 68°F, an *Obelia* colony adds up to 0.8″ (2 cm) in length and develops polyps or medusae from the smallest detectable buds. Individual feeding polyps regress and regenerate over a 3–6 day cycle, depending on temperature. This regression-regeneration cycle, which also includes the theca, is believed to help prevent fouling of the colony by algae and protozoans. *Obelia* is eaten by the sea slug, *Miesea evelinae,* a tiny 0.1″ (3 mm) nudibranch with a translucent whitish-brown body, smooth rhinophores, and few laterally situated cerata with black specks.

Several species of *Obelia* occur in the Southeast but the most common are *O. dichotoma, O. geniculata,* and *O. bidentata. Obelia geniculata,* about 1″ (2.5 cm) in height, shares the smooth-rimmed wine glass-shaped theca around the polyp with *O. dichotoma* but, whereas the stems of *O. dichotoma* are rather straight, those of *O. geniculata* zigzag

Figure 96

from one polyp to the next giving the appearance of an incompletely extended, folding carpenter's rule. The chitinous exoskeleton (perisarc) of *O. geniculata* is much thicker than that of the other two species. *Obelia geniculata* is always small and does not form large bushy colonies. *Obelia bidentata*, which may exceed 6″ (15 cm) in height, resembles *O. dichotoma* but has 10–20 microscopic teeth on the margin of the theca.

Hydroids

Fern Hydroid *Sertularia marginata*

The fern hydroid, *Sertularia marginata*, can be locally abundant on rock jetties in the Southeast where it grows in mats of pale fernlike fronds 2–3″ (5–8 cm) in height. It is also reported to live offshore on "live bottoms." The branches bearing the polyps arise alternately along

Figure 97

the main stem and lie in a single plane. The polyps are arranged pinnately along each of the branches. Little is known about the biology of *Sertularia* except that it does not release its eggs into the sea. Fertilized eggs are brooded in a capsule (gonophore) that resembles a Chinese lantern and a ciliated larva, called planula, is released to find a suitable surface for colonization.

Siphonophores

Portuguese Man-o'-War *Physalia physalis*

Most bathers and beachcombers react with instinctive caution to these dangerous blue and purple sailors. The fragile tentacles suspended below the float can inflict unforgettable pain and cause severe dermatitis even when the animal appears dead and the tentacles are coated with sand. The gas-filled float may reach 12″ (30 cm) in length and the stinging tentacles may extend 65′ (20 m) below it. These animals are complex integrated colonies of specialized individuals, each of which is either a modified polyp or medusa. The feeding members (gastrozooids) are modified polyps whereas the float, the reproductive parts, and a few other specialized individuals are medusae. *Physalia physalis* begins life as a single floating polyp that has one tentacle and a gas-filled medusa-float. All other members of the colony arise by asexual budding from the lower half of the float. The float itself is filled with a gas

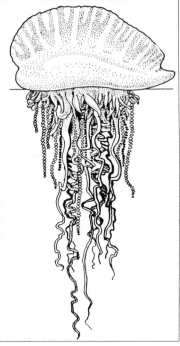

Figure 98

similar to air except that there is an unusually high proportion of carbon monoxide, about 1 to 30%, depending on the colony. The gas is secreted by a special gland in the float. The float of *Physalia,* like the sail of the unrelated by-the-wind sailor, *Velella,* is not set parallel to the long axis of the body but is canted either to the left or the right in about equal proportions of the population. The left- or right-handedness of their sails assures that, in any given wind, half of the population will sail to port and the other half to starboard, assuring wide dispersal of the species. *Physalia* feeds on fishes, stinging them to death with the stinging cells on its contractile tentacles.

Reproductive siphonophores do not release free-swimming medusae and are usually hermaphrodites. *Physalia,* however, is exceptional because colonies are either male or female.

Physalia is preyed on by loggerhead turtles, *Caretta caretta,* the blue glaucus, *Glaucus atlanticus,* and the snail, *Janthina janthina. Glaucus* stores undischarged stinging cells of its prey and can itself sting swimmers. The small, banded, man-o'-war fish, *Nomeus gronovii,* swims unharmed among the fishing tentacles of *Physalia.* It is said that larger fish with an appetite for *Nomeus* swim unwittingly into the tentacles of *Physalia* which promptly subdues them and shares the catch with *Nomeus*. *Nomeus* may also nibble on *Physalia* tentacles. It is not yet clear whether *Nomeus* is immune to the stings of *Physalia* or skillfully avoids contact with the nematocyst-charged tentacles.

Sea Whips   *Color Plate A12*

Sea Whip *Leptogorgia virgulata*

Colorful branched sea whips up to 24" (60 cm) in length wash ashore commonly on southern beaches. They grow abundantly on shelly "live bottoms" in sounds and tidal creeks but can also be found on floating docks, rock jetties, and oyster reefs. The sea whip, *Leptogorgia virgulata,* may be purple, white, orange, yellow or even red. Several colonies are posed together on Plate A12. Undisturbed colonies expand small white polyps from around the stem and branches to feed on minute organisms in the water. When the polyps are retracted, as is always the case when they are washed ashore, their positions are marked by tiny slits in the hard, colorful, living tissue. Colonies attach to hard surfaces with a tough and tenacious protein holdfast while the springy tough branches sway in the currents. *Leptogorgia* uses two devices to hold itself upright and to avoid breakage. First, it has a tough, proteinaceous, internal skeleton, or axial rod, that looks and feels like a black or brown wire in dead specimens. Second, the living tissue covering the axial rod between polyps is filled with calcareous spicules that toughen and stiffen the branches. They are also responsible for the color of the colony.

Leptogorgia is the home or prey for some specialized associates. The Atlantic wing oyster, *Pteria colymbus,* can be found attached to one of the branches. *Conopea galeata,* a narrow, triangular, brown barnacle, is found only on *Leptogorgia* where it is often overgrown by host tissue. The shrimp, *Neopontonides beaufortensis,* presumably eats host tissue and acquires the prey's particular color, which may then act as camouflage to hide the shrimp from its own predators. The snail, *Simnialena uniplicata,* with its spindle-shaped glossy shell, creeps along the branches eating the host and, like *Neopontonides,* incorporates host pigment into its shell. The predatory sea slug, *Tritonia wellsi,* has gills that mimic the expanded polyps of its prey. Dead colonies of sea whips, reduced to their axial rods, are often overgrown with a thick coating of grey, stiff, translucent jelly (lower part of colony in photograph). This is the bryozoan, *Alcyonidium hauffi.*

Another species, *Leptogorgia setacea,* is common from Chesapeake Bay to Brazil. Its yellow, orange, or purple colonies are unbranched or have one or two long flexible branches. It sometimes occurs unattached and is one of the few gorgonians that does so.

Sea Pansies   *Color Plate A13*

Sea Pansy *Renilla reniformis*

The sea pansy, *Renilla reniformis,* is one of the most unusual and beautiful of our anthozoans. Like its close relatives, the sea pens, each sea pansy is a colony of polyps, but the polyps of *Renilla* have several forms and functions. A single, giant, primary polyp, up to 2″ (5 cm) in diameter, forms the anchoring stem (peduncle) and pansylike body which bears the many, small, anemonelike feeding polyps shown in Plate A13. A cluster of several tentacles-less polyps forms an outlet valve that releases water to deflate the colony. The small white dots between the feeding polyps are polyps too, but they do not extend or feed. Instead, they are water pumps that expand the deflated colony. *Renilla* is common on current-swept sand flats in protected areas where it is distributed from low tide level into the subtidal. It anchors in the sand with the peduncle, whose end can be distended for better anchorage, while the heart-shaped primary polyp lies flat on the sand. Extended feeding polyps secrete a sticky mucus net which captures tiny organisms suspended in the water. During spring low tides, when some sea pansies are stranded and exposed, the colonies are always deflated and covered with a thin film of silty sand, making them difficult to spot. The rigidity of the deflated body and the purple color are caused by calcium carbonate spicules, similar to those of sea whips, in the tissue of the animal. *Renilla* is also strikingly bioluminescent when disturbed at night.

The striped sea slug in the photograph is *Armina tigrina,* a predator on *Renilla.* Feeding by *Armina* is one of the stimuli that elicits bioluminescent activity by the pansy. When not feeding on *Renilla,* the slugs, which are 1.2″ (3 cm) in length, bury themselves just below the surface of the sand.

Anemones   *Color Plate A14*

Stinging Anemone *Actinia bermudensis*

This elegant red anemone is common on rocks just below the low tide mark in northern Florida and throughout the West Indies and Bermuda. The specimen in the photograph is fully expanded and is attached by its pedal disk, which is approximately 1″ (2.5 cm) in diameter. Specimens are known from Bermuda that reach 1.6″ (4 cm) and 2″ (5 cm) in height. Immediately outside and below the outermost whorl of tentacles is a row of low spherical bulges, called acrorhagi, that are covered with irregular dense patches of stinging cells. Stinging cells occur elsewhere on the surface of the animal but those associated with the acrorhagi are used to repel encroachment of one polyp onto the territory of another. This rarely results in death but often causes retreat of the intruder. The acrorhagi are reported to be blue in most Bermudian and Caribbean specimens, but those from St. Augustine are pink. When handled, this anemone can cause a burning irritation that may develop into persistent red welts on the skin. *Actinia bermudensis* reproduces asexually by a lengthwise division of the body, a process known as fission. This sort of reproduction enables the species to quickly colonize desirable surfaces. All offspring of the asexual parent are genetically identical clone-mates. *Actinia* also reproduces sexually and many species have internal fertilization. Young are brooded in the coelenteron and eventually released as tiny anemones.

Anemones   *Color Plate A15*

Armored Anemone *Anthopleura carneola*

Few who are not searching for it will notice this well-disguised species. The armored anemone, *Anthopleura carneola,* occurs in large numbers intertidally on exposed rocky shores in northern Florida where it attaches shell fragments to its column with rows of adhesive warts (verrucae). The verrucae are visible on the columns of the anemones in the photograph and often are marked with red pigment. At low tide, when the animals are exposed, the tentacles are withdrawn and only the shell fragments are visible. Aggregations of these anemones under rock overhangs coat the rock with a thick veneer of broken shells and are unrecognizable as anemones except to an informed or astute observer. Expanded individuals are about 0.4″ (1 cm) in height, less than 0.2″ (5 mm) in width across the disk, and have 30 to 60 tentacles. *Anthopleura* is variable in color. It can be reddish, pink, olive green, or pale brown. The oral disk usually is speckled with white spots. This anemone reproduces asexually by longitudinal fission.

Another species, the gulfweed anemone, *Anemonia sargassensis,* attaches to floating gulfweed (*Sargassum*). It is brown or greenish, 0.2″ (5 mm) in height and 0.3″ (8 mm) in width across the oral disk. There are 40–50 tentacles which may be marked with yellow, brown, green, and lavender. The column is smooth and lacks verrucae and cinclides.

Anemones

Warty Anemone *Bunodosoma cavernata*

A walk to a rock jetty or groin on one of our swimming beaches will invariably reveal a few greenish-brown or black specimens of the warty anemone, *Bunodosoma cavernata,* our largest anemone, either attached to a rock in a shady crevice or buried in sand so that only the flowerlike tentacles show on the beach surface. *Bunodosoma* is a common inhabitant near the low tide mark in these areas, and expanded individuals can

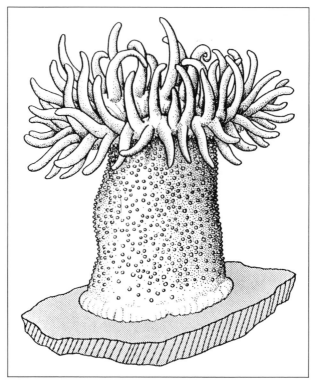

Figure 99

be identified by 40 vertical rows of small warts on the pale column. The tentacles are numerous (almost 100), short compared to the size of the animal; they are marked with red stripes near the mouth. Yellow-white acrorhagi are present between the bases of the outermost tentacles and are used in territorial defense. When exposed to air at low tide, warty anemones contract and withdraw their tentacles and are not easily identified as anemones, looking instead like globs of slick black tar. *Bunodosoma* reaches 3.5″ (9 cm) in height and can be 2″ (5 cm) in diameter across the oral disk. These anemones are very mobile and have sticky tentacles. Individuals that are detached from the substratum can support their body weight in air with tentacles attached by sticky nematocysts to a willing finger. In areas where scorched mussels, *Brachidontes exustus,* are abundant, *Bunodosoma* is often found with mussel valves in its gastrovascular cavity, suggesting that mussels may be part of its diet.

Anemones

Sea Onion *Paranthus rapiformis*

Sea onions are familiar to many beachcombers and naturalists. When washed out of its sandy burrow, *Paranthus rapiformis* adopts the size, shape, and opalescent glossy sheen of a freshly peeled onion and drifts at the mercy of the currents. Someone, however, must have thought that *Paranthus* resembled a turnip rather than an onion because *rapiformis* is Latin for turnip-shaped. *Paranthus* is a burrowing anemone, although it has the ability to drift when washed out of the sand. It accomplishes this by closing its mouth and shortening its body without expelling water. As it shortens, it rounds up until it is almost a perfect sphere or ovoid. Because *Paranthus* is neutrally buoyant, it is bounced along by currents until it settles on a suitable beach. When burrowing in soft

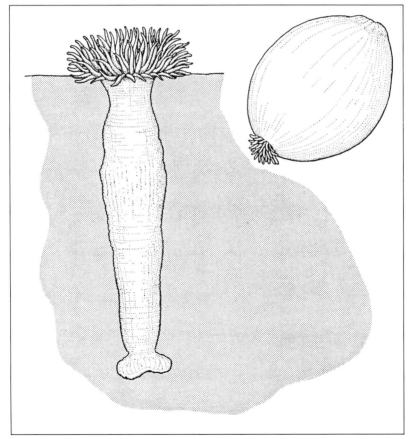

Figure 100

sand, *Paranthus* extends its column downward 14″ (35 cm) or more and adopts a wormlike appearance. It does not always burrow so deeply however, perhaps because it encounters coarse, resistant layers of sand or shell. Under these circumstances, the animal is not so dramatically elongated. *Paranthus* anchors in the sand with the base of the column, which flares out mushroomlike and adheres to the sand, while the numerous brownish-green tentacles are extended at the sand surface. The brown color of the tentacles is caused by zooxanthellae which probably supplement the nutrition of this animal. *Paranthus rapiformis* has up to 180 tentacles and a smooth, pinkish or cream column. It may also be reddish-brown or greenish grey.

Anemones

Red-Spotted Anemone *Aiptasiogeton eruptaurantia*

Red-spotted anemones belong to a family (Aiptasiidae) which includes several species of warm-water anemones. Of them, only species of *Aiptasiogeton* and *Aiptasia* extend northward beyond the subtropics. Species in this family, such as *Aiptasia pallida* and *Aiptasiogeton eruptaurantia,* are animals with well-developed oral and pedal disks and numerous smooth pointed tentacles. Each of the many mesenteries that

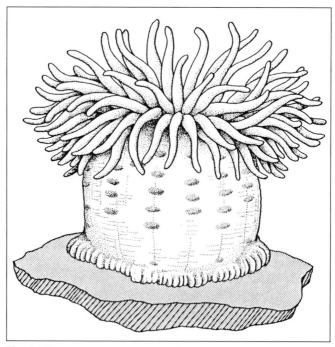

Figure 101

vertically partitions the internal cavity produces a long internal thread, called an acontium. These can be seen clearly in the photograph of *A. pallida*. The acontia are covered with cells containing stinging capsules, or nematocysts, which are used in feeding and defense. When red-spotted or brown anemones (*A. pallida*) are disturbed, they spew the stinging threads from their mouths and from pores in the column, called cinclides. The two to five rows of cinclides in *A. eruptaurantia* are characteristically marked with red pigment, making this one of the easiest anemones to identify.

The red-spotted anemone and the brown anemone occur in similar habitats but red-spotted anemones are less common and smaller (1″; 2.5 cm). The column is cream, the oral disk is usually purplish-brown, and there are three circles of up to 64 tentacles, the inner circle producing the longest tentacles.

Another small (0.8″; 2 cm) anemone, *Diadumene leucolena,* is common on hard surfaces in our water. Like *Aiptasiogeton* and *Aiptasia,* it has zooxanthellae and well-developed oral and pedal disks, mesenteries, acontia, and cinclides. It is smaller than *Aiptasia* and lacks the red spots of *Aiptasiogeton.* The column is tan-orange, greenish, grey, or cream and marked with vertical, white, parallel lines.

Anemones   *Color Plate A16*

Brown Anemone *Aiptasia pallida*

A visit to a well-established floating dock will often reveal exquisite gardens of these brown anemones. The mouth is surrounded by up to 96 long graceful tentacles while two rows of cinclides, through which acontia can be protruded, circle the middle of the column.

The brown color of *Aiptasia pallida* is caused by a unicellular photosynthetic alga, *Symbiodinium microadriaticum,* that lives within the tissues of the anemone's body. The many intracellular algal cells, known as zooxanthellae, get their color from a brown pigment, fucoxanthin, that masks their green chlorophyll. This alga, which is a dinoflagellate, is a close relative of the organism responsible for red tides. Like other plants, *Symbiodinium* uses energy from the sun to convert carbon dioxide and water into sugar and oxygen. It is believed that the same species of dinoflagellate is present in almost all cnidarians that have zooxanthellae. The intimate association of *Symbiodinium* with *Aiptasia* is beneficial to both organisms and is an excellent example of mutualism. The algae secure a home and obtain basic salts and carbon dioxide from the host while the anemone consumes carbohydrates and perhaps oxygen produced by the guest. The cells of *Aiptasia* cultivate these zooanthellae gardens and the anemone feeds itself simply by exposing the algae to sunlight. Under ideal conditions, in partial shade and in clear water, *Aiptasia* may have a tentacle spread of 3″ (8 cm) or more. *Aiptasia* also grows in darkness under rocks. When it occurs in dark places it is not brown, but rather a pure pallid white, which accounts for the second half of its Latin name. *Aiptasia* makes a splendid aquarium animal, especially if kept near a sunny window. Because it reproduces prolifically from fragments of its adhesive pedal disk, it can soon become a weed in an otherwise orderly aquarium.

Aiptasia pallida is the favorite food of two of our prettiest sea slugs, *Berghia coerulescens* (Pl. B18) and *Spurilla neapolitana*.

Anemones

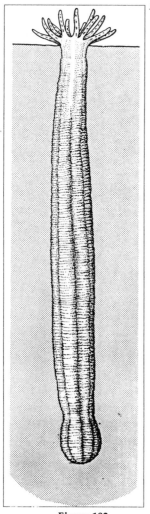

Figure 102

Edwardsia elegans

When freshly collected from one of our muddy sand flats, this long thin anemone, only 0.8–0.1″ (2–3 mm) in diameter and 0.8–4″ (2–10 cm) in length, looks remarkably like the small burrowing sea cucumber, *Leptosynapta tenuis*. *Edwardsia elegans* quickly rolls its oral end inward when it is disturbed and within minutes the much shortened specimen resembles a similarly retracted sipunculan, such as the rock boring sipunculan, *Themiste alutacea,* with which it can be confused. After a few days of undisturbed rest in an aquarium filled with seawater, the anemone will re-extend like the one shown here. It is then possible to see the 14–16 translucent tentacles with white and brown spots and the digging bulb, or physa, on the lower end of the opaque rusty column. When placed on sand, *Edwardsia* burrows slowly using its physa until the entire animal, except for the tentacles, is below the surface of the sand. When viewed from above, the transparent tentacles are perfectly camouflaged against the sand by the mottling of white and brown spots.

A similar species, *Nematostella vectensis,* is a small, translucent, brown, smooth anemone, 0.8–1.2″ (2–3 cm) in length, that burrows in salt marsh sediments. It has 16 tentacles and 8 lengthwise grooves on the column.

Anemones   *Color Plate A17*

Orange-Striped Anemone *Haliplanella luciae*

This lovely anemone, named by the American naturalist, A. E. Verrill, for his daughter, Lucy, is an introduction from the western coast of the Pacific Ocean at about the turn of the century. It is now widespread on the Gulf and east coasts of the United States from Maine to the tropics. As might be expected of a "weed," *Haliplanella luciae* is remarkably tolerant of variations in temperature and salinity and of desiccation. Individuals are often found exposed in the intertidal zone among fragile barnacle (*Chthamalus*) and oyster (*Crassostrea*) shells where they appear as shiny, slick, black spots 0.2–0.4″ (5–10 mm) in diameter. The column of *Haliplanella* is dark green and is marked with parallel orange, white, yellow, cream, or green vertical stripes. There are 25–50 long, delicate, pale-green tentacles which are sometimes tinged with white. *Haliplanella,* like the brown anemone (*Aiptasia*), the redspotted anemone (*Aiptasiogeton*), and the hermit crab anemone (*Calliactis*) expels stinging threads (acontia) from its stomach. In *Haliplanella,* the acontia spew out spaghettilike from the mouth whereas, in *Calliactis, Aiptasia,* and *Aiptasiogeton,* the column is provided with cinclides through which the threads escape. *Haliplanella* individuals may have 1–18 specialized tentacles close to the mouth called "catch" tentacles. These are highly extensible nonfeeding tentacles that sweep the area around the animal and sting other anemones attempting to intrude on its territory. This reflex is similar to the acrorhagial response described for the stinging anemone, *Actinia bermudensis.* Although *Haliplanella* can reproduce sexually, it typically reproduces asexually by lengthwise fission, as in *Actinia,* or by pedal laceration, as in *Aiptasia.* Regardless of the reproductive pattern employed, *Haliplanella* often colonizes a local habitat unexpectedly and may, after enjoying a period of rapid population growth, disappear just as suddenly.

Anemones

Ghost Anemone *Haloclava producta*

Between mid-tide level and the low water mark on protected sand or shelly sand beaches, one occasionally sees craterlike burrows flush with the surface, 0.4–0.6″ (1–2 cm) in diameter, and with a loose scattering of shell fragments around them. The openings are produced by *Haloclava producta,* a highly contractile burrowing anemone. *Haloclava* has about 20 short tentacles with swollen brown tips. The ghost white column bears approximately 20 rows of bumps (adhesive verrucae) corresponding to the number of tentacles. Sand and shell particles may adhere to the verrucae. The individual in the left drawing is almost fully extended,

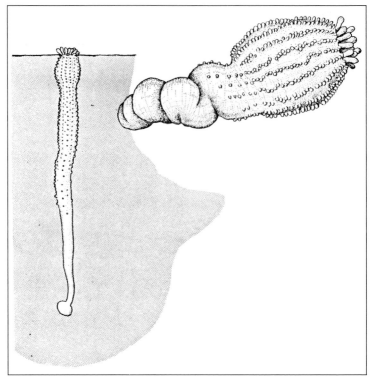

Figure 103

as *Haloclava* typically appears when freshly dug. Fully extended specimens are very long (8″; 20 cm or more) but when removed from sand they shorten and wrinkle (above, right). The slender column terminates in a swollen anchoring physa that looks like an inverted mushroom cap. As in the tube anemone, *Ceriantheopsis americanus,* there is a small pore at the base of the column leading from the stomach to the exterior. The pore is a water outlet and water escapes from it and the mouth when the animal contracts to withdraw into its burrow.

Anemones   *Color Plate A18*

Hermit Crab Anemone *Calliactis tricolor*

This colorful anemone is normally attached to hermit crab shells, especially those of the flat-clawed hermit, *Pagurus pollicaris,* the giant red hermit, *Petrochirus diogenes,* and rarely the striped hermit, *Clibanarius vittatus.* It also attaches directly to the carapace of the calico box crab, *Hepatus epheliticus.* Large numbers of isolated *Calliactis* sometimes wash ashore in areas where flotsam accumulates. Presumably, they have been unwillingly dislodged from their hosts by waves or currents. The column of *Calliactis tricolor* is usually dull brown with cream streaks, although it may be pink with similar markings. There are two circular rows of pores (cinclides) near the base of the column that allow stinging threads (acontia) to be expelled from the coelenteron when the animal is disturbed. The numerous (up to 200) short tentacles are usually white but may be shocking pink or orange. Pigmentation around the mouth and onto the oral disk is tricolored, as indicated in the Latin name, in bands of vivid yellow, red, and pink-purple. *Calliactis* reproduces asexually by a lengthwise division of the column.

Calliactis lives in a symbiotic relationship with its host that is beneficial to both partners. The anemone gains a mobile surface free of competition with other species of anemones and probably can share in scraps of food that drift its way from the sloppy eating habits of the host. The crab probably gains camouflage and protection from the anemone's stinging capsules. The presence of the anemone on the hermit's shell is reported to protect the crab from attacks of *Octopus* and the flamed box crab, *Calappa flammea.* When the hermits, *Petrochirus* and *Pagurus,* move to a larger snail shell they often help the anemone shift from the old shell to the new. *Calliactis* can, however, shift to a new shell under its own power and frequently does so.

Corals

Ivory Bush Coral *Oculina arbuscula*

Our shallow coastal waters support two species of stony corals; star coral, *Astrangia danae,* and ivory bush coral, *Oculina arbuscula.* Neither of these species forms reefs. Individual colonies of *Oculina arbuscula* live in aggregations of spherical heads on rock surfaces. Some of the individual colonies reach 3' (1 m) or more in diameter. While alive, they are dark reddish because of symbiotic algae (zooxanthellae) in their living tissues. A colony is composed of many branches bearing noticeably raised coral cups. *Oculina arbuscula* is a shallow-water species found only in the Carolinas.

Oculina is host to a number of symbionts. Among the more spectacular is the sea spider, *Pycnogonum cessaci,* and the cirratulid polychaete, *Dodecaceria concharum* (1"; 2.5 cm), with its striking green body and orange head appendages.

Reef-forming corals, known as hermatypic corals, are usually restricted to clear, warm water that does not fall below an average, minimum, annual temperature of about 75°F (24°C). There are, however, some exceptions to this rule. The hermatypic coral, *Siderastrea radians,* occurs offshore in the Southeast where temperatures drop below 68°F (20°C) and the coral reefs in Bermuda are exposed briefly to winter temperatures of 63–64°F (17–18°C).

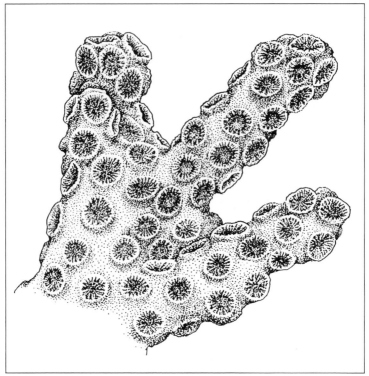

Figure 104

Corals

Star Coral *Astrangia danae*

The star coral, *Astrangia danae,* is the most common stony coral found in shallow water in our area. It attaches tenaciously to hard surfaces, including shells, in small, low, unbranched patches usually not exceeding 2″ (5 cm) in diameter. Efforts to remove this species from rocky surfaces are usually unsuccessful, result in complete destruction of the colony, and are not recommended. Star coral usually is white but is brownish when large numbers of symbiotic algae (zooxanthellae) are present in its tissues. Recent research, however, suggests that *Astrangia* does not derive major nutritional benefits from its symbiotic algae in contrast to most other corals. When expanded, the diaphanous white or brownish polyps of *Astrangia* are speckled with tiny white bumps which are batteries of stinging capsules used in prey capture. This species is distributed northward to Cape Cod and tolerates an annual temperature range of 28–72°F (2–22°C).

52

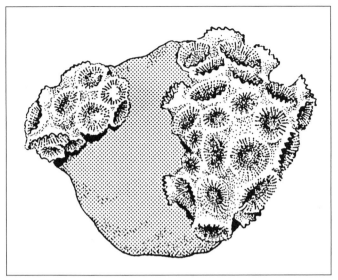

Figure 105

Astrangia reproduces in the summer by broadcasting eggs and sperm into the water where fertilization occurs. The fertilized eggs develop into tiny larvae, less than 0.004″ (0.1 mm) in length. They eventually settle on suitable surfaces and become the first polyps in new colonies. Growth occurs by budding of new polyps at the margin of the colony.

Tube Anemones
Color Plate A19

Tube Anemone *Ceriantheopsis americanus*

This spectacular tube-dwelling animal is not an anemone although it looks very much like one. True anemones are members of the order Actiniaria whereas *Ceriantheopsis* belongs to a related but different group, the Ceriantharia. Cerianthids differ from anemones in their tube-dwelling habit, the occurrence of two distinct whorls of tentacles, and the presence of an open pore at the swollen base of the column, which lacks a pedal disk. The pore is sometimes referred to as an anal pore but it probably does not function in defecation but as a valve to release water when the body shortens as the animal withdraws into its tube. Cerianthids, like anemones, regurgitate solid wastes. The tube of *Ceriantheopsis americanus,* which may be up to 20″ (50 cm) in length and about 1.5″ (4 cm) in diameter, is tough and silky. It is produced by specialized stinging capsules, called ptychocysts. These release long thin threads which do not sting but entangle to weave the tube. In appearance and texture, it is very similar to the spun tube of the sea wolf,

CNIDARIA / Tube Anemones

Polyodontes lupinus, which also occupies the same muddy sand flats as *Ceriantheopsis.* When cerianthid tubes are exposed at spring low tides, the upper part of the tube collapses on the sand and the tips of the tentacles hang limply from the end of the tube. Cerianthids feed by spreading their tentacles on the sand surface to gather food.

Occasionally, the tube fabric is colonized by sabellid polychaetes, called feather duster worms, and large white phoronids, probably *Phoronis australis.*

CTENOPHORA

Comb Jellies

Warty Comb Jelly *Mnemiopsis mccradyi*

Figure 106

At certain times of the year, large numbers of ctenophores appear in coastal waters where they delight the eye with their transparency, iridescence, and striking bioluminescence. Comb jellies do not sting and are extremely fragile. Most species are severely damaged if lifted from the water or even swirled in currents at the end of an oar. They escape storm damage by sinking well below the surface.

Close observation of comb jellies in sunlit water is rewarded by the shimmering colors of their eight comb rows. Each row is a series of small paddles and each paddle is composed of thousands of tiny cilia. Collectively, the cilia produce a color spectrum in much the same way as a diffraction grating or the surface of a compact disk. Disturbance of these animals in the water on moonless nights causes an intense green glow from the vicinity of the eight comb rows. The bioluminescence is produced by specialized light-producing organs located beneath each row.

Mnemiopsis mccradyi is the least fragile of our local comb jellies. Its faintly greenish jelly is stiff and not damaged if handled carefully. The body is more or less ovoid with slightly flattened sides. It reaches about 4″ (10 cm) in length and like all ctenophores is carnivorous, in this case

55

feeding primarily on small crustaceans and larval molluscs which it traps in a mucus film on the inner sides of its two large lobes. The food is then moved to the mouth by cilia and the small tentacles surrounding the mouth. *Mnemiopsis* is eaten by the jellyfishes, *Chrysaora quinquecirrha* and *Cyanea capillata,* and also by another ctenophore, *Beroe ovata. Mnemiopsis mccradyi* has small microscopic warts on its body.

Four similar species of ctenophores occur in our area. *Mnemiopsis leidyi* is similar to *M. mccradyi* in size and shape but lacks the whitish warts on the surface of the body, lacks the greenish opalescence, and has less firm jelly. *M. gardeni* is smaller, reaching only 1.4–1.6″ (3.5–4 cm) in adult length, has warts, and is slightly bluish in color. It may be the juvenile of *M. mccradyi. Bolinopsis vitrea* is a warm water species that reaches 2.4″ (6 cm) in length. Its pinkish or transparent colorless body has two wide lobes with broad shoulders set off distinctly at midbody.

Beroe ovata (to 4.8″; 12 cm), is bell-shaped but is strongly compressed from side to side and lacks the two lobes of *Mnemiopsis* and *Bolinopsis.* Its shape resembles a bishop's miter. *Beroe* tends to be pinkish but young specimens have brown or yellowish spots over the main circulatory canals and around the mouth. It is common in estuaries in winter.

HEMICHORDATA

Acorn Worms

Golden Acorn Worm *Balanoglossus aurantiacus*
Helical Acorn Worm *Saccoglossus kowalevskii*
Banded Acorn Worm *Ptychodera jamaicensis*
Pink Acorn Worm *Schizocardium brasiliense*

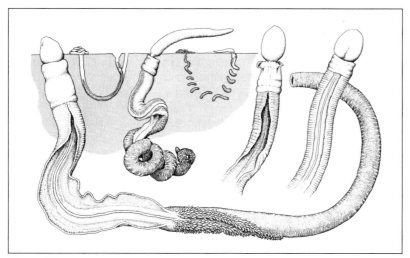

Figure 107

All of our acorn worms are burrowing deposit feeders that live in protected sand and mudflats but only the golden acorn worm, *Balanoglossus aurantiacus,* and the helical acorn worm, *Saccoglossus kowalevskii,* are common. The presence of *Balanoglossus aurantiacus* on a tidal flat can be detected by its large sandy fecal casts piled in soft ropy mounds approximately 2.5″ (6 cm) in width by 1.5–2.5″ (4–6 cm) in height. *Saccoglossus kowalevskii* also makes a fecal cast but it is less than 0.8″ (2 cm) in diameter and often, but not always, lies in a flat open coil. Each coil is about the thickness of mechanical pencil lead.

Balanoglossus aurantiacus reaches 3′ (1 m) in length but it is rarely, if ever, collected entire because the fragile trunk breaks easily. *Balanoglossus* occupies a deep U-shaped burrow about 0.2″ (5 mm) in diameter that opens to the surface at both ends of the U. One burrow opening is used for defecation while the other admits a water current for gas exchange. When the animal feeds, it digs a tunnel off the head end of the burrow and swallows sediment just below the surface. This causes the surface sediment to slump and produces a craterlike depression,

1–2″ (2.5–5 cm) in diameter, above the proboscis of the animal. The nutrient-rich organic material that accumulates at the sediment surface continuously tumbles into this depression and is eaten by the animal. The giant acorn worm, *Balanoglossus gigas* (not illustrated), resembles the golden acorn worm but is much larger (6.5′; 2 m or more). It burrows in clean, current-swept sand flats and produces thick (0.5–1″; 1–2.5 cm), coiled, firm, cylindrical fecal casts.

Saccoglossus kowalevskii, which is much smaller and only reaches 6–8″ (15–20 cm) in length, constructs a helical U-shaped burrow that is not as deep as the burrow of *Balanoglossus,* and there are no feeding shunts developed off the head end of the U. When *Saccoglossus* feeds, it extends its long proboscis over the surface of the sand and with it collects organic material. It then withdraws the proboscis and re-extends it in a new direction. Several repetitions of this behavior result in a surface trace, called a feeding rosette, that resembles spokes radiating from the hub of a wheel. The coiling of the burrow, which perhaps helps anchor the worm, is reflected in a permanent twist of the animal's trunk.

The red-banded acorn worm, *Ptychodera jamaicensis* (12″+; 30 cm+), resembles *Balanoglossus* but is distinguished from it by reddish-brown bands of pigment encircling the trunk, like tiger stripes. It occurs on fine sand flats often with *Balanoglossus.*

The pink acorn worm, *Schizocardium brasiliense* (10″; 25 cm or more) is pinkish with a short, pointed, red proboscis. It burrows in soft muds.

Balanoglossus and *Ptychodera* have flaps (genital wings) that extend outward from the trunk and bear the gonads. In *Saccoglossus* and *Schizocardium,* genital wings are absent and low genital ridges occur instead. The gonads are orange in males and grey in females.

CHORDATA

Tunicates *Color Plate A20*

Constellation Tunicate *Aplidium constellatum*

The dome-shaped colonies of *Aplidium constellatum* are found occasionally on rock jetties and floating docks in high salinity areas. The colonies are typically 1.3″ (3.5 cm) or more in diameter and have red individuals (zooids) embedded in the pale, soft, thick tunic. The tiny zooids are arranged in irregular meandering systems encircling the atrial siphons. The zooids appear white in the photograph because of the accumulated, reflective, fecal material.

Two other species of *Aplidium* are encountered in similar habitats in our area, *A. stellatum* and *A. exile*. Tough cartilagelike plates of *Aplidium stellatum,* known as sea pork, frequently wash ashore and often litter beaches, particularly near inlets. It is primarily a subtidal species but it occasionally grows on rock jetties. When alive, *A. stellatum* typically has red zooids in regular, nearly circular groups in its pink tunic. After death, the zooids pop out, the tunic bleaches to creamy white, and the lifeless tunic resembles salt pork or fatback, hence the common name, sea pork. *Aplidium exile* grows on hard surfaces in high salinity areas in northern Florida where it forms exquisite, semi-transparent, blue colonies.

Tunicates *Color Plate A21*

Paintsplash Tunicate *Didemnum duplicatum*

A colony of *Didemnum duplicatum* resembles a splash of thick white paint. It is a common tunicate in high salinity areas on rock rubble and other firm surfaces, including seaweeds. *Didemnum* colonies are only 0.08–0.1″ (2–3 mm) in thickness but can exceed 4–8″ (10–20 cm) in diameter. The colony appears smooth and glossy, but it often feels gritty because of numerous microscopic calcareous spicules embedded in the tunic. The large number of spicules not only stiffens the tunic and imparts its white color but also adds another unpalatable element to the already indigestible cellulose fibers. *Didemnum* plays another trick to further reduce its attractiveness to predators and perhaps to assist in competition for space. It concentrates sulfuric acid and vanadium in bladder cells in its tunic. When the tunic is damaged by any animal, such as a grazing fish, both substances are released. Vanadium inhibits many basic functions of living cells and like sulfuric acid, which is released in a concentrated form with a pH near 1, is distasteful to most fish. Some scientists, however, downplay the idea that the acid vanadium-containing bladder cells are defenses against predation. They argue instead that vanadium is an important element needed for proper formation of the tunic. Release of sulfuric acid by *Didemnum* is easily observed by damaging the tunic. This releases the acid which reacts with the calcareous spicules liberating small bubbles of carbon dioxide from the vicinity of the wound. Other sea squirts in our area, especially the honeysuckle tunicate, *Perophora viridis,* the translucent tunicate, *Ascidia interrupta,* and the orange tunicate, *Ecteinascidia turbinata,* sequester vanadium in their blood cells.

The white colony in the photograph is *D. duplicatium* whereas the yellow colony on the right may be an undescribed and unnamed species of *Didemnum.* The yellowish-green animal in the lower right is the translucent sea squirt, *Ascidia interrupta,* which is discussed elsewhere.

Tunicates

Chocolate Tunicate *Didemnum psammathodes*

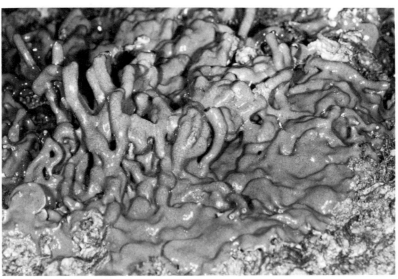

Figure 108

This glossy, smooth, smoky brown, compound tunicate is common in northern Florida growing on rocky surfaces in high salinity water but has not been reported north of St. Augustine. During spring low tides it can be completely exposed in shaded crevices among rocks. The colonies reach a very large size, often 1' (30 cm) or more in width, but not more than 0.2" (4–5 mm) in thickness. The specimen shown in the photograph was growing on the underside of a flat rock. When growing under overhangs or encrusting worm tubes such as those constructed by the segmented worm, *Sabellaria,* the colonies resemble stalactites of melting chocolate or a ropy convoluted mass. *Didemnum psammathodes* is sometimes used for camouflage by the sponge crab, *Dromidia antillensis.* The stiff tunic of this species contains myriads of starlike calcareous spicules similar to those found in the paintsplash tunicate, *Didemnum duplicatum.* The superficial area of the tunic is charged with vanadium and sulfuric acid-containing cells as described for *Didemnum duplicatum.*

Tunicates   *Color Plate A22*

Colorwheel Tunicate *Distaplia bermudensis*

This species is the most colorful tunicate on the southeastern coast. It grows in low rounded masses on hard surfaces in areas of high salinity. The color of *Distaplia bermudensis* is extremely variable as is apparent from the photograph of several colonies collected from a single floating dock in northern Florida. Other colors are common. *Distaplia* grows as stiff, slick, tough, low, rounded mounds or as closely set truncated heads, particularly in young colonies. As the young colonies mature, the heads merge together into a continuous smooth surface. *Distaplia* often overgrows other tunicates, such as the rough sea squirt, *Styela plicata,* whose two open unfouled siphons can be seen in Plate A22. The rest of its tunic is fouled with colonies of *Distaplia.* These colonies, which are typical in size for the species, are 1.6–2.4″ (4–6 cm) in diameter and approximately 0.4–0.6″ (1–1.5 cm) in thickness. In this colonial species, several zooids grow together, surround, and share a common exhalent aperture (cloaca). The anterior part of the atrial siphon of each zooid is enlarged and contributes to the shared cloaca.

Tunicates   *Color Plate A23*

Sandy Lobed Tunicate *Eudistoma carolinense*
Sea Liver *Eudistoma hepaticum*

By enclosing themselves in tunics composed of cellulose, the carbohydrate of which wood and other indigestible plant fibers are made, the tunicates render themselves unpalatable to most predators. In *Eudistoma carolinense,* unpalatability is carried further by impregnating the cellulose tunic with sand. In fact, the tunic of this colonial animal is so densely filled with sand that it and the individual members (zooids) are very difficult to see. The result is what must be one of the world's most indigestible animals. The colonies are hard, brittle, up to 8″ (20 cm) in diameter, 4″ (10 cm) in thickness, and sprout irregular, closely packed, fingerlike lobes the color and texture of sand. Sometimes the colonies may be almost perfectly hemispherical. Zooids are microscopic and embedded deeply in the tunic.

61

The considerable interstitial space created by the growth form of the sandy-lobed tunicate provides habitat for many smaller animals including the polychaetes, *Dorvillea sociabilis, Phyllodoce fragilis, Podarke obscura, Nereis falsa,* and the bivalves, *Chione grus* and *Musculus lateralis.*

The large, rubbery, slippery lobes of *Eudistoma hepaticum* inspired its discoverer to assign the species name, *hepaticum,* which means "liver." Colonies of this animal can be extensive, often thickly covering entire submerged panels of floating docks or large surfaces of boulders on rock jetties. When healthy, it is uniformly purple in color because of many pigment cells in the tunic. The brownish microscopic zooids are completely embedded in the common tunic. Each group of eight or more zooids is arranged in a system, 0.08–0.1″ (2–3 mm) in diameter, surrounding a common exhalent aperture. This species, like *E. carolinense,* occurs year round but becomes moribund in winter, loses its purple color, and turns white. The folds and creases in the surface of the colony are often occupied by juvenile crabs such as the stone crab, *Menippe mercenaria,* which is purple at this age, and the hairy crab, *Pilumnus sayi.* Occasionally the tunic is speckled with a few tiny orange spots. These are orange-red copepods, *Botryllophilus brevipes,* embedded in the surface of the tunic. *Eudistoma* presumably releases some substance to minimize fouling and fouled colonies are rarely seen even though the tunic is a large and apparently inviting surface for potential colonists.

Tunicates   *Color Plate A24*

Light Bulb Tunicate *Clavelina oblonga*
Honeysuckle Tunicate *Perophora viridis*

Clavelina oblonga is an elegant, club-shaped, colonial tunicate that can be found growing in clumps on jetties and floating docks in high salinity areas during the warmer months of the year. The long clear zooids, up to 1.6″ (4 cm) in length, are joined together at their bases by a common tunic but extend upward individually. The two siphons are marked with an opaque white pigment. The endostyle, the evolutionary precursor of the thyroid gland, is the fine, vertical, white line on the ventral side of the large branchial (gill) sac. Scattered spots of opaque white pigment are present throughout the branchial region. The stalk, or abdomen, of *Clavelina* contains the stomach, intestine, and gonads. The intestine seen in the photograph is filled with tan silty feces which will be released into the atrium and out the atrial siphon. *Clavelina* broods its white eggs to the tadpole stage of development in the atrium or sometimes in a specialized, small, atrial pouch. The tunic of *Clavelina* has the consistency of stiff gelatin and seems to be tougher at the common base of the zooids. As the water cools in the fall of the year, the zooids die back to the base of the colony and persist through the winter as dormant buds which regrow in the spring.

A similar species, *Clavelina picta,* is found with *C. oblonga* in tropical and subtropical areas such as the Florida Keys and Bermuda. It is also reported from offshore in the Southeast. *Clavelina picta* has the same organization as *C. oblonga* but its siphons and endostyle are outlined with a dazzling lavender pigment.

The diminutive, green, colonial tunicate, *Perophora viridis,* in Plate A24, frequently overgrows other encrusting organisms like honeysuckle in a flower garden or kudzu in a forest. The zooids, which are usually less than 0.1″ (3 mm) in length, are attached like tiny emeralds on a vinelike stolon. The zooids are transparent and reward observation with a hand lens or microscope. They are excellent animals for observing the normal and periodic reversal of blood flow that occurs in all tunicates and the flow of green corpuscles (vanadocytes) in the circulatory system can be seen easily. *Perophora* concentrates large amounts of vanadium from seawater and stores it in these vanadocytes. Zooid buds occur on the advancing stolons at the margin of the colony. The branchial sac of each zooid has four rows of gill slits in *Perophora viridis* whereas in a closely related species, *Perophora formosana,* there are five rows of gill slits. The latter species has not been found in the range covered by this book but is reported from the tropics.

Tunicates   *Color Plate A25*

Orange Tunicate *Ecteinascidia turbinata*

Although this species is best known from tropical and subtropical areas, where it grows attached to mangrove roots, turtle grass, and rock surfaces, it is nevertheless common on some of our temperate floating docks and pilings where it occurs in loose clumps. Each individual zooid is about 1″ (2 cm) long, soft, and enclosed in a thin transparent tunic. Zooids are colorless but orange pigment marks the siphons in our area and in the Gulf of Mexico. Elsewhere entire zooids may be bright orange. Zooids are joined at their bases by a thin rootlike stolon which contains blood vessels and links the zooids into a functionally integrated colony. Eggs are brooded internally in a sequence of developmental stages extending from the ovary, along the oviduct, to the atrium where tadpoles complete their development and are released. The ovary, eggs, and tadpoles are large and bright orange even in lightly pigmented colonies and are easily seen through the transparent tunic. *Ecteinascidia* releases a defensive chemical and the orange color warns potential predators of the danger. One animal, the tiger flatworm, *Pseudoceros crozieri,* feeds on *Ecteinascidia* anyway.

Ecteinascidia is ideal for demonstrating the basics of tunicate anatomy and function. Nontoxic dyes (food colors) or particles (India ink) can be introduced into the oral siphon allowing water flow and feeding to be observed through the tunic. With fine forceps, zooids are easily removed from their tunics permitting excellent views of heartbeat, circulation, and developmental stages.

Solitary Tunicates

Sea Grapes *Molgula manhattensis*
Translucent Sea Squirt *Ascidia interrupta*
Rough Sea Squirt *Styela plicata*

Figure 109

Almost any firm surface in calm estuarine conditions can be colonized by the solitary tunicate, *Molgula manhattensis.* Sea grapes (1–2″; 2.5–5 cm) grow in groups and each resembles a slightly flattened, translucent, scuppernong grape. Often, however, *Molgula* is itself fouled with other organisms such as the bryozoans, *Bugula neritina, Amathia vidovici,* or various hydroids. The compressible but tough tunic can also be covered with silt or sand, obscuring its milky white translucency. *Molgula* apparently completes its life cycle in one year. It spawns its gametes at night and is reported to be reproductive throughout the year although reproductive output is most intense during warmer months.

A second species, *Molgula occidentalis* (not illustrated), is encountered occasionally in shallow water in our area and is very common south of it. The body is larger than that of *M. manhattensis,* the tunic is tough, wrinkled, tan to reddish-brown, and the mantle tissue is bright orange at the siphons. In southern Florida, the tunic is almost always covered with mud or sand. It is eaten by the tulip snail, *Fasciolaria hunteria.*

Ascidia interrupta is a large (2.4″; 6 cm) solitary tunicate which attaches to shells, floats, boat bottoms, pilings, and rocks. It is one of the most common large tunicates in North Carolina and northern Florida but is rare in South Carolina and Georgia. The tunic of *Ascidia* is translucent and usually slightly green because of green cells in its blood which contain a high concentration of vanadium. The tunic is firm, easily torn, and glassy. *Ascidia* is usually flattened laterally but, depending on the type of attachment surface and degree of crowding, individuals may assume a wide variety of shapes. Attachment is usually on the left side of the body, but other positions occur frequently. This species is apparently restricted to very shallow water. *Ascidia* is probably reproductive throughout the year and is a good source of gametes for laboratory studies of tunicate development. A color photograph of *Ascidia* can be seen in that of the paintsplash tunicate, *Didemnum duplicatum* (Pl. A21)

Styela plicata, our largest solitary tunicate, is described elsewhere.

Tunicates

Rough Sea Squirt *Styela plicata*
***Polyandrocarpa zorritensis* (overgrowing *Styela*)**

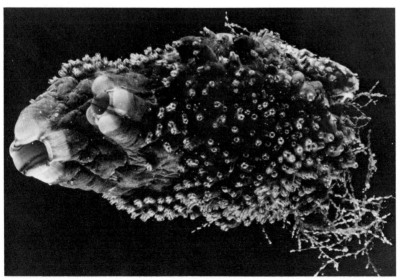

Figure 110

Great lumpy aggregations of *Styela plicata* (Figs. 109, 254), our largest solitary tunicate, often cover ropes, boat bottoms, pilings, floating docks, and other firm surfaces in protected areas with good water movement. Individuals of *Styela* reach 4″ (10 cm) in height although lengths of 2.5–3″ (6–8 cm) are more typical. The tunic is thick, convoluted, very tough, and often encrusted with other organisms such as the honeysuckle tunicate, *Perophora viridis*, or *Polyandrocarpa zorritensis* (pictured), or the bryozoan, *Bugula neritina*. Viewed from above, the siphons are 4-lobed and are marked with purple lines in the shape of a cross over the opening. *Styela* ranges from North Carolina to both coasts of Florida. Like several other tunicates, *Styela* sequesters vanadium but unlike them it also concentrates two other rare heavy metals, niobium and tantalum. It does well in marine aquaria particularly if fed fresh clam juice and supplemented with crumbled, cooked, egg yolk. Spawning of eggs and sperms is stimulated by light at sunrise but there is a time delay so that actual release does not usually occur until afternoon. Fertilized eggs develop through the night into swimming larvae which settle and begin metamorphosis during the next day. *Styela* is reproductive year round.

A second smaller species, *Styela partita,* is encountered rarely in shallow water in the Southeast. It is smaller than *S. plicata,* usually 1.2–2″ (3–5cm) in height, with a rough, reddish, pebbly tunic. Internally, *S. partita* possesses a pair of gonads on each side of the viscera whereas *S. plicata* has two on the left and as many as seven on the right. The inside lining of the tunic (mantle) in *S. partita* is bright orange. *Styela partita* is common in New England and in parts of the tropics, including Bermuda.

Polyandrocarpa zorritensis resembles an aggregation of miniature individuals of *Styela* and the two genera are indeed closely related. *Polyandrocarpa,* however, is a very small (0.4″; 1 cm) colonial species with individual zooids interjoined by a rootlike stolon. Sometimes the tunic is heavily encrusted with sand. The single large *Styela* in the photograph is covered by hundreds of small *Polyandrocarpa* zooids.

Tunicates   *Color Plate A26*

Symplegma rubra

The orange-yellow to cherry-red colonies of *Symplegma rubra* make brightly colored patches on rocks and seawalls of some of our jetties. Although true colonies, the crowded individual zooids each have a distinct oval outline and two tubular siphons opening on the upper surface. The colonies are soft, at least 0.5″ (1 cm) in thickness, and can reach 4″ (10 cm) in diameter. The tunic is a gelatinous transparent film that invests the zooids and allows their bright colors to show through. *Symplegma* grows by developing short rootlike stolons at the margin of the colony. Zooids develop from these stolons and extend the horizontal extent of the colony. Although hermaphrodites, each colony of *Symplegma rubra* is composed at any given time of either mature male or mature female zooids.

A similar species, *Symplegma viride,* occurs in the tropics and has been reported from the Southeast. It resembles *S. rubra* in general appearance but the tunic is dark and a yellow or orange patch occurs between the two siphons of each zooid. Colonies of *S. viride* simultaneously contain mature male and female zooids.

Tunicates   *Color Plate A27*

Royal Tunicate *Botryllus planus*
Frog Egg Tunicate *Diplosoma listerianum*

The regal gold and purple compound tunicate in the photograph is the royal tunicate, *Botryllus planus,* a close relative of *Styela* and *Polyandrocarpa.* This colony is 2″ (5 cm) in width and about 0.1″ (2–3 mm) in thickness. The zooids are arranged in starlike circular to oval systems. The oral siphon of each zooid opens on the perimeter of the system and is enclosed by a loop of gold pigment. The zooids in each system share a single, central, atrial siphon opening to the outside of the colony. The amphipod, *Corophium* can be seen on the *Botryllus* in the photograph, and several of its muddy tubes are visible on the right.

The frog egg tunicate, *Diplosoma listerianum,* is a thin, soft, slimy, gelatinous colony on other fouling organisms such as hydroids and bryozoans, but it also grows directly on the undersurfaces of rocks, floating docks, and grass blades. The colony in the photograph is growing on the green alga, *Bryopsis plumosa.* The tunic is transparent, soft, and structureless. The arrangement of compact greenish-grey zooids in it resembles the appearance and texture of an amphibian egg mass. Colonies are 0.08″ (1–2 mm) in thickness and 4″ (10 cm) or more across. Zooids are not arranged in clear-cut systems but the atrial siphons open into extensive common chambers (cloacal cavities) within the tunic. The chambers are vented to the outside through a few scattered large apertures. The name *Diplosoma* ("two bodies") refers to the fact that the tadpole larva, which will become the first zooid in the future colony, already contains a bud that has precociously formed the second zooid. Each *Diplosoma* tadpole, therefore, has two oral siphons and two branchial sacs.

Lancelets

Amphioxus *Branchiostoma caribaeum*

Fishlike and streamlined, amphioxus (2″; 5 cm) is a close relative of the fishes and other vertebrates. Like the tunicates and the vertebrates,

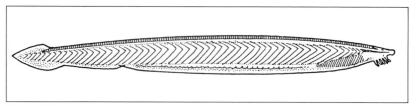

Figure 111

amphioxus has gill slits, dorsal hollow nerve cord, and a backbone-like skeletal rod called a notochord. It is not a fish because it lacks a true backbone, eyes, and a skull. Zoologists regard amphioxus as an evolutionary link between invertebrate and vertebrate animals.

Amphioxus swims much like a fish but only in short bursts of activity. Its swimming motion consists of rapid side-to-side undulations, like a frantic minnow stranded in wave swash, and it can also swim backwards. When amphioxus stops swimming, it sinks to the bottom and rests stiffly on one of its sides, or makes a quick swimming movement and burrows into the sand. Amphioxus probably swims infrequently unless it is disturbed. It is normally found offshore in current-swept sand with only its head projecting above the surface of the sediment. Amphioxus feeds in this position by pumping water into its mouth, through the pharynx and gill slits, and out a large pore situated on the belly. Plankton and other small food particles are trapped in the pharynx and passed on into the gut for digestion. The anus is a small opening on the belly just in front of the tail. The paired gonads are cream-colored blocks along the sides of the body. In early spring, male and female amphioxus spawn their eggs and sperm into the sea. The fertilized eggs soon develop into a transparent, asymmetric, swimming larva, only a few millimeters (0.1″; 2 mm) in length, that remains planktonic for several weeks before settling to the bottom and transforming to a small amphioxus.

Amphioxus occurs in high densities offshore, and because the animals are very muscular and lack bones, consideration has been given to the development of a commercial fishery in the Southeast. An amphioxus fishery has existed for centuries in the village of Liuwutien in southern China. Using hand methods, about 400 fisherman catch an average of 2,600 pounds of amphioxus per 4-hour working day. They are eaten cooked or dried.

ECHINODERMATA

Sea Stars *Color Plate A28*

Grey Sea Star *Luidia clathrata*
Margined Sea Star *Astropecten articulatus*

These two sea stars, which average 3–5″ (8–12 cm) in diameter, are abundant on sandy bottoms in shallow offshore areas from North Carolina to the tropics. Unlike the common sea star, *Asterias forbesi,* and other sea stars found on rocky surfaces, the tube feet of these two species lack suckers and have rounded or pointed tips, enabling them to poke into the sand so they can pole the animals over the sand surface. *Luidia clathrata* and *Astropecten articulatus* are the fastest sea stars in our area, reaching top speeds of approximately 30″ (75 cm) per minute. Both species burrow into sand with their tube feet in search of food and for concealment. Small clams are preferred and large quantities of these are swallowed whole. *Luidia* is reported to overeat if given the opportunity. When it does, the disk bulges conspicuously and may even rupture. Both species lack an anus and regurgitate indigestible shells, sand, and other material from the mouth. The upper surface is covered with plates (paxillae) which, when examined with a magnifier, have the appearance of a field of daisies. Each paxilla consists of an upper plate with a fringe of petal-like spines. The plate is supported by a stalk which grows out of the upper surface of the sea star's body. Interdigitation of spines on adjacent places prevents sand from entering the space between the plates and the surface of the body when the animal burrows. Gills extend into the protected sand-free space where a current of fresh oxygen-rich seawater flows over them. A polychaete worm, *Podarke obscura,* is reported to live in the ambulacral grooves among the tube feet.

Sea Stars *Color Plate A29*

Common Sea Star *Asterias forbesi*

Asterias forbesi is probably the most familiar of the southeastern sea stars. It is usually encountered at low tide on rocky surfaces and frequently washes ashore after storms. It reaches 6″ (15 cm) or more in diameter and is a carnivore with an insatiable appetite. Although it often feeds on the scorched mussel, *Brachidontes exustus,* in South Carolina, individuals will eat nearly anything when confined to an aquarium. Common sea stars probably feed on many species of sessile invertebrates under natural conditions. Unlike *Astropecten* and *Luidia,* which swallow their food whole, *Asterias* embraces the prey with its five arms and holds tightly with its suckered tube feet. The stomach then everts through the mouth to surround and digest the prey. The stomach has the appearance of a thin whitish membrane, and the sea star can cover its prey with it and insinuate it through small spaces. When feeding on bivalves, the stomach can enter the slightest gap (0.004″ or 0.1 mm) between the valves. It is said that when *Asterias* feeds on a large quahog, it can apply approximately 12 lb. (5.5 kg) of force to fatigue the muscles of the clam and open its two valves. The photograph also shows a branched reddish-purple bryozoan, *Bugula neritina,* a typical purple juvenile of the stone crab, *Menippe mercenaria,* and some of the small scorched mussels mentioned above.

Asterias is a major predator of the eastern oyster, *Crassostrea virginica,* in the Northeast and sometimes consumes quantities equal to half the commercial catch. As many as 1000 adult starfish have been removed from a single acre of oysters. *Asterias* rapidly disperses to new oyster beds by drifting with the tide. The star curls up the tips of the arms, releases its hold, and drifts just above the bottom. In this manner, it can travel much faster than it could under its own power and can recolonize oyster beds laboriously cleaned of stars only 24 hours earlier. *Asterias* is excluded from oyster beds in the upper reaches of estuaries by its intolerance of salinities lower than 16 to 18 parts per thousand.

Brittle Stars   *Color Plate A30*

Smooth Brittle Star *Ophioderma brevispinum*
Blood Brittle Star *Hemipholis elongata*

The smooth brittle star, *Ophioderma brevispinum,* occurs commonly in shallow subtidal grass beds. It is usually olive green but color variations are common. The disk is covered above with tiny spherical granules, often displays patches of contrasting colors such as black, yellow, or rust, and the arms may be banded. *Ophioderma* measures up to 3″ (7.5 cm) in diameter and is easily identified by its sleek shape and small spines on the arms that feel rough if a finger is drawn over them toward the disk. *Ophioderma brevispinum* is an omnivore.

The blood brittle star, *Hemipholis elongata* (4″; 10 cm) burrows in oxygen-poor sediments and is sometimes associated with the buried portion of the tube of the polychaete worm, *Diopatra cuprea.* Most species of burrowing brittle stars in our area wave their arms in the overlying water to ventilate the burrow and make pumping movements with the disk to irrigate the gills (genital bursae). *Hemipholis* lacks genital bursae and does not pump its disk. To compensate for the reduced gill area, it has red blood cells containing hemoglobin in its water vascular system. Internally, specialized branched vessels from the water ring of the water vascular system transport the red blood cells to the viscera. Presumably, *Hemipholis* uses this system to improve oxygen transport from the surface water to its buried body. The red corpuscles cause the tube feet to appear red, making identification of *Hemipholis* very easy. A much smaller brittle star, *Ophiactis rubropoda* (1″; 2.5 cm), also has hemoglobin in its tube feet but has six arms instead of five and lives epibenthically and not infaunally.

Brittle Stars

Six Arm Brittle Star *Ophiactis rubropoda*
Spiny Brittle Star *Ophiothrix angulata*
Brooding Brittle Star *Axiognathus squamatus*

Figure 112

There are three common epibenthic brittle stars in shallow water on our coast. All are associated with the community of organisms on hard substrata, such as pilings, oysters, and rocks. *Ophiactis rubropoda* (1″; 2.5 cm) occurs in the southern part of the range covered by this book. It is identified by its small size, six arms, and red tube feet. *Ophiactis* reproduces asexually by disk division. Following division, arms regenerate on the torn edges of the disk. As a result, individuals often have three long original arms and three short, new, regenerating arms as illustrated above. *Ophiactis* is light green but has hemoglobin in its water vascular system and, as a result, its tube feet are bright red.

The six arm brittle star, *Ophiactis rubropoda,* and the brooding brittle star, *Axiognathus squamatus,* are the two smallest brittle stars in our area, reaching about 1″ (2.5 cm) in diameter. Although *Axiognathus* belongs in the Amphiuridae, a family of predominantly burrowing brittle stars, it occurs in large numbers on rock jetties associated with compound tunicates such as the sandy-lobed tunicate, *Eudistoma carolinense.* Its disk is reddish-brown or tan and its arms are white. It feeds on deposited and suspended food particles. *Axiognathus* is an hermaphrodite and is unusual among our local species because it broods its young in ten sacs beneath its disk, called genital bursae, until it gives birth to tiny juvenile brittle stars. *Axiognathus squamatus* is distributed worldwide and is bioluminescent.

The spiny brittle star, *Ophiothrix angulata,* is our most common, conspicuous, and colorful brittle star, reaching a diameter of 2.5″ (6 cm). Body colors may be green, grey, red, or bright orange. It is usually associated with fouling animals such as tunicates, bryozoans, and sponges. *Ophiothrix* has long, bristly, glassy arm spines with which it clings and suspension feeds.

Brittle Stars

Burrowing Brittle Stars
Ophiophragmus wurdemani
Microphiopholis gracillima
Microphiopholis atra

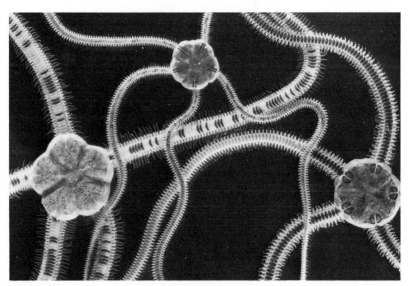

Figure 113

These three brittle stars all have very long thin arms which they use to burrow in fine sand or mud. *Ophiophragmus wurdemani* is our largest shallow-water brittle star, reaching a diameter of 16″ (40 cm), and its arms are often strikingly banded with brown pigment. The upper surface of the pale tan disk is surrounded by a fringe of short papillae that is characteristic of the genus. *Ophiophragmus septus* and *O. filograneus* are similar southeastern species. *Ophiophragmus septus* is reported from offshore and is recognized by a dark stripe along the upper surface of each arm. *Ophiophragmus filograneus* is reported south of Cape Canaveral and in the Gulf of Mexico. It differs from *O. wurdemani* by the grey color of its disk and indistinct banding on its arms.

Microphiopholis gracillima is smaller (6″; 15 cm) and less robust than its relative, *M. atra* (8″; 20 cm), and has longer thinner arms. When disturbed, it readily casts off its disk, which contains its gut and gonads. The lost parts are regenerated later. The small paired plates (radial shields) on the upper surface of the disk also distinguish the two species. The shields are long and narrow in *M. gracillima* and short and wide in *M. atra.* Both species are grey and are common in the Southeast.

Ophiophragmus wurdemani is reported to be a suspension-feeder, whereas *Microphiopholis* species may be deposit- or suspension-feeders. Food particles are caught on two or three arms held upright in the water while the disk and other arms are buried in the sediment. Tube feet transport food along the arms to the mouth located centrally on the underside of the disk.

A tiny red scaleworm, *Malmgrenia lunulata* (0.4″; 1 cm), usually occurs atop the disk of both species of *Microphiopholis.* It often crawls to the edge of the disk and curls its head down between two arms onto the oral surface, perhaps to steal incoming food. A minute symbiotic clam, an unidentified and unnamed species of *Mysella,* occasionally attaches itself to the brittle star arm spines by secreted byssal threads. The clam probably takes advantage of the ventilating water flow created by the host for feeding and gas exchange. Tiny brittle stars, presumably juveniles, sometimes are found on the disk of both species of *Microphiopholis.* Large numbers of rotifers, or wheel animalcules, *Zelinkiella synaptae* (Fig. 159, upper right), attach occasionally to the tube feet of *Microphiopholis* with their peculiar suckerlike stalks.

Another burrowing brittle star, *Amphioplus abditus* (6″; 15 cm), occurs occasionally on our coast. It is brownish-grey without a distinctive pattern on its disk or arms. The radial shields in each pair do not abut each other but diverge like open scissor blades and are separated except at their bases.

Sea Urchins

Purple Sea Urchin *Arbacia punctulata*

The purple sea urchin, *Arbacia punctulata,* is a common, reddish-purple, shallow-water sea urchin of hard substrata, especially groins and

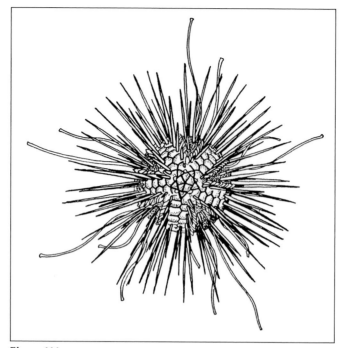

Figure 114

jetties, in the Southeast. The shell, or more correctly, the test, of *Arbacia* is small (2″; 5 cm) and the spines are long. Another common southeastern urchin, the short-spined sea urchin, *Lytechinus variegatus,* has a large test (3.5″; 9 cm) and short spines. *Arbacia* spines are pointed and very sharp except for those on the oral surface which are spatulate and blunt.

Long, suckered tube feet extend beyond the spines of *Arbacia* and other urchins. With these, the animal attaches firmly to hard surfaces in wave-pounded areas where it grazes on algae and encrusting animals, including sponges. The spherical shape of the body also helps to minimize the wave shock experienced by the animal. The long spines help protect sea urchins from predators and also may protect the fragile test by absorbing energy and breaking when struck by suspended rubble or shifting rocks. When a shadow is cast on the test, as might occur when a potential predator passes by, *Arbacia* points its spines in the direction of the object, concentrating its armament on the intruder.

Sea Urchins   *Color Plate A31*

Short-Spined Sea Urchin *Lytechinus variegatus*

The short-spined sea urchin, *Lytechinus variegatus,* occurs abundantly on shallow subtidal bottoms where it feeds on seagrasses. Although the dominant color of *Lytechinus* in the Carolinas is white, it may be pink, red, or lavender in the southern part of the area covered by this book. In addition to the short spines, the test (3.5″; 9 cm) has tiny pincers (pedicellariae). Unlike those of *Arbacia punctulata* or the sea star, *Asterias forbesi,* some *Lytechinus* pincers have swollen glandular tips that secrete poison. Fortunately they are ineffective against humans. *Lytechinus* often holds shell or plant fragments over its upper surface with its long adhesive tube feet, as shown in the photograph. Although the significance of this behavior is not completely understood, experiments suggest that the animals cover themselves in response to light, possibly to protect themselves from sunburn. Others suggest that the covering is camouflage. A small cryptically colored polychaete, *Podarke obscura,* is often found crawling among the spines of *Lytechinus.*

The pencil urchin, *Eucidaris tribuloides,* may be encountered occasionally in our region. *Eucidaris* is a sluggish urchin that uses its thick, pencil-like spines to wedge itself into rock crevices. At night, it may roam more freely. *Eucidaris* is said to feed on algae, bryozoans, and the boring sponge, *Cliona.* A close inspection of the primary spines of the pencil urchin may reveal small galls, 0.2″ (5 mm) in diameter. These are caused by a tiny snail reported from tropical regions, *Mucronalia nidorum,* which bores into the spines.

Sand Dollars

Sand Dollar *Mellita quinquiesperforata*

This splendid animal, or at least its dried skeleton, symbolizes the joys of vacationing on the southeastern coast. Sand dollars are flattened cousins of regular sea urchins. When alive, they are covered with a brown felt of very short spines but when dead and sun-bleached they are smooth and grey or white. The animals move slowly through sand in current-swept areas while buried just below the surface. Food particles such as diatoms and microbe-coated sand grains are conveyed to the mouth by specialized tube feet. The mouth is located in the center on the underside of the dollar. Five, hard, bird-shaped jaws crush the diatoms and sand grains before they enter the stomach. The five openings in the test, called lunules, help to prevent sand dollars from being washed out of the sand. The lunules reduce the hydrodynamic lift imparted to the winglike dollars by water currents. Other functions have been suggested for the lunules. They may be shortcuts for transport of food from the upper to the lower side of the dollar or they may allow passage of sand upward as the dollar burrows. The flowerlike pattern on the upper (aboral) surface that is faintly visible in living dollars but conspicuous in dried tests is where special tube feet extend into the overlying seawater for gas exchange.

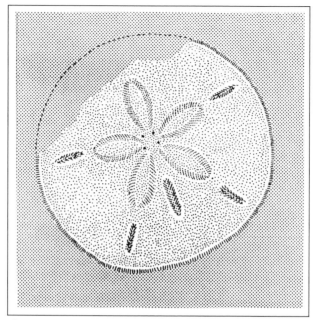

Figure 115

A tiny crab, *Dissodactylus mellitae* (Fig. 235), often lives in pairs near the lunules of sand dollars, where they apparently feed on mucus and food gathered by the host. Dead sand dollar skeletons provide a home for the spoon worm, *Lissomyema mellita*.

Heart Urchins   *Color Plate A32*

Heart Urchin *Moira atropos*

Heart urchins are bilaterally symmetrical relatives of regular, spherical, sea urchins. One of the 5 rows of tube feet is deeply cleft which imparts a heart-shaped profile to the test. Like other irregular urchins, such as sand dollars, heart urchins are specialized burrowers.

The heart urchin, *Moira atropos,* attains a length of approximately 2.5" (6 cm). The scattered black structures visible among the spines are pincers (pedicellariae) that produce a toxic secretion and presumably help protect the animal. *Moira* burrows in soft, subtidal, muddy bottoms and feeds on surface and subsurface deposits of organic material. As *Moira* digs into the mud, the apical spines, which are arranged in a circle, plaster a stabilizing layer of mucus on the walls of a vertical shaft joining the animal's burrow with the overlying water, 4–6" (10–15 cm) above. The shaft is used to transport oxygenated seawater to the urchin and to provide access to surface sediments rich in organic nutrients.

Moira maintains the shaft and gathers overlying sediments with a few remarkably extensible tube feet with expanded flowerlike ends. As the animal moves forward slowly through the mud, these same tube feet excavate new vertical shafts. *Moira,* with its shaggy spines and bilateral symmetry, is sometimes called a "sea porcupine."

Sea Cucumbers

Brown Sea Cucumber *Sclerodactyla briareus*
Green Sea Cucumber *Thyonella gemmata*

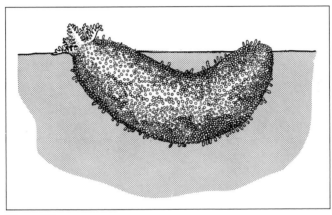

Figure 116

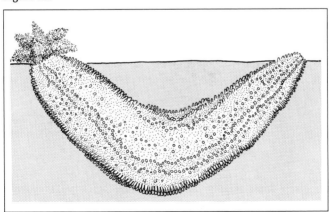

Figure 117

Nearly every beachcomber who walks the waterline after storms has seen the grey-brown bloated or limp bodies of the brown sea cucumber, *Sclerodactyla briareus* (4″), rolling up and down the beach in the swash or stranded at the high tide line. Under these conditions, the unfortunate animals often have their scattered brownish tube feet sanded away revealing a glossy, unhealthy-looking, whitish skin. Normally, *Sclerodactyla* burrows in sand just below the surface, anchors its tube feet to sediment particles, and extends both ends of the body upward into the water. Ten branched tentacles, eight long and two short, extend from the front end of the body to feed on suspended plankton and other organic material. The eight long sticky tentacles withdraw, one at a time, and wipe off the attached food on the two shorter tentacles. These transfer the food to the mouth. At the opposite end the intestine opens through the anus, as does a pair of internal, hollow, branched gills (respiratory trees). Water moves in through the anus to inflate the gills, and after oxygen is absorbed, the gills deflate and water moves back out. The tube feet of *Sclerodactyla* are scattered in profusion over the body surface. *Sclerodactyla* is reportedly eaten by loggerhead turtles (*Caretta caretta*).

The green sea cucumber, *Thyonella gemmata* (10″; 25 cm), also burrows but prefers muddier sand than does *Sclerodactyla*. The body of freshly dug specimens is flexed sharply and reflects the shape of the animal's semipermanent burrow, which has two circular openings about 1–3″ (3–8 cm) apart. *Thyonella* feeds and breathes in the same manner as *Sclerodactyla*. Both species have red cells in their tube feet containing the blood pigment, hemoglobin. The tube feet in *Thyonella*, however, are not scattered widely over the surface of the body but are more or less concentrated in five rows.

Sea Cucumbers

White Synapta *Leptosynapta tenuis*
Cucumber Clam *Montacuta percompressa*

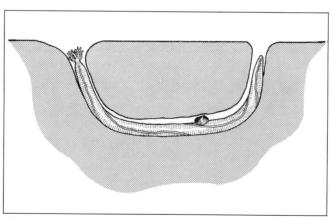

Figure 118

The white synapta, *Leptosynapta tenuis* (6″; 15 cm) is a fragile wormlike sea cucumber that lacks tube feet, except for the five branched oral tentacles which surround the mouth. It also lacks the internal gills (respiratory trees) characteristic of most larger cucumbers, and *Leptosynapta* absorbs oxygen through its thin skin instead. It occupies silty sandflats throughout the Southeast. Like the two unrelated worms, *Balanoglossus aurantiacus* and *Arenicola cristata, Leptosynapta* constructs a U-shaped burrow. The bottom of the U is located 4–5″ (10–12 cm) below the surface and the oral end of the animal extends upward into a funnel-shaped depression opening to the surface. Here the sticky digits on the oral tentacles collect sand and deposited organic material which are pushed into the mouth by the tentacles. The anal end of the animal projects into the other burrow opening and periodically defecates a soft pile of indigestible sand on the sediment surface. Tiny anchor-shaped ossicles in the skin grip the walls of the burrow and also stick to human skin. *Leptosynapta* ventilates its burrow by producing peristaltic waves of the body wall. Respiratory water is pulled in the feeding funnel and exits through the sandy fecal mound where plankton and other organic material may be filtered out. Occasionally, *Leptosynapta* turns around in its burrow and ingests the fecal mound, perhaps to extract food collected on the sand filter. It has been estimated that large populations of *Leptosynapta* overturn 10 to 60 tons of sediment per acre per year through their feeding and burrowing activities. By comparison, earthworms in an acre of fertile soil till about 10 tons of soil per year. A similar but rare pink species, the pink synapta, *Epitomapta roseola,* 4″ (10 cm) in length, also occurs in our area.

The tiny bivalve, *Montacuta percompressa* (0.2″; 5 mm; Fig. 159), shown attached to the body of *Leptosynapta* by byssal threads, is found nowhere else except with this cucumber. It takes advantage of the protection afforded by the burrow and feeds from the water flow produced by the host. This clam is an adult female. Males are dwarfs and parasitic on their spouses. Figure 159 (upper left) shows a female clam attached to *Leptosynapta.*

PHORONIDA

Phoronids *Color Plate A33*

Phoronis architecta

Phoronids are beautiful fragile animals aptly named after the fair Phoronis, a charming girl of Greek mythology who underwent some unlikely metamorphoses. Most phoronids develop from a transparent pelagic larva that does not resemble an adult. When the larva settles, it undergoes a complex metamorphosis to give rise to the adult body.

Phoronis architecta (4″; 10 cm) is a shallow-water species that occurs in sand. It constructs and occupies a straight, slender, stiff, hard tube (6″; 15 cm) of neatly cemented sand grains. The tube is oriented vertically and the animal extends out of the upper end to collect suspended food particles with its horseshoe-shaped crown of tentacles (lophophore). The mouth is at the base of the tentacles and the gut can be seen through the transparent skin as a narrow whitish stripe. The anus opens just outside the lophophore at the open end of the tube. The red pigment is hemoglobin in cells of the animal's blood vessels and is a provision for transporting oxygen from the exposed end of the organism to the rest of the body.

Large populations of feeding phoronids resemble gardens of flowers and are grazed by small fishes. Under such conditions, phoronids withdraw rapidly into their tubes and voluntarily jettison their lophophores. A new lophophore is regenerated in two to three days.

The two other species, *Phoronis psammophila* and *P. muelleri,* occur in the Southeast and resemble *P. architecta* in size, shape, and tube construction, although *P. muelleri* tends to live in muddier sediments than the other two species. Careful observation is required to distinguish these three species. *Phoronis psammophila* broods its embryos externally on the lophophore and has conspicuous organs for this function. *Phoronis architecta* and *P. muelleri* liberate their eggs directly into the water and lack lophophoral organs. *Phoronis muelleri* is separated from the other two species by technical internal characteristics.

Phoronis ovalis is a much smaller species (0.2″; 5 mm) that inhabits galleries in oyster shells resembling those excavated by boring sponges. Its crown of tentacles is nearly circular when viewed from above. *Phoronis australis* (2″; 5 cm) is a white phoronid with a spiral lophophore that is found embedded in the tube of the tube anemone, *Ceriantheopsis americanus.* A species of *Phoronopsis,* probably *P. harmeri,* inhabits sand flats in North Carolina. It is a large species with tentacles arranged in two spirals, each a mirror image of the other. A collar occurs at the base of each spiral.

BRACHIOPODA

Lamp Shells

Glottidia pyramidata

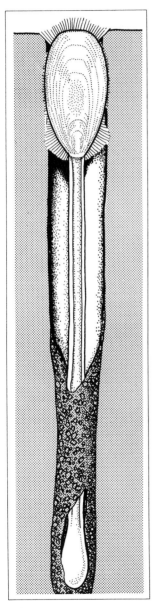

Figure 119

The lamp shell, *Glottidia pyramidata*, resembles a clam because of its bivalved shell, burrowing habit, and filter-feeding mode of nutrition. It is not a mollusc, however, but a member of an ancient group, the Brachiopoda, which is unrelated to molluscs. The brachiopods have lived on our planet for at least 600 million years. Fossils of species with the same body form as *Glottidia* have been found in rocks 500 million years old.

Brachiopod valves are positioned top and bottom with respect to the major body axis of the animal rather than left and right as in clams. Most brachiopods also produce an attachment stalk, called a pedicle or "little foot," that is a living part of the body instead of an inert secretion from the foot, as is the byssus of bivalves.

Glottidia valves are about 1″ (2.5 cm) in length and do not have a hinge. They are held together only by muscle and other soft tissues. The valves gape slightly while feeding and, because a rigid hinge is absent, shear across each other like scissors blades as it burrows. *Glottidia* orients itself in a vertical burrow with the swollen tip of the pedicle anchored at the bottom and the gape of the valves nearly flush with the sediment surface at the keyhole-shaped burrow opening. While feeding, long bristles, or setae, form three siphons that allow entry and exit of seawater and suspended food particles while excluding sand grains. Ciliated tentacles inside the valves pump water into the mantle cavity through the two side siphons. The tentacles trap food particles, convey them to the mouth, and probably also function as gills. Water leaves the mantle cavity through the center siphon. If *Glottidia* is disturbed while feeding, it contracts the muscles in the pedicle and withdraws into its burrow.

BRYOZOA

Moss Animals

Rubbery Bryozoan *Alcyonidium hauffi*

Figure 120

Grey rubbery colonies of *Alcyonidium hauffi* often overgrow the axial rods of the sea whip, *Leptogorgia virgulata,* as shown above. One often finds large colonies washed ashore which exceed 4–6″ (10–15 cm) in extent and resemble mopheads. The fingerlike lobes of the colony are approximately 0.25″ (6 mm) in diameter and are stiffly rubbery. Thousands of nearly microscopic individuals (zooids) are embedded in the rind of this flexible common skeleton. When the colony is in seawater and left undisturbed, the zooids extend, unfurl a minute funnel-like crown of tentacles, and begin to filter-feed by pumping seawater and suspended particles through the tentacles. Some of the extended zooids are seen magnified in the inset. A small (0.2″; 5 mm), cryptic, flat, circular sea slug, *Doridella obscura,* is found commonly on the surface of the colony where it feeds on zooids and lays tightly coiled, white egg masses. Two other species of *Alcyonidium* are reported from our area, *A. mammillatum* and *A. polyoum.* These species are difficult to identify and require further study by specialists. The shells of dove snails in the genus *Costoanachis* are often covered by a thin layer of *Alcyonidium.*

Moss Animals   *Color Plate A34*

Bushy Bryozoans
Amathia distans
Bugula neritina
Anguinella palmata
Zoobotryon verticillatum

There are many species of branching bushlike (arborescent) bryozoans inhabiting hard substrata on our coast. The four species discussed here are the most common. Colonies of *Amathia distans* are common on firm estuarine surfaces including floating docks, pilings, and oyster reefs. The bushy colonies are approximately 2.5″ (6 cm) in height. The individuals, or zooids, are arranged in double rows that spiral partly around the stems. The related species, *A. vidovici* and *A. convoluta,* are similar to *A. distans* in general appearance but the zooids in *A. vidovici* are in small clusters that spiral partly around the stem, whereas those of *A. convoluta* are in double rows and spiral completely around it. A small nudibranch (0.3″; 8 mm), an undescribed species of *Okenia,* feeds on *Amathia.*

Anguinella palmata (2.5″; 6 cm) is very common on firm surfaces in the intertidal zone where the exposed colonies hang like grey-brown, silty, wet, limp clumps when the tide is out. Each zooid in the colony extends from the end of a short tubular exoskeleton (zooecium).

Bugula neritina, which forms bushy reddish-purple colonies up to 3–4″ (8–10 cm) in diameter, is one of our most common and easily recognized bryozoans. Its zooids are arranged in two rows along the stems and branches. *Bugula* grows abundantly around and below the low water mark throughout our area. It is the only species of purple bushy bryozoan in the Southeast. Older or moribund colonies, however, are a dirty greenish-brown but usually retain traces of their original color. *Bugula neritina* is by far our most common *Bugula* but two other species occur with some regularity on hard surfaces in high salinity water. Both resemble *B. neritina* in growth form but colonies are usually

83

smaller. *Bugula stolonifera* is tan or beige whereas *Bugula fulva* is yellow or yellow-brown. Both species have microscopic pincers (avicularia), which are not present in *B. neritina*.

Large colonies of the loosely branched *Zoobotryon verticillatum*, which may exceed 12″ (30 cm), are reminiscent of transparent noodles found in oriental cuisine. *Zoobotryon* occurs abundantly in quiet water, as found in some of the deeper tide creeks and harbor areas, but also may be found on more exposed sites. The zooids in this species are in two rows, one on each side of the stem and branches.

Moss Animals

White Crust, *Membranipora tenuis*

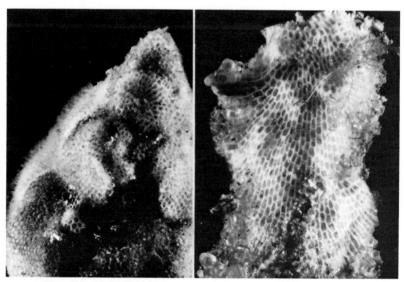

Figure 121

Many of our bryozoans form thin calcareous crusts on submerged objects, such as shells, seaweeds, or arthropod carapaces. We have several species and their identification usually requires magnification. Only common and easily recognized species are discussed on these pages.

Thin, white, hard, calcified crusts of *Membranipora tenuis* are common on hard surfaces throughout our area (right photo). The colonies in the photographs are approximately 1″ (2.5 cm) in diameter but others can be much larger. Colonies of *Membranipora,* and other encrusting bryozoans, consist of hundreds of individual members, or zooids, each enclosed in its own calcareous boxlike exoskeleton, the zooecium. The

84

upper surface of each *Membranipora* zooecium is not calcified, rather a flexible membrane stretches across the top like a tight drumhead. Muscles attach to the inner surface of this membrane and bow it inward when they contract. This raises the internal pressure and extends the retracted feeding tentacles, which pop up like a Jack-in-the-box. Extended feeding tentacles are visible along the shell margin in the left photograph.

Membranipora tuberculata is a similar species that encrusts leaves of the gulfweed, *Sargassum,* which frequently washes ashore after storms. *Membranipora arborescens* is an uncommon species in shallow water where it also forms white crusts. With a microscope, it can be distinguished from *M. tenuis* by its larger aperture, a brown line around the aperture, and by spines on the frontal, or upper, wall.

Moss Animals

Orange Crust *Schizoporella unicornis*
Lettuce Bryozoan *Thalamoporella floridana*

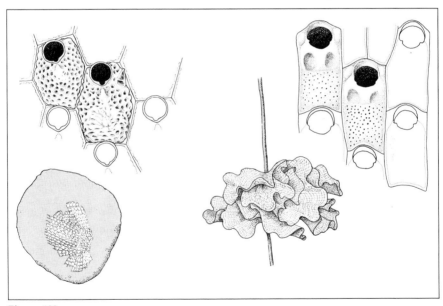

Figure 122

Schizoporella unicornis is an orange or white encrusting bryozoan common throughout our region. The calcified skeleton of each individual (zooid) has a circular aperture through which a crown of feeding tentacles protrudes, a perforated frontal wall, and a single bump behind the aperture. In addition to the typical feeding zooids, there are two specialized zooids in the colony. The first is a pincer (avicularium) that

85

may function to protect the colony from intruders by pinching them. The avicularia are keyhole-shaped and adjacent to some of the feeding apertures. There is a lid on the avicularium that opens and snaps shut like a diminutive mousetrap. The second specialized zooid, called an ovicell, is a spherical swelling on the frontal wall of some feeding zooids (see Fig. 122, right zooid). The ovicells are calcified brood chambers for a single developing egg produced by a feeding zooid. In some bryozoans such as *Bugula neritina,* there is a placenta between the feeding zooid and the developing eggs in the ovicell.

A similar species, *Parasmittina nitida,* forms pink-orange or white calcified crusts. The frontal wall in this species bears numerous, low, rounded bumps and peripheral pores, and the aperture is circular with two posterior sinuses not found in *Schizoporella. Parasmittina* becomes yellow when removed from the water and allowed to dry. *Schizoporella* does not change color when so treated.

Thalamoporella floridana grows as brittle lacy ruffles usually in the form of thin sheets but also in massive heads exceeding 7″ (18 cm) in diameter. Such colonies are reminiscent of open-headed varieties of lettuce. The lettuce bryozoan is calcified and as fragile as a thin potato chip. Colonies overgrow other organisms, frequently seaweeds and the bare axial rods of the sea whip, *Leptogorgia virgulata.* The largest colonies occur in tide creeks and sounds attached to *Leptogorgia.* Young colonies of *Thalamoporella* begin as crusts and superficially resemble colonies of *Membranipora tenuis.* Soon, however, the growing edges of the colony grow away from the surface as double sheets of individuals and their exoskeletons (zooecia). Microscopic examination of the frontal wall of the zooecium is necessary to distinguish *Thalamoporella* from *Membranipora.* The frontal (upper) surface of *Membranipora* is open and covered by a flexible membrane, that of *Thalamoporella* is completely calcified except for tiny perforations.

Conopeum seurati is another white, erect, lacy bryozoan in our area. The thin ribbonlike colonies do not form heads and the zooecia lack frontal walls. The aperture is very large and has a beaded rim.

KAMPTOZOA

Nodders

Barentsia laxa

Figure 123

Kamptozoans are typically microscopic animals but *Barentsia laxa,* a large colonial species, reaches 0.5″ (1.3 cm) in height and is visible without a hand lens. The colony in the photographs, however, is small and its largest individuals are only 0.1″ (3 mm) high. The body, which is called the calyx, is white and cup-shaped. It rests atop a long, flexible, muscular stalk which is smooth and lacks spines (left photograph). Up to 25 short ciliated tentacles project upward into the water. As in all kamptozoans, the tentacles are arranged in a horseshoe-shaped ring (right photograph). The base of the stalk enlarges into a muscular bulb and forms a flexible joint with the creeping rootlike stolon. The stolon interjoins all members of the colony. The stalks of living individuals sway, bend, nod, and twist. When an individual is disturbed, the stalk bends rapidly and presses the individual against the substratum, per-haps to avoid predation. Calyxes are sometimes lost or discarded leaving only a naked stalk (left photo). These stalks regenerate the missing calyx.

Barentsia colonies form by continuous budding from the stolon. Sexual reproduction results in larvae that are brooded on the calyx and eventually released into the sea.

KAMPTOZOA / Nodders

The ciliated tentacles of kamptozoans produce a water current that passes upward through the tentacles as in feather duster worms but opposite the direction of flow in moss animals and their relatives. Suspended food particles are trapped on the inner sides of the tentacles and conveyed to the mouth by cilia. Both the mouth and anus lie within the crown of tentacles.

There are many other species of kamptozoans in shallow coastal waters. *Pedicellina cernua* resembles *B. laxa,* but it is smaller, has spines on the calyx and stalk, and lacks the muscular basal bulb. Several microscopic, solitary, commensal species occur in our waters. *Loxosomella cricketae* grows on sponges, such as the garlic sponge, *Lissodendoryx isodictyalis. Loxosomella tethyae* grows on the red sponge, *Cyamon vickersi. Loxosomella bilocata* is found on the setae of the sea wolf, *Polyodontes lupinus,* while *L. worki* attaches to the inside of its tube. *Loxosomella minuta* attaches to the skin of the hermit peanut worm, *Phascolion strombus,* and *Loxosoma spathula* lives in the tubes of the polychaete, *Petaloproctus socialis.*

SIPUNCULA

Peanut Worms

Hermit Sipunculan *Phascolion strombus*

Figure 124

This sipunculan lives in shells of gastropods, such as the Atlantic auger, *Terebra dislocata* (1.2″; 3 cm), shown in the photograph. *Phascolion strombus* and its adopted home lie partially buried in bottom sediments while the long introvert, shown in the photograph, extends onto the surface to feed on deposited organic material. *Phascolion* lines the interior of the snail shell with a tube of cemented sand grains. The tube has two openings, one for the introvert and another near the siphonal canal of the shell for the flow of respiratory water.

The unique sipunculan introvert is the retractile anterior end of the body. The mouth is located at the end of it and is surrounded by a ring of feeding tentacles which are visible only when it is fully extended. Strong longitudinal retractor muscles extend from the introvert back into the trunk of the body where they attach to the inner side of the body wall. Contraction of these muscles pulls the introvert back into the body. The introvert is extended by circular muscles in the body wall. Contraction of these muscles puts coelomic fluid under pressure and forces the introvert out of the coelomic space where it was stored.

89

One of the smallest known bivalves, *Mysella cuneata* (0.04″; 1 mm), is found in the siphonal canal of shells occupied by *Phascolion strombus,* and two can be seen in the photograph. The clam takes advantage of the water flow produced by the worm for feeding and gas exchange. Other animals also occur with *Phascolion.* These include the commensal hydroid, *Stylactis hooperi,* shown in the photograph, the commensal kamptozoan, *Loxosomella minuta,* which attaches to bumps on the sipunculan's skin, and a polychaete, *Exogone dispar.*

Peanut Worms   *Color Plate B1*

Rock-Boring Sipunculan *Themiste alutacea*

The rock-boring sipunculan, *Themiste alutacea,* is about 0.8″ (2 cm) long and lives associated with calcareous surfaces. It is found with the coral *Oculina* where it reportedly occupies the angles between the branches. *Themiste* also bores into limestone rocks and it occurs in the interstices between other animals in the epifaunal community. The borehole consists of a deep polished cavity with a narrow opening at the surface of the rock. The introvert and its tentacles extend through the opening for feeding and gas exchange. It is not thoroughly understood how *Themiste* bores into rock, although it has been suggested that chemical reactions and mechanical abrasion are involved. When *Themiste* is disturbed, the tentacles and introvert are withdrawn and the trunk swells. The swollen trunk wedges so securely against the wall of the cavity that it cannot be removed without damaging either the animal or the rock. Freshly collected *Themiste* contract to become smooth, pear-shaped, and pinkish-grey with a papilla at the posterior end. The introvert is not visible until the animal relaxes and extends it. The mouth lies at the tip of the introvert and is surrounded by six, short, branched tentacles. There are scattered brown hooks on the base of the introvert.

The peanut worm in the photograph has been removed from its burrow and posed atop a mat of the scorched mussel, *Brachidontes exustus.*

Peanut Worms

Burrowing Sipunculan *Sipunculus nudus*

This large pinkish-tan worm, which reaches 12″ (30 cm) in length, is a burrower in coarse and fine sand flats. *Sipunculus* does not establish a permanent burrow but, like an earthworm, moves more or less continuously through the sediment ingesting organic material and sand as it proceeds. Freshly collected animals held in bowls of seawater defecate large amounts of sand. Like all burrowing sipunculans, *Sipunculus*

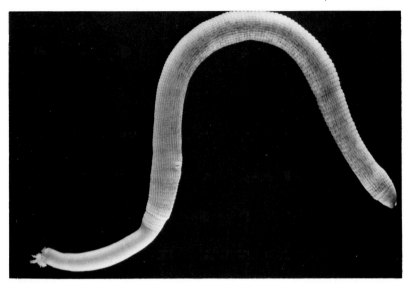

Figure 125

moves through sand using its introvert, which is the short uncheckered end of the body. It proceeds by alternately extending, anchoring, and retracting the introvert to pull the body forward. Several short branched tentacles surround the mouth at the end of the introvert and help sort edible detritus from inedible sand grains. *Sipunculus* swims awkwardly by sharply flexing the anterior end of its body rearward.

Most sipunculans occupy burrows with a single opening to the environment. If the anus of a sipunculan were situated at the end of its body in the blind end of the burrow, it would be difficult to maintain a tidy home. To avoid sanitation problems, the gut loops back on itself and the anus opens anteriorly near the base of the introvert to discharge waste at the burrow opening. The anus of the individual in the photograph is visible as a transverse groove just behind the introvert.

MOLLUSCA

Chitons and Limpets

Cayenne Keyhole Limpet *Diodora cayenensis*
(far left and right)
Eastern Beaded Chiton *Chaetopleura apiculata*
(center)

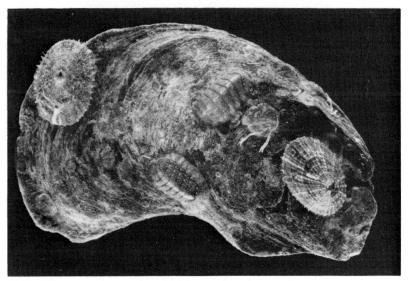

Figure 126

The chitons belong to their own class of molluscs, the Poly-placophora, and are easily recognized by their unusual shell which consists of eight overlapping dorsal plates. The group is adapted for a grazing life on wave-beaten rocky coasts. Chitons have a large ventral foot for holding to rocks and the rounded back presents a reduced profile to the crashing waves. Like the snails, they have a rasplike arrangement of teeth, known as radula, which they use to scrape algae from rocks. Our species have these features but do not live on rocky coasts, rather occur subtidally on old shells on the bottoms of creeks and sounds. By far the most common chiton in our area, *Chaetopleura apiculata,* is a small species about 1″ (2.5 cm) long and dull yellow, brown, or greenish in color. With magnification, one can see that each dorsal plate bears several orderly longitudinal rows of distinct peglike bumps. A tropical species, *Ischnochiton striolatus,* has recently been reported from North Carolina, but it is not common. It resembles

92

Chaetopleura but is smaller and its dorsal bumps are small and scattered irregularly over the plates. In addition, the fleshy girdle encircling the plates laterally is distinctly scaly (under magnification).

The limpets are grazers and have a broad creeping foot and low profile like the chitons. They are snails however, belonging to several families in the class Gastropoda, and as such they have a shell composed of a single piece. The limpet shell is a broad-based cone and is not coiled like that of most snails. The only species in our area is the Cayenne keyhole limpet, *Diodora cayenensis.* The family Fissurellidae, to which these keyhole limpets belong, is characterized by the possession of a small opening, or anal aperture, at the apex of the shell. The anal aperture is an outlet for water flowing over the gills and for wastes from the intestine and kidney. Our species is often found on subtidal creek bottoms along with our chiton but it is not restricted to that habitat and is also found on oyster reefs, floating docks, seawalls, and rock jetties.

South of Jacksonville, there is another limpetlike gastropod, the striped false limpet, *Siphonaria pectinata* (Fig. 215). Although superficially similar to *Diodora,* it is a pulmonate snail and the two are only distantly related.

Another group, the true limpets in the family Acmaeidae, is related to the keyhole limpets but resembles the false limpets in having no apical aperture. There is a species in this family in the northeastern United States (*Acmaea testudinalis*) and another in southern Florida (*Acmaea pustulata*) but none in our area.

Top Snails

Beautiful Top Snail *Calliostoma pulchrum*

Most of the snails in the family Trochidae on our coast belong to the genus *Calliostoma.* They are grazers, feeding on attached epibenthic organisms, including sponges. The family has several western Atlantic species but only a few of them occur in shallow water close to the shore. The trochid shell is shaped like a child's top and is ornamented with beaded spiral ridges. They have a thin, horny, circular operculum, and there may or may not be a cavity, the umbilicus, in the center of the base beside the aperture. Of the two species that are occasionally found in shallow water, *Calliostoma euglyptum,* the sculptured top snail, is the more common and occurs subtidally on rocks or sand. The shell is a broad, low, reddish-brown cone reaching 1″ (2.5 cm) in height. In profile, the sides are nearly flat with each whorl being slightly convex and separated from adjacent whorls by a shallow groove. *Calliostoma pulchrum,* the beautiful top snail, is smaller (0.6″; 1.5 cm) and has a slightly higher, narrower spire. It is yellowish- or reddish-brown and has a spiral row of small, discrete, dark red-brown spots. There are sometimes white spots beside the red ones and there may be larger diffuse

Figure 127

reddish blotches. The shell is rough in outline, with the lowest bead row on each whorl larger than those above it, forming a conspicuous ridge which separates successive whorls. Neither of these species has an umbilicus.

Turbans

Chestnut Turban *Turbo castanea*

The turbans belong to the family Turbinidae and are related to the top snails. There is only one species in our area, *Turbo castanea,* and it is not often seen. It has a heavy rough shell that is usually more or less top-shaped with convex, swollen whorls. The interior is iridescent and the operculum is thick and calcareous. *Turbo castanea* reaches about 1.5″ (4 cm) and has a rough shell with a large round aperture. The color is variable, and the shell is covered by spiral rows of irregular beads. The heavy circular operculum is white and brown. Other species, including the long-spined star snail, *Astraea phoebia* (2″; 5 cm), occur in deeper waters offshore. *Astraea* is flattened with a low spire and has distinctive, flat, triangular projections from the sides of the whorls.

Another family, the Neritidae, is a tropical group essentially absent from our area but one species, *Neritina reclivata,* the olive nerite, has been reported once from a salt marsh near Beaufort, North Carolina. It is common in south Florida and the Gulf of Mexico. Its shell is about 0.6″ (1.5 cm) high, obliquely ovoid, and dark greenish or olive with fine

94

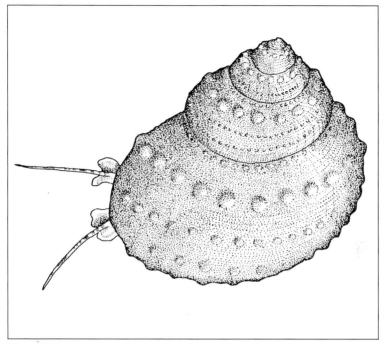

Figure 128

dark lines. The operculum is dark and irregular. It inhabits brackish or freshwater marshes and is herbivorous. The common bleeding tooth, *Nerita peloronta,* one of several species in the Florida Keys, is probably the best known representative of the family but it does not occur in our area. The nerites have strong oblong shells with a smooth, broad, often toothed, inner aperture lip. There is a very large body whorl and a large aperture, but the remaining whorls are small and inconspicuous.

Periwinkles

Marsh Periwinkle *Littorina irrorata*

The marsh periwinkle, *Littorina irrorata* (1″; 2.5 cm), is one of the characteristic animals of *Spartina* salt marshes along the southeastern coast of the United States. These globular pointed snails are a nondescript grey or beige color sometimes with spiral brown lines or wavy brownish blotches. The aperture is creamy white. They are tolerant of desiccation and are usually seen attached to grass stems above the water or sediment. They are herbivores that feed on algae and detritus on the sediment surface while the tide is out. They avoid immersion in water, presumably to minimize predation by blue crabs, which nevertheless,

95

Figure 129

are reported to shake periwinkles off their perches. The periwinkles belong to the Littorinidae, all of which have strong shells with a large body whorl and moderately high pointed spire. There is no umbilicus and the operculum is dark and horny. The shell may or may not be sculptured. There are many east coast periwinkles, all associated with habitats along the water's edge but only the marsh periwinkle is likely to be found in most of the area covered by this guide. A rocky coast species, *Littorina ziczac* (0.5″; 1.3 cm), is common south of our range and is rarely found as far north as Wrightsville Beach, North Carolina. This species is light grey with many zigzag reddish-brown lines on the whorls. The spire is high and there is a spiral ridge on the body whorl. *Littorina saxatilis* (0.5″; 1.3 cm), which is common on rocks and pilings in the northern United States, has been reported as far south as Harker's Island, North Carolina, but it is rare in our province. Its color is variable, often orangish, brown or grey, with a dark brown aperture and a deep suture. Another rocky coast species, *Littorina littorea*, is common in the northern United States and Europe and is eaten by Europeans. It does not occur in our area.

Scale Snails   *Color Plate B2*

Scale Snail *Cochliolepis parasitica*

Despite the specific name, these tiny snails are commensals, rather than parasites, which live with the giant tube-dwelling scaleworm, *Polyodontes lupinus* (Fig. 193). The snails are less than 0.2″ (5 mm) in diameter and, in life, have a perfectly transparent, colorless, flat, glass-like shell. Upon the death of the animal, however, the shell becomes opaque. The intense red of the living animal is due to the respiratory pigment, hemoglobin, in the tissues and is not the color of the shell. The snails are found with *Polyodontes,* usually under its scales, and apparently feed on particulate organic matter brought into the tube by the worm's respiratory water currents. *Cochliolepis* belongs to the Tornidae, all of whose members are tiny snails with oval opercula.

A similar snail, *Cyclostremiscus pentagonus,* is about the same size as *Cochliolepis* but lacks hemoglobin and has a more angular shell. It belongs to the Vitrinellidae whose members resemble the tornids but have a circular operculum. It lives on the mud walls of the burrow of the mantis shrimp, *Squilla empusa.* We have other tiny snails in the families Tornidae and Vitrinellidae but most of them live offshore and their identification is difficult.

Caecums

Caecum pulchellum

The snails in the family Caecidae are distinctive and easily recognized but are usually overlooked because of their small size. The shell of a caecum is not spiraled like those of other snails, but is a short slightly curved tube open at one end. *Caecum pulchellum* (0.2″; 5 mm) is a common inhabitant of grass beds. It has about 25–30 evenly sized circular ridges around the shell and is white or cream. The circular ridges of *C. floridanum* (0.2″; 5 mm) are not even and are larger near the aperture. *Caecum cycloferum* (0.3″; 8 mm) lacks circular rings and has longitudinal ridges instead. *Caecum carolinianum* (0.2″; 5 mm) is smooth, lacking rings or ridges on the shell.

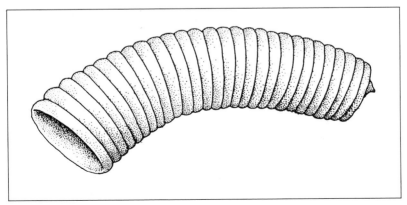

Figure 130

Several species of tiny, inconspicuous, coiled snails (0.1–0.3″; 2–8 mm) inhabit the intertidal surface of salt marshes, sometimes in high densities. These snails are detritivores belonging to two families, the Hydrobiidae and Assimineidae. Members of these families have similar shells with high spires and opercula. The hydrobiids have two long head tentacles with an eye at the base of each, whereas the assimineids have two short tentacles with an eye at the apex of each. *Assiminea succinea* (0.1″; 3 mm) is the common assimineid in our area and we have many species of hydrobiids, not all of them described. The assimineids are much more tolerant of desiccation than are the hydrobiids.

Miniature Ceriths

**Greens Miniature Cerith *Cerithiopsis greeni*
Awl Miniature Cerith *Cerithiopsis emersoni*
Adams Miniature Cerith *Seila adamsi*
Grass Cerith *Bittium varium***

Members of the Cerithiopsidae are small snails with high, pointed auger- or awl-shaped shells with an oval aperture and a distinct siphonal canal. The shells are usually brown, grey, or tan and strongly sculptured. The operculum is horny and oval. In the area covered by this guide there are three important shallow-water species, two in the genus *Cerithiopsis* and one in *Seila*. The two *Cerithiopsis* are dark brown, have spiral rows of beads, and are nearly identical. *Cerithiopsis emersoni,* the awl miniature cerith, reaches 0.8″ (2 cm), but is usually smaller, and has straight sides and a more or less square aperture. *Cerithiopsis greeni,* Greens miniature cerith, reaches only 0.3″ (8 mm), has slightly convex sides,

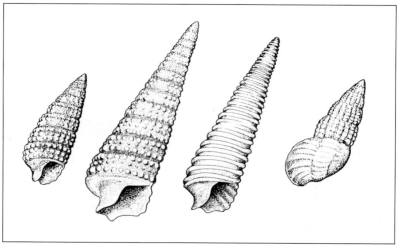

Figure 131

98

and a rounder aperture. The differences are subtle but are apparent in the drawing and can be used reliably with experience. Our other common shallow-water cerithiopsid, *Seila adamsi,* or Adams miniature cerith, is easily recognized. It is about 0.4″ (1 cm) long and has smooth, unbeaded, spiral ridges. All of these species are found in epibenthic, or fouling, communities on hard bottoms.

The Diastomatidae are small snails closely related to the cerithiopsids and cerithiids. They are elongate with a high pointed spire and have an oval aperture with an indistinct siphonal canal (the siphonal canal of the cerithiids and cerithiopsids is well developed and easily seen). We have one inshore species, the grass cerith, *Bittium varium,* and it is abundant in submerged grass beds. These dark brown snails reach only 0.2″ (5 mm) in length. They resemble our three cerithiopsids but, unlike them, have a thickened longitudinal ridge, or varix, on the body whorl.

Ceriths

Florida Cerith *Cerithium atratum*

Members of the Cerithiidae have tall-spired pointed shells much like those of the Cerithiopsidae. Most of the cerithiids have an oval aperture with anterior siphonal canal and posterior anal canal at opposite sides of the aperture. The cerithiopsids do not have an anal canal. The operculum is oval, dark, and has few whorls. Most of the Atlantic cerithiids

Figure 132

are tropical but the Florida cerith, *Cerithium atratum* (1.3"; 3 cm), occurs from North Carolina to the tropics. It is a subtidal species inhabiting shallow water and is dull grey and often stained. The whorls have several longitudinal ribs and spiral rows of small beads. There is usually a varix (a thick longitudinal ridge) on the body whorl. The tiny (0.2"; 5 mm) smooth, unsculptured, thin-shelled, yellow-brown sargassum snail, *Litiopa melanostoma,* occurs on floating gulfweed (*Sargassum*) and is a cerithiid.

Members of the Potamididae (horn snails) resemble the cerithiids but inhabit brackish water and have round opercula. The ladder horn snail, *Cerithidea scalariformis,* is about 1" (2.5 cm) long and is pale reddish-brown with spiral white lines. There is no siphonal canal and the whorls bear small vertical ribs but no varices. The aperture lip is strong and smooth. These snails may be common in the upper intertidal zone of muddy salt marshes.

Several other families in the superfamily Cerithiacea have representatives in our offshore waters but are not found alive inshore. *Turritella exoleta* (1"; 2.5 cm) in the family Turritellidae has a sharp elongate spire and resembles the Atlantic auger, *Terebra dislocata,* but the two are not related. *Turritella* has no radial sculpture and its whorls each bear two spiral ridges separated by a concavity. One of the worm snails which occurs off our coast, *Vermicularia knorrii* (3"; 8 cm), begins life as a turritella-like snail with tightly coiled whorls, but the older whorls depart from this pattern and are loosely and irregularly coiled so that they do not touch each other. Another worm snail, *Siliquaria squamata* (4"; 10 cm), belongs to the related family Siliquariidae and has a shell that is loosely and irregularly coiled over its entire length. In addition, it has a long row of small pores or slits along the whorls. Both worm snail species live in sponges offshore.

Pyramid Snails

Oyster Mosquito *Boonea impressa*

One of the many parasites that plague oysters is the tiny pyramidellid snail, *Boonea impressa.* These snails are only 0.2" (5 mm) in length but are often present in large numbers on the outside of oyster shells. They position themselves along the gape of the oyster, insert the tubular proboscis through the gape into the mantle, and suck the blood from the oyster. The left-most individual in the photograph is in the feeding position on the edge of an oyster and its proboscis can be seen extending over the edge of the shell. The snail's small size and blood-sucking habits are reminiscent of mosquitos, hence the fanciful common name. *Boonea* inhibits oyster growth not only by consuming the blood of its

Figure 133

prey but also by interfering with its feeding. Infested oysters close their valves much more frequently and have slower feeding rates than uninfected individuals.

The pyramidellids are a large group of very small snails. The biology of this group is poorly understood but they are presumed to be predators or parasites of other marine invertebrates. Many species are present on our coast, but their hosts are mostly unknown. The classification of pyramidellids is currently in confusion and their identification is difficult. The oyster mosquito is the most common of our species and, fortunately, can be readily identified by its shape, white color, and unbroken spiral ridges. Another species, *Boonea seminuda,* parasitizes scallops and slipper snails. It is white, usually has about 4 (2–6) spiral rows of beads per whorl. Some of these snails can be seen on Plate B23.

Janthinas   *Color Plate B3*

Common Janthina *Janthina janthina*

Several species of animals are specialized for life at the surface of the open ocean. They are not normally seen by land-bound observers but occasionally may be blown ashore by storms. Among these interesting animals are the violet snails in the family Janthinidae. Three species may occur on our coast and all have fragile purple and white shells about 1″ (2.5 cm) high or a little larger. They are predators of the floating colonial cnidarians *Velella* (by-the-wind sailor), *Physalia* (Portuguese man-o'-war), and *Porpita* (blue buttons), which are also adapted for life

101

at the surface of the sea. The snails are heavier than water and construct a durable raft of air bubbles entrapped in mucus to keep themselves at the surface and in the vicinity of their food. Their eggs are laid in the bubble raft. The species most often found on beaches is the common janthina, *Janthina janthina.* The easily recognized shell is pale lavender or white above and purple below. At sea, the animals usually orient themselves with the purple half up and the pale half down, presumably making themselves inconspicuous to predators in either the air or water. An aerial predator would see a purple shell against the deep blue of the sea while an aquatic predator would be looking at a pale shell against the sea's shimmering, silvery, lower surface. *Janthina* releases a purple pigment when disturbed. The shell is wider than high and the lower lip of the aperture is smoothly rounded. The elongate janthina, *Janthina globosa,* is entirely purple and higher than wide. It has a distinct rounded point on the lower lip of the aperture. The pallid janthina, *Janthina pallida,* is a paler purple than the other species and has a very large aperture with a smoothly rounded lip.

Wentletraps

Humphreys Wentletrap *Epitonium humphreysi*

The wentletraps (Epitoniidae) are mostly offshore animals and only a few species will be found alive in water of wading depth. Their empty shells, however, are a favorite home of small hermit crabs and may often

Figure 134

be found on our outer beaches. The family is a large one whose members are all relatively small, awl-shaped, pointed snails. They have smooth, globose, strongly convex whorls with strong, distinct widely spaced axial ribs and no other sculpture. The aperture is round or oval, there is no siphonal canal, and the aperture lip is heavy and strong. The operculum is thin and horny. Many species are reported to feed on anemones or corals. There is some experimental evidence that the snails apply an anesthetic to the prey, thus preventing retraction of the polyps while the snail feeds. Wentletraps have a very long proboscis. The egg string is unusual and resembles a string of beads. A few species occur in shallow water on our coast but they are rarely seen. Humphrey's wentletrap (*Epitonium humphreysi,* 0.7″; 1.8 cm), the angulate wentletrap (*E. angulatum,* 0.4″; 1 cm), the brown-banded wentletrap, (*E. rupicola,* 0.8″; 2 cm), the many-ribbed wentletrap, (*E. multistriatum,* 0.6″; 1.5 cm), and Krebs wentletrap (*E. krebsii,* 0.6″; 1.5 cm) may occasionally be found at wading depths. Because of the large number of similar species their identification may be difficult.

Slipper Snails

Common Atlantic Slipper Snail *Crepidula fornicata*
White Slipper Snail *Crepidula plana*

The family Calyptraeidae includes the cup and saucer snails, which are not found at wading depths in our area, and the slipper snails, which

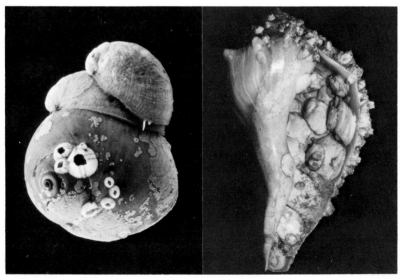

Figure 135

are common in shallow water. The slipper snails superficially resemble limpets but retain a tiny coiled apex at one end of the shell. Inside, there is a characteristic shelf extending partially across the opening, a feature that is absent in all limpets. Adult slipper snails are filter feeders and do not move about in search of food as do browsing or predatory snails.

We have two common species in our area and they are easily distinguished from each other. *Crepidula fornicata* (1.8"; 5 cm) has a strongly arched shell that is pale with dark spots or entirely dark. It often occurs in stacks on hard surfaces, such as oyster shells or the outside of the shells of hermit crabs, as in the photograph above. The encrusting bryozoan on the shell in the photograph is *Membranipora tenuis*. In tall stacks, the oldest and largest snail is located at the bottom of the stack and ultimately becomes a female. Younger and smaller individuals toward the top of the stack are males. The snails begin life as small males and eventually change sex to become females as they grow. Because it takes so much less energy to be a male and make sperm than to be a female and make yolky eggs, many animals adopt the strategy of being male while young and small, female when old and large. The stacking habit is more pronounced in northern populations than in the South.

Our other common species, the white slipper snail, *Crepidula plana* (1.4"; 3.5 cm), has a flat white shell and is often found inside the aperture of hermit crab shells or on other flat smooth surfaces such as broken bottles. This species does not form stacks but a single tiny male can often be seen atop a much larger female. There are many white slippers in the photograph on the right.

Crepidula aculeata (spiny slipper, 1.4"; 3.5 cm) is occasionally found on rocks, especially in the south of our area. It has a rough shell and the shelf bears a central longitudinal ridge. It is often overgrown by sponge. *Crepidula convexa* (convex slipper, 0.5"; 1.3 cm) is a small, dark, reddish-brown species whose apex is curved into a strong hook. It is found on the outside of hermit crab shells.

Simnias

Single-Toothed Simnia *Simnialena uniplicata*

Sea whips support a characteristic community of specialized animals, most of which are found nowhere else. Some, such as the barnacle, *Conopea,* and the clam, *Pteria,* use the whip solely as a site of attachment but many others are specialized predators utilizing the host for food as well as living space. Among these predators are the single-toothed simnia, *Simnialena uniplicata,* and the common West Indian simnia, *Cymbula acicularis.* These are distinctive snails, not likely to be confused with anything except each other. Our most common species, *Simnialena uniplicata,* is about 0.8" (2 cm) in length, and spindle-shaped, with pointed ends. The color of the shell normally matches that

Figure 136

of the host. The shell is smooth and has a long slitlike aperture running along its length. When extended, the transparent black and white mantle covers the shell as in the photograph above. The inner edge of the aperture bears a small fold at one end. The other species found in the Southeast, *Cymbula acicularis,* looks very much like *S. uniplicata* but has no fold on the aperture margin. It is occasionally found as far north as North Carolina.

The simnias belong to the family Ovulidae whose members are relatively small, elongate, and usually brightly colored snails with a long slitlike aperture and no operculum. The shell is glossy and covered by a large, often strikingly colored, mantle. Simnias feed on sea fans and sea whips. Another ovulid, the flamingo tongue, *Cyphoma gibbosum* (1"; 2.5 cm), eats sea fans and has a brightly colored mantle. The smooth shell is blunt at each end, has a raised ridge across its middle and is off-white with an orange border. This species is common in the tropics and occurs offshore in the Southeast.

The cowrie family, Cypraeidae, is poorly represented in the Carolinian province but one species, *Cypraea spurca acicularis* (Atlantic yellow cowrie, 1.2"; 3 cm), may occasionally be found under stones or coral rubble, especially in the South of our range. Cowries have glossy, domed, spireless shells with a long slitlike aperture toothed on both margins. Our species is flattened with a pure white base and speckled orange-brown dome.

Most members of the trivia family, Triviidae, resemble cowries but have transversely ridged shells. They feed on compound tunicates. *Trivia candidula* (little white trivia, 0.3"; 8 mm) is a small, ridged, pure

105

white, cowrielike species that may be found in shallow water, especially in the South. *Erato maugeriae* (0.2″; 5 mm) is a tiny predator of the compound tunicate, *Botryllus*. It is smooth and grey with a low pointed spire and looks more like a marginella than a cowrie but has teeth on both sides of its long narrow aperture.

Moon Snails

Baby's Ear *Sinum perspectivum*
Atlantic Moon Snail *Polinices duplicatus*

The family Naticidae includes the moon snails and baby's ears, which have very large feet and mantles, live in sand, and prey on other molluscs. Naticids make a distinctive egg case, called a sand collar, composed of a layer of eggs sandwiched between two thin layers of sand. The layers are held together by mucus and the resulting collar is shaped rather like a large-mouth funnel. The Atlantic moon snail, *Polinices duplicatus* (2″; 5 cm), is one of the most familiar animals of the southeastern coast. The shell is smooth and rounded with a low spire. Shells can be seen in plate A18 and Figure 135. The aperture is large and there is an opening, the umbilicus, extending up into the columella, but it is partially plugged by a large brown growth of shell. The operculum is horny and flexible. Living moon snails, their empty shells, and shells inhabited by hermit crabs are common on our coast. The snails are predators on molluscs, including other *Polinices*, which live in the silty sand of protected beaches. The snail drills a neat beveled hole through

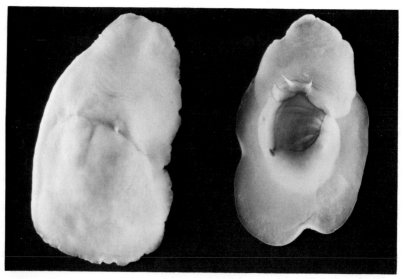

Figure 137

the shell of the prey to reach the soft tissues within. *Polinices* spends most of its time beneath the sand in search of its prey. When cruising near the sand surface it makes a telltale wandering furrow in the sand. Its shell is protected from abrasion by the extensive mantle and foot that almost completely cover it when the snail is underway, as is the one in the photograph. The anterior part of the foot is used for digging and, with the mantle, gives a streamlined profile for burrowing. The expanded foot has about four times the volume of the retracted foot. Expansion of the foot is accomplished by the influx of seawater into numerous small pores at the posterior end. Water can be seen leaving these pores when the animal retracts the foot into the shell. The expanded foot provides a stable base in soft sediments and accomplishes locomotion via cilia or waves of muscle contraction. The sand collars of *Polinices* are 3–4″ (8–10 cm) in diameter.

A close relative, the white baby's ear, *Sinum perspectivum,* has a flattened, white, much reduced shell that is completely covered by the mantle and foot. It has no operculum. While the moon snail's shell is only partly enclosed by the mantle, that of the baby's ear is entirely hidden by soft tissue when the snail is burrowing through sand. On close examination, the apparently shapeless white mass in the photograph can be seen to have mantle, foot, and small tentacles similar to those of *Polinices.* The shell, from which the name "baby's ear" derives, is small, more or less ear-shaped, and quite unable to accommodate the entire mantle and foot. It is hidden within the mass of soft tissue in the photograph. Like *Polinices,* these snails live beneath the sediment surface and are predators on other molluscs, especially bivalves. Another species, *S. maculatum* (brown baby's ear), lives offshore and has a yellow-spotted brownish shell that occasionally washes ashore. The soft tissues of this species are spotted with purple.

Rock Snails and Drills

Florida Rock Snail *Thais haemastoma floridana*
Atlantic Oyster Drill *Urosalpinx cinerea*
Thick-Lipped Drill *Eupleura caudata*
Tinted Cantharus *Pisania tincta*

The large and diverse family Muricidae includes the murex snails, which are not often found in the inshore waters of most of our area, and the oyster drills, which are. The muricids have heavily sculptured, usually dull-colored shells with a horny operculum. The siphonal canal is well developed and is often long and the aperture frequently bears teeth. Muricids are shallow-water tropical or subtropical predators on snails, bivalves, and barnacles.

Figure 138

The Atlantic oyster drill (1.5″; 4 cm) is a predator of juvenile oysters in higher salinity waters. The shell is rough, has broad axial ribs, and is variably colored. Oyster drills are usually the most common snail on estuarine oyster beds where they use a combination of mechanical and chemical methods to drill a hole in the upper valve of oysters. They are especially destructive of young oysters with thin shells but actually prefer barnacles when available.

The thick-lipped drill, *Eupleura caudata,* reaches about 1″ (2.5 cm) in length and resembles its relative *Urosalpinx. Eupleura* is more common subtidally and is rarely found in the intertidal. It has one or two flattened, bladelike longitudinal ridges, or varices, extending from the sides of the large body whorl and is easily distinguished thereby from *Urosalpinx.*

The Florida rock snail, *Thais haemastoma floridana,* is much larger and heavier than the other species and reaches 3″ (8 cm) in length. The shell is heavy and rough but variable in shape. There is a notch at the upper corner of the aperture. The columella, or inner edge of the aperture, is cream or salmon colored. This snail is an important oyster predator that is sometimes placed in a separate family, the Thaididae.

In the Southeast, the whelk family Buccinidae is represented primarily by the tinted cantharus, *Pisania tincta* (1.2″; 3 cm), which is common on rocks, oysters, and grass beds in North Carolina and Florida. *Pisania tincta* closely resembles the juvenile Florida rock snail but lacks the orange aperture of the muricid. The two have similar shapes and both have a groove in the upper corner of the aperture. The only other buccinid likely to be found in our area is *Cantharus multangulus,* which resembles *Urosalpinx* but occurs in grass beds where it eats barnacles.

108

Dove Snails

Color Plate B4

Lunar Dove Snail *Astyris lunata*
Greedy Dove Snail *Costoanachis avara*
Well-Ribbed Dove Snail *Costoanachis lafresnayi*

The Columbellidae, or dove snails, are very common in our area but are often overlooked because of their small size. All columbellids are small, usually less than 1″ (2.5 cm) long, and are more or less spindle-shaped, being pointed at both ends and thicker in the middle. The aperture is long and narrow, usually about half or more of the length of the shell, which may be sculptured or smooth. There is a horny brown operculum that is an elongate oval with one narrow curved end. Our species are found on algae and bryozoans and other organisms growing on hard bottoms. Most common is the lunar dove snail, *Astyris lunata*. These are tiny, fat, smooth, brown snails reaching 0.2″ (5 mm) in length. The shell is marked by zigzag dark lines or pale spiral bands and is smooth and unsculptured. These snails are very common on some of the branching bushlike bryozoans. The greedy dove snail, *Costoanachis avara*, and the well-ribbed dove snail, *Costoanachis lafresnayi*, are similar and easily confused. Both reach about 0.6″ (1.5 cm) and are slender spindles with narrow aperture, high spire, and ribbed surface. *Costoanachis avara* is a little fatter and has a slightly lower spire. Its ribs are smooth and it has teeth on the inside of the outer lip of the aperture. Its whorls have convex sides. *Costoanachis lafresnayi* has a higher spire with nearly straight sides. It has strong spiral ridges and grooves between the axial ribs and the aperture lip is not toothed. The two species are easily distinguished once both have been seen. The shells of these two snails are often completely overgrown by a soft encrusting bryozoan in the genus *Alcyonidium* or by a coralline red alga.

Two other small columbellids live offshore but may occasionally be found in shallow water. The smooth *Astyris raveneli* (0.4″; 1 cm) resembles *A. lunata* but is translucent white with no markings. The similarly shaped *Parvanachis obesa* (0.3″; 8 mm) has a rough, radially ribbed, grey shell with spiral brown lines.

Mud Snails

Eastern Mud Snail *Ilyanassa obsoleta*

The eastern mud snail, *Ilyanassa obsoleta* (0.8″; 2 cm), is one of the most common gastropods on our coast. It lives on muddy beaches and salt marshes, and forms dense aggregations of thousands of individuals segregated according to age. These nondescript snails are gregarious and rarely occur alone. When traveling they leave a mucus trail containing a chemical marker which other mud snails recognize and follow, thus

Figure 139

maintaining the aggregation. On the other hand, *Ilyanassa* reacts negatively to a substance released by injured individuals and will quickly leave the vicinity. Mud snails have heavy, ovoid, black shells that are often eroded. The snails are omnivores and will eat algae, detritus, and dead or moribund animals but mostly they feed by ingesting mud.

Ilyanassa belongs to the Nassariidae, a family of small omnivorous or carnivorous snails with smooth or sculptured shells. The operculum is horny and often bears teeth along its edge, although it does not in *Ilyanassa.* There is a siphonal canal. In the early spring, females produce many translucent, bristly, irregular egg cases about 0.1″ (3 mm) in diameter which they attach to hard substrata. The capsules may sometimes be present in such abundance that they obscure the underlying surfaces.

Ilyanassa obsoleta is the intermediate host of the schistosome parasite, *Austrobilharzia variglandis,* whose adult stage is a blood fluke of shorebirds. Larvae released into the water from the snails penetrate the skin of birds and enter the blood where they mature. Whereas birds are the natural host of the adult fluke, the larvae will also penetrate the skin of wading or swimming humans. In this inappropriate host they are unable to enter the blood but remain briefly in the skin where they cause an allergic response known as swimmer's itch.

Nassa Snails

Eastern Nassa *Nassarius vibex*
New England Nassa *Nassarius trivittatus*

Although *Ilyanassa obsoleta* is the most common and best known of

Figure 140

our mud snails, we have other species in our area. These species belong to the genus *Nassarius,* all of whose members have toothed opercula and two pointed, fleshy, posterior processes on the hind edge of the foot. Of them, only *Nassarius vibex,* the eastern nassa (0.7"; 1.8 cm) is common. This species occurs intertidally on sandy flats, sometimes with *Ilyanassa.* It is easily recognized by its pointed squat shape and the broad, glossy, flat plate (parietal shield) beside the aperture. Its shell is sculptured with bumpy axial ribs and the outer lip of the aperture is toothed along its inside margin. The shell is pale grey or greenish-grey.

Nassarius vibex eats the eggs of the polychaete worms, *Axiothella mucosa, Diopatra cuprea,* and *Arenicola cristata,* as well as carrion and detritus. When feeding on worm eggs, the proboscis is inserted into the jelly mass surrounding the eggs which are then extracted by suction. The snail eats only the eggs, not the jelly, and can remove all eggs from the mass. It appears to prefer eggs to carrion or detritius. *Ilyanassa obsoleta* has also been seen eating the eggs of *Arenicola.*

The New England nassa, *Nassarius trivittatus* (0.7"; 1.8 cm), lives on subtidal sand offshore and is rarely seen in the Southeast in water of wading depth. The shell is distinctive with precisely aligned rows of beads, a deep suture, and a beaded shelf between whorls. It is a northern species, rare in the Southeast and not found south of Georgia.

Another species, *Nassarius albus* (variable nassa, 0.5"; 1.3 cm), inhabits offshore sands in the Southeast but is not normally seen in water of wading depth or less. It has a pale white or grey shell, sometimes with brown spots or spiral brown lines, strong longitudinal ribs, and a narrow parietal shield.

111

Whelks

Knobbed Whelk *Busycon carica*
Channeled Whelk *Busycon canaliculatum*

The fulgur whelks in the genus *Busycon* belong to the family Melongenidae. They are major predators of clams, which they open using their foot and shell. We have three important species in shallow water on our coast and they are easily distinguished from each other. Complications are introduced by the presence of less common species, the alleged existence of subspecies and varieties, and a very confused and conflicting taxonomic situation. Considering the situation at it simplest however, we have:

1. *Busycon carica,* the knobbed whelk. This is a dextral (aperture on the right) species with strong knobs on the shoulders of mature individuals. Juveniles, such as the individual in the photograph, have brown stripes on the shell but these are lost in adults. This species reaches 10″ (25 cm) in length and has a bright, glossy, orange aperture when mature. The shell is illustrated with the hermit crabs in Figure 226 and Plate C21.

2. *Busycon contrarium* (or *B. perversum* of some authors), the lightning whelk, is sinistral (aperture on the left) and is also striped when juvenile but not when adult. Mature specimens reach over 16″ (41 cm) and have glossy white apertures. The knobs on the shoulders are small or absent.

Figure 141

3. *Busycon canaliculatum,* the channeled whelk, reaches almost 8″ (20 cm), has no knobs on the shoulders, has a deep U-shaped or flat-bottomed spiral channel marking the position of the suture between successive whorls. It has a fuzzy periostracum and is dextral.

4. *Busycon spiratum,* the pear whelk, also has a fuzzy periostracum and deep sutural channel but is smaller (5″; 13 cm) and its sutural channel is V-shaped. It is not one of our common species. It is dextral.

These whelks lay long proteinaceous strings of thick disklike egg capsules that resemble poker chips on a string. The strings may be almost 1 yard (1 m) in length and about 1.5″ (3.8 cm) in diameter and are often seen washed ashore on beaches. The female snail anchors the string in sand but after the eggs hatch the strings break loose and often drift ashore.

Crown Conchs

Crown Conch *Melongena corona*

The family Melongenidae includes the crown conchs (*Melongena*) and the fulgur whelks (*Busycon*). All members of the family are medium to large carnivores with heavy shells and horny opercula.

Melongena corona (2″; 5 cm) is a distinctive and common species in south Florida and the Gulf of Mexico. It is not found in the area covered by this guide except in northern Florida where it lives in shallow water near the shores of quiet estuaries and sounds and is often associated with mangroves or oyster beds. At least part of its diet consists of oysters

Figure 142

and snails but it is a scavenger as well. *Melongena* tolerates a variety of salinities and exhibits a wide range of variations in shell architecture. Typically, it has a low spire and the top of the body whorl is armed with a row of sharp conical teeth. It usually has broad purplish spiral bands on the body whorl. Melongenid embryos develop in waferlike egg capsules to become young snails. Neither *Melongena* nor *Busycon* has a swimming, planktonic, dispersal stage as do most other marine snails.

Tulip Snails   *Color Plate B5*

True Tulip *Fasciolaria tulipa*
Banded Tulip *Fasciolaria hunteria*

The tulip snails and their close relative, the horse conch, *Pleuroploca gigantea* (Figure 144), belong to the Fasciolariidae and are carnivores that prey on other molluscs, including oysters. The thick sculptured lip of these snails is used to chip a hole in the prey's shell through which the proboscis is inserted. These are large snails pointed at both ends, with a high spire and long siphonal canal. Our two tulips have smooth spindle-shaped shells with dark lines spiraling around them. The most commonly seen species over most of our range is the banded tulip, *Fasciolaria hunteria*. The shell has solid uninterrupted spiral lines and there is a spiral ridge *inside* the aperture near its upper corner. Banded tulips reach about 3″ (8 cm) in length and are often found in shallow water. Our other common species, the true tulip, *Fasciolaria tulipa,* is more common in the south and reaches much larger sizes (8″; 20 cm). The color is variable and dark spiral lines are present but interrupted. There is no ridge inside the aperture.

The tulips and horse conch produce distinctively shaped egg capsules. Those of the tulips are about 0.7″ (1.8 cm) and are shaped like laterally flattened cones. They are made of translucent protein and each contains many eggs. Those of the horse conch are similar but a little larger. All are attached to firm surfaces.

Olive Snails   *Color Plate B6*

Lettered Olive *Oliva sayana*

The Olividae, or olive snails, have long, narrow shells with a very large body whorl. This last whorl accounts for most of the shell and the spire is short, inconspicuous, and pointed. The aperture is long and narrow and extends almost the entire length of the body whorl. The inner margin of the aperture bears numerous wrinkles or folds. Olivids live in sand with the shell surrounded by the large foot and mantle. Thus protected from abrasion, the shell remains smooth and glossy. The lettered olive, *Oliva sayana,* is often found on outer beaches and offshore in sand. In the surf zone it feeds on coquina clams and mole crabs which it asphyxiates with its foot. It is large, reaching 2.5″ (6.4 cm), and its shiny brown shell is marked with V-shaped darker brown lines that look like writing. It has no operculum.

The olive snails have elongate shells whose long axis is held parallel to the long axis of the crawling animal. The overall appearance is one of bilateral symmetry and, even though they are as asymmetric as other snails, they are functionally balanced and streamlined for motion through sand.

Olive Snails

Variable Dwarf Olive *Olivella mutica*

The variable dwarf olive, *Olivella mutica,* is much smaller (0.4″; 1 cm) than its more conspicuous relative, the lettered olive. It lives in silty sand or sandy mud in shallow water and has an operculum. It makes a narrow, shallow furrow in the surface of moist intertidal sand and is reported to swim by flapping the lateral margins of the foot. At least one species of *Olivella* feeds by burying in sand and casting two mucus nets from its foot into the swash. The nets collect food and are periodically ingested. The color pattern of the glossy seed-shaped shell of *O. mutica* is variable but is usually some combination of white with broad brown or brownish-purple spiral stripes. The spire is relatively larger than that of the lettered olive. There is a narrow, smooth, glossy parietal shield on the columella next to the upper part of the aperture.

Figure 143

Other shallow-water species in our area are the rice olive, *Olivella floralia,* which is all white and more slender than *O. mutica* but about the same length or a little larger. The snowy dwarf olive, *Olivella nivea,* is larger (1″; 2.5 cm) and has a slender, off-white shell with brown or purple-brown markings. It resembles *O. mutica* but lacks the parietal shield of that species.

Marginellas *Color Plate B7*

Dewy Marginella *Marginella roscida*

Some of the marginellas (family Marginellidae) occasionally occur in shallow water on sandy bottoms in our area. They are small, often brightly colored, and have shiny glossy shells. The body whorl is large, dominating the shell, and the aperture is long and narrow. There is no operculum. They have large, patterned mantles that envelop the shell when the animal crawls. The animal in the photograph is *Marginella roscida* (0.5″; 1.3 cm). It has a very large body whorl that is widest at the top. The outer lip of the aperture bears a few dark spots and the shell is often covered by white speckles. The most common species in our shallow waters is *Marginella apicina,* the common Atlantic marginella. It reaches about 0.4″ (1 cm) in length and closely resembles *M. roscida* but lacks the speckles on the shell and is a little broader.

The tiny (0.2″; 5 mm), fat, ovoid, white or grey teardrop marginella, *Granulina ovuliformis,* has no spire, the apex being hidden by the top of the aperture which is as long as the shell. The inner margin of the aperture lip is finely toothed. The oat grain marginella, *Hyalina avena,* is very slender with a tiny low spire. It is white with three spiral orange stripes and reaches 0.5″ (1.3 cm). The tiny gold-lined marginella, *Marginella aureocincta* is only 0.2″ (5 mm) long. It is slender and has a relatively high spire for a marginellid, being almost equal to half the height of the body whorl. The shell is cream or white with two spiral orange stripes. The outer lip is finely and sparsely toothed.

Sozons Cone *Conus delessertii*
Horse Conch *Pleuroploca gigantea*
Scotch Bonnet *Phalium granulatum*

These three unrelated snails are common offshore species that may occasionally wash ashore on outer beaches. Sozons cone (4″; 10 cm) is one of about four cone species (family Conidae) in our area. The cone snails are predators on a variety of invertebrates (and fishes in the Pacific) and are equipped with a harpoonlike radula and poison glands. Although none of our species is known to have a toxin fatal to humans (as do some Pacific species), no living cone should be handled carelessly.

Figure 144

The horse conch (Fasciolariidae) above is a juvenile about 4″ (10 cm) long. Adults reach almost 24″ (61cm) and are our largest snails. Adults look like the juvenile above but are covered with a conspicuous dark brown periostracum that makes them darker. Small individuals may occur in shallow inshore or estuarine water. Horse conchs feed on other molluscs and small ones are sometimes found on oyster beds. The tulip snails (Pl. B5) belong to this family.

The scotch bonnet, *Phalium granulatum* (3″), belongs to the helmet snail family, Cassidae, which includes the king and emperor helmets. The bonnet shell is more or less egg-shaped with a sharp spire, squarish brown blotches, and a broad glossy area (parietal shield) beside the aperture. The outer lip of the aperture is thick and toothed. The helmets, *Cassis madagascariensis* (emperor helmet, 12″; 30 cm) and *C. tuberosa* (king helmet, 8″; 20 cm), also live offshore and are often caught in nets by commercial fishermen. They are much larger than *Phalium* and have long narrow apertures and broad, glossy parietal shields. The cassids are predators on echinoderms such as sand dollars, sea biscuits, and sea urchins. While feeding, they dissolve the calcareous tests of their prey with a secretion containing sulfuric acid. Then they quickly cut an opening through the softened skeleton to expose the edible flesh.

Augers

Atlantic Auger *Terebra dislocata*

The elongate and sharply pointed Atlantic auger, *Terebra dislocata,* reaches 1.5″ (3.8 cm) in length and is most commonly encountered on

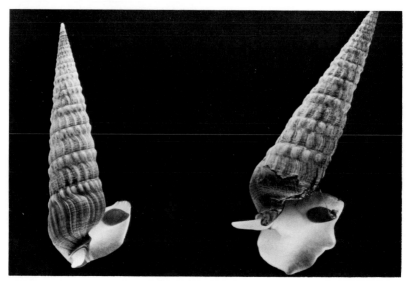

Figure 145

quiet silty-sand beaches and creek bottoms. It preys on the golden acorn worm, *Balanoglossus aurantiacus,* and several snails often accumulate atop the sandy fecal mound of a worm, where they await its return. When moving across intertidal flats, they make shallow furrows. The color varies from pale grey to dark grey or reddish brown. The whorls bear numerous fine axial ribs and a single deep spiral groove that cuts across the ribs. *Terebra dislocata* belongs to the Terebridae and is the only common member of its family in shallow waters in our area. Both snails in the photograph are *T. dislocata.*

Terebra concava (0.8″; 2 cm) occurs just offshore and can sometimes be found alive on our outer beaches. It is smaller than *T. dislocata* and differs from it in having concave whorls. Terebrids have long, slender, pointed, awl-shaped shells with a relatively small aperture equipped with a siphonal canal. The operculum is teardrop-shaped. Many terebrids lack a radula or have a harpoonlike radula with a poison sac like that of their relatives, the cone snails.

The related family Turridae is very large and contains a few small southeastern species, none of which are often encountered intertidally. The taxonomy and classification of the turrids is confused and their identification is difficult. Turrids usually have rather rough shells with moderately high spires. Most species have a distinct "turrid" notch at the posterior end of the aperture, opposite the siphonal canal. Some species do not have an operculum. Like the cones they have poison glands.

118

Marsh Snails

Florida Marsh Snail *Detracia floridana*
Common Marsh Snail *Melampus bidentatus*

The small, brown, bean-shaped *Melampus* is usually less than 0.5″ (1.3 cm) in length and is a characteristic and common feature of the salt marsh. *Melampus* can usually be found in salt marshes on vegetation or beneath litter near the high tide line. It belongs to the family Melampidae in the subclass Pulmonata, which includes the land snails and garden slugs, and is not closely related to marine snails. Unlike most marine snails, the marsh snails respire in air, rather than water, and use a lung, rather than a gill, for this purpose. They are more or less omnivorous, feeding on detritus, dead animals, and the algae and microscopic animals growing on marsh grasses. They have several predators, including killifish, and are tolerant of a wide range of salinities but prefer areas of higher salinity. Even though *Melampus* is a pulmonate air-breathing snail related to terrestrial snails and false limpets, it nevertheless has a planktonic larva like most of the truly marine snails.

A similar species, the Florida marsh snail, *Detracia floridana,* is common throughout our range but is restricted to lower salinity marshes which are mostly avoided by *Melampus.* The two species are hard to tell apart. They coexist in brackish marshes but *Detracia* is excluded from high salinity marshes. *Melampus* is larger, has a lower

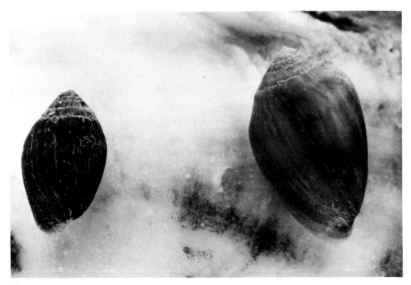

Figure 146

119

spire, has two teeth on the inner edge of the aperture and about 4 ridges on the inside of the outer lip. *Detracia* has a higher spire, one large and one small tooth on the inner lip of the aperture, and about 10 ridges on the inner surface of the outer lip.

Bubble Snails   *Color Plate B8*

Solitary Paper Bubble *Haminoea solitaria*

The bubble snails (order Cephalaspidea) are represented in shallow Carolinian waters by a few small and infrequently encountered species. *Haminoea solitaria,* shown above, has a spirally grooved, fragile, white shell about 0.5″ (1.3 cm) long. The mantle is well developed and envelops the shell when extended. The shell is domelike with a very broad aperture. It is visible on the right side of the photograph. To the left is the head with its flattened cephalic shield, which is used for burrowing. This shield is a characteristic of the order Cephalaspidea although it is not present in all species. *Haminoea* can be found plowing through the sediment in silty sand flats.

A larger species, *Bulla striata,* the common Atlantic bubble snail, has a stronger, more inflated, larger, brownish shell. It reaches about 0.8″ (2 cm) in length and lives in grassy sand and mud flats in south Florida and the Gulf of Mexico.

Barrel Bubbles   *Color Plate B9*

Channeled Barrel Bubble *Acteocina canaliculata*

Acteocina canaliculata is a small snail-like species of Cephalaspidea. Its coiled shell has a low conical spire and an elongate narrow aperture and is stronger than the shells of *Bulla* and *Haminoea*. It superficially resembles a tiny olive snail and is usually less than 0.2″ (5 mm) long. The shell is white and orange and the tissues are pinkish. It is found in shallow waters in silty sand but also occurs offshore to depths of about 120′ (37 m). There are several species of *Acteocina* in the Southeast, but the others do not typically occur in shallow inshore waters.

Seaweed Seaslugs   *Color Plate B10*

Spanish Tenor *Placida dendritica*

Members of the order Sacoglossa are superficially nudibranch-like and usually lack a shell although there are some fascinating tropical species with a clamlike bivalved shell. Sacoglossans are usually small, mostly less than 1″ (2.5 cm), and have a pair of rhinophores on the head. The back often bears numerous fingerlike cerata and each contains a branch of the gut. Gills are sometimes present. Sacoglossans feed on algae and some of them refrain from digesting the chloroplasts of their

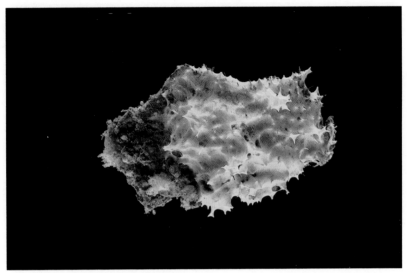

A1. Sulfur sponge, *Aplysilla longispina*

A2. Eroded sponge, *Haliclona loosanoffi*

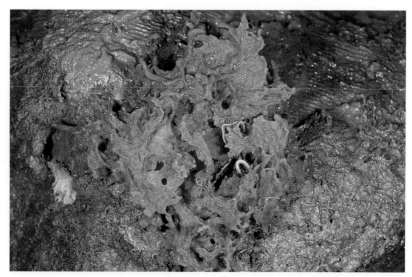

A3. Flabby sponge, *Mycale americana*

A4. Red beard sponge, *Microciona prolifera*

A5. Bread sponge, *Halichondria bowerbanki*

A6. Sun sponge, *Hymeniacidon heliophila*

A7. Lion's mane jelly, *Cyanea capillata*

A8. Cannonball jellyfish, *Stomolophus meleagris,* **and the spider crab,** *Libinia dubia*

A9. Hydroids, *Eudendrium carneum* **(left),** *Bougainvillia rugosa* **(right)**

A10. Hydroid, *Tubularia crocea*

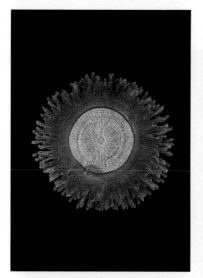

A11. **Blue button,** *Porpita porpita*

A12. **Sea whips,** *Leptogorgia virgulata*

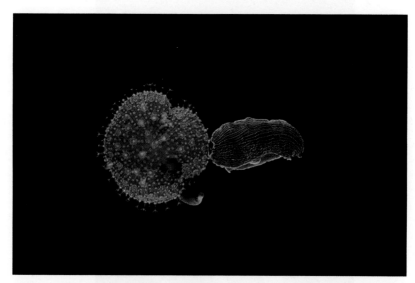

A13. **Sea pansy,** *Renilla reniformis,* **and its predator, the striped sea slug,** *Armina tigrina*

A14. Stinging anemone, *Actinia bermudensis*

A15. Armored anemone, *Anthopleura carneola*

A16. Brown anemone, *Aiptasia pallida*

A17. Orange-striped anemone, *Haliplanella luciae*

A18. Hermit crab anemone, *Calliactis tricolor,* **and long-wristed hermit crab,** *Pagurus longicarpus*

A19. Tube anemone, *Ceriantheopsis americanus*

A20. Constellation tunicate, *Aplidium constellatum*

A21. Paintsplash tunicate, *Didemnum duplicatum* (white), unnamed tunicate, *Didemnum* sp. (yellow), and translucent sea squirt, *Ascidia interrupta* (lower right)

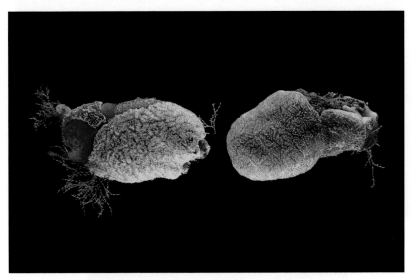

A22. Colorwheel tunicate, *Distaplia bermudensis*

A23. Sandy lobed tunicate, *Eudistoma carolinense* (left), and sea liver *E. hepaticum* (right)

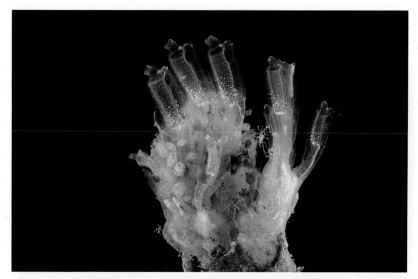

A24. Light bulb tunicate, *Clavelina oblonga,* and honeysuckle tunicate, *Perophora viridis*

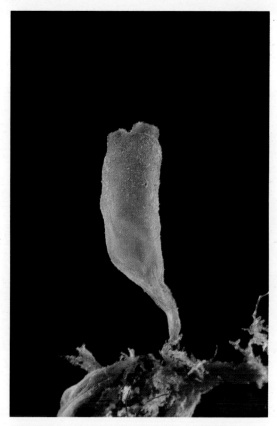

A25. Orange tunicate, *Ecteinascidia turbinata*

A26. Tunicate, *Symplegma rubra*

A27. Royal tunicate, *Botryllus planus* (gold and purple), and frog egg tunicate, *Diplosoma listerianum* on the green alga, *Bryopsis plumosa*

A28. Grey sea star, *Luidia clathrata* (left), and margined sea star, *Astropecten articulatus* (right)

A29. Common sea star, *Asterias forbesi,* moss animal, *Bugula neritina* (reddish brown), scorched mussel, *Brachidontes exustus,* and juvenile stone crab, *Menippe mercenaria*

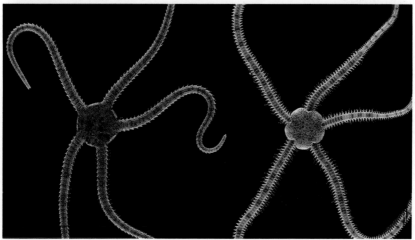

A30. Smooth brittle star, *Ophioderma brevispinum* (left), and blood brittle star, *Hemipholis elongata* (right)

A31. Short-spined sea urchin, *Lytechinus variegatus*

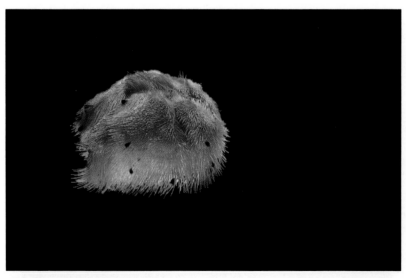

A32. Heart urchin, *Moira atropos*

A33. Phoronid, *Phoronis architecta*

A34. Bushy moss animals, *Amathia distans* (upper left), *Anguinella palmata* (top center), *Zoobotryon verticillatum* (bottom center), and *Bugula neritina* (far right)

prey. Instead they keep these photosynthetic organelles alive and encourage them to continue photosynthesizing to produce food for the slug.

Placida dendritica is occasionally abundant in local patches on algae such as *Bryopsis* and *Codium. Placida* is usually about 1″ (2.5 cm) long but may be larger. The body is yellowish but the cerata may be intensely green due to algal chloroplasts contained within. These animals are broad and flat with numerous cerata and the rhinophores each bear a longitudinal groove. The anterior corners of the foot are rounded, a common condition in sacoglossans.

Elysia chlorotica, the eastern emerald elysia, is a bright green or brown species found on vegetation such as *Vaucheria, Caulerpa, Cladophora, Halimeda, Ruppia, Ulva,* and *Zostera,* especially in low salinity water. It is less than 1″ (2.5 cm) in length. The head has a pair of longitudinally grooved rhinophores but there are no cerata on the body. Instead, there are two large winglike flaps (parapodia), one on each side of the body. It has been shown that this species incorporates chloroplasts from its food into its own cells and that these chloroplasts continue to conduct photosynthesis. The slugs presumably utilize the resulting carbohydrates.

Sea Hares   *Color Plate B11*

Sooty Sea Hare *Aplysia brasiliana*

The sea hares are our largest opisthobranchs and species on our coast reach 8″ (20 cm) in length. Members of the order are massive soft animals with a distinctly rabbitlike appearance when viewed head on. They often have a pair of lateral winglike swimming flaps, or parapodia, and the head bears two pairs of tentacles. One pair, the rhinophores, is located on top of the head just behind the eyes whereas the second pair is simply the elaborated anterior margin of the head. Both pairs are visible in the photograph in which the animal's head is on the left. The shell is small, flattened, and at least partly embedded in the tissue of the back. It is at the surface and can easily be seen and felt without dissecting the animal. The shell is visible in the photograph. Sea hares are herbivores that graze on seaweeds on rock jetties, pilings, creek bottoms, sea walls, and grass beds. They lay large, tangled masses of spaghettilike egg strings and some release clouds of dark ink when threatened.

Two species common on our coast are *Aplysia brasiliana* (the sooty sea hare) and *Bursatella leachii,* the ragged sea hare. *Aplysia* is the larger and reaches 8″ (20 cm) in length. It is smooth-bodied, usually reddish-purple or greenish with a pair of large swimming parapodia. *Bursatella* is usually smaller and its body is covered by numerous, long, branched,

121

filamentous processes. It lacks the large winglike parapodia of *Aplysia* and has no shell as an adult. A California species is 30″ (76 cm) long, weighs 35 lbs. (16 kg), and is the largest known gastropod.

Sea Slugs   *Color Plate B12*

Lemon Drop *Doriopsilla pharpa*

The nudibranchs are a large and diverse group of shell-less, uncoiled, and untwisted snails known collectively as sea slugs. Unlike most terrestrial slugs, they are often brightly colored and exquisitely beautiful. All are carnivores and most specialize in eating one, or a few, species of sponges, bryozoans, or cnidarians. The Southeast is not known for its nudibranch fauna, but it is nevertheless rich and varied although little studied. There are at least 50 species in shallow water along the coasts of the Carolinas. There are four suborders, all of which are represented on our coast.

Nudibranchs are more or less slug-shaped and have a broad creeping foot lying beneath the body of the animal. The head always bears at least one pair of dorsal appendages, the rhinophores. These are sensory and may be adorned with bumps, collars, sheaths, or lamellae, or they may be smooth. Small eyes may be present beneath the bases of the rhinophores. There may be other processes on the head but there is only one pair of rhinophores. Often there are gills located somewhere on the animal and the back may bear numerous fingerlike processes called cerata. Each true ceras contains a branch of the gut and sometimes a capsule, the cnidosac, at the tip.

The suborder Doridoidea is mostly composed of slugs with broad flattened bodies which lack cerata and have a circle of retractable gills around the dorsal anus. The rhinophores usually have lamellae and can be withdrawn into the mass of the head. The back may be smooth or bumpy and its skin often contains irregular calcareous spicules similar to those of sponges.

We have several doridoideans on our coast but they are not often encountered. *Doriopsilla pharpa* is probably the most common, and is certainly the most conspicuous. It is a smooth-backed, flattened, orange or yellow oval reaching 1″ (2.5 cm) in length. The gills are arranged in a circle at the posterior of the back. *Doriopsilla* feeds on the boring sponge, *Cliona celata,* and like the sponge, is common on old oyster shells.

The photograph shows *Doriopsilla* on the left of a shell inhabited by *Cliona.* Many papillae of the boring sponge are visible on the right of the shell. The slug has its rhinophores extended but the gills are retracted.

Sea Slugs *Color Plate B13*

Sponge Slug *Doris verrucosa*

Doris verrucosa (1.5″; 3.8 cm) belongs to the Doridoidea, a group of nudibranchs with flat oval bodies. Its back is covered with soft warts. It feeds on several species of sponges and its color depends on the type of sponge it has been eating. If the red beard sponge, *Microciona,* is the prey, the slug is grey. If the food is the eroded sponge, *Haliclona loosanoffi,* or the garlic sponge, *Lissodendoryx,* then the predator is yellow. Slugs feeding on the felt sponge, *Craniella,* are green. The sponge in Plate B13 is *Lissodendoryx isodictyalis.* The slug uses its radula to cut small cubes from the sponge which it then ingests. Note the lamellate rhinophores on the head (left), papillate back, and the posterior circle of dorsal gills (right) on the slug in Plate B13.

Anisodoris prea is an uncommon, large (2″; 5 cm), dark greenish or greyish species. It resembles *Doris verrucosa* in shape and in having a warty back, but in this case the back and warts are very firm and hard, whereas those of *Doris* are soft. Living specimens can be recognized by a distinctive order of cedar or napthalene, which seems to be released as a milky fluid. They probably feed on sponges, perhaps on *Hymeniacidon.*

Many sponge-eating nudibranchs, including *Doris verrucosa* and *Anisodoris prea,* have spicules in their skin which superficially resemble those of their sponge prey. It is tempting to assume that the slugs simply appropriate the spicules of their prey the way other opisthobranchs appropriate stinging cells or chloroplasts but this is not the case, at least not with *Doris* and *Anisodoris.* The slugs' spicules are not shaped like those of the prey and they are made of calcium carbonate, whereas those of the sponge (in this case) are made of silicon.

Sea Slugs *Color Plate B14*

Harlequin *Polycera chilluna*

Some nudibranchs, such as the Polyceratidae and Goniodorididae, have thick sluglike bodies with numerous tentacles extending from the back. Like *Doris,* they have a dorsal circle of gills and usually have lamellate rhinophores, although they may not be retractable. They often feed on bryozoans. *Polycera hummi* (1″; 2.5 cm) is our only common polyceratid, and it is often found on the bryozoan, *Bugula neritina.* *Polycera hummi* resembles the shape of *Polycera chilluna* in the color plate but is shorter and thicker. It has a mottled grey body with bright blue and yellow bands around the dorsal tentacles. *Polycera chilluna* (1.5″; 4 cm), which is shown because of its striking coloration, is rare in shallow water and its prey is unreported. *Polycerella emertoni* is an

123

uncommon species that feeds on a variety of bryozoans including *Bugula* and *Amathia.* It is a tiny (0.2″; 5 mm) white species with brown spots and smooth rhinophores.

Sea Slugs   *Color Plate B15*

Rainbow Slug *Okenia sapelona*

The members of family Goniodoridae usually resemble the poly-ceratids in having thick, sluglike bodies and numerous dorsal tentacles, which are arrayed around the periphery of the back. *Okenia impexa* is a common, but tiny (0.3″; 8 mm), white and brown species that lives and feeds solely on the bryozoan, *Anguinella palmata.* It has a thick, sluglike body like most polyceratids and goniodorids. *Okenia sapelona* (1″; 2.5 cm), which is shown in Plate B15, is a very rare, brightly colored species whose prey is unknown. Unlike the other goniodorids, it is flat rather than thick-bodied and sluglike. This translucent animal has intense chrome-yellow spots on the back and pale yellow and blue tentacles. *Ancula evelinae* is another small (0.5″; 1.3 cm) uncommon species with unknown prey. It is shaped like *Polycera* but is pure white with neat, dark, purple-brown blotches. Two tentacles arise at the base of each rhinophore.

Doridella obscura (Corambidae) is a small (0.5″; 1.3 cm), almost circular, species that lives and preys on the large bryozoan, *Alcyonidium hauffi* (Fig. 120). It is pale grey with brown speckles and is almost impossible to see when at home on its prey. *Doridella* is a flattened oval with a smooth gill-less back. The small gills are located under the posterior overhang of the back and are hidden from view. This species is very common but is easily overlooked. The coiled white egg strings are easier to see than the animals themselves.

Sea Slugs   *Color Plate B16*

Sea Whip Slug *Tritonia wellsi*

Tritonia wellsi (0.6″; 1.5 cm) is a colorless, white species that feeds on the sea whip, *Leptogorgia.* The head (facing to the right in Plate B16) has a transverse row of six anterior tentacles in addition to the rhinophores. The rhinophores of this group of nudibranchs have a sheath or collar around the base. The highly branched arborescent gills are arranged in two longitudinal dorsolateral rows and resemble the polyps of the prey. An egg mass of the nudibranch is visible in the photograph as are expanded polyps of the sea whip. A similar species, *Tritonia bayeri,* is also reported from the area. It differs from *T. wellsi* in small details.

Doto chica (0.8″; 2 cm) is occasionally found living and feeding on the large hydroid, *Eudendrium carneum. Doto* species have sluglike bodies with a row of short, thick, unbranched, but very bumpy cerata along each side of the back. Another species lives on the hydroid, *Halocordyle disticha,* but is undescribed. It has bushy gills arising from the inside face of the anterior cerata. *Doto* species suck fluids from the prey and do not actually ingest the polyps.

Sea Slugs   *Color Plate B17*

Sargassum Sea Slug *Scyllaea pelagica*

The sargassum sea slug, *Scyllaea pelagica,* is one of the characteristic members of the specialized community living on floating gulfweed (*Sargassum*). These slugs prey on hydroids living on *Sargassum. Scyllaea* is a distinctively shaped brown or yellow slug that reaches 2.5" (6.3 cm) in length and is common on floating *Sargassum.* The rhinophores are leaf-shaped and there are large projections on the sides of the back. *Scyllaea* apparently ingests the spherical *Sargassum* floats which may then improve the slug's buoyancy and help keep it at the surface near the floating weed and its food. Three of the floats can be seen inside the slug in Plate B17. The slug in the center of this photograph has recently deposited a string of yellow eggs which can be seen to the left of the animal. Beside its head, on the right, is a small sargassum goose barnacle, *Lepas pectinata.* The sargassum fronds are covered with hydroids.

The suborder Arminoidea is represented on our coast by a single common species, *Armina tigrina,* which is shown on Plate A13 with its prey, the sea pansy, *Renilla reniformis. Armina* is a smooth, flattened, elongated oval that is sometimes mistaken for a flatworm. It has no dorsal processes other than a pair of small lamellate rhinophores. Its gills are located under the overhang of the back and are not visible from above. *Armina* reaches about 1.5" (3.8 cm) in length and is distinctively marked with longitudinal black and white stripes. It lives in silty sand on protected beaches and feeds exclusively on sea pansies. The slugs may become bioluminescent from eating *Renilla,* which is itself bioluminescent.

Sea Slugs   *Color Plate B18*

Anemone Sea Slug *Berghia coerulescens*

One of our best represented and most colorful groups of nudibranchs, the Aeolidoidea, consists of slugs specialized for preying on cnidarians. The head bears a pair of rhinophores and usually a pair of tentacles as well, and the back is covered with numerous cerata which store the stinging capsules of the prey. We have several species on our coast but only the most common can be discussed here. The beautiful species in Plate B18, *Berghia coerulescens,* is usually less than 1.5" (3.8 cm) long and feeds on the anemone, *Aiptasia pallida. Berghia benteva* is a little

125

smaller and much less colorful. It is recognized by its pink cerata and red cnidosacs. Its prey is unknown. All *Berghia* species have rhinophores with bumps on their posterior surfaces. A related species, *Spurilla neapolitana,* reaches 2.5″ (6.3 cm) and also feeds on *Aiptasia pallida. Spurilla* stores the zooxanthellae as well as the nematocysts of *Aiptasia.* It has lamellate rhinophores and is orange with white spots.

Cratena pilata is one of our most common sea slugs. These nudibranchs, about 1″ (2.5 cm) long, are pale ivory or grey, and have indistinct orangish patches on the top and sides of the head. They have smooth or slightly wrinkled rhinophores and are usually found on the hydroid, *Tubularia crocea,* but sometimes on *Halocordyle disticha.* Another fairly common species, *Learchis poica* (0.6″; 1.5 cm) is orangish-brown and has rhinophores with fleshy rings around them. The cerata have dark brown cores and are especially dark at their bases. *Fiona pinnata* (1.5; 3.8 cm) is a pelagic species that may sometimes be found on barnacle-covered flotsam on the outer beach. It eats the goose barnacle, *Lepas,* in which case it is brown, or the pelagic hydrozoans, *Velella* and *Porpita,* in which case the slug is blue. *Fiona* also eats the pelagic snail, *Janthina.* The anterior foot corners are rounded, not tentaclelike, and each ceras has a wavy longitudinal ridge on its inner side.

Octopods

Common Octopus *Octopus vulgaris*

Octopods and squids belong to the mollusc class Cephalopoda, so named because the foot is developed into a set of eight or ten arms and tentacles associated with the head and surrounding the mouth. Members of this class tend, like many vertebrates, to be large active predators with well-developed locomotory, nervous, and sensory systems. They have eyes almost identical to those of the vertebrates. The class includes the chambered and paper nautilus, squids, cuttlefishes, and octopods in numerous families. In most, the shell is reduced or absent but in the primitive members of the class, such as the chambered nautilus, it is large, external, and well developed. Squids have an internal shell, and octopods have no shell at all.

We have two species of octopus in our shallow inshore waters. *Octopus vulgaris* is the common octopus, but despite its name it is rarely seen. It is common enough, but lives secretively under rocks where it is difficult to find. It reaches about 24″ (61 cm) in diameter and has eight suckered arms extending from the head. The body is soft and globular. It has a rich supply of color cells in the skin that are under precise nervous control so that it can alter its color rapidly and dramatically. This species reportedly has a life span of only one year. *Octopus briareus,* the

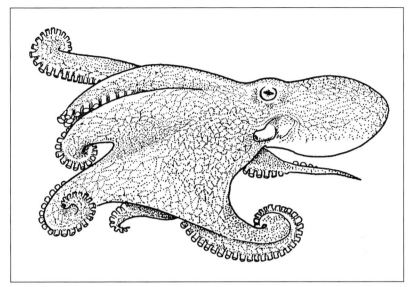

Figure 147

briar octopus, also occurs on our coast but is smaller. The two species are distinguished on technical differences in the tip of the male sexual arm.

The pelagic paper nautilus, *Argonauta argo,* is an octopus that occurs offshore. The thin calcareous shell is really an egg case and is secreted by two arms of the female. It sometimes washes ashore. Males have no shell.

Squids

Atlantic Brief Squid *Lolliguncula brevis*

Squids are torpedo-shaped cephalopods streamlined for rapid swimming. They have firm, cylindrical bodies and a pair of fins at the pointed end. They have eight arms and two long tentacles. The shell is internal and differs from family to family. Members of the family Spirulidae have a chambered spiral shell that is often washed ashore on beaches. The Sepiidae, or cuttlefish, have an oval calcareous plate and the Loliginidae have a flexible, cartilagelike rod or pen. The most commonly encountered species on our coast is *Lolliguncula brevis,* a small (8″; 20 cm) member of the Loliginidae. This squid is abundant in tidal creeks, sounds, and estuaries but is a rapid swimmer and is rarely seen unless captured in a trawl or large net. It is delicate and dies rapidly when removed from the water. The fins are short, about half the length of the body, and rounded apically. The body is covered with pigment cells that can change the color from translucent white to dark brown.

127

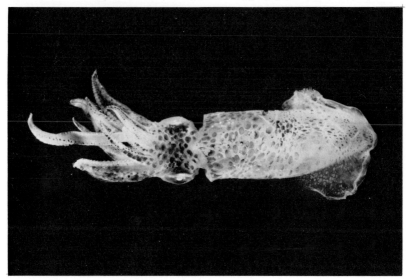

Figure 148

Loligo pealeii, the longfin squid, may reach 24″ (61 cm) in length and has pointed fins that are well over half the length of the body. It lives in shallow coastal waters.

Illex illecebrosus, the northern shortfin squid, is also found in shallow offshore water and resembles *Loligo.* It has, however, a long body with very short pointed fins. The fins are much less than half the length of the body. The eyes of *Illex* are nearly hidden and are inconspicuous.

Spirula spirula, our only species of spirulid squid, has a flat, spiral, internal shell about 1″ (2.5 cm) in diameter. The shell is a chambered, coiled cone with its whorls lying in a single plane and not touching each other. *Spirula* is a pelagic offshore species whose distinctive shell is sometimes found on our beaches.

Nut Clams

Atlantic Nut Clam *Nucula proxima*

Nucula proxima, the Atlantic nut clam, is a primitive bivalve belonging to the family Nuculidae (nut clams). These are small clams, about 0.4″ (1 cm) long, that have an obliquely oval shape in side view. The valves bear irregularly spaced concentric growth ridges and the periostracum is strong, smooth, and pale greenish brown. The interior is smooth and pearly and the inner margins are finely toothed. The hinge consists of an arched row of many small similar teeth. They occur in small numbers in the high subtidal in muddy sand where they live in burrows. Another species, *Nuculana acuta* (pointed nut clam, 0.5″; 1.3

128

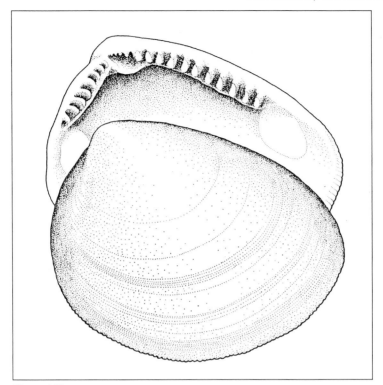

Figure 149

cm), resembles the Atlantic nut clam but has a shell with a sharply pointed posterior end and regularly spaced concentric ridges. It is common offshore.

The nut clams are deposit feeders that use a pair of long tentacles located beside the mouth to find particles of organic material and transport them to the mouth. Food particles in the sand stick to the mucus on the tentacles and are moved to the mouth by cilia. The clams orient themselves in the mud with the anterior end up and then move horizontally just below the sediment surface.

Awning Clams   *Color Plate B19*

Atlantic Awning Clam *Solemya velum*

Solemya velum, the Atlantic awning clam, belongs to the Solemyidae. Individuals reach lengths of 1″ (2.5 cm) and have thin, fragile, elongate valves that together form an open-ended and slightly compressed cylinder. The periostracum is strong, glossy yellow or yellowish brown and overgrows the margins of the valves to form curved awninglike over-

129

hangs. The valves of mature individuals are dark brown and strongly marked with alternating radial rays of light and dark. Younger individuals are yellow and have much less conspicuous rays. There are no hinge teeth, and the foot is cylindrical with a circular, sharply scalloped end, as can be seen in the younger individual on the left of plate B19. *Solemya* lives in intertidal and high subtidal silty sand in a Y-shaped burrow system unique among bivalves. The two upper arms of the Y open to the surface and the vertical arm extends 8″ (20 cm) or more into the sediment. The flared foot provides the purchase needed to move the clam through the burrow.

Solemya velum has a reduced, scarcely discernible gut that plays little or no role in feeding; there is a species on the Pacific coast, *S. reidi,* that has no gut at all. *Solemya velum* maintains large populations of intracellular chemosynthetic bacteria in its gill filaments. These bacteria derive energy from the oxidation of sulfur compounds, such as hydrogen sulfide, which are abundant in the anerobic sediments around the bottom of the burrow. The energy derived from this oxidation is shared with the clam which uses it as its primary energy source and for maintenance and synthesis. The oxygen needed for this process is available only at the top of the burrow. When in that region, *Solemya* uses hemoglobin to trap and store oxygen. It then moves to the oxygenless lower portions of the burrow where the stored oxygen is used by the clam for respiration and by the bacteria to oxidize sulfur compounds.

Solemya can swim by rapidly closing the valves and retracting the foot to force a jet of water posteriorly from the valves. It is thought that this behavior may be used to move through the burrow and to flush debris from the burrow. The commensal crab, *Pinnixa sayana,* and an undescribed amphipod in the genus *Listriella* have been found with *Solemya.*

Mussels

Musculus lateralis

The marine mussels belong to the family Mytilidae whose members have strong thin shells with weak or absent hinge teeth. They are often pointed at the anterior end and flared posteriorly. The umbos are displaced far towards the anterior end and sometimes may be the anteriormost part of the valve. The interior of the shell is pearly, iridescent, and glossy. The animals use protein threads (byssus) to attach to hard surfaces. They are usually epifaunal but some species bore into the calcareous rock and others live in soft sediments. The foot is small and the anterior adductor muscle is small or absent.

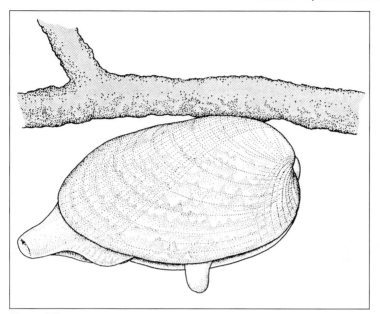

Figure 150

One of our more unusual and less noticeable species is *Musculus lateralis*. It is a small fat clam whose greenish valves are marked with fine zigzag brown lines. These clams are less than 0.5″ (1.5 cm) long and often occur in the fouling community on rocks or shells in inshore waters. They are primarily a subtidal animal though, and are more common offshore. The inflated valves bear very fine concentric striations and have weak radial ribs on the anterior and posterior ends. The middle region of each valve is free of radial ridges and they are best recognized by this feature although a lens is needed to see it clearly. *Musculus* lives attached to other organisms such as arborescent bryozoans and hydroids. Some species of *Musculus* retain eggs in the mantle cavity and brood their young on their gill filaments.

Mussels

Scorched Mussel *Brachidontes exustus*

One of our most common mussels is the small (1″; 2.5 cm) scorched mussel, *Brachidontes exustus*. It may also be seen in Plate B1. This intertidal species uses a strong protein byssus to attach to hard surfaces, especially rocks, where it may dominate the zone just above the low tide line and below the oyster zone. It forms the lowest of the three intertidal zones (barnacle, oyster, mussel) characteristic of hard substrata on our

Figure 151

coast. Under ideal conditions these mussels form dense mats of closely packed animals that provide living sites for several other invertebrate species. They have dark blackish, yellowish, greenish, or brownish ribbed valves with tiny teeth along the interior margins. The anterior end of the valves extends past the umbo and there are up to four small teeth in the hinge.

Another species, *Ischadium recurvum,* the hooked mussel, is similar. It is larger (2″; 5cm) and the umbo extends anteriorly past the end of the shell and is recurved to form a hook. Hooked mussels too are intertidal and are often found with oysters.

The common blue mussel, *Mytilus edulis,* is a northern species reported from as far south as South Carolina. It is not common in our area, but small stunted individuals occur here occasionally. Blue mussels may be found in North Carolina in the winter but are killed by summer temperatures. In the North they occupy a habitat similar to that of *Brachidontes* and are harvested commercially for food. These mussels reach 3″ (7.6 cm) in length in the North and have smooth, ribless, slate-blue or blue-black (sometimes brown) valves with fine concentric ridges.

Mussels   *Color Plate B20*

Atlantic Ribbed Mussel *Geukensia demissa*

Geukensia demissa is our largest mussel, and it reaches about 4″ (10 cm) in length. It has yellowish-brown or greenish-brown valves with strong radial ribs. The umbos are located slightly posterior to the extreme anterior end of the shell. *Geukensia* is a characteristic member of the salt marsh community where it lives embedded in mud around the stems or roots of *Spartina* grass, to which it attaches with a byssus. The plant in Plate B20 has been uprooted, washed, and posed with *Geukensia* beside it. Normally the mussel is almost entirely buried in mud or sand with only the wide posterior end extending above the sediment surface. The umbos are often eroded. *Geukensia* also occurs intertidally on pilings, seawalls, and oyster reefs.

Because it lives fairly high in the intertidal, *Geukensia* is exposed to air more than it is submerged in water and it is one of the most terrestrial of all North American bivalves. When it is exposed, it gapes and breathes air. Evaporation of water from the mantle cavity helps cool the animal in the hot summer marsh and partial burial in mud helps reduce desiccation. It is tolerant of a wide range of temperatures and salinities. *Geukensia* closes its valves when a shadow falls across it. Vibrations from the closing of one mussel are transmitted to others in the clump causing them to close also.

Mussels

Tulip Mussel *Modiolus americanus*
Mahogany Date Mussel *Lithophaga bisulcata*

The tulip mussel, *Modiolus americanus,* has a smooth reddish or yellow-brown shell with a heavy felty periostracum with stringlike hairs

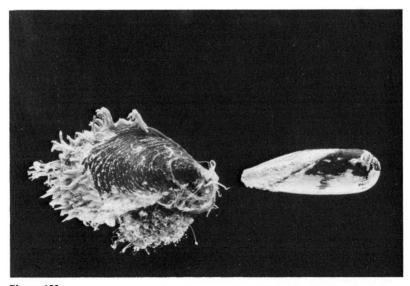

Figure 152

extending from it. The valves have fine concentric growth rings but no radial ribs. Brown or purple posterior rays appear on the outside of the valves which are rosy inside. The umbos are pink or orange. Tulip mussels reach 3″ in length and are a subtidal species found attached by a byssus to submerged grass, in sand, or on rocks. In soft sediments they completely bury themselves and in grass beds they attach to roots and stolons below the sediment surface.

The mahogany date mussel, *Lithophaga bisulcata,* is colored and shaped more or less like a date seed. It inhabits a chamber excavated in limestone or thick shell. The chamber closely conforms to the size and shape of the mussel that made it and is enlarged as the animal grows. Communication with the exterior is maintained via the siphons, which extend to the surface through openings that are smaller than the chamber itself so that the mussel is permanently enclosed. *Lithophaga* differs from other mussels in having a posterior end smaller than the anterior. The valves are brown and ribless. There is an oblique ridge running across each valve which separates the anterior from posterior ends. The posterior is usually encrusted with limy deposits, perhaps the precipitated products of the boring process. These mussels may reach 2″ (5 cm) in length. A similar species, *Lithophaga aristata* (scissor date mussel, 2″; 5 cm) also bores into calcareous material. Unlike *L. bisulcata* its valves bear limy posterior extensions which cross each other scissorslike. A greyish calcareous encrustation usually obscures the underlying brown color of the shell.

Arks

Ponderous Ark *Noetia ponderosa*

The arks, in the families Noetiidae and Arcidae, have several southeastern species but most are subtidal as adults and will not often be encountered alive unless it is possible to dredge or dive for them. This primitive group of bivalves is characterized by heavy radially ribbed valves and a long, straight hinge line. The hinge teeth are small, numerous, and similar to each other, a condition referred to as taxodont. There is an external, proteinaceous, hinge ligament between the umbos that is sometimes useful in identification. A heavy, dark, fuzzy periostracum is usually present but may be eroded away in places to reveal the underlying shell. Many species have hemoglobin in the blood which gives their tissues a red or pink color.

Members of the genus *Noetia* (Noetiidae) have heavy valves of equal size and they close tightly, leaving no opening for a byssus. Our species, *Noetia ponderosa* (2.5″; 6.4 cm), is fairly common subtidally in the sand of creek bottoms. Its heavy equal valves are strongly inflated and meet evenly, without overlapping. The umbos are located anteriorly but point posteriorly. There is a large, flat, black, transversely striated

Figure 153

ligament between the umbos. The valves are rounded anteriorly and tapered posteriorly. The ribs are strong and each is subdivided by a fine groove running along its length. The valleys between ribs are transversely striated. Inside, the valves are white and the posterior muscle scar is raised to form a low platform.

Ponderous arks live infaunally in soft subtidal bottoms but, as with all arks, the siphons are poorly developed and the posterior end of the clam must extend above the sediment surface into the water. So exposed, the valves provide an attractive attachment site for many epibenthic species, especially sea whips.

Arks

Transverse Ark *Anadara transversa*
Blood Ark *Anadara ovalis*

Some of our southeastern arks belong to the genus *Anadara* (Arcidae), whose members have slightly unequal valves and no gap for the byssus. *Anadara ovalis,* the blood ark (2.5″; 6.4 cm), is about as high as it is long and has a roughly oval shape. Its valves are inflated and heavily ribbed, but are not so heavy as those of *Noetia.* The left valve slightly overlaps the right ventrally and the ribs are smooth, lacking grooves, beads, or ridges. The periostracum is heavy, dark, and feltlike although it is often worn away in places to reveal the underlying white shell. The external ligament is very narrow and inconspicuous and the umbos point ante-

Figure 154

riorly. The tissue contains hemoglobin and is pink. It is a common species, living in the low intertidal or high subtidal in sand, although juveniles are often found attached to rocks by a weak byssus. These small clams can climb vertical surfaces by pulling themselves up by byssal threads attached above them. In sand they burrow shallowly with the posterior end of the valves exposed at the sediment surface.

Anadara transversa, the transverse ark (1.5″; 3.8 cm) is a smaller species with elongate, more or less rectangular valves. They are longer than high and the dorsal and ventral edges are roughly parallel while the anterior and posterior margins are rounded. The ribs of the left valve are beaded but those of the right usually are not. The left valve overlaps the right. Transverse arks are fairly common and sometimes live attached to rocks or in silty sand.

Anadara floridana (cut-ribbed ark, 5″; 13 cm) occurs uncommonly in shallow water, and small specimens are difficult to distinguish from *A. transversa.* The ribs of *A. floridana* are headed and strongly grooved, and its valves do not overlap, although the left is slightly larger than the right. Fine concentric lines are present between the ribs.

Turkey Wings and Arks

Zebra Turkey Wing *Arca zebra*
Incongruous Ark *Anadara brasiliana*

The turkey wings in the genus *Arca* have long narrow valves with a conspicuous ventral gap, or notch, to accommodate a large byssus which they use to attach to rock or coral. *Arca zebra,* the zebra turkey wing, reaches 3″ (7.6 cm), has a small byssal gap, and conspicuous

136

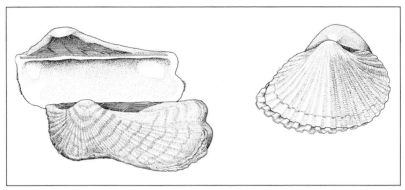

Figure 155

diagonal zebra stripes on the valves. *Arca imbricata,* the mossy ark, reaches 2″ (5 cm), has a large byssal opening, and lacks zebra stripes. Neither species is intertidal but *Arca imbricata* is more likely to be found in shallow water than *A. zebra.* Valves of both species wash ashore. Turkey wings live attached to firm objects offshore and are often themselves overgrown by other sessile organisms such as barnacles. The drawing shows the straight hinge and numerous similar taxodont teeth that characterize the Noetiidae and Arcidae.

Anadara brasiliana, the incongruous ark, reaches about 2″ (5 cm) in length. Its shape resembles that of *Noetia* and *Anadara ovalis* but its left valve strongly overlaps the right ventrally, and the ribs are covered by transverse ridges especially on the left valve. The ribs of the right valve are smooth posteriorly but anteriorly are ridged like those of the left valve. The periostracum is rather thin but there is a large, dark, external ligament similar to that of *Noetia.* The umbos point toward each other, the valves are not as heavy, and the posterior adductor muscle scar is not elevated. In profile, the valves have a sharp posterior angle and are not smoothly rounded like those of *A. ovalis.*

Wing Oysters   *Color Plate B21*

Atlantic Wing Oyster *Pteria colymbus*

The Atlantic wing oyster, *Pteria colymbus,* belongs to the family Pteriidae which includes the commercially important pearl oysters. Members of this family usually have a long straight hinge with a posterior winglike projection. The shell is strong, lustrous, and shiny inside, and covered on the outside with a thin dark periostracum. These oysters are epibenthic and have a strong byssus with which they attach to hard objects. *Pteria colymbus,* which is the only important representative of this family in our area, attaches with a byssus to sea whips in the shallow subtidal. The clams may reach lengths of 3″ (7.6 cm) and are yellowish or dark brown with a long, narrow, posterior wing and a broadly rounded, obliquely oval, posterior lobe. The left valve is swollen, the right is flatter, and the byssus passes through a large notch in the latter. They occasionally produce small pearls of no commercial value.

The southern Atlantic pearl oyster, *Pinctada imbricata,* has been reported from as far north as North Carolina but it is not a common inhabitant of our area. It is flattened like *Pteria* but has a very short posterior wing. Its valves are thin with a scaly periostracum and lustrous interior. It lives attached to rocks and gorgonians.

Pen Clams

Sawtooth Pen Clam *Atrina serrata*

Figure 156

The large clams in the family Pinnidae (pen clams) have distinctive wedge or fan-shaped valves and live partially buried in the intertidal and high subtidal of sand flats and grass beds. They have a tiny foot and use it to spin a byssus (visible in the lower right of the photograph) to attach to hard objects beneath the surface of the sand. The narrow end of the shell points downward with the flared upper end extending into the water above the sediment. There is a small anterior adductor muscle at the pointed end of the shell and a large posterior adductor near the center. The valves are thin, flexible, translucent, fragile, and adorned with spines. The valves are shiny and pearly over part of the inside surface. Unlike most other bivalves, pen clams close the shell by flexing it. Contraction of the adductor muscles causes the thin valves to bend, resulting in their closing. When the muscles relax the elastic valves spring back to their original shape, thus opening the shell. The hinge is not involved.

We have three species in our shallow waters. The valves of *Atrina serrata* (7″; 18 cm), shown above, have numerous relatively small spines in closely spaced rows. *Atrina rigida* and *A. seminuda* (both 8″; 20 cm) are much alike and both have larger and less numerous spines in widely spaced rows. These two differ from each other in the position of the posterior adductor muscle scar with respect to the pearly region of the interior of the valve. In *A. rigida* the scar is at the edge of the pearly area, whereas in *A. seminuda* it is entirely surrounded by the pearly area.

Pen clams support interesting communities of fouling organisms on the exposed portions of their valves, and two decapod crustaceans live commensally inside the valves. These are the pea crab, *Pinnotheres maculatus,* and the shrimp, *Pontonia domestica.*

File Clams   *Color Plate B22*

Pellucid File Clam *Lima pellucida*

The file clams (Limidae) have oval valves and are more common in the tropics than in our region. We have one species, the pellucid file clam, *Lima pellucida,* that is seen occasionally on hard substrata in shallow water. The file clams are epibenthic animals that attach to the substratum by a bundle of strong protein threads (byssus). They are about 1″ (2.5 cm) long and the oval valves are thin and pellucid with radiating ribs. The soft tissues are often pinkish and the mantle margin bears numerous, long, graceful, beaded tentacles. Like the scallop, they can swim by forcefully closing the valves to eject jets of water. *Lima* builds and inhabits nests constructed of debris held together by byssal threads.

Another species, more common south of our area, is *Lima scabra,* the rough file clam. It is much larger than *L. pellucida* and reaches 2.5″ (6.3 cm) in length. The radial ridges on the valves usually are strong and

139

coarse with overlapping shinglelike scales but sometimes they are nearly smooth. The soft tissues are spectacularly colored bright red or orange. *Lima scabra* lives on rocks and coral attached by a weak byssus, usually in crevices or on the lower surface of the rock. When disturbed, the clam releases the byssus and swims away. This species has been reported from offshore North Carolina where it lives under rocks at depths of about 100′ (30 m).

Oysters

Eastern Oyster *Crassostrea virginica*

Members of the oyster family Ostreidae are epibenthic species that attach permanently by one valve to hard substrata, often to other oysters. We have two common species on our coast. The most common is the eastern oyster, *Crassostrea virginica,* which is harvested in huge quantities. This species is primarily intertidal and often forms large reefs on mud, sand, or rocks. These oysters are found in sounds, estuaries, salt marshes, and tidal creeks and tolerate low salinity water. It is a large species, typically reaching 6″ (15 cm) or more in length and has long, grey, irregular, asymmetric valves, one of which is cemented to a hard surface. The muscle scars on the glossy white interior are purple and there is no row of small teeth around the inner margins of the valves. The edges of the valves are very thin and razor sharp so that handling them without being cut is difficult.

Figure 157

Our other common inshore species is the horse oyster, *Ostrea eques-tris.* Horse oysters are smaller (2″; 5 cm) and tend to be circular rather than elongate. They are less common than eastern oysters and live subtidally on hard substrata in higher salinity water. They do not form reefs as do eastern oysters. The interior of the valves is greenish, and the muscle scars are not purple. The lower, or attached, valve has high wavy walls, and the inner margin of the upper valve bears a marginal row of tiny teeth or bumps. The sponge oyster, *Ostrea permollis,* lives inside sponges offshore.

Scallops   *Color Plate B23*

Bay Scallop *Argopecten irradians*

The scallop family (Pectinidae) is a well-known group with over 300 species worldwide and about seven in our area. Members of the family are, in general, characterized by having a single, large, fused, adductor muscle instead of the two smaller ones found in most bivalves. This muscle is the edible part of the scallop. The valves are more or less circular in outline with processes, called ears, on either side of the umbo, which give the entire valve a fanlike appearance. Scallops have no siphons and live unattached, resting on the bottom. They can swim by rapidly and forcefully closing the valves to generate spurts of water.

Our most common shallow-water, sometimes intertidal, species is *Argopecten irradians,* the bay scallop (3″; 7.6 cm). These scallops lie on sandy bottoms in protected waters and are especially fond of grass beds. The two ears of the valves are about the same size and both valves are arched and bear strong wide ridges. The upper (left) valve is dark brown or grey while the lower (right) is white. Scallops are famous for their numerous iridescent blue eyes arrayed along the mantle margin. The tiny parasitic snail, *Boonea seminuda,* can be seen in the color plate feeding on the mantle margin.

The calico scallop, *Argopecten gibbus,* is about 2″ (5 cm) in diameter. It also lives subtidally in grass beds in shallow protected waters but usually has colorful (yellow, lavender, red-orange) *mottled* upper valves. Like the bay scallop, it has a white lower valve and the two ears are similar in size.

The mossy scallop, *Aequipecten muscosus,* has very large hinge ears and lacks mottling on its solidly colored valves. It is about 1.5″ (3.8 cm) in diameter and its strong ribs are scaly. This colorful species is often covered by sponge.

Another small species. *Chlamys sentis* (1.5″; 3.8 cm), the thorny scallop, can be immediately distinguished from our other species by its vastly unequal ears, a characteristic of its genus. The radial ribs are fine, numerous, and covered with small prickly scales. The color is variable, and it lives beneath rocks.

The lion's paw, *Lyropecten nodosus* (6″; 15 cm), sometimes washes ashore on outer beaches but normally lives on the calico scallop beds offshore. Its valves are like those of other scallops but have very wide, flat-topped, bumpy ribs. It is usually orange.

Jingles   *Color Plate B24*

Common Jingle *Anomia simplex*

The well-known common jingle, *Anomia simplex* (1″; 2.5 cm), is the only common member of the family Anomiidae (jingle clams) on our coast. Members of this family are attached epibenthic species with two quite dissimilar valves. The lower (right) valve is attached to a hard surface and is perforated by a large hole through which a limy byssus passes. This valve is thin and flat. The upper (left) valve is arched, thin, glossy, irregular, and translucent. The upper valve of *Anomia simplex* can be orange, beige, yellow, silver, or black, and its inner surface bears a white muscle scar that resembles a baby's footprint. These jingle clams may reach 1.5″ (3.8 cm) in diameter but are usually smaller. The valves are more or less circular in outline although there may be much variability in shape. The clams are usually found in shallow subtidal water attached to hard objects. Three muscles, the left foot retractor, the left foot protractor, and the adductor, work together to close the valves. The left foot retractor is attached to the substratum by the byssus, which passes through the hole in the right valve. The foot is visible extending from beneath the upper valve in Plate B24. Short sensory mantle tentacles can be seen around the margins.

Pododesmus rudis (false Atlantic jingle, 1″; 2.5 cm) also attaches to hard substrata and resembles *A. simplex* except that it has a rough, ribbed, non-glossy upper surface. It is not common.

The Atlantic thorny oyster, *Spondylus americanus,* is an offshore species occurring in waters deeper than 50′ (15 m). It belongs to the family Spondylidae and is closely related to the scallops. Thorny oysters reach about 4″ (10 cm) in length and their variously colored valves bear long flat spines. They are beautiful and spectacular but will not be found in shallow water in our region.

Jewel Boxes   *Color Plate B25*

Corrugated Jewel Box *Chama congregata*

The Chamidae, or jewel boxes, are epibenthic species that live attached by one valve to firm surfaces. The valves are asymmetric with the deeper, attached, lower valve forming a box to enclose the animal while the flatter upper valve acts as a cover. Our most common species is probably *Chama congregata,* the corrugated jewel box. The left valve of this species forms a deep cup and the flatter right valve is the lid. The outer part of the shell is very rough and ornamented with scaly radial ridges. The color is variable but is often white and red-purple. These clams are about 1″ (2.5 cm) in diameter and are usually found subtidally. A commensal pea crab, *Pinnotheres chamae,* has recently been reported living with *Chama congregata* on coral in North Carolina.

Another species, the leafy jewel box, *C. macerophylla,* is similar but the scales are much longer and form long, flat, leaflike processes extending from the valves. This species is larger, reaching about 2″ (5 cm) or more in diameter.

Lucinas and Diplodons

Cross-Hatched Lucina *Divaricella quadrisulcata*
Many-Lined Lucina *Lucina multilineata*
Atlantic Diplodon *Diplodonta punctata*

There are several small clams with circular profiles that live infaunally in silty or muddy sand on protected beaches and subtidal bottoms. The most commonly encountered species belong to the related families Lucinidae and Ungulinidae. Neither has incurrent siphons or a pallial sinus, but both have a long wormlike foot which is used to construct an incurrent tube of sand and mucus. Our three most common species are illustrated.

Members of the Lucinidae have an excurrent but no incurrent siphon and the family is represented on our coast by two fairly common species. *Lucina multilineata* (many-lined lucina) is small (0.4″; 1 cm),

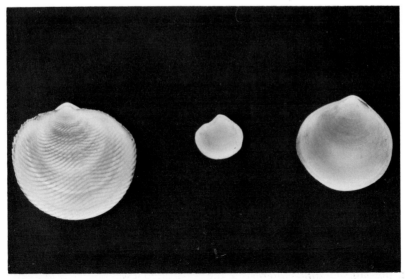

Figure 158

143

dull white, and swollen. In side view the valves are circular in outline except for a distinct depression beside the umbo. Surface sculpture consists of fine concentric striations and the inner margins of the valves are finely toothed. The valves are heavier and more inflated than those of *Diplodonta punctata.*

Divaricella quadrisulcata (cross-hatched lucina) is a larger lucinid, reaching 0.8″ (2 cm), with glossy white valves. The inner margins are finely toothed and the outer surface is ornamented with strong, criss-crossing, concentric and wavy V-shaped ridges. The valves are circular in outline except for a slight dorsal flattening, and are moderately inflated.

Anodontia alba (buttercup lucina, 2″; 5 cm) is common offshore in water more than 3′ (1 m) in depth. It has roughly circular inflated valves that are dull and chalky white outside and pale orangish yellow within. Empty valves often wash ashore but living animals are rarely seen. This species is widely used in the manufacture of shell jewelry.

Members of the Ungulinidae have two cardinal teeth in each hinge, one of which is split into two parts. They have no siphons, neither incurrent nor excurrent. Our most common species is *Diplodonta punctata,* the Atlantic diplodon. These clams may reach 0.8″ (2 cm) in diameter but are usually smaller. They have smooth, fragile, white or brownish valves which are moderately swollen. The outer surface bears microscopic concentric striations and the inner margin is smooth. They are circular in outline with central umbos.

Diplodonta semiaspera, the pimpled diplodon, is a smaller and less common species. It is circular in outline and very fat, with an almost spherical, chalky, greyish-white shell and visible concentric growth rings. The rings are subdivided into rows of tiny microscopic bumps. The valves are heavier and stronger than those of *D. punctata.* It is found on limestone rocks or coral.

Commensal Clams   *Figure 159*

Montacuta percompressa
Mysella sp C
Entovalva sp A
Entovalva sp B
Lepton sp
Mysella cuneata
Aligena elevata

The superfamily Leptonacea contains a number of interesting clams specialized for a commensal existence with other invertebrates. We have several species on our coast, many of which have not yet been

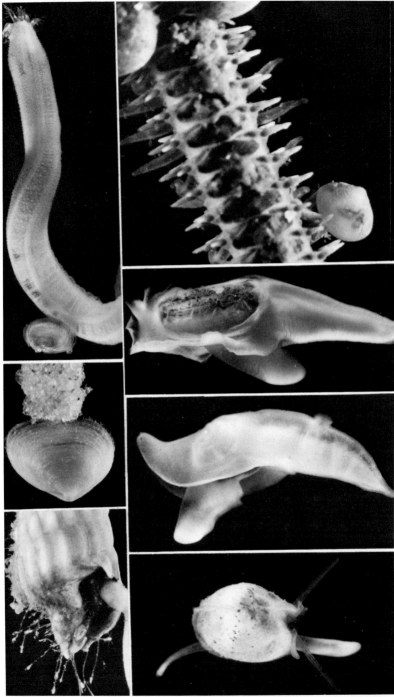

Figure 159. *Montacuta percompressa* (top left); *Mysella* sp C (top right); *Entovalva* sp A (right upper middle); *Entovalva* sp B (right lower middle); *Lepton* sp (bottom right); *Mysella cuneata* (bottom left); *Aligena elevata* (middle left).

145

assigned names. Several of them are shown here and many are also illustrated with their hosts on other pages. The animals in the photograph are not shown at the same scale.

The host specificity of these clams often makes identification easy. In most cases it is necessary only to know the identity of the host to know the name of the clam, so specific are their relationships to their hosts. The giant capitellid worm, *Notomastus lobatus* (Pl. C5), has three species of leptonacean clams in its burrow, none of which has been described and named. *Entovalva* sp A has a well-developed shell (shell length 0.3″; 8 mm) and begins life under the scales of the scaleworm, *Lepidasthenia varia* (Fig. 192), itself a commensal in the burrow of *Notomastus*. *Entovalva* sp B (Fig. 159; Pl. C5) has a drastically reduced shell and looks more like a worm than a clam so overdeveloped is its mantle (shell length 0.2″; 5 mm, total length 1.2″; 3 cm). Females live attached to *Notomastus* and dwarf males live in the mantle cavity of the females. A rare species, known only from three individuals, montacutid sp A (not shown), has strong valves and a poorly developed mantle. Nothing is known of its biology.

Aligena elevata (Figs. 159, 206; 0.2″; 5 mm) is a tiny fragile species that lives outside the tube of the bamboo worm, *Clymenella torquata*. *Montacuta percompressa* (0.2″; 5 mm; Figs. 159, 118) lives with the burrowing sea cucumber, *Leptosynapta tenuis*. *Montacuta floridana* (0.4″; 1 cm, not shown) lives with the large onuphid polychaete, *Americonuphis magna,* in Florida and North Carolina. The tiny *Mysella cuneata* (0.1″; 3 mm; Figs. 159, 124) lives with the peanut worm, *Phascolion strombus*. There are several undescribed species of *Mysella,* each with a different host. *Mysella* sp A occurs with an undescribed burrowing sea cucumber, *Mysella* sp B with the spoon worm, *Thalassema hartmani, Mysella* sp C (Fig. 159) with the brittle stars, *Microphiopholis atra* and *M. gracillima,* and *Mysella* sp D (not shown, 0.2″; 5 mm) with *Leptosynapta tenuis.* The commensal rotifer *Zelinkiella synaptae,* can be seen on the tube feet of the brittle star in upper right of Fig. 159. *Lepton longipes* (0.3″; 8 mm) was described as inhabiting the "holes of marine worms and fossorial crustaceans in South Carolina" and has since been reported from the burrows of *Callianassa major* and *Upogebia affinis.* A small undescribed species of *Lepton* inhabits the burrows of the mantis shrimp, *Squilla empusa,* in North and South Carolina and perhaps elsewhere. These two species are snail-like in appearance and habits. Each has a long, narrow, creeping foot like a snail and crawls about with the shell held above the foot, snail-fashion. Further, the anterior mantle margin has a pair of long sensory tentacles that resemble the head tentacles of snails. There is a third, less conspicuous, posterior, median, mantle tentacle.

The leptonaceans show a high degree of adaptation for their commensal existence in the burrows of other animals and are a good example of the way natural selection can modify species for special ecological conditions. All leptonaceans are small so that they can live in the burrow or tube of another animal without interfering with the host. These clams show great host specificity and have appropriate anatomical and behavioral mechanisms for finding and remaining with their proper host. The leptonacean foot is adapted for creeping, rather than digging. These animals do not need to dig since they crawl around inside a burrow already constructed by the host. The leptonaceans retain a byssus throughout life, something few of their close relatives do. The byssus is used to maintain contact with the host or its tube. The mantle is often elaborately developed, a luxury not affordable to clams living in unprotected situations. The shell is usually thin and fragile and is sometimes drastically reduced. Again, this is possible only for clams living in protected places such as the burrows of other animals. The leptonaceans show a wide variety of reproductive adaptations designed to get the sexes and gametes together, something not easily accomplished by small, relatively immobile animals living isolated from others of their species. Some species are hermaphrodites, with each individual being both male and female, either simultaneously or sequentially. Hemaphroditism, which is common in some molluscs such as the opisthobranchs and pulmonates, is rare in bivalves. Some species have dwarf parasitic males that live attached to the female. In one species, *Montacuta percompressa,* nothing remains of the male except its testis, which is embedded in the tissue of the female. Females of many leptonacean species retain the eggs in the mantle cavity where they hatch and begin development. This is called brooding and it allows the adult to give the developing young a greater degree of shelter and care early in life. This too is rare among marine bivalves although it is the rule in freshwater species.

Cockles   *Color Plate B26*

Giant Atlantic Cockle *Dinocardium robustum*

The large and important cockle family, the Cardiidae, has several representatives on our coast but empty valves are encountered far more often than living specimens. Members of this family are heart-shaped when viewed from either end and some are very large.

Our most common cockle species is the giant Atlantic cockle, *Dinocardium robustum,* which is found in shallow, occasionally intertidal, waters. Its empty valves are a familiar feature of our outer beaches. It is a large species (4″; 10 cm) that lives in clean unstable sand in shallow water, usually just offshore. Its valves are inflated, brown or pinkish-brown, and marked by strong flat radial ribs. They have a narrow, L-shaped foot and use it to burrow quickly and also to leap vigorously. The siphons are short, separate, and bear numerous fine processes.

Trachycardium muricatum, the yellow cockle, may also be found occasionally, sometimes washed ashore on outer beaches. It is a smaller species, reaching about 2.5″ (6.4 cm). It is not as fat as *Dinocardium* and has a very slender heart-shaped profile when viewed end on. Viewed from the side, the valves are nearly circular. It can be recognized immediately as a member of its genus by its rough scaly ribs. In this species only the anterior and posterior ribs are scaly while the ribs of the upper and middle portions of the valves are smooth. The external color is variable but is often yellowish, sometimes with brown mottling. The valves are yellow inside.

Trachycardium egmontianum, the prickly cockle, has more elongate, oval valves whose ribs are scaly over the entire surface. It is usually grey outside with a pale pink blush inside.

Members of the genus *Laevicardium* (egg cockles) have smooth, inflated shells without spines or discernible ribs. *Laevicardium laevigatum* (2.8″; 7 cm) is common in shallow water in the Southeast. It is taller than long, variously colored, and has about 50 fine radial ribs that cannot be detected by touch.

Surf Clams

Dwarf Surf Clam *Mulinia lateralis*

The surf clams, in the family Mactridae, are common in shallow waters although, in spite of the common name, most of them do not live

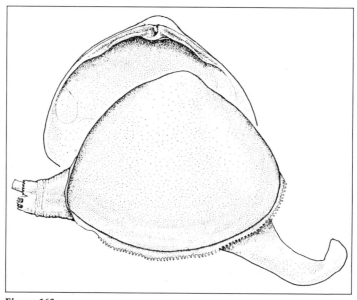

Figure 160

in the surf. The empty valves of several species are commonly found washed ashore on ocean beaches. The hinge of a mactrid shell has a characteristic, usually triangular, pitlike chondrophore which houses a large internal pad of protein, the resilium. The elastic resilium pushes the valves apart when the clam relaxes its muscles. An external ligament is also present but is small. The valves usually have centrally located umbos.

The species most often encountered in estuaries is the dwarf surf clam, *Mulinia lateralis*. It is our smallest surf clam, reaching only 0.6″ (1.5 cm) in length. It is characteristic of fine silty sand bottoms of shallow, quiet waters and is not found in clean unstable sands. It can live in waters with salinities as low as 15‰, roughly half the concentration of sea water. It is white with solid strong valves. The valves are moderately inflated and roughly triangular with the umbos located in the middle of the dorsal margin. The posterior slope bears a radial ridge on each side. It has short siphons. Its pale cream-white color should be sufficient to distinguish it from juvenile *Spisula,* which it resembles. Further, the lateral teeth of *Spisula* bear fine sawtooth denticles which are lacking in *Mulinia.*

Surf Clams

Fragile Surf Clam *Mactra fragilis*
Atlantic Surf Clam *Spisula solidissima*
Channeled Surf Clam *Raeta plicatella*
Dwarf Surf Clam *Mulinia lateralis*

Three of our surf clams live in offshore shallow sands and are rarely seen alive near the water's edge. Their empty valves, however, are a common sight on our outer beaches, especially after storms. Members of this family are easily recognized as such by the large pitlike chondrophore in the hinge of each valve. In life, the chondrophore houses an elastic resilium which opposes the adductor muscles and opens the shell. *Mactra fragilis* (2.5″; 6.4 cm), the least common of the three, has smooth, off-white, sometimes slightly yellowish valves. The umbos are central and the valves are an elongate oval with a wide posterior gape. As in *Mulinia,* each valve bears a posterior radial ridge close to the upper margin. *Mactra* is an intertidal and high subtidal species that prefers sandy areas.

The most common of these three species is *Spisula solidissima,* which may exceed 8″ (20 cm) in length but is usually less than 4″ (10 cm). The valves are smooth and roughly triangular, again with central umbos. The white shell is covered by a thin, glossy, yellow periostracum. *Spisula* prefers unstable shifting sand in tidal channels or on outer

Figure 161

beaches where it is found in the high subtidal and low intertidal. Populations south of Cape Hatteras are considered by some biologists to belong to a separate species, *Spisula raveneli.*

Raeta plicatella (2.8″; 7 cm) is unmistakable with its fragile, white, grooved, and ridged valves. Each of the valves is sculptured with wide concentric channels and high ridges. The sculpture is visible inside the valves as well but here the ridges become channels and vice versa. *Anatina anatina* (smooth surf clam, 2″; 5 cm) has similar valves but lacks the wide concentric channels and ridges of *Raeta.* Each valve has a strong posterior radial rib. This species is not illustrated but may occasionally be found washed ashore on outer beaches. An adult *Mulinia lateralis* is included at the bottom of the photograph for comparison with its larger relatives.

Surf Clams and Marsh Clams

Wedge Rangia *Rangia cuneata*
Carolina Marsh Clam *Polymesoda caroliniana*

Another surf clam likely to be encountered in shallow southeastern

150

Figure 162

waters is the common brackish-water species, *Rangia cuneata. Rangia* has the chondrophore and resilium characteristic of the family. It is common infaunally in low salinity water and is a fat dark clam. It has heavy wedge-shaped (cuneiform) valves which are rounded anteriorly and pointed posteriorly. The posterior dorsal surface behind the umbos is somewhat flattened. It is similar in size and shape to the Carolina marsh clam, *Polymesoda caroliniana.* Although the two are unrelated they occur in similar habitats and may be confused with each other.

Polymesoda (2.5″; 2.5 cm) belongs to the family Corbiculidae and is the only marine member of that family on our coast. These clams have almost circular outlines and fat (inflated) valves. The valves are dull white with a heavy, dark brown, sometimes greenish, periostracum. The periostracum is usually worn away from the umbonal region so the underlying white shell is exposed and eroded. *Polymesoda* lacks the pitlike chondrophore in the hinge that is present in *Rangia,* and it has an almost circular outline as opposed to the wedge-shaped outline of *Rangia.* It is common on sandy or muddy bottoms in brackish waters, especially in the intertidal region of low salinity salt marshes and may extend upstream to areas inhabited by cypress trees. A freshwater

151

species, *Corbicula manilensis,* was introduced into the United States in 1938, has spread rapidly, and now causes serious economic and ecological damage by clogging water supplies, ditches, intakes, and pumps, and by eliminating native bivalve species in natural waters.

Razor Clams

Color Plate B27

Atlantic Razor Clam *Ensis directus*
Green Razor Clam *Solen viridis*

The razor clams of the families Cultellidae and Solenidae are so named because of their resemblance to a straight razor. We have two common species in our area and in life they are easily distinguished. The more common species, *Ensis directus,* a cultellid, is long and narrow with a thin, glossy, green, brown, and purple periostracum. Its siphons, which can be seen in the photograph, are short, fringed at the ends, and separate, not fused. The elongate shell is slightly curved and may be as long as 6″ (15 cm) but is usually much shorter. Its empty valves are often found on beaches. Cultellids have umbos near, but not at, the anterior end of the valves. The left hinge has a double cardinal tooth. *Ensis* lives in the high subtidal and low intertidal where it prefers fine, slightly muddy sand and strong currents. It burrows rapidly and although it positions itself near the surface when feeding, it withdraws into the burrow at low tide. Any disturbance, such as the footsteps of an approaching collector, will cause it to withdraw even deeper in the burrow.

Solen viridis, a solenid, is a smaller species, about 2″ (5 cm) at the most, that has a glossy greenish-yellow periostracum and less curved valve margins. Alive, it can be recognized immediately by its long, fused, jointed siphons. The siphons are readily broken at the joints, and when seen alone may be mistaken for some new and unknown phylum of segmented worms. The openings of the siphons are guarded by small tentacles. These are present at each joint so that wherever the siphon breaks the opening will be guarded. In the solenids, the umbos are terminal, or nearly so, and there is a single tooth in the hinge of each valve.

Both species live infaunally in silty sand, are rapid burrowers, and have valves that gape at both ends. They are common in the intertidal and high subtidal.

Macomas

Elongate Macoma *Macoma tenta*
Baltic Macoma *Macoma balthica*

We have several members of the family Tellinidae on our coast and all of the common ones are in the genera *Tellina* and *Macoma*. The tellinids are active infaunal burrrowers in soft sediments, usually in the

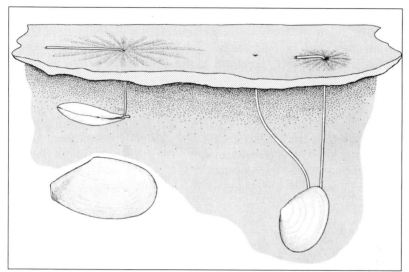

Figure 163

silty sand of protected beaches. They differ markedly from most bivalves in being deposit feeders rather than filter feeders. They burrow horizontally through the sediment to seek fresh deposits. They have exceptionally long mobile siphons which they extend over the surface of the sediment to gather particulate organic material. Because of the length of the siphons the pallial sinus is very large in this group.

We have two common species of *Macoma* and several of *Tellina* in our shallow waters. The two genera are similar but *Tellina* has lateral teeth in the hinge whereas *Macoma* does not but this is not a useful character for field identification. The only two species that are likely to be confused are *Macoma tenta* and *Tellina texana*. A photograph of *Macoma tenta* is included with those of our common *Tellina* species in Figure 164. Our two species of *Macoma, M. tenta* and *M. balthica,* do not resemble each other, do not occur together, and are not likely to be confused.

Macoma tenta (0.7″; 1.8 cm) has asymmetric white valves with a posterior twist to the right. It lies in the sediment a little less than 1″ (2.5 cm) below the surface and, like most tellinids, lies on its side with the convex left side down so that the posterior twist is directed upwards. The animals, which are deposit feeders, extend about 1″ (2.5 cm) of the incurrent siphon along the sediment surface to seek food particles. The siphon is alternately extended and withdrawn during this search. This activity results in a surface pattern of shallow grooves radiating outward, like the spokes of a wheel, from the central opening. The excurrent siphon is not extended to the surface, rather reaches only about 0.1–0.2″ (2–3 mm) from the posterior end of the clam and discharges directly into the surrounding sediment.

Macoma balthica (1″; 2.5 cm) is common north of Georgia in muddy intertidal and shallow subtidal sediments of quiet waters of low salinity (less than 18 ‰). *Macoma balthica* has deep oval valves with central umbos. The valves are white, sometimes pink, with an enormous pallial sinus. Adults live 2–8″ (5–20 cm) deep in the sediment and are oriented vertically rather than horizontally. They extend both siphons to the sediment surface and feed by moving the incurrent siphon over it. Intertidal animals are thought to be suspension feeders when the tide is in and deposit feeders when it is out.

Tellins

Tellina aequistriata (far left)
Macoma tenta (lower middle left)
Tellina texana (upper middle)
Tellina versicolor (middle right)
Tellina alternata (far right)

Identification of tellinids is difficult but our common species can usually be separated from each other. Among the most common of our species are *Tellina texana* and *Macoma tenta*. Both are small, about 0.6″ (1.5 cm) in length, and similar in appearance. They often occur

Figure 164

together and are best distinguished by the profile of the posterior end. *Tellina texana* is steeply sloped posterior to the hinge while *M. tenta* has a more gentle slope, with a snoutlike appearance. This snout is deflected to the right and there is often a bit of rusty-orange color around the margins of the valves. The *Macoma* in the photograph is a small individual.

Tellina versicolor resembles *T. texana* in size and shape but is usually pink, whereas *T. texana* is always white. In profile, the valves of *T. versicolor* are straight along the ventral margin and there is an inconspicuous dorsal concavity (for the ligament) located just behind the umbo. *Tellina iris* (which is uncommon and is not shown) reaches about 0.6″ (1.5 cm) in length and is white like *T. texana*, but it has distinctive oblique grooves that cross the concentric growth rings. These grooves are most evident anteriorly.

The two other species in the photograph are much larger and are not so common as *T. texana* and *M. tenta*. *Tellina alternata* has glossy, elongate (3″; 7.6 cm) valves with strong, smooth, concentric growth ridges. *Tellina aequistriata* has shorter (1″; 2.5 cm) valves that are a dull chalky greyish-white. They too have strong, concentric growth ridges but in addition have one or two strong radial ridges on the posterior ends of the valves.

Jackknife Clams

Common Sand Clam *Tagelus plebeius*
Divided Sand Clam *Tagelus divisus*

Our two common representatives of the Solecurtidae have elongate rectangular valves and superficially resemble the razor clams in the family Solenidae. Unlike them, the solecurtids have very long, separate siphons. Both of our species are intertidal filter feeders that construct deep burrows in fine sediments. They inhabit permanent burrows in mud or muddy sand and extend the two siphons to the sand surface where they make a characteristic pair of openings 1–3″ (2–8 cm) apart. The siphons must be long enough to extend distances many times the length of the clam in order to reach the sediment surface. The valves have a large pallial sinus to accommodate the retracted siphons.

The more common of the two species, *Tagelus plebeius*, is relatively large, reaching 3″ (7.6 cm) in length. It may be abundant on muddy intertidal flats where the burrows of large individuals extend as much as 20″ (51 cm) into the sand. The valves are wider than those of the razor clams and, in adults, the dark periostracum is eroded to reveal the chalky white shell beneath. Juveniles have a yellowish, uneroded periostracum (like that of adult *Tagelus divisus*). *Tagelus plebeius* is often called the "spit clam" in reference to its habit of squirting water into the

Figure 165

air when the tide is out. Juveniles of the commensal crab, *Pinnixa chaetopterana,* often occupy the burrow of this species. The ribbon worm, *Cerebratulus lacteus,* is a major predator of *T. plebeius.*

Our other species, *Tagelus divisus,* is smaller, about 1.5″ (3.8 cm) at most, with rounded, less rectangular valves that are glossy yellow through life. The central region of each valve bears a faint purple wedge-shaped radial band running from the umbo to the edge. Inside, the middle of each valve bears a radial ridge which is lacking in *T. plebeius.* It too is common on intertidal flats and builds a burrow similar to that of *T. plebeius* except that it is often J-shaped with the deep end curved upward. Burrows of this small species do not exceed 8″ (20 cm) in depth.

Semelids

Atlantic Abra *Abra aequalis*
Tellin-like Cumingia *Cumingia tellinoides*

These two clams belong to the Semelidae whose members are easily confused with the tellins. The family is more important in the tropics but there are a few species in the Southeast. Two of them are found with some regularity in shallow, subtidal sand flats. Many of the semelids are colorful, but these two are not. They are usually infaunal in sand or mud in shallow water, and, like the tellins, they are deposit feeders with long siphons and a large pallial sinus. They differ from the tellins primarily in their possession of a hinge with an internal chitinous pad, or resilium, in

156

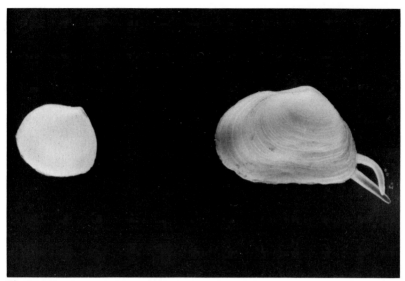

Figure 166

addition to the external ligament. This resilium is a circular or narrow oval pad of protein and chitin lying in a similarly shaped pit, the chondrophore, just posterior to the cardinal teeth in the hinge.

Cumingia tellinoides (0.8″; 2 cm) is usually found in sand or on rocks. It is best recognized by its circular resilium lying in a spoon-shaped chondrophore, which is much like that of the surf clams (Mactridae). The valves are a dull white with concentric ridges and the periostracum is thin and yellowish. The umbos are a little behind the middle, the posterior-ventral angle is sharp, and the anterior is rounded. The valves have a single cardinal tooth each. The pallial sinus is rounded and deep, but not so deep as that of *Abra*. The valves are sometimes slightly irregular and may be twisted posteriorly.

Abra aequalis (0.4″; 1 cm) is a common species and very tellinlike in appearance. It has shiny, translucent, smooth, white valves with a lopsided oval shape. The resilium is long, narrow, and inconspicuous and there are two cardinal teeth in the right hinge. The pallial sinus is deep and rounded, nearly reaching the anterior adductor muscle. The umbo is a little behind the middle of the valve, the posterior slope is steep, and the anterior slope gentle and rounded.

Two subtidal species, *Semele proficua* and *S. purpurascens,* also occur in the area but are rarely found in the intertidal. *Semele proficua* (1.2″; 3 cm) is nearly circular in profile. Its valves are white, sometimes with pink rays, and are sculptured with weak, irregularly spaced, concentric rings and microscopic radial grooves. *Semele purpurascens* (1.2″; 3 cm) has lopsided oval valves and is variously colored dull purple or brownish orange. It has concentric and radial sculpture.

Coquina Clams   *Color Plate B28*

Coquina *Donax variabilis*

Members of the wedge clam family, Donacidae, are small clams that live in sand, usually in the surf of outer beaches. Their umbos are displaced posteriorly giving the shell a wedge shape when viewed from the side. Our most familiar species is the coquina clam, *Donax variabilis,* that is very common intertidally on outer beaches. Coquinas reach about 0.8″ (2 cm) in length and come in a variety of pretty pastel colors including lavender, yellow, pink, blue, and white. They often have bands of darker color radiating from the umbo to the margins of the valve. The valves are sculptured with fine concentric ridges and distinct radial ribs, which are strongest posteriorly. The inner margins are finely toothed and the valves are strong and glossy and, of course, wedge-shaped. Like the mole crabs, coquinas are filter feeders that live in the sand and migrate up and down the beach to maintain an optimum position with respect to the waterline.

Another form, *Donax parvulus,* is apparently a distinct species although some authors consider it to be a variety of *D. variabilis.* The two are similar in shape and ecology but exhibit some important differences. *Donax parvulus* is smaller than *D. variabilis* and lacks radial ribs on its valves. In North Carolina, where both species have been studied, the two share the intertidal beach during the spring and summer after colonizing it as juveniles in late winter. During the spring and early summer both species migrate up and down the intertidal beach with each tide but in late summer these tide-related migrations cease and *D. parvulus* moves into the subtidal for the winter. *Donax variabilis* remains in the intertidal but now allows itself to be stranded by each ebbing tide, perhaps to avoid crowding by mole crabs or predation. *Donax variabilis* eventually moves into the subtidal in late fall. Both species spawn subtidally in the winter and juveniles recolonize the intertidal beach in late winter.

A tuft of the hydroid, *Lovenella gracilis,* is growing on the posterior end of one of the clams in the photograph. Several fishes as well as ghost crabs, speckled crabs, shimmy worms, and humans prey on *Donax.*

Venus Clams

Northern Quahog *Mercenaria mercenaria*

The family Veneridae (venus clams) has many southern representatives, most of which are easily recognized. Venerids in general are characterized by the presence of a distinctive, external heart-shaped, dorsal area, the lunule, located anterior to the umbos, and they usually have a similar but more elongate area, the escutcheon, posterior to the

Figure 167

umbos. Quahogs, or hard-shell clams, *Mercenaria mercenaria,* are the commercial clam of our coast and are variously known as littleneck, cherrystone, or chowder clams depending on their size. They have large, heavy, chalky, grey or brownish valves. With the exception of two smooth areas, near the umbos, the entire outer surface is covered with fine concentric growth ridges. The interior is glossy white with intense purple areas near the posterior edge and hinge. They are infaunal filter feeders, that live shallowly buried in a variety of sediment types from clean sand to mud. The larvae require the presence of large shell fragments or pebbles before they will settle out of the plankton. Position in the sediment depends on sediment type. Clams in sand usually live about 1″ (2.5 cm) below the surface, strain water through the overlying sand, and grow rapidly. Individuals in mud live closer to the sediment surface, apparently have problems with fouling of the gill surface by silt, and do not grow as rapidly. Clams in the intertidal zone live deeper in the sediment than those in the subtidal, apparently to reduce the danger of being dislodged by scouring. Large individuals reach 5″ (13 cm) in length.

Mercenaria mercenaria was eaten by east coast American Indians before and after European colonization. Woodland Indians made beads, called wampum, from the purple and white valves. The word "wampum" was translated to mean "money" hence the scientific name *mercenaria* for these clams. The Iroquois name *quayhon* eventually became the English common name "quahog" (pronounced co-hog).

A second species, *M. campechiensis,* the southern quahog, reaches 6″ (15 cm) and closely resembles *M. mercenaria* except that it has no purple inside and there is no smooth area on the outside of the valves.

Venus Clams

Cross-Barred Venus *Chione cancellata*

The cross-barred venus, *Chione cancellata,* lives intertidally or subtidally in clean or slightly silty sand in shallow water, often in creek bottoms or grass beds. It is less than 1.5″ (3.8 cm) in length and a gridwork of strongly raised radial and concentric ridges makes it unmistakable. It is one of our most common and best known venus clams. The shell has a long, flattened oval escutcheon behind the umbo and a small, distinctly heart-shaped lunule in front of the umbo. Although *Chione* has been collected up to 24″ (61 cm) below the sediment surface, it has very short siphons and its normal living position is at the surface with the posterior end of the valves protruding into the overlying water. In this position it is frequently exploited as an attachment site by seaweeds and sea whips. These clams are slow and apparently weak burrowers that enter the sediment with difficulty, often moving horizontally as they try to effect penetration. *Chione cancellata* avoids coarse sediments, probably because of the increased difficulty of burrowing into them. Population densities of over 150 per square meter have been

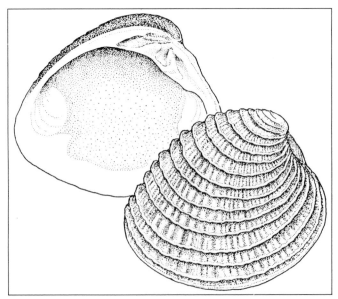

Figure 168

160

recorded intertidally. Papillae at the ends of the short siphons appear to be light sensitive and are responsible for a shadow response resulting in retraction of the siphons when a shadow falls across them.

Pitar fulminatus, the lightning venus (1.5″; 3.8 cm), resembles *Mercenaria* in shape. It is a subtidal species not often encountered in shallow water. The valves have large full umbos and closely spaced concentric growth rings, but there is no radial sculpture. The exterior is a dull white or grey with zigzag brown markings arranged in radial bands. The lunule is large and outlined by an incised line. The inner margins of the valves are not crenulate.

Venus Clams   *Color Plate B29*

Gem Clam *Gemma gemma*
Grey Pygmy Venus *Chione grus*

At 0.2″ (5 mm) *Gemma* is one of the world's smallest saltwater clams. In outline the valves are roughly triangular and are glossy white with variable amounts of purple or red-violet. The lower inside margin of the valves bears a row of tiny teeth and the outside is ornamented with microscopic concentric ridges. These clams should not be confused with juvenile *Mercenaria mercenaria,* which have strong, sharp, bladelike concentric ridges. *Gemma* may be exceedingly abundant on sand flats in the Northeast but is less common in the Southeast where it is found in sandy salt marshes and on sandy protected beaches. This clam is a venerid but it lacks an escutcheon and the lunule is faint. The umbos are often eroded. It broods eggs and releases tiny clams instead of larvae.

Another small species, the grey pygmy venus, *Chione grus,* is a member of the epifaunal community of hard substrata and is also found on protected beaches. It is less than 0.5″ (1.3 cm) in length, oblong and variously colored, grey, pink, or salmon on the outside, with some purple on the interior. The surface of the valves bears strong concentric ridges but radial ridges, while present, are weak.

Venus Clams   *Color Plate B30*

Sunray Venus *Macrocallista nimbosa*

The sunray venus is sometimes common intertidally or subtidally in clean sand tidal flats. It prefers areas exposed to wave scouring but avoids high energy beaches with heavy surf. The valves are long, strongly compressed, smooth, and shiny. They are glossy lavender or brown with a sunburst of dark bands radiating from the umbo to the periphery. The clams are large and may reach 5″ (13 cm) in length. Both clams in the photograph are *M. nimbosa,* the sunray venus. The clam burrows rapidly by moving forward as it penetrates the substratum. As with many venerids, but unlike most other bivalves, the juveniles live deeper in the sediment than the adults. This apparently is due to the greater likelihood that the young will be swept from the sediment by scouring.

A second species in the genus, *M. maculata,* the calico clam, is smaller and more or less egg-shaped in outline, being much less elongate. It reaches about 2″ (5 cm) in length and is brown with darker brown spots that impart a checkered appearance. It is less common and occurs in slightly deeper water than the sunray venus.

Venus Clams

Disk Venus *Dosinia discus*

The disk venus has almost circular, glossy, creamy white valves that may be as large as 3″ (7.6 cm) in diameter. It is very strongly flattened and disklike. The umbos are centrally located and point anteriorly. The glossy valves have about 50 strong concentric growth rings per inch (20 per cm). The valves are normally shiny white but when freshly dug from anaerobic sediments they may be stained black. Another species, the elegant venus, *Dosinia elegans,* is almost identical to *D. discus* but has coarser concentric rings, of which there are only about 25 per inch (10 per cm). *Dosinia* species have no escutcheon, but the lunule is distinct and well defined. There is a thin, yellowish, glossy periostracum. *Dosinia* valves, still held together by the ligament, are frequently washed ashore on outer beaches. The two species have similar ecological re-

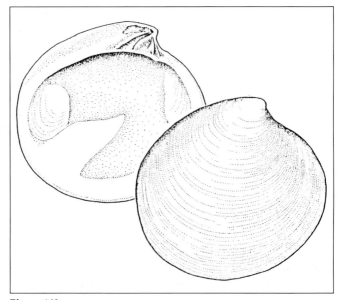

Figure 169

quirements and prefer sandy tidal flats with tidal currents but no surf. They burrow rapidly, slicing the thin shell through the sand with a rocking motion, until they reach a position about 4″ (10 cm) below the sediment surface where they live with the posterior end pointed up.

Another flat, circular venerid, *Cyclinella tenuis,* reaches about 0.8″ (2 cm) in diameter and superficially resembles juvenile *Dosinia.* Its valves are circular in outline with central, anteriorly pointed umbos, but the concentric growth rings are not nearly so regular nor so obvious as those of *Dosinia* and its valves are not glossy. A lunule is present but it is not well defined. *Cyclinella* also resembles the semelid, *Semele proficua,* which is circular in outline with central umbos. As a venerid, *Cyclinella* has no resilium or chondrophore as does *Semele.* It is also a little fatter than *Semele* and lacks the microscopic radial lines of that species. Neither *Cyclinella* nor *Semele* is glossy like *Dosinia* nor are the concentric rings evenly spaced. *Cyclinella* inhabits muddy subtidal sediments in estuaries and lagoons. It has a long pointed foot like that of a lucinid.

False Angel Wings

False Angel Wing *Petricola pholadiformis*

We have two species in the family Petricolidae on this coast: *Petricola pholadiformis* and *Rupellaria typica. Petricola pholadiformis,* the false angel wing, is an intertidal species often found boring into clay or peat or, as juveniles, on rocks and pilings in the spaces between mussels. The

Figure 170

valves are elongate and superficially similar to those of the angel wing, *Cyrtopleura costata.* The valves are thin and have strong, scaly, radial ribs. The umbos are anterior and the valves have large fingerlike cardinal teeth, which the true angel wings do not have. False angel wings reach about 2″ (5 cm) in length and are much longer than high. Adults are white but juveniles are pink or brownish purple, and this color may persist as a small spot near the umbo of slightly older, otherwise white, individuals. They have long separate siphons and a large pallial sinus. The foot and siphons are visible in the photograph.

The false angel wings, or false piddocks (Petricolidae), superficially resemble the angel wings (Pholadidae) but differ from them in many important respects. Both families are borers and they exhibit similar characteristics, developed in response to the requirements of similar life styles. The hinge of petricolids lacks the complex assortment of accessory plates found in the pholadids and has hinge teeth, which the pholadids lack. There are no inner processes for muscle attachment (apophyses) associated with the petricolid hinge as there are in the pholadids. Like the pholadids, the petricolids have white, sculptured, often deformed valves with umbos displaced toward the anterior end.

Rock Borers

Atlantic Rock Borer *Rupellaria typica*

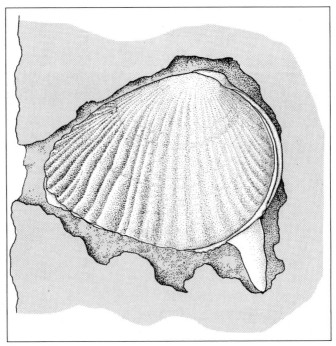

Figure 171

Rupellaria typica, the Atlantic rock borer, bores into soft calcareous rock and coral in the intertidal and high subtidal. It is short, only a little longer than high, and has heavy, irregular, variable valves ornamented with widely spaced, wavy radial ribs. The concentric growth lines are widely and irregularly spaced. These borers reach about 1.2″ (3 cm) in length and are inflated and rounded anteriorly while compressed and tapering posteriorly. The valves are dirty chalky white on the outside and stained buff or brown inside. The shell has a posterior gape and the pallial sinus is large.

Softshell Clams

Antillean Sphenia *Sphenia antillensis*

Figure 172

In the Northeast, the Myidae or soft shelled clams are represented by the well known and widely appreciated steamer clam, *Mya arenaria.* Although this large species has been reported as far south as the Carolinas, it is rare in our region and not often encountered. We do, however, have a tiny member of the family, *Sphenia antillensis,* which is less than 0.5″ (1.3 cm) in length. The myids in general have chalky greyish-white valves with a wide posterior gape. They have a large flat or spoon-shaped chondrophore in the hinge of the left valve (mactrids and semelids have a chondrophore in both valves) and their siphons are fused. *Sphenia antillensis* is sporadically common on hard surfaces along our coast. These small dirty-white clams live nestled in the

165

confining spaces between other epibenthic organisms such as tunicates and mussels, or they may form dense mats on hard surfaces. They tie themselves to the substratum with protein threads. The valves are roughly rectangular, irregular, variable, and deformed by pressure from neighboring organisms. They are fragile and thin, with coarse irregular growth lines and a posterior gape. The left valve is smaller than the right. This clam has a narrow foot and large pallial sinus.

Paramya subovata (0.4″; 1 cm) is commensal with the landlord echiuran, *Thalassema hartmani,* and is shown with that species (Fig. 185). It is a small, obese, chalky, white clam with a posterior gape, and often has a rusty brown margin around the valves. *Paramya* lives beside the burrow of *Thalassema* and inserts its short siphons into the interior of the burrow to avail itself of the food- and oxygen-rich water provided by the worm. A similar species, *Cryptomya californica,* lives similarly with the west coast innkeeper echiuran, *Urechis caupo.*

Box Clams

Box Clam *Corbula swiftiana*

There are several species of box clams in the family Corbulidae on our coast but their classification is confused and specific identification is difficult. Members of this family are easily recognized as such, however,

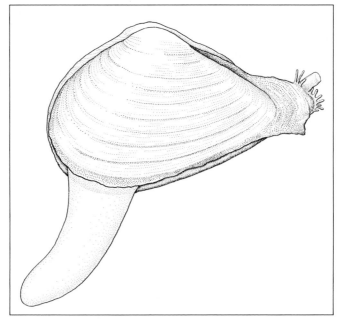

Figure 173

and have right valves larger than the left. The right valve overlaps the left, especially posteriorly and ventrally, and the left fits neatly inside it. The valves are thick with rounded concentric ridges and the shell is swollen. The umbos are usually central, the anterior margin broadly rounded, and the posterior margin pointed and sometimes ribbed. There is an internal resilium but no external ligament. The valves are usually white, but sometimes pink or yellow, and, viewed from above, the hinge of the left valve has a distinct V-shaped notch beside the umbo. The species in the drawing is *Corbula swiftiana.* It is about 0.3″ (8 mm) long, lives infaunally in soft silty sand; it is our most common box clam.

Gaper Clams

Burrowing Gaper Clam *Gastrochaena hians*

Gastrochaena hians (0.6″; 1.5 cm) is an inhabitant of mollusc shells, coral, and limestone. It bores in calcareous substrata to form bottle-shaped chambers. Living bivalves infested with *Gastrochaena* often secrete additional shelly material over the thin walls of the chamber resulting in recognizable roughened bulges on the valve. *Gastrochaena* communicates with the exterior with its siphons. Excavation of the chamber is thought to be accomplished with a combination of mechanical abrasion by the surface of the valves and chemical secretions of the epithelium of the foot, siphons, and mantle. The valves are reduced, thin, fragile, chalky, and incapable of enclosing the entire animal. They are pointed anteriorly, broadly rounded posteriorly, and there is a small winglike process extending anterior to the umbos. There are no hinge teeth and the anterior gape is wide. The ligament is external. The ventral

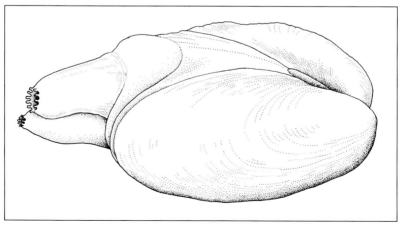

Figure 174

mantle margins are fused over part of their length but there are anterior and posterior openings for the disk-shaped foot and fused siphons respectively.

Gastrochaena ovata, a less common species, occurs from South Carolina southward. It resembles *G. hians* but has a more elongate shell and lacks the anterior winglike process of that species. The umbos are the anteriormost part of the shell. Juveniles of *Diplothyra smithii,* which also bores into limestone, have poorly developed accessory plates and are easily confused with *Gastrochaena.* The valves of *Gastrochaena,* however, lack the concentric ridges and oblique groove of *Diplothyra.*

Angel Wings

Angel Wing *Cyrtopleura costata*

The unusual bivalve family Pholadidae (angel wings or piddocks) has several southeastern representatives including the well-known angel wing. Pholadids usually have long, white, highly sculptured valves and a hinge without teeth (the similar petricolids have hinge teeth). The valves gape widely and cannot completely enclose the soft parts of the animal, and a unique set of external calcareous or chitinous plates is present to assist them. The hinge has no ligament to open the valves which, instead, are pushed apart by the bulging tissue mass inside. The inner hinge area does, however, possess a conspicuous process for the attachment of foot muscles. This process, called an apophysis, is fragile, easily broken, and often missing from the empty valves found on the

Figure 175

beach. Angel wings bore into clay and firm mud by rasping away the bottom of the burrow with the fine teeth on the anterior end of the valves.

The angel wing, *Cyrtopleura costata* (5″; 13 cm) bores into silty sand or clay in the high subtidal. It has thin, white, elongate valves that are rounded anteriorly and posteriorly. The valves bear strong, scaly, radial ribs. The apophysis is broad and spoonlike, and the fused siphons are many times the length of the valves. The siphons in Figure 175 are partially retracted.

The fallen angel wing, *Barnea truncata* (3″; 7.6 cm), is similar to the angel wing and lives in similar habitats, but it has weaker radial ribs and scales and is more boxlike than the angel wing. Its valves are truncate, not rounded, posteriorly and the apophyses are narrow and fingerlike.

An offshore species, *Pholas campechiensis,* the Campeche angel wing (4″; 10 cm), also resembles *Cyrtopleura,* but it has about a dozen distinctive vertical partitions under the reflected lip of each umbo.

Borers

Smiths Piddock *Diplothyra smithii*

Pholadids in the genera *Diplothyra* and *Martesia* bore into rock and wood respectively. To accomplish this, they anchor themselves with the suckerlike foot and use the teeth on the anterior end of the shell to rasp into the substratum. They are small wedge-shaped clams with strongly inflated anterior ends and compressed tapered posteriors. As pholadids they have accessory plates associated with the hinge. The two genera are distinguished on rather technical characteristics but for our purposes the nature of the substratum can be used to recognize them. In general, if the animal bores into rock or shell it can be assumed to be *Diplothyra,* if into wood, *Martesia.*

Diplothyra smithii is common in limestone, oyster, and clam shells. It is small 0.6″; 1.5 cm), and the largest accessory plate (mesoplax) covering the hinge is oval or shield-shaped. The anterior region of the valves bears fine denticulate concentric ridges and is separated from the posterior region by a shallow oblique groove. Posteriorly, the ridges are weak and not denticulate. This is our only *Diplothyra* species.

Martesia species closely resemble *Diplothyra smithii* but may be much larger (2″; 5 cm). There are several species along the southeastern coast. *Martesia cuneiformis* is fairly common and has coarse concentric ridges anteriorly and posteriorly. The anterior, but not the posterior, ridges are denticulate and a strong groove separates the two regions. The accessory plate (mesoplax) above the hinge is shield-shaped and has grooves extending outward from a broad, shallow, central groove. The posterior end of the valves may be extended by shelly deposits and the valves are dirty white or grey in color. *Martesia cuneiformis* can be seen

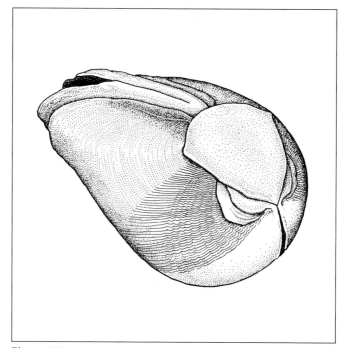

Figure 176

on Plate B31. *Martesia striata* and *M. fragilis* are similar to *M. cuneiformis,* but both have a more or less oval or heart-shaped mesoplax plate. That of *M. fragilis* bears concentric grooves while that of *M. striata* does not.

Shipworms   *Color Plate B31*

Shipworm *Bankia gouldi*

The shipworms (Teredinidae) are wormlike and bear little superficial resemblance to other bivalves. Close inspection of these unusual clams, however, shows them to have valves, siphons, and other features like their close relatives, the angel wings (Pholadidae). Their two valves, which are greatly reduced and rasplike, are used to bore extensive tunnels and galleries in marine timbers. The clam is very long, delicate, and wormlike and relies on the wooden gallery wall, rather than its shell, for protection. The clam lines the tunnels with a coating of lime. Shipworms bore continuously and maintain communication with the surrounding sea via the two siphons which extend from small exterior openings in the wood. The siphons bring oxygen into the burrow and remove wastes from it.

Shipworms are not filter feeders and do not strain food from the respiratory current. Instead, they eat the wood excavated from the burrow. Wood is composed primarily of cellulose, a carbohydrate that is notoriously difficult for animals to digest and that is also a poor source of nitrogen. The shipworms are thought to have solved the problems of an all-wood diet by maintaining populations of bacteria that produce the enzymes necessary to digest cellulose, as do the protozoan symbionts of termites, and that also convert molecular nitrogen to compounds that can be used for protein synthesis, as do the bacterial symbionts of leguminous plants. Among the many wood-boring bivalves only the teredinids can use wood as a food source and they are the marine equivalents of termites. The pholadid wood-borers, such as *Martesia,* do not use their borings for food.

The posterior end of a shipworm bears a pair of shelly or chitinous pallets which are used by the clam to close the external opening and by biologists to identify the clam. There are many species in the three genera *Bankia, Teredo,* and *Nototeredo* but their identification requires the use of specialized literature. Shipworm species tend to be worldwide in distribution, perhaps because of transport by wooden sailing ships.

A contracted specimen of *Bankia gouldi* (1″; 2.5 cm contracted) can be seen in the center of Plate B31. It looks like a worm and its anterior end and small valves are on the right. Its two pallets are visible at the posterior end (left). The valves and anterior end of a second individual can be seen above the pallets. The pholadid wood borer, *Martesia cuneiformis,* is present in the photograph also. A large individual lies just to the right of the shipworm, and there are several smaller specimens scattered about in the wood.

Glass Clams

Pearly Glass Clam *Lyonsia beana*

Two species of the family Lyonsiidae (glass clams) occur sporadically in shallow water on our coast. The family is characterized by its fragile, thin, glassy valves, minutely papillate periostracum, gaping posterior, elongate shape, and toothless hinge. They have an elongate internal ligament which is associated with a small, calcified ossicle under the umbos. Neither of our species is common.

Lyonsia beana (1″; 2.5 cm) has white valves covered by a dark brown periostracum which is often worn away over the umbos. The valves are thin, irregular, and unequal with anterior umbos. The anterior end is squarish and swollen, the posterior is flattened laterally. These clams superficially resemble mussels and occur on rocks or other hard surfaces.

171

Figure 177

Lyonsia hyalina (0.8″; 2 cm) is easily recognized by its thin, fragile, glasslike valves. This species is irregular, swollen anteriorly, and laterally compressed posteriorly. It is often sand-encrusted. The posterior margin is diagonally truncate. The length is about twice the height. This clam has a long narrow foot and usually lives in subtidal muddy sand, especially in grass beds, but can occasionally be found on rocks. The periostracum is wrinkled. *Lyonsia* burrows slowly and uses a weak byssus to attach to sand grains. In its normal position in the sand the posterior tip of the shell and the short siphons extend above the sediment into the water.

Pandoras

Three-Lined Pandora *Pandora trilineata*

The family Pandoridae is primarily a northern group represented in the Southeast by the uncommon *Pandora trilineata,* the three-lined pandora (1″; 2.5 cm). It is a white, extraordinarily flat, laterally compressed clam with a glossy, pearly interior. It is so flat that the entire clam, consisting of two valves and the living animal, is easily mistaken for a shell fragment. This species is dipper-shaped and is about twice as long as high with a narrow blunt posterior end and broadly rounded anterior end. There is a distinctive rounded ridge running lengthwise along the dorsal edge posterior to the umbo. Pandorid clams are laterally flattened and lie on the surface of sandy bottoms in quiet waters with the concave left valve facing down.

172

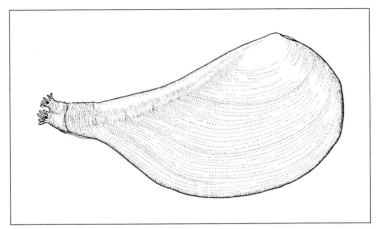

Figure 178

Members of the Periplomatidae (spoon clams) are characterized by thin valves, a rib on the inner surface of each valve, a broad, oblique, spoon-shaped chondrophore in each valve, and a small unattached ossicle above the chondrophore. The only southeastern species, *Periploma margaritaceum,* (unequal spoon clam, 1″; 2.5 cm) is almost never found in water less than 6′ (2 m) deep on our coast although it is very common in Texas. It is compressed with unequal, oval, white valves.

Tusks

Ivory Tusk *Dentalium eboreum*

The tusk and tooth molluscs belong to their own class, the Scaphopoda. They are unlike other molluscs in their possession of a one-piece, hollow, conical shell open at both ends. They may have evolved from bivalves in which the two valves fused together dorsally and ventrally but remained open anteriorly and posteriorly. They are infaunal animals which live in sediments with the large anterior end pointed downwards and the narrow posterior end protruding a little above the sediment surface. They feed on small shelled protozoans (Foraminifera) using filamentous oral tentacles called captacula. Water for respiration is circulated in and out the small posterior end. They are mostly restricted to subtidal or offshore waters but *Dentalium eboreum* occurs in silty sand in shallow, even intertidal, water. It has a translucent white or pinkish shell about 2″ (5 cm) long. It is smooth over most of its length but the small end bears fine longitudinal ridges and a single short slit. The shell is round in cross section and slightly curved. *Dentalium texasianum* (1.5″; 3.8 cm) is hexagonal (occasionally pentagonal) in cross section with ridged flat sides. It may occur subtidally in high

173

salinity estuaries. Among our deeper water species, *D. meridionale* (4″; 10 cm) is grey and has an oval cross section. *Dentalium laqueatum* (2.5″; 6.3 cm) has fluted sides.

Tooth molluscs, which belong to the genus *Cadulus* in the family Gadilidae, are much smaller than most of the tusks and are less than 0.5″ (1.3 cm) long. Rather than being a long tusk-shaped cone, the shell is expanded near the middle and resembles a canine tooth. *Cadulus carolinensis* is swollen near the middle and has four short slits at the small end. *Cadulus quadridentatus* is less swollen and the small end has four deep notches. Both occur subtidally in the Southeast but are rarely encountered.

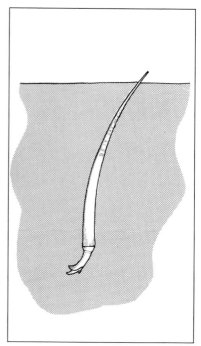

Figure 179

NEMERTEA

Ribbon Worms

Milky Ribbon Worm *Cerebratulus lacteus*

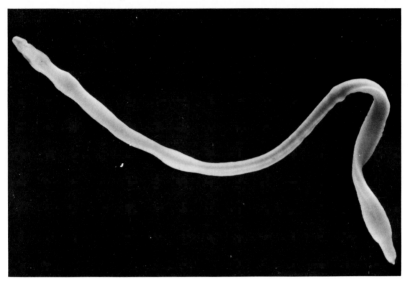

Figure 180

This non-segmented worm is an infrequent but conspicuous predator on sandflats throughout our region. Reaching 20″ (51 cm) or more in length (*Cerebratulus lacteus* is reported to reach 20′ (61 m) in extended length north of our area), *Cerebratulus* burrows in soft sediments and launches subterranean attacks on its prey with a long, protrusible, sticky proboscis. The mouth of *Cerebratulus* is large and distensible allowing the worm to ingest its prey. When feeding on bivalves such as the razor clam, *Ensis directus, Cerebratulus* is reported to attack the foot of the clam first, thus preventing withdrawal of the animal into its burrow. *Cerebratulus* attacks larger bivalves by entering the shell through one of the clam's siphons. It probably also feeds on polychaetes.

Cerebratulus burrows by generating peristaltic waves along its body, some of which can be seen along the front half of the worm in the photograph. It also swims vigorously by flattening its body, top to bottom, and writhing like an eel. *Cerebratulus* normally swims at night and returns to the sand by day. Its ability to swim, its large flat body, its well-developed, longitudinal, lateral cephalic grooves, and its lack of a stylet on the proboscis are useful characteristics in identifying this

175

species. It also has a threadlike caudal filament (cirrus) which is commonly missing in collected specimens. The regenerating caudal cirrus appears as a small bump on the tail end (right) of the individual in Figure 180 and can be clearly seen in Figure 282. *Cerebratulus* fragments itself voluntarily, usually into two pieces. When freshly dug from the sand, the flattened posterior end often separates from the rest of the body and wriggles vigorously like a minnow out of water. With a predator's (or collector's) attention focused on the more active tail part, the head end burrows quickly back into the sand.

Ribbon Worms   *Color Plate B32*

Pink Ribbon Worm *Micrura leidyi*

The pink ribbon worm, *Micrura leidyi* (3–5″; 7.5–13 cm), resembles a small milky ribbon worm (*Cerebratulus*) except that it is always pink, salmon, or orange and does not swim. It has a marked tendency to fragment into many sausage-shaped pieces, often within seconds after the animal is collected. The specimen in the photograph is complete and shows one of the two cephalic grooves on the head and a short, unbroken, threadlike caudal cirrus at the opposite end of the animal. *Micrura* burrows in sand around the low water mark on protected sand flats throughout our area. When disturbed, and when feeding, *Micrura* everts its long, threadlike, whitish, sticky proboscis.

Ribbon Worms

Burrowing Ribbon Worms
Carinoma tremaphoros
Zygeupolia rubens
Paranemertes biocellata

Ribbon worms are common predators in sandy beaches along our coast. All burrow by generating peristaltic waves along the front of the body. Their burrowing movements resemble those of many polychaetes with which they may be confused by beginners. Unlike polychaetes, nemerteans lack segments and the body is smooth although the serial arrangement of gonads, which is visible through the translucent skin, may falsely suggest segmentation. Most of our species are small and threadlike and do not exceed 2″ (5 cm) in length but a few, such as *Cerebratulus lacteus* and *Micrura leidyi,* are large. The three species shown above are 2–3″ (5–7.5 cm) in length.

Carinoma tremaphoros is translucent, white anteriorly, and cream or tan posteriorly. The head is conical and acute in active animals but rounded anteriorly and spatulate in relaxed specimens. The head lacks eyes and sensory grooves and the mouth is ventral, behind the bilobed

Figure 181

brain. The tail is broad and flattened. When placed in a dish of fresh seawater, *Carinoma* initiates burrowing movements. It is common in current-washed sand flats protected from waves.

The head of *Zygeupolia rubens* is white, the proboscis region is pinkish, and the genital region is tan and flattened. The head is sharply pointed anteriorly and lacks eyes and other sensory structures. The mouth is ventral behind the brain. A long, threadlike cirrus is present on the tail. *Zygeupolia* is an active burrower in clean sand beaches exposed to waves and currents. It resembles *Carinoma* in size, body shape, and burrowing habit but is distinguished from it by the sharply pointed head, cirrus, and rosy hue. *Zygeupolia* is distinguished from *Micrura* by its lighter color, lack of cephalic grooves, flattened posterior, longer cirrus, acutely pointed head, and production of rapid burrowing waves on the front end of the body.

Paranemertes biocellata is an opalescent pinkish-white ribbon worm with a tapered bullet-shaped head and a flattened tail. The anterior tip of the head bears two inconspicuous and nearly microscopic eyespots. A faint, dorsal, transverse groove occurs behind the eyes. The brain is red unlike those of *Carinoma* and *Zygeupolia,* which are colorless. The mouth is anterior, terminal, and opens at a pore shared with the proboscis. The proboscis bears a piercing stylet. Replacement stylets are produced and stored in up to 6 reserve sacs. Living individuals exude a milky mucus when placed in culture dishes containing seawater. *Paranemertes* occurs in protected sand flats throughout our area.

Ribbon Worms

Epibenthic Ribbon Worms
Lineus socialis
Evelineus tigrillus
Lineus bicolor
Nemertopsis bivittata
Zygonemertes virescens
Amphiporus cruentatus
Tubulanus rhabdotus

Ribbon worms are important but often overlooked members of epifaunal communities throughout the Southeast. Some intertidal species, such as *Lineus socialis* and *Nemertopsis bivittata,* may occur by the thousands and dominate part of the intertidal zone. All of the nemerteans illustrated and discussed below are threadlike and their identification usually requires magnification.

Lineus socialis (3″+; 7.5+ cm) is brownish-red anteriorly and dark brown posteriorly. A long, deep, lengthwise groove occurs on each side of the head as do two lengthwise dorsal rows of 2–8 dark eyespots each. The mouth is ventral and located well behind the brain. The trunk has approximately 10 more or less evenly spaced, narrow, unpigmented,

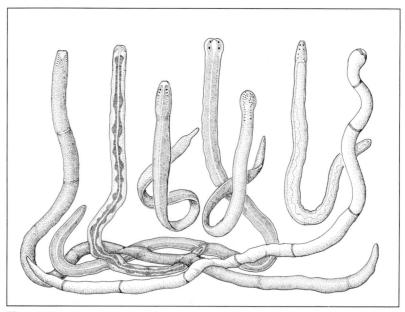

Figure 182

transverse bands. *Lineus socialis* is elongate, sticky, and sluggish but when disturbed it coils into a helix. It is common to abundant in *Brachidontes* mussel mats.

Evelineus tigrillus (2″; 5 cm) is strikingly marked with a longitudinal stripe of bright orange flanked by black on a background of translucent white and pale yellowish. It has longitudinal grooves on both sides of the head. This is a tropical species that is sometimes found in northern Florida.

Lineus bicolor (1–2″; 2.5–5 cm) is greenish or grey anteriorly and tan posteriorly. The body has a middorsal creamy-white stripe. The head has two straight rows of eyespots and two deep lateral grooves. The mouth is ventral near the head constriction.

Nemertopsis bivittata is a long (6″; 15 cm) stylet-bearing species and, like *Lineus socialis,* is abundant in mussel mats. The body is olive except for a white middorsal stripe and the head has 4 dark eyespots at the corners of an imaginary square. A weak transverse groove passes between the eyes and continues ventrally. Another stylet-bearing species, *Prosorhochmus americanus* (1″; 2.5 cm, not shown) also has 4 eyes which, unlike those of *Nemertopsis,* lie at the corners of a low rectangle not a square. Its yellow-orange body lacks a middorsal stripe. It is viviparous and lives on hard bottoms beneath barnacles, mussels, and oysters in the intertidal zone.

Zygonemertes virescens (2″; 5 cm) is a common stylet-bearing nemertean. It is greenish, yellowish, or white. The ovoid head has many scattered dark eyespots which extend posteriorly in two lateral longitudinal lines, one in each of the two nerve cords. Two oblique grooves occur ventrally on the head. *Zygonemertes* is found in the lower intertidal and subtidal zones where it feeds on amphipods.

Amphiporus cruentatus (4″; 10 cm) occurs subtidally on shelly bottoms. It is tan or yellowish and three red lines (blood vessels) are visible running lengthwise through the trunk. The head has two rows of eyespots, the first pair of which are the largest. *Amphiporus ochraceus* (1″; 2.5 cm) is a common species similar to *A. cruentatus* but lacks the red blood vessels and has a red brain. There is a dorsal transverse groove behind the eyes, and two ventral oblique grooves behind the first pair of eyes. The eyespots of the two *Amphiporus* species do not extend posteriorly as they do in *Zygonemertes.*

Tubulanus rhabdotus (4″ +; 10+ cm) has no stylet and lives in a thin, transparent, cellophanelike, fragile tube which it attaches to compound tunicates. The anterior margin of the head has a transverse dark brown band and similar bands occur along the trunk. *Tubulanus pellucidus* is a tiny (0.5″; 1.3 cm) translucent species which occurs in habitats similar to those of *T. rhabdotus.* It has no brown bands, but instead has two shiny white bands on the head. The proboscis region is inflated and the trunk is distinctly annulated so that it appears segmented.

PLATYHELMINTHES

Flatworms

Zebra Flatworm *Stylochus zebra*
Mutable Flatworm *Coronodena mutabilis*

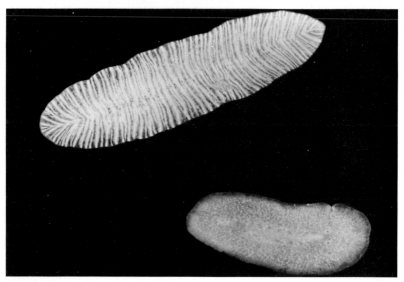

Figure 183

The aptly named *Stylochus zebra* occurs predominantly as a symbiont of some hermit crabs, particularly the flat-clawed hermit, *Pagurus
pollicaris,* and the giant red hermit, *Petrochirus diogenes,* both subtidal
species. In our area, usually only one flatworm occurs with each hermit
but two or more are typical for crabs in the Northeast. *Stylochus* (2″; 5
cm) lives inside the snail shell above the host. It feeds on the eastern
white slipper snail, *Crepidula plana,* which typically grows in the aperture of the shell occupied by the hermit. It has been suggested that
Stylochus may also feed on developing eggs of the host. When reproductive, *Stylochus* cements its egg masses to the inside of the shell above the
carapace of the crab. Young flatworms hatch as small, ciliated, swimming larvae.

Turbellaria, the class name for the free-living flatworms, means "a
disturbance" and no better name could be applied to *Coronodena
mutabilis* (1″; 2.5 cm). *Coronodena* can be found adhering to the
undersurfaces of rocks or shells where it conforms to every surface
irregularity like a living film. Touching any spot along the margin of

180

these well-disguised animals causes an immediate and rapid flow of the affected part away from the annoyance as if the rock surface itself was withdrawing. The species epithet, *mutabilis,* meaning "changeable," also refers to the plasticity of this species' body. *Coronodena* swims by undulating the margins of its body. When much disturbed, it will roll up the margins of its body, like curling a tongue, then bend itself downward into a compact mass resembling a tiny automobile tire, and sink quickly to the bottom. This species is one of several large species of flatworms found in shallow water on our coast. Many of these are difficult to identify, but *Coronodena* is recognized by its brownish color and absence of tentacles. It has many small marginal eyes around the edges of the anterior third of the body and also has two clusters of cerebral eyes on low bumps near the center of the anterior end. Brown species of *Stylochus* in our area may be distinguished from *Coronodena* by the presence of a pair of anterior tentacles on the dorsum.

Flatworms   *Color Plate B33*

Tiger Flatworm *Pseudoceros crozieri*

This splendid large (1.6″; 4 cm) flatworm is found in areas where its prey, the orange tunicate, *Ecteinascidia turbinata,* grows in abundance. Like other members of the family Pseudoceridae ("false horns"), *Pseudoceros* has two tentacles on its head that are formed by folds in the anterior margin of the body and held vertically like rabbit ears, as shown in plate B33. Two elongated clusters of black dots are visible immediately behind the tentacles. These are multiple eyespots (cerebral eyes) in the brain of the animal. The long white area just behind the eyes is the pharynx or foregut. When feeding, the pharynx is protruded from the underside of the body like a large ruffled sleeve which, once in position over the prey, begins swallowing it. The decorative black lines are pigmented areas in the skin. *Pseudoceros crozieri* is a tropical species found throughout the Caribbean, in Bermuda, and as far north as Beaufort, South Carolina.

Flatworms

Variable Flatworm *Oligoclado floridanus*
Shaggy Flatworm *Thysanozoon nigrum*

Oligoclado floridanus (1.6″; 4 cm) is a common flatworm associated with fouling organisms on rock jetties, oyster reefs, creek and sound bottoms, and pilings. Its color may be pinkish orange, bright orange, or grey-brown and depends on the color of ingested prey and extent of digestion. *Oligoclado* is distinguished from our other large flatworms with marginal tentacles by its color and by the presence of marginal eyes between the two anterior tentacles. The pale area behind the brain and

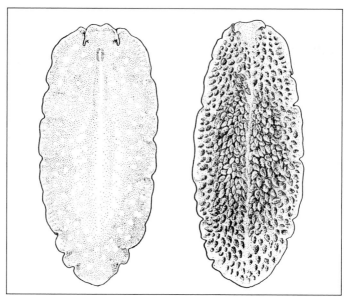

Figure 184

cerebral eyes marks the position of the pharynx which, in this species, is a simple muscular tube. In contrast, closely related flatworms, such as *Pseudoceros,* all have a pharynx that is ruffled and sleevelike. *Oligoclado* is reported to feed on tunicates but occurs on the hydroid, *Tubularia crocea,* and on various other substrata.

A rare species, *Thysanozoon nigrum* (1.2″; 3 cm) is one of the most striking flatworms on our coast. It has a shaggy covering of numerous, dark, fingerlike papillae making identification easy. The papillae contain branches of the gut. Although the prey of *Thysanozoon nigrum* is unknown, it is probably a tunicate because almost all other members of its family, the Pseudoceridae, feed on them. In Bermuda, *Thysanozoon nigrum* eats the tunicate, *Eudistoma olivaceum,* which has not been found on the southeastern coast.

ECHIURA

Spoon Worms

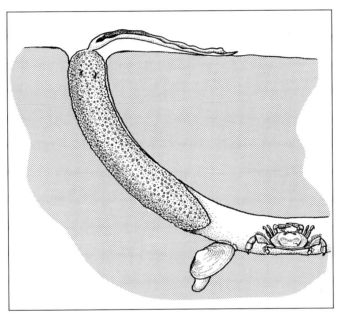

Figure 185

The landlord worm, *Thalassema hartmani* (3–5″; 7.5–13 cm), excavates stable U-shaped burrows in estuarine mudflats. The unsegmented trunk may be greenish or soft pink resulting from an abundance of circulating hemoglobin-containing corpuscles in the body cavity. The front part of the body is a flexible gutter (prostomium) and is used for feeding. While the animal is securely in its burrow, the highly extensible prostomium stretches over the sediment surface, collects deposited organic material, and conveys it back to the mouth at its base. *Thalassema* digs its burrow in an unconventional fashion. A pair of stout hooks, called setae, are located on the front of the trunk near the attachment of the prostomium. While burrowing, *Thalassema* folds back the prostomium, rocks the anterior trunk and setae back-and-forth, and digs downward like a backhoe. *Thalassema,* like many

183

animals that feed on plant material and detritus, has a very long gut to increase the retention time of food. The gut of this species is approximately ten times the length of the body.

A second species, *Lissomyema mellita,* is similar to *T. hartmani* but has a shorter (0.8″; 2 cm), globose trunk lacking the coarse surface papillae. *Lissomyema mellita* occupies the dead tests of the sand dollar, *Mellita quinquiesperforata,* and discarded shells of molluscs in a fashion similar to that of the hermit sipunculan, *Phascolion strombus.*

Thalassema hartmani hosts three species of symbionts in its stable burrow. The small truncated clam in Figure 185 is *Paramya subovata* (0.5″; 1.3 cm), a commensal that occurs in the wall of the host burrow and extends its short siphons into the burrow to feed and respire. Another commensal clam (not shown), *Mysella* sp., is tiny (0.2″; 5 mm), oval, and attaches by byssal threads to the body of the host. The commensal crab, *Pinnixa lunzi,* is a filter-feeder that shares the burrow with *Thalassema.* A similar relationship between a spoon worm, clam, and crab occurs on the California coast. There, the clam, *Cryptomya californica,* and the crab, *Pinnixa franciscana,* share the burrow of the innkeeper echiuran, *Urechis caupo.*

ANNELIDA

Segmented Worms

Green Oyster Worm *Phyllodoce fragilis*

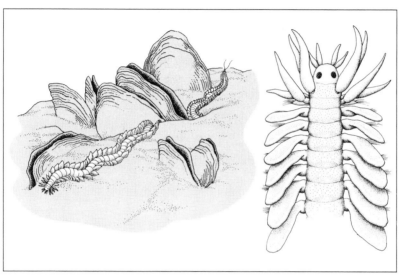

Figure 186

The flattened, leaflike, dorsal paddles (cirri) arranged in pairs along the length of the body are characteristic of species in the family Phyllodocidae. *Phyllodoce fragilis* (2.5″; 6.4 cm) often associates with oysters where it produces mucus-lined burrows in the mud between adjacent shells. In the field, individuals resemble fragile, sticky, yellow or green threads in oyster clumps or beneath oysters on pilings or rocks. Some of the green pigmentation is imparted by eggs which fill the body cavity of mature females. Little is known regarding the biology of *Phyllodoce* although it is assumed to be a carnivore that captures prey, such as other small polychaetes (syllids), with its unarmed, eversible pharynx. *Phyllodoce* normally crawls slowly using its many parapodia but when disturbed, it shimmies vigorously and secretes a copious amount of sticky mucus. Most of the mucus is secreted by glands in the paddles. The mucus contains a toxic substance, perhaps a heavy metal, that discourages predators such as fishes and crabs. The paddles are also gills. Cilia occur on their posterior surfaces and maintain a continuous stream of water over the skin. In other phyllodocids, the paddles are used as gills, swimming fins, and covers for brooded embryos.

185

There are several other phyllodocids on our coast but none are as common as *Phyllodoce fragilis,* and most are much smaller.

Segmented Worms

Bloodworm *Glycera dibranchiata*

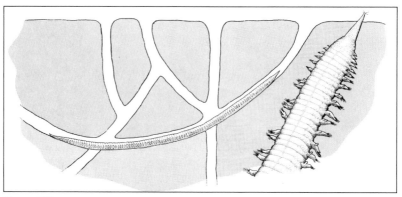

Figure 187

Bloodworms are some of the larger and more familiar polychaetes along our coast. Sport fishermen purchase them alive in bait shops and seafood markets and use them as bait. Most segmented worms are partitioned internally by transverse bulkheads (septa), like large passenger ships and submarines. These septa are primarily important for peristaltic burrowing movements in soft-bodied animals, such as earthworms, but they may also prevent excess fluid loss in wounded animals. The bloodworm body cavity, which contains a bloodlike fluid, is not partitioned by septa unlike that of most other segmented worms. Instead, it is a single continuous and uninterrupted space. As a result, when a bloodworm is pierced by a fishhook it bleeds copiously, justifying its name. Bloodworms do not burrow using waves of peristalsis as do most segmented worms. Instead, they explosively evert a long muscular pharynx which punches into the sediment. Once in place, the tip of the pharynx swells and anchors in the sand. Contraction of the pharynx retractor muscles then pulls the body toward the anchored pharynx and deeper into the sediment. The tip of the pharynx bears four poison glands that open into four fangs and is used to capture and subdue prey. Most fishermen and collectors have experienced bloodworm bites. Bloodworms excavate and occupy galleries (Fig. 187, left) in which they ambush prey. The prey are detected with four tiny, vibration-sensitive antennae (Fig. 187, right). Glycerids swim by whipping their bodies in a

186

rhythmic snakelike fashion which makes prediction of their position and capture very difficult. Swimming occurs primarily at night in late winter when the worms swarm to the surface to release their gametes.

There are several species of glycerids in our area but only two, *Glycera dibranchiata* and *G. americana,* are common in shallow water. *G. dibranchiata* (up to 9″; 23 cm), has a fingerlike, unbranched, unretractable gill above and below each parapodium. This species is collected in Maine and Nova Scotia and sold in bait shops along the east and west coasts of the United States. *Glycera americana* (5″; 13 cm) has one branched, retractile, blood-red gill above each parapodium.

Segmented Worms

Swift-Footed Worm *Podarke obscura*

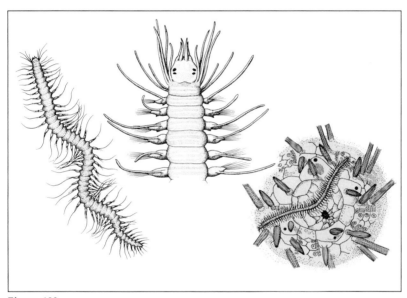

Figure 188

Podarke obscura (0.8″; 2 cm) is the only common southeastern representative of the Hesionidae, a family of active fast-moving worms with an inclination to form symbiotic relationships with larger invertebrates, particularly echinoderms. The leftmost drawing shows the animal in full gait and reveals some secrets of its rapid locomotion. The parapodia and setae are quite long, increasing the stride length of the animal. As undulatory waves pass forward along the body, these further increase the stride by swinging the extending parapodia and setae farther forward and the retracting parapodia and setae farther rearward, much as a sprinter extends his stride with good rotation at the hips. *Podarke* occurs free-living throughout our area in the fouling community on hard surfaces. It is also a commensal with the short-spined sea urchin, *Lytechinus variegatus* (Figure 188, right), and other echinoderms. The lines of dark pigment on the upper surface of the reddish-brown body of *Podarke* camouflage it among the broken patterns of purple on the surface of the test of living urchins.

Two other species of hesionids occur in shallow water in the Southeast. *Podarkeopsis levifuscina* (0.8″; 2 cm) is pale brown and occurs as a commensal in the burrow of the white synapta, *Leptosynapta tenuis*. *Parahesione luteola* (0.6″; 1.5 cm) is brown and is found as a commensal with the mud shrimp, *Upogebia affinis*.

Segmented Worms   *Color Plate C1*

Red, White and Blue Worm *Proceraea fasciata*

Polychaetes in the family Syllidae are small active animals typically found living and feeding among fouling organisms. The syllid head bears three antennae, two or three pairs of eyes, and two rounded ventral palps, which may be fused. *Proceraea fasciata* (1.2″; 3 cm) is larger and more colorful than most members of this family and consequently is more likely to be noticed. The syllids are all predators and many of them suck the juices from hydroids just as aphids suck juices from plants. Some of the many species have a single thornlike tooth on an eversible pharynx that can puncture a hole in the body of a prey animal. Just behind the pharynx is a muscular pump, the proventricle, that provides suction to draw in the nutritious body fluids of the prey. *Proceraea*, however, may ingest larger pieces of tissue, as do some related species of syllids. Its pharynx has a circle of small teeth to tear away small chunks of food which might then be sucked into the gut by the proventricle. The proventricle can be seen in Plate C1 as an orange patch behind the head. The blue of this patriotically colored polychaete is imparted by eggs undergoing maturation in the body cavity of the female.

A noteworthy relative of *Proceraea* is the sponge-eating *Syllis spongicola* (0.5″; 1.3 cm) which occurs, often by the hundreds, in such sponges as the eroded sponge, *Haliclona loosanoffi*, the bread sponge, *Halichondria bowerbanki*, and the garlic sponge, *Lissodendoryx isodictyalis*.

Segmented Worms

Nereis succinea

This polychaete enjoys the widest distribution of any invertebrate species in the Southeast, occurring in all benthic habitats except outer

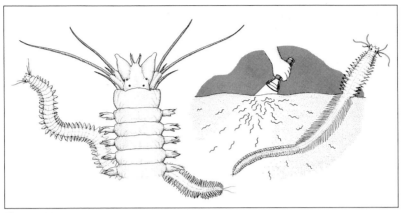

Figure 189

beaches. *Nereis succinea* (3.5″; 9 cm) may be the most abundant poly-chaete in our estuaries and is recognized as an important food of sport fishes. Several factors account for its broad distribution. It is tolerant of a wide range of salinities thus allowing for wide dispersal in the estuary. It has very generalized eating habits, feeding primarily on surface detritus deposits. Surprisingly it has a wide eversible pharynx armed with a formidable pair of ice-tonglike jaws and a battery of small teeth. It uses these for defense and aggression as well as for feeding. *Nereis succinea* spawns during the spring and late summer in a spectacular display involving myriads of rapidly swimming reproductive indi-viduals called heteronereids (Fig. 189, far right). During spawning periods, moonlight or artificial lights near the water attract hundreds of pink fishlike heteronereids to the surface (Fig. 189, middle right). This behavior synchronizes the release of eggs and sperms into the sea.

All members of the family Nereididae, which includes *Nereis suc-cinea,* have conspicuous heads with two short antennae, four eyes, two bulbous palps, and four pairs of long tentacular cirri. There are several similar species of nereidids in our area. *Nereis succinea* has broad, flat, straps on the posterior parapodia which make it the only easily identi-fied species. *Nereis falsa* (2.4″; 6 cm) occurs in slightly higher salinities than *N. succinea* and lacks straps on the posterior parapodia. All species of *Nereis* have two rings of hard little teeth inside the pharynx. *Laeonereis culveri* (3.1″; 8 cm) is found in lower salinity areas than *N. succinea* and lacks hard teeth in its pharynx. Instead, the pharynx bears soft papillae. *Platynereis dumerilii* (2.0″; 5 cm) occurs on the gulfweed, *Sargassum. Ceratonereis irritabilis* (6.3″; 16 cm) is our largest nereidid. It occurs in muddy protected beaches and has only one ring of teeth in its eversible pharynx.

Segmented Worms

Shimmy Worm *Nephtys bucera*

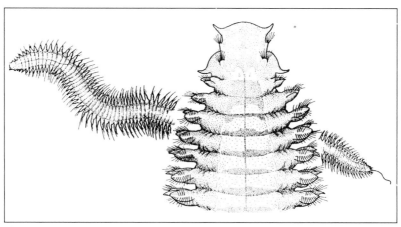

Figure 190

Shimmy worms are burrowing carnivores in wave-pounded swimming beaches and in the current-swept sand around inlets. The British refer to them as "cat worms" because of their feline appearance. The head is small, flattened, eyeless, and bears four short antennae.

Nephtys bucera (5″; 12 cm), our largest species, is characteristic of exposed beaches from about mid tide level into the subtidal zone. There it feeds actively on animals such as the coquina clam, *Donax variabilis,* the mole crab, *Emerita talpoida,* and the polychaete, *Scolelepis squamata.* Shimmy worms burrow rapidly using a combination of vigorous shimmying movements and a protrusible pharynx. Like that of *Glycera,* the pharynx can be forcefully driven into the sand, anchored, and the animal drawn toward the anchored tip. *Nephtys* also swims using the same vigorous undulations of the body. Shimmy worms have the annoying habit, from a collector's point of view, of voluntarily breaking in half when any effort is made to restrain them. This behavior, of course, is of value to the worm when a predator, such as a fish or bird, tries to pull them from the sand. Under these circumstances, the worm gives up its posterior end and regenerates it later. Like bloodworms, sexually mature shimmy worms swarm to the surface at night and burst, releasing their gametes into the sea.

A second species, *N. picta* (3″; 7.5 cm), occurs in silty sand in less wave-stressed areas. The outcurved gills that attach to each parapodium resemble a tiny sickle and begin on setiger 3 in *N. picta* and setiger 4 in *N. bucera.* Another species, *Aglaophamus verrilli* (2″; 5 cm) has incurved rather than outcurved gills beginning on setiger 5 and lacks any pattern on the back. Identification of nephtyid species is unreliable without a microscope.

Segmented Worms

Scaleworms *Harmothoe aculeata*

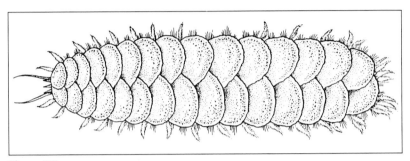

Figure 191

We have three families of scaleworms in shallow water on our coast; the Polynoidae, Sigalionidae, and Polyodontidae. All are dorsoventrally flattened with elaborate heads bearing numerous sensory structures and all have a double longitudinal row of scales on the back. These scales are modified parts of the parapodia and are attached to the body by a short fleshy stalk. This arrangement creates a protected open space between the layer of scales and the animal's back, especially in the polynoids. Water for gas exchange circulates through this space along the length of the body. Polynoids generally occupy very tight places, often the burrows or tubes of other anmals. Their success probably depends on the scaly second skin which maintains an open channel for water circulation regardless of cramped quarters.

The polyodontids construct a tube which excludes sediment from the respiratory current so they are less dependent on the second skin of scales for that purpose. In polyodontids, the scales are reduced and do not completely cover the back. Most of the polynoids are commensals with other invertebrates, the sigalionids usually burrow freely in sediments without constructing a tube, and the polyodontids build tubes in sediment.

Harmothoe aculeata (0.8"; 2 cm) is an inhabitant of oyster reefs, rock jetties, and shelly bottoms and is typical of our many polynoid species. It lives in crevices and under rocks where its dirty reddish-brown color helps in concealment. The setae, scales, and appendages trap silt and detritus which also help to camouflage the body.

191

Segmented Worms

Scaleworms
Lepidasthenia varia
Sthenelais boa

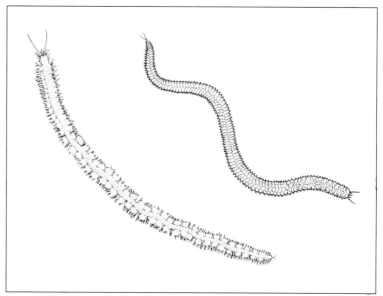

Figure 192

The long (4″; 10 cm) slender body and elegant transparency of the scales of *Lepidasthenia varia* belie its close relationship to the short silty scaleworm, *Harmothoe,* but they both belong to the family Polynoidae. *Lepidasthenia* is a commensal with the maitre d' worm, *Notomastus lobatus.* The scaleworm lies along the length of the thorax of *Notomastus* with its head situated near that of the host. *Lepidasthenia* may feed either on the deposited organic material collected by the host or directly on host tissue. The body is cream with greenish bands. The brain contains non-circulating hemoglobin, is bright red, and visible through the transparent head scales. Similar pigment occurs in the nerve cords and pharyngeal muscles. Respiratory pigments seem to be absent from the blood and coelomic fluids of scaleworms and present only in nerve and muscle tissues. Juveniles of the commensal clam, *Entovalva* sp. A (Fig. 159), attach inconspicuously to the underside of *Lepidasthenia* scales. As they grow larger, the scale is pushed aside and the clam resembles the one shown above. Eventually *Entovalva* detaches from the scaleworm and attaches to the burrow wall of *Notomastus.*

192

Other common polynoids in our area include *Lepidametria commensalis* (2.8″; 7 cm), which is pink or grey with dark bands and lives in the burrow of the spaghetti worm (*Amphitrite ornata*), *Lepidonotus sublevis* (0.8″; 2 cm), which is mottled tan, greenish, or grey and lives in the shells of hermit crabs (and elsewhere), and *Malmgrenia lunulata* (0.4″; 1 cm), which is red or brownish-red and occupies the burrows of the brittle stars, *Microphiopholis atra* and *M. gracillima.*

Sthenelais boa (4″; 10 cm), our most common southeastern member of the family Sigalionidae, burrows in protected beaches. Its pinkish body is arched dorsally and is covered with closely set, overlapping, opaque scales resembling a snakeskin. This attribute, along with its long snaky body and form of locomotion, has earned this *Sthenelais* the specific name of "boa." The scales may be tan, grey, or rust.

Segmented Worms

Sea Wolf *Polyodontes lupinus*

The sea wolf, *Polyodontes lupinus,* at a length of 2′ (60 cm) and width of 1″ (2.5 cm) is the largest and most intimidating of our shallow-water polychaetes. The back bears small flimsy scales in two widely separated longitudinal rows. It occupies muddy, tough, silken tubes that are oriented vertically in silty sands near the low water mark and below. The tubes often project a few inches above the surface of the sand and closely resemble tubes of cerianthid anemones. *Polyodontes* constructs its tube of woven golden threads secreted by internal thread glands that

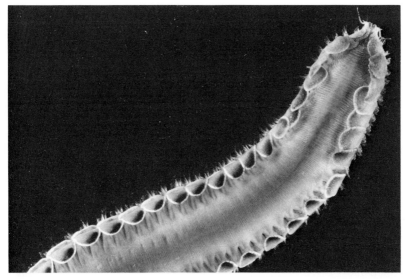

Figure 193

open along the sides of the body. When removed from its tube, as shown in the photograph, *Polyodontes* undulates sluggishly, moves its small scales up and down like clashing cymbals, and begins to spin a new tube. These movements may produce a respiratory water flow over the body when the animal is in its close-fitting tube. A tiny flattened snail, *Cochliolepsis parasitica* (Pl. B2), lives below the scales, presumably to take advantage of the water flow and food suspended in it.

Polyodontes may not always be as docile as it seems when removed from its tube. Its body is very muscular and it has a powerful protrusible pharynx bearing four, strong, chitinous jaws that resemble large fish hooks. It is believed to be a carnivore that extends out of its tube to seize prey.

An undescribed polynoid scaleworm occurs in the tube of *Polyodontes.* Two kamptozoans are reported to be associated with *Polyodontes.* One of these, *Loxosomella bilocata,* attaches to the tips of the setae and has been found in North Carolina and southern Florida whereas the other, *L. worki,* attaches to the lining of the tube and is known only from southern Florida.

Segmented Worms *Color Plate C2*

Caterpillar Fireworm *Amphinome rostrata*

Fireworms (Amphinomidae) are best identified by the bristly appearance of their numerous, long, white, calcareous setae. Amphinomids are called fireworms because the sharp setae easily penetrate human skin, break off, and cause a painful burning irritation. When disturbed, most fireworms erect the white setae, as shown in Plate C2, in a defensive posture. They have small inconspicuous heads and the body may be short and wide or long and narrow.

Amphinome rostrata and its relative, *Hipponoe gaudichaudi,* are offshore pelagic species that live on driftwood and other floating objects encrusted with goose barnacles. *Amphinome* reaches about 5″ (13 cm) in length and 0.6″ (1.5 cm) in width and has the appearance of a large fuzzy caterpillar. It occurs in moderate abundance among clusters of the goose barnacle, *Lepas,* on which it feeds. The muscular pharynx of *Amphinome* lacks teeth, as in other members of the family, and is used as a pump to ingest whole barnacles. A well-fed specimen, such as the one in the photograph, appears lumpy because of barnacles in its gut. *Amphinome* defecates perfectly cleaned barnacle valves. The tufts of orange filaments along the sides of the body of *Amphinome* are its gills.

Hipponoe gaudichaudi is much smaller (0.8″; 2 cm) than *Amphinome* and lives inside the valves of *Lepas.* It is short, wide, soft, pinkish-orange, and grublike. The young of *Hipponoe gaudichaudi* and *Amphinome rostrata* are protected by attachment to the mother's body.

In our area only one species of fireworm, *Pseudeurythoe ambigua,* occurs commonly inshore. *Pseudeurythoe* is long, thin, and pink and reaches 2.8″ (7 cm) in length by 0.08″ (2 mm) in diameter. It burrows in muddy sand on protected beaches and, when collected, coils its body, exposing its white bristly setae. It is a small worm not known to sting humans.

Segmented Worms

Soda Straw Worm *Kinbergonuphis jenneri*

Polychaetes in the family Onuphidae are tube builders and often grow to impressive lengths. They have well-developed heads with numerous sensory structures and a pair of well-developed, black, chitinous jaws. Of the several species on our coast, two, the soda straw worm, *Kinbergonuphis jenneri,* and the plumed worm, *Diopatra cuprea,* are very common and their tubes are characteristic features of most protected beaches.

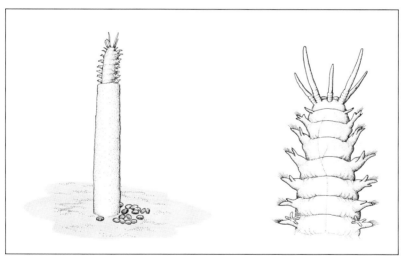

Figure 194

The long, sandy, grey tubes of *Kinbergonuphis jenneri* project vertically a few centimeters above the surface of intertidal sand flats like sandy soda straws. Each tube is approximately 0.2″ (5 mm) in diameter. Although sufficiently rigid to remain upright in air, perhaps because of the sand grains incorporated into the tube material, the tubes are nevertheless soft and compressible. The tubes continue vertically far below the surface of the sand as flimsy, whitish, parchment tubes. Tubes often wash out of the sand and may accumulate in windrows on the beach.

Kinbergonuphis jenneri is pink, lacks eyes on its prostomium, and reaches 28″ (70 cm) in length. Its food is not known but the results of its feeding activity are often apparent. Small, oval, brown fecal pellets, about the size and shape of the chocolate sprinkles used on cupcakes and cookies, accumulate on the surface of the sand around the tube.

The tubes of *Kinbergonuphis* are usually found in anaerobic sediments containing organic matter and hydrogen sulfide. Two species of small worms, a flatworm and a roundworm, are sometimes associated with the outside of the tube and they apparently derive their energy from the oxidation of hydrogen sulfide in the surrounding sediments. Both species are mouthless, with no trace of mouth or pharynx, and have a solid gut composed of large cells filled with endosymbiotic and chemosynthetic bacteria. These endosymbionts are thought to be responsible for oxidation of the sulfur compounds and the resulting release of energy useful to the host. The nematode is relatively large, about 0.6″ (1.5 cm) in length, and whitish. It is *Astomonema jenneri,* and it lives with its mouthless head embedded in the onuphid tube and most of its long slender body projecting into the surrounding sediments. It apparently does not penetrate the tube. The mouthless flatworm is a small species, *Paracatenula urania.* A mouthless oligochaete, *Olavius tenuissimus,* is also reported from shallow southeastern waters.

Onuphis eremita is a smaller (4.7″; 12 cm) but similar species that constructs a similar tube in shallow subtidal areas. It can be distinguished from *Kinbergonuphis* by the number of rings at the bases of the head appendages, 12–23 in *Onuphis* and 4–5 in *Kinbergonuphis.* *Mooreonuphis nebulosa* (6″; 15 cm) is dark brown, constructs an irregular, hard, shell-and-sand tube, and has a pair of eyes on the prostomium.

Segmented Worms

Plumed Worm *Diopatra cuprea*

The large, black shaggy tubes of the onuphid polychaete, *Diopatra cuprea* (12″; 30 cm), are a common sight projecting a few inches above the sediment surface on muddy tidal flats. The conspicuous tubes (Fig. 195, right) are approximately 0.4″ (1 cm) in diameter and are typically composed of plant fibers, shell fragments, seaweeds, sticks, and other debris laced together and bound by a dark secretion. The part of the tube below the surface of the sand lacks a covering of debris and consists entirely of material secreted by the worm. It has the appearance of a smooth, collapsible, straight, grey to white tube. This large stable surface of the shaggy tube cap encourages colonization by seaweeds and small animals upon which *Diopatra* feeds. Where the worms occur in dense aggregations, they emerge from their tubes to feed on their neighbors' gardens as well as their own. The upper end of the tube cap of *Diopatra* is

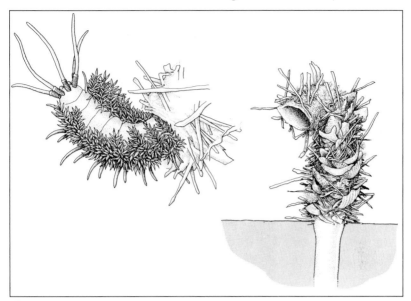

Figure 195

usually downturned like a shepherd's staff. Apparently this orientation helps keep suspended sediment from entering the tube. *Diopatra* is an active omnivorous polychaete with a brilliantly iridescent skin and impressive spiraled gills on its anterior segments. *Diopatra* is sometimes parasitized by juveniles of the arabellid polychaete, *Notocirrus spiniferus.* The blood brittle star, *Hemipholis elongata* (Pl. A30), is sometimes found wrapped around the subsurface part of *Diopatra*'s tube.

Americonuphis magna occurs in slightly more exposed areas and builds a tube similar to that of *Diopatra.* Its tube cap is larger and perhaps has fewer incorporated shell fragments. *Americonuphis* can exceed 28″ (70 cm) in length and reach 0.4″ (1 cm) in width. The front of the body is buff with many dark brown spots. The gills are comblike and extend the length of the body beginning on setigers 6 or 7. Two commensal clams live with *Americonuphis. Montacuta floridana* lives at the bottom of the tube in a fashion similar to that described for *Aligena elevata* and its host the bamboo worm, *Clymenella torquata* (Figs. 159, 206). An undescribed clam, also belonging to the family Lasaeidae, attaches to the body of *Americonuphis.*

Segmented Worms

Ringneck Worm *Eunice antennata*
Rockworm *Marphysa sanguinea*

The family Eunicidae includes a large number of tropical and sub-

Figure 196

tropical species of which many are carnivores. Eunicids have elongate, cylindrical, wormlike bodies with a large heart-shaped prostomium which usually bears 3 or 5 short antennae. Only two species, *Eunice antennata* and *Marphysa sanguinea,* are common in our shallow waters.

The ringneck worm, *Eunice antennata* (4.3″; 11 cm), is a fairly common species on coral (*Oculina*), rocks, and shelly bottoms in our area. It is believed to feed by seizing prey with jaws which are borne on a muscular eversible pharynx. *Eunice antennata* can be distinguished from other eunicids in our area by the white ring behind the head and by the strongly ringed antennae banded with red. The head can also be dark red.

The rockworm, *Marphysa sanguinea,* is a large (12″; 30 cm) muscular polychaete that burrows in soft muddy sediments mixed with clay such as occur in oyster reef areas. *Marphysa* is associated with thick clumps of fouling organisms on floating docks, pilings, and rocks and is more common than *Eunice.* It also occurs in calcareous rocks where access is presumably gained through the holes produced by boring organisms. *Marphysa* is an omnivore. The gills begin on setigers 21 to 24 and are long scarlet-red filaments that arch upward over the back of the animal. Several filaments can be associated with each gill. The microscopic parallel fibers in the cuticle impart an opalescent sheen to the skin.

A small, beautiful polynoid scaleworm, presently known as *Lepidonotus inquilinus* (1.2″; 3 cm), is collected occasionally from the muddy burrows of *Marphysa* in North Carolina. It is pale cream in color with small purple spots and approximately 24 pairs of scales. Each scale is marked with a transverse red-brown bar with an oblique white bar. The head has an anterior purple spot.

Segmented Worms

Opalworm *Arabella iricolor*
Threadworm *Drilonereis magna*

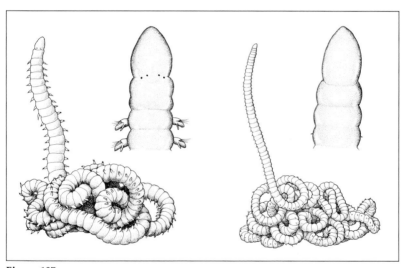

Figure 197

Polychaetes of the family Arabellidae are elongated, cylindrical, earthwormlike animals that burrow in sand and muddy sand on protected beaches. Like earthworms, they have small, pointed, appendage-free heads to facilitate burrowing. The parapodia are reduced and inconspicuous and there are no gills. We have two common species of arabellids, *Arabella iricolor* and *Drilonereis magna.*

The opalworm, *Arabella iricolor,* is a long (12″; 30 cm) slender (0.2″; 5 mm) polychaete with a strikingly iridescent skin, hence its common and specific names. The muscular body is typically brownish red but it can also be brown, creamy pink, or greenish. *Arabella* has well-developed jaws embedded in a protrusible muscular pharynx. It is assumed to be a carnivore although nothing specific is known about its diet. *Arabella* is distinguished from most other arabellids in our area by the presence of four tiny black eyespots situated in a row across the rear margin of its head.

199

Other conspicuous members of the family in this region are in the genus *Drilonereis.* The threadworm, *D. magna,* occurs abundantly on muddy sand flats. Individuals are very long (14″+; 35+ cm), very slender (0.04″; 1 mm), dark red or brown, and easily broken. They look like threads and are called threadworms. It is claimed, facetiously, that they stitch the mudflats together. Although similar to *Arabella* in general shape, *Drilonereis* is more slender and the head lacks eyes. *Drilonereis* possesses jaws but the gut is reported to be filled with sediment, suggesting that it may be a deposit feeder.

The juveniles of another arabellid, *Notocirrus spiniferus,* are parasites in the body cavity of the onuphid polychaete, *Diopatra cuprea.* Adult *N. spiniferus* reach only 2″ (5 cm) in length, have a transparent row of four small eyes on the back of the head, and live in sand. As many as 50 young worms, up to 0.2″ (5 mm) each, have been reported from a single *Diopatra.* Nothing more of the biology of these parasites is known.

Members of the family Lumbrineridae closely resemble the arabellids but are not so long as our two common arabellids. There are several lumbrinerid species on our coast and one of them, *Lumbrineris impatiens,* is fairly common in the sand of outer beaches whereas another, *L. coccinea,* lives on rocks and corals.

Segmented Worms

Millipede Worm *Dorvillea sociabilis*
Ghost Worm *Schistomeringos rudolphi*

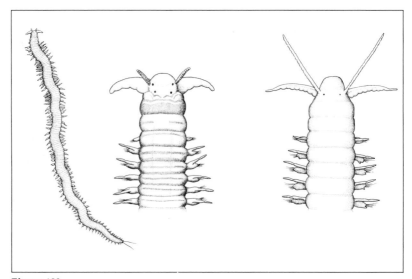

Figure 198

The Dorvilleidae includes several species of southeastern polychaetes that are small and easily overlooked. Dorvilleids have long slender bodies and heads with two short dorsal antennae, and two ventral palps that resemble the antennae. The first two segments following the head lack parapodia. They have complex chitinous mouthparts which include a pair of mandibles. The two largest species are *Dorvillea sociabilis* and *Schistomeringos rudolphi*. Both species can be found among fouling organisms on floating docks, oyster reefs, shelly bottoms, and rocks.

The body of *Dorvillea sociabilis* (1.2"; 3 cm) is reminiscent of some millipedes. It is arched and rounded dorsally, flat ventrally, relatively short, and bears numerous short parapodia. The red bands, usually two per segment, are a constant feature of this species. *Dorvillea* has complex jaws carried in a protrusible, bulbous, muscular pharynx. It is believed to be a carnivore.

Schistomeringos rudolphi is a small (1.2"; 3cm) cadaverous-white polychaete similar to *Dorvillea* but lacking the red banding. It too is believed to be a carnivore although algae and detritus have been found in its gut, suggesting that it may subsist on a varied diet.

Owners of seawater aquaria may sometimes notice infestations of tiny (0.2"; 5 mm), almost microscopic, white worms on the walls of their tanks. These are *Ophryotrocha puerilis,* a dorvilleid species rarely seen in nature because of its size. Examination with a hand lens will reveal its black jaw apparatus. Another tiny worm may also be found in seawater aquaria. It belongs to the family Dinophilidae and in our area is probably *Dinophilus jagersteni*. This species is even smaller than *Ophryotrocha* and lacks the black jaws of that species.

Segmented Worms

Ragged Worm *Orbinia ornata*

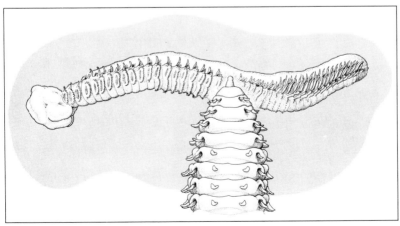

Figure 199

Polychaetes in the family Orbiniidae are usually orangish active burrowers in muddy sand flats. They are recognized by the absence of appendages on the head (prostomium) and by the progressive shift in position of their parapodia from the side of the body at the front end to the back at the hind end. This shift in parapodia and the presence of long fingerlike gills gives many species of this family a somewhat ragged appearance. Species of Orbiniidae burrow actively, ingesting deposited-material with a soft saclike pharynx that can be protruded like a bubble-gum bubble and then withdrawn with organic material adhering to its surface. Figure 199 shows a protruded pharynx bulging outward below the tiny, white, conical head.

The ragged worm, *Orbinia ornata* (10″+; 25+ cm), is the largest orbiniid in our area. The transverse rows of small, whitish, fingerlike papillae on each of the thoracic segments distinguish this species from all other southeastern orbiniids except *O. riseri*. *Orbinia riseri* (2.4″; 6 cm) is smaller and pale green-yellow, and its gill filaments begin on setiger 9 instead of setiger 5, as in *O. ornata*. Other species in our area are placed in the genera *Scoloplos* and *Haploscoloplos*. Two members of the genus *Haploscoloplos*, *H. fragilis* and *H. robustus*, are common animals on southeastern tidal flats and salt marshes. Our most common *Scoloplos* is *S. rubra*.

Segmented Worms

Palp Worms *Scolelepis squamata*

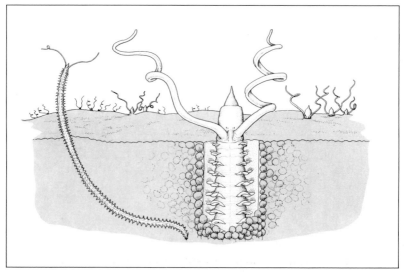

Figure 200

Palp worms (family Spionidae) are typically small tube-dwelling animals with small heads and two long palps used for deposit or suspension feeding. Most spionids have a ciliated groove along the length of each palp that is used to transport deposited organic matter to the pharynx like a tiny conveyor belt. We have many spionid species and the family is represented in most benthic habitats.

Myriads of *Scolelepis squamata* (1.4″; 3.5 cm) live on exposed swimming beaches near the low tide line. Each animal builds an inconspicuous vertical sandy tube, about 6″ (15 cm) by 0.04″ (1 mm), that opens flush with the surface of the beach. Adjacent tubes in the population may be very close to each other, sometimes not more than 0.08″ (2 mm) apart. Unlike other spionids, *Scolelepis* is not a deposit feeder. Instead, it holds its palps (0.2″; 5 mm) up in the swash and catches suspended particles which adhere to the sticky mucus. The palps then retract, coiling like springs, and transfer the particles to the pharynx. *Scolelepis* palps lack the ciliated groove that is characteristic of spionid species living in less wave-stressed habitats. It is also unusual among its relatives because the palps do not break off readily when the animal is disturbed. In other species of spionids, the worms must extend their palps to feed, where passing predators presumably view them as food. It may be in the best interest of these species to shed a threatened palp, and regenerate it later, rather remain attached to it and make the ultimate sacrifice. *Scolelepis,* on the other hand, lives in a physically stressed habitat where there are probably fewer grazing predators and very rapid water currents.

Scolelepis is eaten by the polychaete *Nephtys bucera,* probably also by the nemertean, *Zygeupolia rubens,* various shorebirds, and presumably by various fishes.

Polydora websteri is a spionid that bores into oyster shells and causes the formation of calcareous mud-filled blisters on the inner surface. There are several other species of *Polydora,* one of them, *P. colonia,* builds mud tubes in sponges.

Segmented Worms

Parchment Tube Worm *Chaetopterus variopedatus*

The tapered ends of the distinctive parchment tube of *Chaetopterus variopedatus* (10″; 25 cm) are a common sight on muddy protected beaches at and below the low tide mark where they project a few inches above the sediment surface. This peculiar white animal feeds on plankton and other suspended organic matter by pumping water through its tube and trapping the particles on a secreted mucus net. The three circular flaps in the midbody of *Chaetopterus* are pistons that pump water in the head end of the cylindrical tube, over the animal, and then out the opposite end. Two long projections situated immediately

Figure 201

behind the flattened spatulate head arch up over the back of the body and continuously secrete a sheet of mucus (not shown) that trails backward like a miniature basketball net extending downward from its rim. The lower end of the net is gathered at an organ known as a "food cup," shown in Figure 201 as a white fleshy projection extending downward and in front of the first piston. During feeding, the three pistons pump water through the mucus net on which food particles are trapped. The food cup rolls up the food-laden net into a tiny ball which is then conveyed to the mouth by a fine, lengthwise, ciliated groove on the back of the animal. Black organic material that has been eaten by *Chaetopterus* is visible through the transparent skin in the stomach region of the gut.

Chaetopterus is strikingly bioluminescent, a paradox for a blind animal living in sediment in an opaque tube. The bioluminescence is associated with mucus secreted under direct nervous control. When a tube opening is disturbed, as might occur when a predator expresses an interest, a blue luminous cloud of mucus is quickly released from the opening while *Chaetopterus* withdraws to the opposite end of the tube. The luminescent cloud might startle the predator.

Chaetopterus usually has a pair of crabs belonging to one of two species as permanent house guests. The species shown in the photograph is *Polyonyx gibbesi* (0.6″; 1.5 cm) and it is a member of the family Porcellanidae. Both individuals have their filter-feeding mouthparts (third maxillipeds) exposed and the female (upper left) is

204

carrying an orange egg mass below her abdomen. If *Polyonyx* does not share the tube with *Chaetopterus, Pinnixa chaetopterana* usually does. Although *Pinnixa* is similar in size and feeding habits to *Polyonyx,* it belongs to an unrelated family of crabs, the Pinnotheridae. Occasionally, a third pinnotherid species, *Pinnotheres maculatus,* is found in the tube.

Segmented Worms

Cellophane Tube Worm *Spiochaetopterus oculatus*

Figure 202

This species is easily recognized by its unmistakable ringed tube, a portion of which is shown in the photograph. The tube is transparent and about 6″ (15 cm) in length and 0.04″ (1 mm) in diameter. *Spiochaetopterus oculatus* lives in muddy intertidal sand flats where densities may reach 200–300 per square yard. The tube is oriented vertically in the sediment with only the upper 0.04″ (1 mm) projecting above the surface. The worms are usually oriented head up in the tube. The tube is tough, resembles cellophane and it is often mistaken for a plant root. Each section of the tube represents a successive stage in its construction. Only the ventral side of the worm's head secretes tube material, so each tube section is cast as two half cylinders. The tube can be modified at any time by cutting away portions with bladelike setae on the animal's fourth segment. The related parchment tube worm, *Chaetopterus variopedatus,* uses similar setae to modify its tube. The

205

two long palps on the head of *Spiochaetopterus* betray the close relationship of this family to the family Spionidae. The filter-feeding *Spiochaetopterus*, however, does not usually use its palps for feeding, rather for ejecting fecal material and other unwanted particles from the tube. When the supply of suspended food is limited, the palps may collect deposited organic matter from the surface of the sediment. *Spiochaetopterus* feeds in the same way as *Chaetopterus*, except that the former species simultaneously secretes 12 or more mucus nets to strain plankton from the water pumped through its tube. The mucus nets are produced between successive ruffled flaps (notopodia) visible in the photograph on the upper surface of the animal along the length of the body. Unlike *Chaetopterus*, the much smaller *Spiochaetopterus* has no pistons and water is pumped through the nets by cilia on the margins of the flaps. When the net becomes clogged with food, it is rolled into a small ball by a ciliated cup and transported to the mouth by a ciliated middorsal groove which extends the entire length of the body. Fecal pellets are also transported toward the upper end of the tube by the same middorsal groove. When such pellets reach the head, they are transferred to the two long palps which move them out of the tube.

The only other chaetopterid on our coast is *Mesochaetopterus taylori* which is encountered rarely. Its tube is similar to that of the soda straw worm, *Kinbergonuphis jenneri* (Fig. 194), but it is rusty brown.

Segmented Worms

Shovel Headed Worm *Magelona phyllisae*

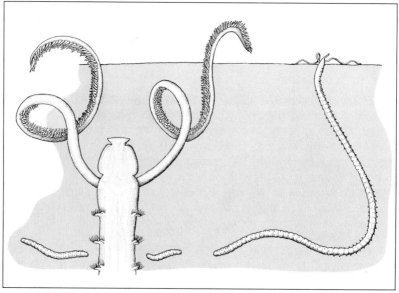

Figure 203

Shovel-headed polychaetes (family Magelonidae) are long (4″; 10 cm or more) slender animals that occur in intertidal and subtidal, silty sand flats, sometimes in high densities. The head is flat like a spatula, and rigid, and it is used in burrowing. Behind the head, the body is divided into two regions, the thorax in front of the ninth segment and abdomen behind it. When animals removed from sediment reburrow, they wriggle their heads from side to side and slice into the sand. All magelonids have two long palps that arise near the mouth and are used for deposit-feeding on the surface of the sand (right). The palps, however, do not transport food to the mouth by way of a ciliated groove as in spionid polychaetes. Instead, large particles and very small animals are collected by the abundant sticky papillae on the palps. The collected food is moved to the mouth by bending the palp and transferring the food to other papillae nearer the head. The process is repeated until food reaches the mouth. The thorax is pink because the heart, which is located there, shows through the transparent skin. The heart and blood vessels contain the respiratory pigment, hemerythrin. Hemerythrin contains iron but is otherwise completely unrelated to the more widely distributed red hemoglobin. Among the annelids, hemerythrin occurs only in the magelonids but it is also found in the phyla Brachiopoda, Sipuncula, and Priapula.

Magelona phyllisae (4″ + ; 10 cm +) is a common species on protected mudflats. The head terminates in two short horns. Females contain violet eggs and their bodies resemble purplish threads when seen in the mud.

Segmented Worms

Unicorn Worm *Aricidea fragilis*

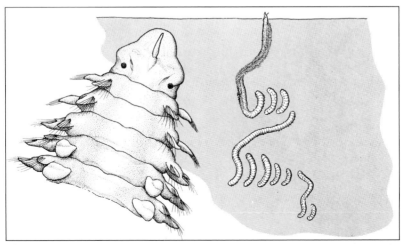

Figure 204

Aricidea fragilis is a long, slender, orange-red polychaete (4″+; 10+ cm) that occurs on sandy protected beaches. This common species superficially resembles some members of the family Orbiniidae because of its ragged dorsal surface and apparent lack of head appendages. *Aricidea,* however, has a single, inconspicuous, small antenna on its head. Gills occur only on the front end of *Aricidea,* whereas in orbiniid polychaetes, gills are found along the entire length of the body except on the very front.

Members of the family Paraonidae, such as *Aricidea,* are burrowers and deposit feeders. The deeper portion of the burrow is spiraled, corkscrewlike, perhaps to provide better anchorage in the sediment. While feeding, the front end of the worm extends onto the surface of the sand and its protrusible saclike pharynx collects deposited food. The production of a burrow with sections thrown into spirals, the restriction of gill surfaces to the front end of the trunk, and the habit of surface feeding near the head end of the burrow are reminiscent of similar patterns in the unrelated acorn worm, *Saccoglossus kowalevskii.*

Segmented Worms   *Color Plate C3*

Orange Fringed Worm *Cirriformia grandis*

This spectacular animal is sometimes common in shallow subtidal sediments on well-protected beaches. *Cirriformia grandis* (2″; 5 cm) burrows in soft silty sand exposing only its filamentous tentacles and gills to the surface. The feeding tentacles and the gills look very much alike. The numerous tentacles are whitish and originate on the anterior segments of the body. In the photograph, they appear in a cluster immediately behind the head. Tentacles can be extended outward in all directions over the surface of the sediment for collection of deposited organic material. Each tentacle has a ciliated groove which runs its entire length and transports food particles to the animal. When the animal is disturbed, the tentacles are quickly withdrawn for their protection. Each segment of the body has a pair of very long reddish-orange gill filaments which extend into the overlying water for gas exchange. The gills are not grooved.

A similar species, *Cirriformia filigera* (1.6″; 4 cm), is found epibenthically on hard substrata and is orange or brown. It has several pairs of tentacles on segments 4 to 7 whereas those of *C. grandis* are located above segments 1 and 2. Another common species of the family Cirratulidae in our region is the tiny red *Tharyx marioni* (0.4″; 1 cm). It has only one pair of tentacles and red, segmentally arranged gills.

The cirratulids have reduced heads that lack appendages. The parapodia are also reduced, being represented by setae, tentacles, and gills. They typically bear a varying number of grooved anterior feeding tentacles, and cylindrical respiratory gills, which resemble the tentacles, along much or all of the length of the body. The feeding mode resembles that of terebellids, to which they are not related.

Segmented Worms $\hfill$ *Color Plate C4*

Sandpaper Worm *Piromis eruca*

This sluggish sand-encrusted polychaete is the only commonly encountered representative of the family Flabelligeridae in our area. *Piromis eruca* (2″; 5 cm) burrows in soft estuarine muds. The body is positioned just below the surface of the sediment and curved slightly into a shallow U which brings opposite ends of the animal in contact with the sediment surface. The head, which consists of a prostomium and peristomium, can be retracted into the front of the body for protection. The very long setae at the front of the animal form a cage (see Plate C4) that is exposed at the surface of the sediment and probably protects the head and gills. Flabelligerids feed by extending a pair of grooved filamentous palps (not visible in the photograph) over the sediment surface beyond the protection of the setal cage. Deposited organic material is transported to the mouth by the ciliated grooves of the palps. The sand grains on the back of this species are firmly attached to the body. They toughen the skin of *Piromis* and may reduce predation by providing camouflage or lowering palatability. A unique feature of the Flabelligeridae is the presence of a dichromatic, hemoglobin-like, respiratory pigment, chlorocruorin, that appears green under some lighting conditions and red under others. The eggs of *Piromis* are also dichromatic. When they are dissected free from the gonads, they change back and forth from green to bright yellow in response to some unknown but presumably chemical stimulus.

Segmented Worms

Lancelet Worm *Armandia agilis*

The lancelet worm, *Armandia agilis* (1.2″; 3 cm) is a pink fusiform polychaete that superficially resembles amphioxus and, like it, is functionally and anatomically fishlike. The body is streamlined, compressed from side to side, and has a flattened tail "fin." When *Armandia* is removed from the sand, it wriggles vigorously and swims rapidly like a tiny eel. *Armandia* also uses these movements to burrow in current-swept sand flats where it is said to be a deposit-feeder. It has a protrusible, soft, pillowlike pharynx. *Armandia* is comparable to amphioxus in other ways: the mouth is surrounded by a fringe of sensory filaments, eyespots occur along the length of the body, and there is a pair of ventrolateral folds of the body that flank a median longitudinal groove.

209

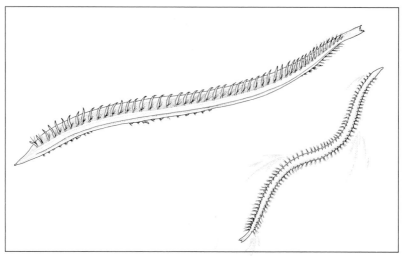

Figure 205

A similar species, *A. maculata,* is also found in shallow southeastern waters. Superficially the two are very much alike but *A. maculata* is smaller, with setae on 29 segments whereas 36 or more segments of *A. agilis* bear setae.

Some other species of opheliids in the Southeast belong to the genus *Travisia,* and although their bodies are tapered at both ends, as in *Armandia,* they are not streamlined for swimming. Instead, they have the appearance of grubs or tiny blimps. They are foul-smelling sluggish burrowers in subtidal sands and muds and are rarely encountered.

Segmented Worms *Color Plate C5*

Maitre d' Worm *Notomastus lobatus*

Our several species of polychaetes in the family Capitellidae are red or purple earthwormlike animals with small reduced appendages. They often occur in muddy sediments where they feed on deposited organic material. Marine sediments that are enriched with organic pollutants often support very high densities of certain species such as *Capitella capitata.*

Notomastus lobatus is the largest (30″; 76 cm) representative of the family. It occurs on soft, sticky, clayey mudflats where it constructs a vertical burrow wound into a perfect helix. The body of the animal is also helically coiled, as shown in Plate C5. The burrow walls are polished and the burrow itself appears to be carefully maintained. The stability of the burrow, the nonaggressive feeding style of the worm, and the movement of water through the burrow encourage colonization by symbiotic animals. *Notomastus* must be a gracious host because there are at least eight symbionts that share its burrow.

These commensals include a polynoid scaleworm, *Lepidasthenia varia* (Fig. 192), that lies against the thorax of *Notomastus,* near the head end of the burrow. The white sluglike animal attached to the body of the worm in Plate C5 is an undescribed clam, *Entovalva* sp. B (0.8"; 2 cm), which has a reduced shell and an enlarged mantle. Several of these bivalves attach to one worm but do not harm it. Another clam, *Entovalva* sp. A (0.4"; 1 cm), has a larger shell and pinkish tissue, and sometimes attaches to the lining of the burrow (Fig. 159). This clam begins life as a commensal of the scaleworm, *Lepidasthenia,* living under its scales (Fig. 192). As it grows, it deserts the scaleworm and resides on the burrow wall. Yet another clam (0.4"), a rare undescribed and unnamed species with a normal shell and pink tissues, occurs deep within the burrow. All three clams belong to the Lasaeidae and are discussed in more detail with the bivalves (Fig. 159). A filter-feeding, pinnotherid crab, *Pinnixa retinens* (0.5"; 1.3 cm), shares the burrow with *Notomastus.* Infrequently, the flattened pilargid polychaete, *Ancistrosyllis commensalis* (0.8"; 2 cm), is found in the burrow. The hesionid polychaete, *Gyptis vittata* (0.4"; 1 cm), is also reported from the burrow as is an undescribed species of the amphipod genus, *Sextonia* (0.6"; 1 cm).

All of our capitellid worms superficially resemble *Notomastus* but the rest are much smaller and some are tiny. The smallest is *Heteromastus filiformis,* which rarely exceeds 2" (5 cm). *Heteromastus* may be very common on protected silty beaches where it produces tiny cindercones of feces at the sediment surface.

Segmented Worms

Bamboo Worm
Clymenella torquata
Aligena elevata
Listriella clymenellae

Polychaetes in the family Maldanidae resemble bamboo canes because their bodies are composed of conspicuous long segments. They construct straight open tubes of sand or mud and orient them vertically with the upper end exposed above the sediment surface. Bamboo worms may be common or even abundant on protected beaches. Each worm lives head-down in its tube and feeds on organic matter and sediment. The upper, or tail, end defecates indigestible material onto the sand surface.

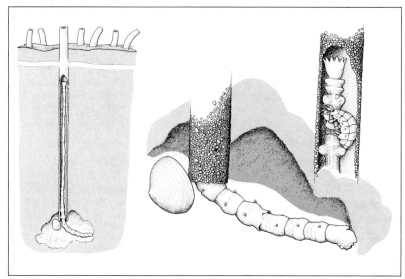

Figure 206

Clymenella torquata (4″; 10 cm) occurs in patches in large numbers on some of our muddy sandflats. Its tube is sandy, fragile, and about 8″ (20 cm) in length. It feeds head down on subsurface sediments or it extends its hind end over the sediment surface and hoes surface deposits into the tube. This hoeing behavior results in a surface trace that resembles the feeding rosette of *Saccoglossus kowalevskii*. Because *Clymenella* lives below the sediment surface where oxygen availability is low, it must pump aerated surface water through the tube with waves of contraction along its body or by moving, pistonlike, up and down its tube. Feeding on sediment at the lower end of the tube creates a cavity in the sand. This space and the ventilating water current are exploited by the small clam, *Aligena elevata* (0.2″; 5 mm), shown in Figures 206 and 159. One to several of these clams attach to the lower end of the tube, like mussels attached to a rock. The clams strain food from the tube water and presumably are protected by living deeper in the sediment than their short siphons would otherwise permit. A symbiotic amphipod crustacean, *Listriella clymenellae* (Fig. 206, 0.2″; 5 mm), and occasionally juveniles of the worm pea crab, *Pinnixa chaetopterana,* occur in the tube.

Clymenella is usually brown, olive, green, or reddish orange and has a thin, flangelike, membranous collar on the fourth segment. A similar species, *Axiothella mucosa,* is usually red and lacks the collar although it has a low fleshy ridge in this position. The green body color of *Clymenella* results from the accumulation in the skin of the bile pigment, mesobiliverdin, a derivative of seaweed pigments. *Axiothella* produces an oval, transparent, gelatinous egg capsule (1.2″; 3 cm) attached to the upper end of the tube that is reminiscent of a small stranded jellyfish (Fig. 35). *Clymenella* releases its gametes into the sea and does not make an egg capsule.

Another bamboo worm, *Petaloproctus socialis,* lives in dense aggregations on coarse-sand flats. Each worm cements sand grains together to form a tube while adjacent worms cement the sand between tubes to from a small hard reef. *Petaloproctus* is long and fragile. Its head end is red, the middle brown, and the hind end pale red. The posterior end is a broad entire flange.

Segmented Worms

Lugworm *Arenicola cristata*
Pinnixa cylindrica

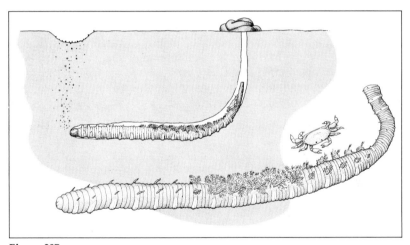

Figure 207

Lugworms are robust, burrowing, sediment-eaters that construct semipermanent L-shaped burrows in sand which they occupy head end down. The common name presumably refers to the sluggish, heavy, and clumsy nature of these animals. A crater develops in the surface of the sand over the head end of the burrow as a result of subsurface feeding. The hind end of the animal emerges occasionally from the burrow opening and defecates a soft coil of sand on the sediment surface. The artifacts of lugworm feeding, a surface crater or funnel and a sandy fecal casting, closely resemble those of unrelated animals that feed similarly, for example, the sea cucumber, *Leptosynapta tenuis,* and the acorn worm, *Balanoglossus aurantiacus*. Like these animals and other sediment-eaters, *Arenicola* is an important tiller of marine soils, much like earthworms in garden soils.

The body of lugworms is usually divided into three regions. The front end (Fig. 207, left end) is robust, muscular, and is used for digging. The middle part is respiratory and covered with bushy red gills. The hind end, which must expose itself to the world outside the burrow during defecation, is weakly developed and, if disturbed, sections of it are readily cast off. The lost hind end is later regenerated. In several parts of the world, lugworms are considered to be choice bait for fish, but our species burrows too deeply to be caught easily.

Arenicola cristata is a large reddish or greenish-red worm, reaching 12″ (30 cm) or more in length and 0.6″ (1.5 cm) in diameter. The green skin pigment is arenicochrome, and represents a class of chemicals called quinones, which have antibiotic properties. The pigment stains human skin when the animals are handled. *Arenicola* burrows on protected intertidal beaches and is common. In early spring, *Arenicola cristata* produces an elongate, amber or pink, gelatinous egg mass up to 1 yard in length that streams outward from the burrow opening. The protected burrow of *Arenicola* is frequently shared by the commensal pea crab, *Pinnixa cylindrica* (0.6″; 1.5 cm). A smaller form of *A. cristata*, which occurs in sandier sediments and produces a small spherical or ovoid egg jelly, in the past was considered to be a distinct species, *A. brasiliensis*.

Segmented Worms

Shingle Tube Worm *Owenia fusiformis*

The shingle tube worm, *Owenia fusiformis* (6″; 15 cm), occurs on protected beaches at and below the low water mark and can be recognized by its distinctive tube. The tube is composed of carefully selected sand and shell particles which are neatly arranged like shingles on a roof. The tube is oriented vertically in the sand and about 0.5″ (1.3 cm) protrudes above the sediment surface. The short, branched, ciliated tentacles extend from the mouth of the tube, create a water current, and trap suspended food particles. They can also bend over and sweep deposited organic material from the surface of the sand. Although the lower end of the tube opens at a minute pore, *Owenia* does not eliminate wastes through it. Instead, the worm turns around in the tube and defecates from its upper end. Each of the shell fragments and sand grains in the tube is attached along a single edge to the membranous tube lining. This arrangement allows *Owenia* to bend and shorten the tube while maintaining a protective armor, like a suit of medieval mail. The tube is actually a functional second skin. The worm can shorten the tube three to four times its extended length and even burrow through sedi-

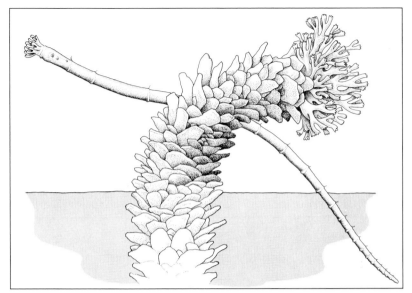

Figure 208

ment with it. The free edges of the flat particles are always directed upward. This helps anchor the animals in the sand, like flanges on some fenceposts, and may help resist shorebird or fish predation.

This splendid animal is named after Sir Richard Owen, a nineteenth-century zoologist and paleontologist who, among other achievements, discovered the roundworm that causes trichinosis, the debilitating parasitic disease contracted from eating raw or inadequately cooked pork.

Segmented Worms   *Color Plate C6*

Ice Cream Cone Worm *Cistenides gouldii*

Cistenides gouldii is our only shallow-water representative of the ice cream cone worms. They occur, sometimes commonly, on protected beaches throughout our region and reach 2″ (5 cm) in length.

Tube construction in these animals is elevated to an art. The walls of the hollow tube are exactly one sand grain thick. As the animal grows, the tube is enlarged at the wide end by the addition of new courses of carefully selected and perfectly fitted sand grains which are mortared in place. The completed tube is rigid and fragile. The head end of the tube is to the right in Plate C6, the hind end to the left.

Cistenides feeds below the surface of the sand on deposited organic material. Its tube is open at both ends and oriented vertically or obliquely within the sediment. The wide end projects down and the

215

narrow end up, protruding slightly above the surface. Ice cream cone worms loosen the sediment for feeding with stout golden bristles projecting from the head. The bristles are also used as a protective plug to seal the tube when the animal withdraws. Grooved, retractile, oral tentacles move microbe-coated sand grains to the mouth. Selected grains are swallowed and the organic material adhering to them is digested. Feces and sand grains of unsuitable sizes for consumption are released at the sediment surface from the upper end of the tube.

Unrelated animals that play similar ecological roles, like chimney swifts and bats, are often convergently similar. Ice cream cone worms and tusk molluscs illustrate this phenomenon.

Segmented Worms

Mason Worms *Sabellaria floridensis*

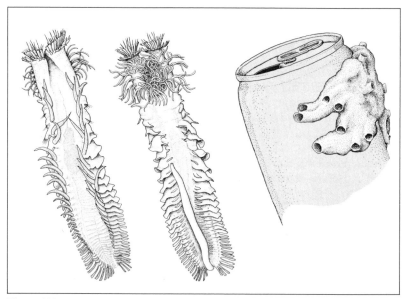

Figure 209

Polychaetes in the family Sabellariidae construct and occupy hard, strong, sand tubes sometimes alone and sometimes in dense aggregations. They are attached to hard surfaces such as shells, rocks, pilings, beverage cans (Fig. 209, right), and other sabellariid tubes. The masses of tubes are usually in small patches, 2–3″ (5–7.5 cm) in diameter in our area, but in southeastern Florida and along the coast of California, some species build extensive reefs. Some of these are intertidal and large

216

B1. Rock boring sipunculan, *Themiste alutacea,* **on scorched mussels,** *Brachidontes exustus*

B2. Scale snail, *Cochliolepis parasitica*

B3. Common janthina, *Janthina janthina*

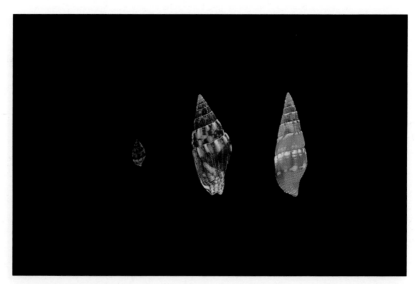

B4. Lunar dove snail, *Astyris lunata* (left), greedy dove snail, *Costoanachis avara* (center), and well-ribbed dove snail, *Costoanachis lafresnayi* (right)

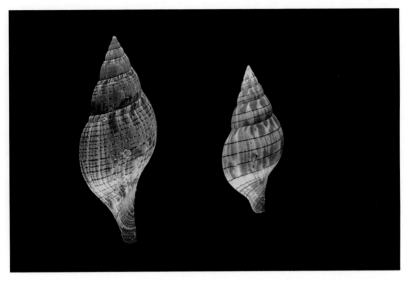

B5. True tulip snail, *Fasciolaria tulipa,* and banded tulip snail, *F. hunteria*

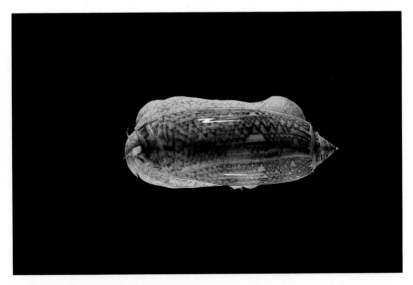

B6. Lettered olive snail, *Oliva sayana*

B7. Dewy marginella, *Marginella roscida*

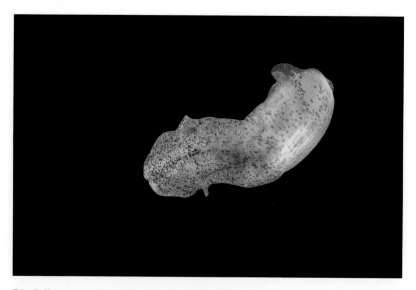

B8. Solitary paper bubble snail, *Haminoea solitaria*

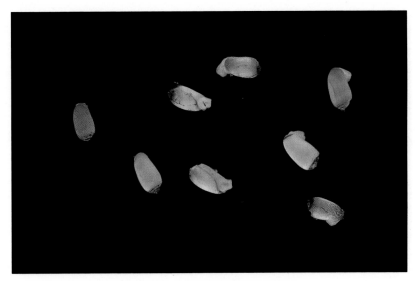

B9. Channeled barrel bubble snail, *Acteocina canaliculata*

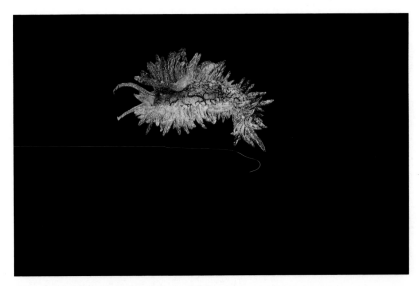

B10. Seaweed sea slug, *Placida dendritica*

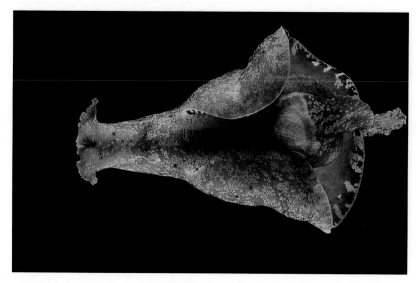

B11. Sooty sea hare, *Aplysia brasiliana*

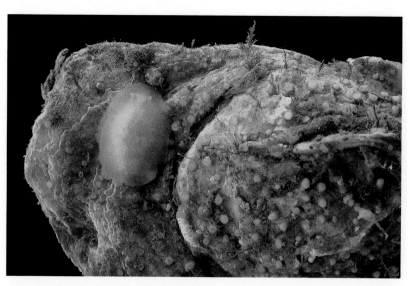

B12. Lemon drop sea slug, *Doriopsilla pharpa,* on the boring sponge, *Cliona celata*

B13. **Sponge slug,** *Doris verrucosa,* **on the garlic sponge,** *Lissodendoryx isodictyalis*

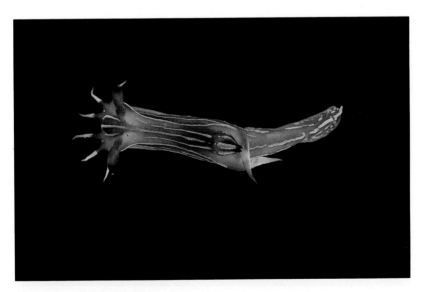

B14. **Harlequin,** *Polycera chilluna*

B15. Rainbow slug, *Okenia sapelona*

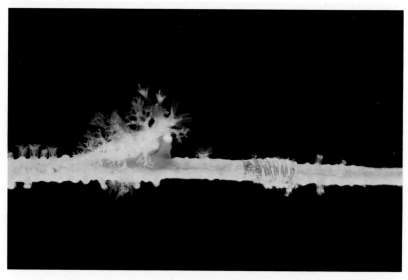

B16. Sea whip slug, *Tritonia wellsi,* on the sea whip, *Leptogorgia virgulata*

B17. Sargassum sea slug, *Scyllaea pelagica* (center), on gulfweed, *Sargassum*

B18. Anemone sea slug, *Berghia coerulescens*

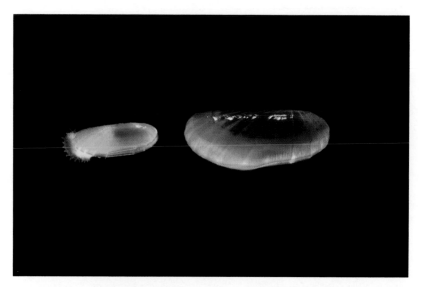

B19. Atlantic awning clam, *Solemya velum*

B20. Atlantic ribbed mussel, *Geukensia demissa*

B21. Atlantic wing oyster, *Pteria colymbus,* on the sea whip, *Leptogorgia virgulata*

B22. Pellucid file clam, *Lima pellucida*

B23. Bay scallop, *Argopecten irradians,* and the parasitic snail, *Boonea seminuda*

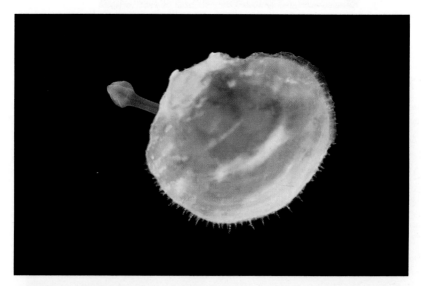

B24. Common jingle, *Anomia simplex*

B25. Corrugated jewel box, *Chama congregata*

B26. Giant Atlantic cockle, *Dinocardium robustum*

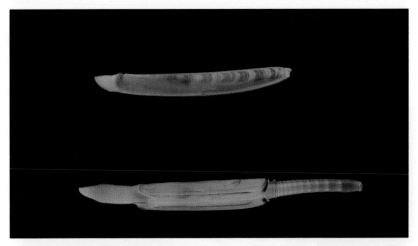

B27. Atlantic razor clam, *Ensis directus* (top), green razor clam, *Solen viridis* (bottom)

B28. Coquina clam, *Donax variabilis,* with attached symbiotic hydroid, *Lovenella gracilis*

B29. Gem clam, *Gemma gemma* (left), and grey pigmy venus, *Chione grus* (right)

B30. Sunray venus, *Macrocallista nimbosa*

B31. Shipworm, *Bankia gouldi* (wormlike, center), pholadid borer, *Martesia cuneiformis* (right and elsewhere in wood)

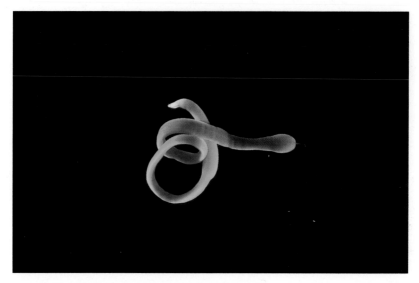

B32. Pink ribbon worm, *Micrura leidyi*

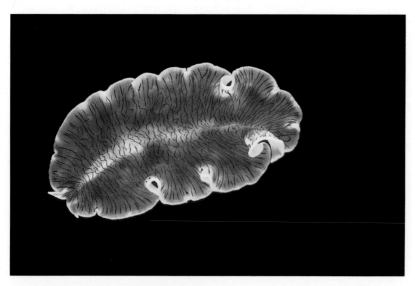

B33. Tiger flatworm, *Pseudoceros crozieri*

enough to walk on. Reef building by sabellariids has stimulated interest in using them as a means of natural erosion control along southeastern beaches.

Sabellariids feed by trapping suspended food particles on numerous short mucus-covered tentacles on the head (Fig. 209, center). Because these animals occupy a tube with only one opening and do not turn around in the tube, an extraordinary provision is found to maintain tube sanitation. The hind end of the body is reduced to a long thin duct containing little more than the intestine. When the animal is in its natural orientation, this duct (Fig. 209, center) doubles back beneath the body, extends toward the head, and releases fecal material at the opening of the tube. The feces do not foul the feeding tentacles because they are compacted in the intestine into pellets that are too large to be collected by the tentacles. The paired elongate filaments along the animal's back are red gills (Fig. 209, left).

Sabellaria floridensis (Fig. 209) and *S. vulgaris* (both 1.2''; 3 cm) are similar species occurring in shallow water throughout the region covered by this book. They can be distinguished only on the basis of technical features associated with the two clusters of golden bristles on the head, which are used as an operculum to seal the opening of the tube when the animals withdraw.

Segmented Worms

Spaghetti Mouth Worm *Melinna maculata*

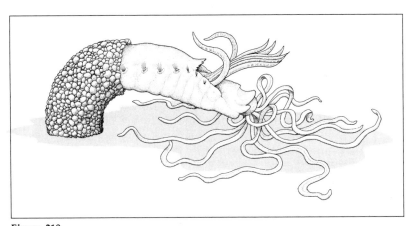

Figure 210

The spaghetti mouth worms in the family Ampharetidae resemble the spaghetti worms (Terebellidae), discussed below. Unlike them however, the ampharetids can completely withdraw the whitish feeding

217

tentacles into the mouth whereas the terebellids can shorten the tentacles but cannot completely withdraw them. Ampharetids are sedentary and construct sandy or muddy tubes in which they orient themselves head up. The animals emerge from the tubes to feed, as shown above. Some species, like *Melinna maculata* (1.2″; 3 cm), live in sediment on protected beaches while others live on the surfaces of animals and their artifacts, such as worm tubes. The highly mobile wormlike tentacles extend over the surface of the sediment and collect deposited food particles. Each tentacle is ciliated and behaves as a miniature conveyor belt to transport food back to the mouth. While feeding, the reddish or greenish gills are held up in the water above the sediment. Spaghetti mouth worms are uncommon in shallow water but abundant in the deep sea. *Melinna maculata* occurs occasionally on protected beaches in our area.

Segmented Worms   *Color Plate C7*

Spaghetti Worm *Amphitrite ornata*
Worm Pea Crab *Pinnixa chaetopterana*

Spaghetti worms (Terebellidae) are spectacular crevice, burrow, or tube-dwelling polychaetes with very long mobile tentacles, and usually with conspicuous gills on the head. Many terebellids are large, stout worms, reaching 12″ (30 cm) or more in some tropical species. Such animals can extend their tentacles 1 yard (1 m) or more in all directions while feeding in, on, and above the submerged substratum.

Amphitrite ornata (6″; 15 cm) is the largest of about 10 common shallow-water species in the Southeast. In prefers to colonize protected muddy areas in sounds, tide creeks, oyster reefs, and salt marshes where it constructs and occupies a stable, U-shaped, mud burrow with a polished mucus lining. *Amphitrite* feeds on surface deposits of fine particles which it collects with its stringlike tentacles. The tentacles have a lengthwise tract of cilia which moves individual particles to the mouth like a conveyor belt. Larger clumps of food, or a heavily-coated tentacle, are pulled in by shortening one to several of the tentacles and wiping them clean on the lips flanking the mouth. *Amphitrite* feeds alternately from both openings of its burrow. Seen from above, the burrow is often a smooth-sided mound with a hole, the burrow opening, in the center. Sometimes, however, the burrow opens on flat sediment without a mound.

The ridges visible along the sides of the body bear hundreds of microscopic hooks, like the tiny hooks on one half of a Velcro closure, which *Amphitrite* uses to grip the walls of its burrow. The hooks on the front and rear halves of the body face in opposite directions, presumably making it difficult to remove the animal from its burrow by pulling either end.

Amphitrite shares its burrow with several symbionts, including the scaleworm, *Lepidametria commensalis* (2.8″; 7 cm), the worm pea crab, *Pinnixa chaetopterana* (0.6″; 1.5 cm, shown in Plate C7), and the tiny rotifer, *Zelinkiella synaptae* (Fig. 159), which attaches to the red gills.

Segmented Worms   *Color Plate C8*

Feather Duster Worm *Sabella melanostigma*

Three families of polychaetes, the Sabellidae, Serpulidae, and Spirorbidae, are sometimes called feather duster worms. Of these, the sabellid polychaetes, including *Sabella melanostigma,* are our largest and most colorful. They are striking animals in marine aquaria and are easy to maintain provided that they are fed occasionally with fresh clam juice or finely mashed, hard boiled, egg yolk.

Sabellids produce and occupy membranous tubes into which shell, sand, or mud may be incorporated. Most of the larger species are permanently confined to their tubes but smaller species, such as *Fabricia sabella* (0.5″; 1.3 cm), can abandon them and crawl backwards. *Fabricia* has eyes on its hind end to facilitate this activity. Sabellids extend their flowerlike crown of tentacles into the water to feed, as shown in the Plate C8, and trap small suspended particles. The tentacles have a thick coating of cilia and produce a strong current that flows through the crown, from left to right in the photograph. This water current not only transports food to the animal but aids in gas exchange. When a sabellid is touched or when a shadow passes over the tentacles, it rapidly retreats into its tube. The small, paired, maroon spots on the tentacles of *Sabella* are light-sensitive eyespots that trigger the shadow response.

The feather duster of *Sabella melanostigma* is approximately 1″ (2.5 cm) in diameter. The aggregated muddy tubes (3″; 7.5 cm in length) of this species are found in tangles on intertidal and shallow subtidal rocks. Two other common sabellids in our area are *Demonax microphthalmus* (2″; 5 cm) that occupies a sandy tube and sports a green or white and brown fan with irregularly scattered red-brown eyes and *Notaulax nudicollis* (5″; 13 cm) that bores into limestone, has a striking purple and white fan, an orange body, and a dark transparent tube.

Segmented Worms

Fan Worm *Hydroides dianthus*

The fan worms, or feather duster worms, comprise three families of polychaetes in the Southeast, the Sabellidae, the Serpulidae, and the Spirorbidae. The sabellids occupy membranous tubes onto which sediment may be attached and lack an operculum to seal the tube (see *Sabella melanostigma*). The serpulids, such as *Hydroides,* secrete cal-

219

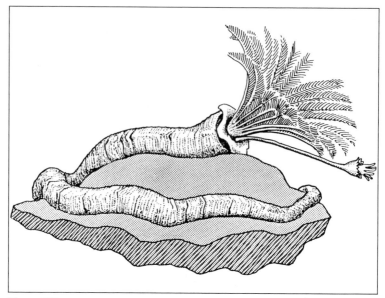

Figure 211

careous tubes and have an operculum. The minute spirorbids are similar to serpulids but coil their calcareous tubes clockwise or counterclockwise in a more or less flat spiral.

The fan worm, *Hydroides dianthus* (1.2″; 3 cm), and other serpulids permanently occupy their secreted tubes. They emerge partially from the tubes to expand the array of tentacles, or fan, for feeding and gas exchange. Fan worm tubes open only at the head end and this raises the question of how these animals, which do not turn around in their tubes, avoid fouling the tube with fecal material. The sanitation problem is solved by a ciliated groove that runs from the anus to the head along the back of the worm. Fan worms avoid reingesting the waste by first compacting it into pellets which are too large to be selected by the fan. The openings of the kidney ducts are also near the base of the fan, as in *Sabella*. A club-shaped structure behind the fan, resembling a golf tee, is a plug, the operculum, which seals the opening of the tube when the fan is withdrawn. The operculum is one of the featherlike tentacles which, during development, becomes modified for its special function. *Hydroides* is found throughout the year in the Carolinean region on virtually any firm surface.

Filograna implexa (2″; 5 cm) forms networks of long, very narrow, white, calcareous tubes which together give the impression of fine lace. *Filograna* is a gregarious species that reproduces asexually by transverse division. The tubes of many worms coalesce to form large lacelike masses often rising above the surface of the substratum. These worms are common in North Carolina and Florida.

220

The family Spirorbidae is closely related to the Serpulidae and consists of tiny worms that construct and inhabit coiled calcareous tubes about 0.1" (2 mm) across the coil.

Leeches

Fish Leech *Calliobdella vivida*

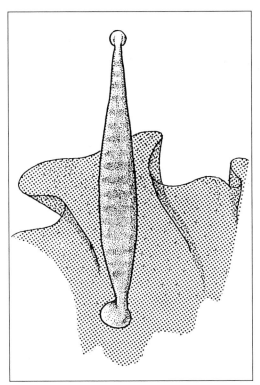

Figure 212

The green marine leech, *Calliobdella vivida* (1.2"; 3 cm), can be common in high salinity water on oyster reefs and sea lettuce, *Ulva lactuca,* in the cold months of the year. Like many, but not all, leeches, *Calliobdella* is a blood-sucking parasite. It parasitizes several species of fishes in our region, particularly Atlantic menhaden, *Brevoortia tyrannus,* and it usually attaches with its front and rear suckers to the inside of the mouth. More than twenty of these leeches have been collected from the mouth of a single unfortunate fish. An epidemic of *Calliobdella* on menhaden occurred in South Carolina in 1971. During that year, commercial fishermen working with menhaden reported that their decks,

221

feet, and hands were covered with leeches. The leeches may be responsible for transmitting a kind of fish malaria to menhaden caused by a single-celled organism called *Hemogregarina brevoortiae.*

Calliobdella reproduces in late winter and early spring. It leaves its host, as do all fish leeches, and searches for a substratum for attachment of its cocoons, perhaps oyster shells or sea lettuce. The young hatch as miniatures (0.1″; 2 mm) of the adults and "search" when a shadow passes over them. While searching, they adopt the posture shown in Figure 212 with the front sucker waving to and fro in the water. Adults and juveniles are excellent swimmers and can even attach their suckers to the surface of the water to rest or to await their hosts.

Most of our marine leeches belong to the fish leech family, Piscicolidae. In brackish water the most common species is *Myzobdella lugubris,* which also occurs in fresh water. This species infests a wide variety of marine and freshwater bony fishes as well as blue crabs and shrimps. It is common in shallow brackish lagoons. *Calliobdella* has 11 to 13 pairs of lateral pulsatile respiratory vesicles which are lacking in *Myzobdella.*

Sharks in our area are often infested with *Stilbarobdella macrothela,* which lacks lateral vesicles but has wartlike tubercles scattered over the body. Skates and rays are often parasitized by *Branchellion* species, *B. torpedinis* in the North and *B. ravenelii* in the South. Both species have lateral unbranched gills, 33 pairs in the former, 31 in the latter. In our area marine turtles support two species of *Ozobranchus* in the family Ozobranchidae. *Ozobranchus branchiatus* has 7 pairs of branched gills and is restricted to the green turtle, *Chelonia mydas. Ozobranchus margoi* has 5 pairs of branched gills and is found on several species of marine turtles including the green, loggerhead, and leatherback.

ARTHROPODA

Horseshoe Crabs

Horseshoe Crab *Limulus polyphemus*

Figure 213

The horseshoe crab, *Limulus polyphemus* (24″; 61 cm), belongs to an ancient, little changed group of arthropods that is now almost extinct. Its shape is distinctive and there is no other animal on our coast with which it could possibly be confused. The body is divided into a large, anterior, horseshoe-shaped head and thorax and a posterior abdomen. There are small eyes on the head. The mouth and its several pairs of appendages are on the lower surface. Most of these appendages have weak pincers which are used to gather the small clams, worms, and crustaceans these animals prey upon. The first leg of males is a large swollen hook used to grasp the female during mating. The hind pair of legs lacks a pincer and is used to push the creature slowly and methodically forward in sand or mud.

The under surface of the abdomen bears large flat book gills consisting of numerous thin sheets adapted for absorbing oxygen from the water. The abdomen has a long spike at the end. The book gills of older individuals often support large populations of the small white flatworm, *Bdelloura candida*. In spite of their suckered and leechlike appearance,

223

these worms are commensals, not parasites. Another small white flat-worm, *Syncoelidium pellucidum,* occurs in smaller numbers on horse-shoe crabs. It does not have a posterior sucker.

Horseshoe crabs mate in the spring when they can often be seen traveling in tandem, female in front, smaller male behind as in Figure 213. Up to 80,000 eggs are deposited in large bowl-like depressions in the intertidal region of quiet protected beaches. The eggs are consumed by numerous predators, including several species of birds, fishes, and seashore mammals.

In spite of their common name, horseshoe crabs are not crabs but chelicerates, more closely related to spiders, scorpions, ticks, and sea spiders than to crabs and shrimps. While they look fearsome, horseshoe crabs are entirely harmless. Their pincers are weak and can deliver only a gentle pinch, but you might want to keep your fingers out of the spiny food groove between the bases of the legs. The long spikelike tail is not used offensively and you would have to go out of your way to hurt yourself with it. Their safety lies in their armor, not in active defense or aggression.

Sea Spiders   *Color Plate C9*

Black Sea Spider *Anoplodactylus lentus*

Superficially the sea spiders look much like true spiders and, because of this resemblance, are easily recognized. Although their evolutionary relationships are not well understood, they are probably related to spiders and they have some features in common with them. We have several species on our coast but only one, *Anoplodactylus lentus,* is large and common enough to be noticed by casual observers. These gangly black or dark purple animals are about 1.5″ (3.8 cm) across and are almost all legs, with a tiny narrow body. The sea spiders in Plate C9 are on the hydroid, *Eudendrium carneum,* their favorite prey.

The sea spiders are carnivores that feed on bryozoans or hydroids, from which they suck the juices. They are commonly found in the fouling community on docks, pilings, rocks, and creek bottoms. Because of the extreme reduction in the size of the body, the ovaries are located in the legs, the only place there is room for them. After the eggs are released and fertilized they are carried by the male on a special pair of legs. A sea spider with visible egg masses, such as the one in the lower right of the photograph, is a male, not a female. Females may also have a similar pair of legs but use them for grooming, as do males when not carrying eggs.

Another common species, *Tanystylum orbiculare,* is much smaller (0.2″; 5 mm) white or tan, and is rarely noticed. *Achelia sawayai* is almost identical to *Tanystylum* and can be distinguished from it only on detailed technical grounds. It is common also. Yet another common species, *Callipallene brevirostrum,* is a small delicate animal with very long gangly legs like those of *Anoplodactylus.* It is much smaller and is transparent and colorless. It is often found on the hydroid, *Plumularia floridana.*

Copepods   *Color Plate C10*

Lernaeenicus radiatus

The large crustacean class Copepoda includes over 8,000 species, many of which occur in the Southeast in various habitats. They are mostly microscopic, or nearly so, and lie outside the interest of most coastal visitors. Their small size belies their importance, however, and they are of immense ecological significance. The planktonic species form a vital link between the photosynthetic phytoplankton and the carnivorous fishes. In recognition of their position in the food chain they are often called the "cows of the sea" with the phytoplankton being the marine equivalent of grass.

Most copepods will pass unnoticed by laymen but some of the parasitic species are large and conspicuous, especially those that attach to fishes. *Lernaeenicus radiatus* (1″; 2.5 cm), shown in Plate C10 on an anchovy, one of its many hosts, is a common parasitic copepod. It is highly modified for this existence and bears no obvious similarity to the other, nonparasitic, copepods. The head of the animal in the photograph is embedded in the tissue of the fish and the neck, body (red), and two egg strings trail behind. This individual is a female. The parasite feeds on the blood of the host and this species is known to parasitize about 15 species of fishes. Three other species of *Lernaeenicus* occur in the Southeast and are similar to *L. radiatus.* Sometimes the exposed parts of these copepods are overgrown by hydroids which give them a bushy appearance.

Anomalocera ornata, a large, blue, planktonic, calanoid copepod, sometimes washes ashore in such numbers that it forms windrows several miles long on outer beaches. At sea uncountable numbers of these animals sometimes strike the water surface from below so that it appears to be raining. This is a nearshore species.

Barnacles   *Color Plate C11*

Goose Barnacle *Lepas anatifera*

Barnacles are crustaceans, related to shrimps, crabs, copepods and beachhoppers, but they are highly modified for a sedentary existence, usually as filter feeders, although some are parasitic, and some consume larger prey. Most live attached to firm surfaces such as rocks, grass stems, seaweed, pilings, oysters, turtles, or even whales. Most barnacles are covered by a set of hard limy plates, four of which are movable and

225

serve as doors that, when open, allow the featherlike legs to emerge and capture food. There are two types of common barnacles; goose barnacles and acorn barnacles. The body of a goose barnacle, with its protective plates, is located atop a flexible stalk which is attached to a hard surface. The acorn barnacles, on the other hand, have no stalk and the body, which is completely enclosed by the plates, is attached directly to the substratum.

Most of the many species of barnacles in inshore waters are acorn barnacles and the goose barnacles present are mostly washed in from offshore habitats. An exception is the tiny (0.1″; 2 mm), worldwide, commensal species, *Octolasmis muelleri,* which lives attached to the gills of coastal and estuarine crabs. Dissection of a mature blue crab will often reveal these tiny stalked barnacles on the gills. The crab loses its barnacle guests each time it sheds its exoskeleton. Consequently, barnacles are most common on adult female crabs that have ceased molting. Several other species of *Octolasmis* occur in our area but *O. muelleri* is the most common and occurs on the largest number of hosts. *Octolasmis hoeki* may sometimes be found on the outside, as well as in the gill chamber, of its hosts. It has a more heavily calcified shell than *O. muelleri.*

Lepas anatifera, which is the large (1.5″; 3.8 cm) species pictured in Plate C11, lives on floating objects at sea, including the floating snail, *Janthina.* Contrary to the reputation barnacles have as filter feeders, *Lepas anatifera* is reported to feed on small fishes and the floating pelagic cnidarians *Velella, Porpita,* and *Physalia,* as well as microscopic planktonic organisms. Boards and bottles covered with *Lepas* often wash ashore and should be inspected for the worm, *Amphinome rostrata* (Plate C2), a large, bristly, red-brown predator of whole barnacles; for *Hipponoe gaudichaudi,* a smaller pink worm, and for the sea slug, *Fiona pinnata,* which also eats *Lepas.* A smaller goose barnacle, *Lepas pectinata* (1″; 2.5 cm), is common on floating *Sargassum* weed and can be seen in Plate B17.

Barnacles

Ivory Barnacle *Balanus eburneus* (left)
Fragile Barnacle *Chthamalus fragilis* (middle)

Among the many species of acorn, or stalkless, barnacles on the southeastern coast the most common and noticeable are the two shown in Figure 214. Ivory barnacles are large (1.2″; 3 cm) white barnacles commonly found on oysters, pilings and seawalls near or below the low tide line. The much smaller (less than 0.4″; 1 cm) fragile barnacle is probably the most common barnacle on this coast. Of all our barnacles, it is the most tolerant of desiccation and consequently lives higher in the intertidal zone of rocks, walls, pilings, and the stems and leaves of marsh

Figure 214

grass than any other marine animal. These small barnacles form a dense belt above the oyster and mussel zones on hard intertidal surfaces. Another species, the star barnacle, *Chthamalus stellatus,* occurs in similar situations in the southern part of the Carolinian Province where the two species coexist. Star barnacles are illustrated in Figure 215. The two *Chthamalus* species are distinguished by differences in the margin of the base of the shell. That of *C. stellatus* is sinuous and scalloped with a starlike outline, while that of *C. fragilis* is smooth, with a circular or oval outline. In Figure 214 the large barnacles are *Balanus eburneus* and the small ones are *Chthamalus fragilis.* An isopod crustacean, *Sphaeroma quadridentata,* is a common member of the intertidal community and one appears in the photograph.

There are several other acorn barnacles in the Southeast. *Balanus improvisus* and *B. subalbidus* are common, small (0.5″; 1.3 cm), smooth, white species that are easily confused with each other and with juvenile *B. eburneus.* Four of our barnacle species have red or purple on the shell. The largest of these is an enormous pinkish barnacle, *Megabalanus antillensis* (2″; 5 cm), which occurs on hard surfaces in the low intertidal and subtidal of the tropics. It extends northward into northeastern Florida. *Balanus trigonus* (0.8″; 2 cm) has a rough shell with a more or less triangular opening and deeply pitted closing plates. It is very common in shallow water in Florida but less so in the Carolinas. The other two colored species are small (0.4″; 1 cm) and are very hard to identify without dissection. They are *B. venustus,* with more or less evenly spaced narrow reddish lines, and *B. amphitrite,* with irregularly spaced, wider, reddish bands.

A large white barnacle, *Chelonibia testudinaria,* is common on the backs of sea turtles where it lives attached to the surface. A second species, *C. caretta,* also occurs on sea turtles but is rare in the Southeast. It resembles *C. testudinaria* but is firmly embedded in the bone of the turtle's shell. Another species in this genus, *C. patula,* lives on the backs of crabs and horseshoe crabs and is shown on Plate C27. All members of this genus are low and wide with open fleshy apertures.

Barnacles   *Color Plate C12*

Seawhip Barnacle *Conopea galeata*

Seawhip barnacles (0.6″; 1.5 cm) are easily identified by virtue of their obligate commensal relationship with the seawhip, *Leptogorgia,* and by their unusual shape and color. They are found only on seawhips and are brown with white markings. The basal plate is boat-shaped and is attached to the host. More often than not, the living tissue of the seawhip overgrows the barnacle, covering it with a layer of orange, white, yellow, or purple tissue. In such cases the normal profile and color of the barnacle is obscured and it looks like an inanimate lump on the seawhip. The aperture through which the barnacle feeds and respires is not overgrown however, and the lump will always have an opening if the barnacle is alive. The barnacles on the left of the photograph (Pl. C12) are attached to the dead axial rod of the seawhip and are not overgrown by seawhip tissue. The barnacles in the center and right are on living seawhips and have been overgrown. The aperture of the barnacle in the center is clearly visible as are the feeding appendages of the specimen on the right.

Like other acorn barnacles, individuals of this species are simultaneously male and female (hermaphroditic) but are unusual in having dwarf males in addition to the large conspicuous hermaphroditic animals. The dwarf males cluster around the apertures of the large hermaphrodites where they are available to ensure cross fertilization. This arrangement is apparently a necessary adaptation in this species because the large distance separating any two hermaphroditic individuals is too great to be traversed by the penis of the hermaphrodite.

The barnacle order Acrothoracica contains small, unbarnacle-like animals that bore into calcareous objects. It is represented in the Southeast by *Kochlorine floridana* (0.2″; 5 mm) which forms chambers in the shells of molluscs, barnacles, calcareous bryozoans, serpulid worm tubes, and red calcareous algae. Its presence is revealed by a tiny (0.1″; 2 mm) elliptical slit at the surface.

Barnacles

Striped False Limpet *Siphonaria pectinata* (lower left)
Volcano Barnacle *Tetraclita stalactifera* (center)
Star Barnacle *Chthamalus stellatus* (right)

Volcano barnacles, *Tetraclita stalactifera,* are large (1.6″; 4 cm),

Figure 215

tropical, grey barnacles whose range extends to northern Florida. They are circular in cross section with steep rough sides and a small round opening. The opening of the volcano barnacle is maintained by erosion and its size is variable. In most other barnacles, this opening is made when the side plates grow and expand laterally. Volcano barnacles are characteristic of the intertidal zone of rocks in high salinity water and are often found with *Chthamalus stellatus* (the star barnacle), *Siphonaria pectinata* (the striped false limpet), and the anemone, *Anthopleura carneola.* All of these animals are tolerant of desiccation and heat and can withstand the periodic exposure to air that is characteristic of the intertidal zone. Three star barnacles are attached to the sides of the volcano barnacle in the photograph and several others are scattered about on the rock where they can be recognized by their scalloped margins. Star barnacles are the tropical equivalent of the southeastern *Chthamalus fragilis.*

Siphonaria pectinata also appears in the photograph and there is a single small individual on the lower left slope of the volcano barnacle. Several others are concentrated in the lower left corner of the frame. This limpetlike snail has a pale, conical, uncoiled shell with dark vertical stripes. It has an air-breathing lung and a gill in the lung cavity so that it can breathe in either air or water. It resembles the keyhole limpets but, unlike them, has no opening at the apex of the shell. Limpets in the genus *Siphonaria* graze on algae and return to a "home site" or "scar" on the rock during low tide. The home sites are depressions in the rock that conform closely to the contours of the limpet's shell and are believed to help reduce predation, dislodgment, abrasion, and desiccation by insuring a close fit to the rock surface. False limpets are pulmonates and are closely related to the land snails and only distantly related to the other limpets.

Mantis Shrimps
Color Plate C13

Mantis Shrimp *Squilla empusa*

Squilla empusa belongs to a group of crustaceans known collectively as the mantis shrimps because of their resemblance to praying mantises. These crustaceans are flattened top to bottom and have a pair of large powerful claws which they hold beneath the body as if they were praying. Like their terrestrial namesakes, they are fierce predators that use these claws to prey, not pray. The motion of the claws is one of the fastest recorded animal movements. The many species of mantis shrimps are similar to each other but there are only three common species in shallow southeastern waters. One of these is the large *Squilla empusa* which is shown in Plate C13. This robust and prickly animal reaches 6″ (15 cm) in length and inhabits a U-shaped burrow in soft mud. In the North, burrows may extend as much as 12′ (4 m) into the sediment but in the Southeast they are only about 20″ (51 cm) deep. The animals are grey with a little yellow on the tail appendage. A rare relative, *S. neglecta,* has white rather than yellow on the tail. A jagged row of sharp teeth arises from the hind margin of the tail of both species. *Squilla* is especially common in muddy creek bottoms where it lurks in the burrow mouth and ambushes its prey. The tiny snail, *Cyclostremiscus pentagonus,* and the undescribed, minuscule, snail-mimicking clam, *Lepton* sp., live on the walls of *Squilla* burrows. Another mantis shrimp, *Chloridopsis dubia,* occurs on estuarine mud bottoms from South Carolina south. In resembles *Squilla empusa* but is brightly colored with blue, green, and red.

Coronis excavatrix is a common species that lives on partly protected silty-sand beaches where there is reduced wave action. It is smaller and more delicate than *Squilla,* reaching only about 2.5″ (6.4 cm) when adult. It can change its color and may vary from transparent and almost colorless to dark brown. The hind margin of the tail lacks squilla's formidable row of teeth but does have a few tiny spines arising from below the margin. *Coronis* digs a vertical burrow about 0.5″ (1.3 cm) in diameter and over 3′ (1 m) deep. The sandy walls of the upper burrow are often rusty in color. Most of the small holes in the lower intertidal zone of silty beaches are the burrow openings of either *Coronis* or the mud shrimp, *Callianassa.* The openings of *Coronis* burrows are usually larger than those of *Callianassa,* even though the latter is the larger animal. *Callianassa* burrows taper near the surface while those of *Coronis* do not.

230

Isopods

Wharf Roach *Ligia exotica*

Isopoda is a crustacean group that includes many marine and fresh-water representatives in addition to the better known terrestrial pill bugs or woodlice. There are several marine species on our coast but most are small and inconspicuous and easily escape notice. In general, our shallow-water isopods are less than 1″ (2.5 cm) long and are flattened top to bottom. They are closely related to the amphipods which are usually flattened side to side. One of the two pairs of antennae, the seven pairs of legs, and the single pair of uropods that characterize the isopods are visible in Plate C14. The uropods are the hindmost pair of appendages. The isopods have one pair whereas the amphipods have three.

The largest and most conspicuous isopod on our coast is the large wharf roach, *Ligia exotica* (1.5″; 3.8 cm). This fast grey isopod is common on wharf pilings and rock jetties where it lives above the water line. It is an evolutionary descendent of terrestrial, rather than marine, isopods and lives close to, but usually not in, the water. It belongs to the terrestrial suborder Oniscoidea as do the familiar pill bugs or roly-poly bugs (woodlice) in your woodpile. As the common name implies, it resembles a cockroach in size, shape, and agility.

Isopods

Smooth Seaweed Isopod *Idotea baltica*
Sand Isopod *Chiridotea caeca*
Rough Seaweed Isopod *Erichsonella filiformis*

Many of the common isopods on our coast belong to the suborder Valvifera whose members have two doors below the abdomen that protect their delicate gills. Many of these animals are long and slender. Several species are common in vegetation. Among them are *Idotea baltica* (0.8″; 2 cm) and *Erichsonella filiformis* (0.4″; 1 cm), both of which may be encountered on seaweeds on rock jetties. Both are long and slender but *Idotea* has smooth sides whereas *Erichsonella* has irregular sides. *Idotea baltica* has a truncate abdomen with two indentations and a small point on the end. *Erichsonella* has a bluntly pointed abdomen. *Idotea* is an herbivore that lives in marine vegetation. It deposits the pigments from its food in its own exoskeleton so that its color matches that of the seaweed that is currently its home and food. Another species, *Erichsonella attenuata,* is also common in vegetation in the Southeast.

Chiridotea caeca (0.6″; 1.5 cm) is a small, flat, wide species commonly found intertidally in the sand of our outer beaches. *Chiridotea* has a pointed abdomen and is white with black markings. Several other

231

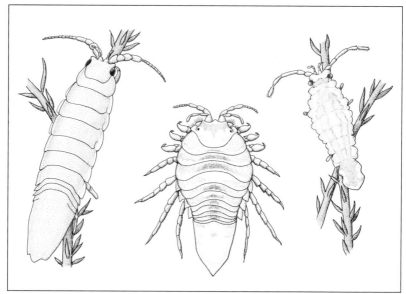

Figure 216

species of *Chiridotea* live in other sandy or silty habitats but are not common. *Edotea triloba* (0.4″; 1 cm) is a common species on silty sand subtidal bottoms. It is flatter and wider than any of our valviferans with the exception *Chiridotea*. It does not have the color pattern of *Chiridotea* but does have a pointed abdomen.

Cleantis planicauda (1.2″; 3 cm) lives in quiet water, usually on subtidal creek bottoms, inside the hollow decaying sections of old *Spartina* stems. It is long, slender, and brown.

The suborder Anthuridea is also represented in our area and contains isopods with long, very narrow bodies. Several anthurideans live in silty sand and may be difficult to identify without more specialized literature, or even with it in some cases. In high salinity water *Apanthura magnifica* is a common species. This is a small (0.4″; 1 cm), pure white species with a very slender, elongate, almost wormlike body. *Cyathura polita* is larger (1″; 2.5 cm) and may be common in silty sand in low salinity water. *Cyathura burbancki* is common in similar habitats where salinities are greater than 20 parts per thousand.

Isopods

**Marine Roly-Poly *Sphaeroma quadridentata*
Thorn Isopod *Ancinus depressus***

There are several species of aquatic isopods that resemble backyard pillbugs and, like them, can roll themselves into little balls. Unlike the

232

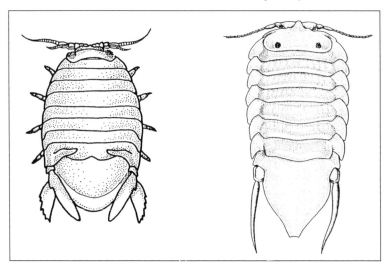

Figure 217

pillbugs, they belong to the marine suborder Flabellifera and not to the terrestrial group Oniscoidea. There are several common members of this group in the Southeast. *Sphaeroma quadridentata* (0.8″; 2 cm) is illustrated above and also in the photograph of *Balanus eburneus* (Fig. 214). *Sphaeroma walkeri* (0.4″; 1 cm) resembles *S. quadridentata* but is smaller and has many bumps on the posterior part of the body. It is a tropical Atlantic species that extends into northern Florida where it lives intertidally on rocks around and under the valves of oysters. Like many marine isopods, it occurs in several different colors including green, brown, and orange. *Sphaeroma destructor* (0.8″; 2 cm) bores into dead wood and damages marine timbers and construction in Georgia and Florida. *Paracerceis caudata,* whose males have rough backs and long curved uropods, is common in the fouling community. *Exosphaeroma diminuta* (0.1″; 3 mm) is a tiny species that looks like *S. quadridentata* but is much smaller. It lives on outer beaches in the sand.

Ancinus depressus lives on sandy, shallow, subtidal, bottoms in high salinity water along outer beaches and inlets. It is about 0.3″ (8 mm) long and white or cream in color. The body is depressed and very hard, with a heavily calcified and rocklike exoskeleton. The abdomen (pleotelson) is solid and posteriorly pointed. The uropods (last abdominal appendages) are uniramous, long and pointed. The animal can roll into a ball and lock its head into grooves on the underside of the abdomen so that it is virtually impossible to unroll against its will. The resulting ball is like a small thorny rock and is presumably unappetizing to potential predators.

A minute, flat, oval, brown sphaeromatid, *Cassidinidea ovalis* (0.2"; 5 mm), is found on intertidal oysters and in salt marshes in South Carolina and to the south. It has a truncate posterior end and the outer branch of the uropod is very small.

Isopods in the genus *Limnoria* (the gribbles) bore into wood in the intertidal zone and may be responsible for extensive damage and economic loss. Two species of these tiny (0.1"; 2 mm) isopods, *L. tripunctata* and *L. lignorum,* are reported from the southeastern coast. The boring activity of *Limnoria* and *Sphaeroma destructor* removes wood from the intertidal region of pilings resulting in a characteristic hourglass-shaped constriction near the waterline.

There are many other species of flabelliferans but, like the amphipods, they usually escape notice and their identification is difficult.

Isopods

Gill Louse *Lironeca ovalis* adult (top) and juvenile (bottom)

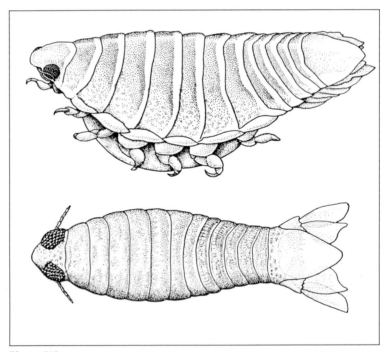

Figure 218

Unlike their close relatives the amphipods, many groups of isopods have adopted parasitic modes of existence. Some, such as the epicaridean isopods, parasitize other crustaceans and are highly modified for a parasitic existence. Others, such as the many fish parasites in the family Cymothoidae (suborder Flabellifera), are only slightly modified for parasitism and are similar to free-living isopods. These species live on the skin, gill chambers, or mouths of fishes and show relatively little anatomical adaptation for parasitism, although their legs are modified for clinging and the body is often asymmetrical. One of these, *Lironeca ovalis* (1″; 2.5 cm), is a common southeastern species that is found on the gills of several species of fishes. The juvenile stages are free-swimming and do not closely resemble the adult, the latter being asymmetrical. Until recently, the juveniles were thought to be a separate species and bore the name *Aegathoa oculata,* in reference to their very large eyes. Recent studies, however, indicate that *Aegathoa* is the juvenile stage of one or more species of cymothoid isopod, probably *Lironeca ovalis.* Another species, *Olencira praegustator* (1″; 2.5 cm), is common in the mouth cavity of menhaden (*Brevoortia*). There are many other species of cymothoid fish parasites in the Southeast.

The isopods in the suborder Epicaridea parasitize other crustaceans and those in the family Bopyridae live on crabs and shrimps where they are almost always found in the gill chamber. They are specialized for parasitism and the female bears little resemblance to an ordinary isopod. There are many species in the Southeast, each parasitizing a different species of decapod crustacean. The female attaches beneath the carapace of a shrimp or crab of the proper species, and in the case of shrimps, causes the formation of a conspicuous blister on the side of the animal. The male is much smaller than the female and retains a recognizable isopod shape. The parasites always live in pairs with the male attached to the female. The mud shrimp in Figure 225 is parasitized by bopyrid isopods. A few bopyrid species attach below the abdomen of the host rather than in the gill chamber. The snapping shrimp, *Synalpheus longicarpus,* which itself inhabits the water canals of offshore sponges, is infested with the bopyrids *Hemiarthrus synalphei,* which lives beneath the abdomen, and *Synsynella deformans,* which inhabits the gill chamber. This unfortunate shrimp is host to several other species of bopyrid parasites.

Beachhoppers

Saltmarsh Beachhopper *Orchestia grillus*

Amphipods are small, inconspicuous, rarely noticed crustaceans. They are usually less than 0.8″ (2.0 cm) in length, usually have laterally flattened, shrimplike bodies, and inhabit a variety of habitats. They are closely related to the isopods. We have almost 100 species of these abundant and ecologically important animals in our shallow coastal waters but they are almost entirely unknown to casual observers. A few species, however, may be more familiar, either because of their larger

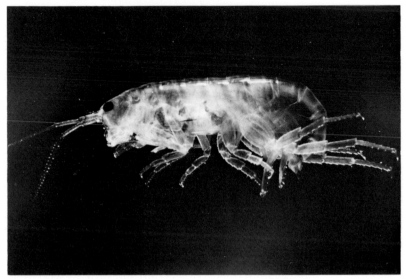

Figure 219

size or because they occur in more accessible habitats. Some of the amphipods are semiterrestrial, or even terrestrial, and inhabit the land at the edge of the sea. The semiterrestrial species are known as beach-hoppers because of their erratic hopping mode of locomotion. Most visitors to southern beaches are familiar with the beachhoppers which live beneath driftwood and stranded seaweed at the high tide line. They can often be found by overturning flotsam stranded on damp sand. When exposed, the amphipods hop furiously for a few seconds and then disappear suddenly. The species shown above, *Orchestia grillus* (0.7"; 1.8 cm), is common around the edges of higher salinity salt marshes. Another species, *Uhlorchestia uhleri* (0.5"; 1.3 cm), is found beside low salinity or freshwater tidal marshes. Still another, *Uhlorchestia spartinophila* (0.4"; 1 cm), lives in the salt marsh rather than on its edge. On outer beaches, the beachhoppers are larger and belong to the genus *Talorchestia*. Our two species are *Talorchestia megalophthalma* (0.8"; 2 cm) and *T. longicornis* (1.2"; 3 cm). Two truly terrestrial species, *Talitroides alluaudi* and *T. topitotum,* have been reported from the Charleston area and can be found there in humus and leaf litter near residences and in deciduous forests. These are Indo-Pacific species that have been introduced with exotic plants into greenhouses and sub-tropical areas of the United States.

Epifaunal Amphipods

Bigclaw Amphipod *Dulichiella appendiculata*

Almost every inshore benthic habitat supports several species of amphipod crustaceans, often in large numbers, but because of their

236

Figure 220

small size they are usually overlooked. Most species are similar to each other and specific identification is difficult. Only a few of the most common or distinctive species are discussed here. The epifaunal, or "fouling," community of sponges, bryozoans, hydroids, and tunicates, so widespread on hard bottoms, supports a wide variety of amphipod species. These epibenthic species, which are mostly about 0.5″ (1.3 cm) long or less, can be seen scurrying about on their sides over sponges and bryozoans that have been removed from the water. Many of them build tubes of mud, debris, algae, and their own secretions, whereas others roam freely over the surface.

Dulichiella appendiculata, shown above, is only one of the many common species in this habitat. Males of this species are easily recognized even in the field by their single enormous claw. No other amphipod in the Southeast has such a structure.

A number of small amphipods in the family Corophiidae build and inhabit mud tubes on hard substrata. Our several species of *Corophium* are grey, dorsoventrally depressed amphipods that resemble small isopods. They can be abundant and their tubes may form thick layers of mud on submerged objects. A *Corophium* and some of its tubes are present in Plate A27 with *Botryllus planus.*

Infaunal Amphipods

Spectacled Amphipod *Ampelisca verrilli*
Beach Digger *Haustorius canadensis*

Many of our amphipod species burrow into soft sandy or muddy

Figure 221

bottoms. Some inhabit more or less permanent burrows; others do not. Many of these species belong to the families Haustoriidae or Ampeliscidae. Sandy or silty sand beaches support many species of fat, soft-bodied, white, burrowing amphipods in many genera of the family Haustoriidae. They can be collected by passing sand, from either oceanic or protected beaches, through a fine sieve. These small crustaceans are usually less than 0.4″ (1 cm) in length and are often mistaken for immature mole crabs. *Haustorius canadensis* (0.5″; 1.3 cm) is the largest of these haustoriids. It is a characteristic member of the outer beach fauna where it inhabits intertidal sands. Other species are also found on outer beaches, and there are several species in the sand of protected beaches.

Another infaunal species, *Ampelisca verrilli* (0.6″; 1.5 cm), is a laterally compressed animal that lives in protected sand flats. It is the largest and most common of our *Ampelisca* species. *Ampelisca* species have four eyes, each with a thickened lens.

Skeleton Shrimps

Skeleton Shrimp *Caprella penantis*

The most distinctive of the benthic amphipods are the skeleton shrimps. These relatives of the beachhoppers have lost the abdomen and are modified for clinging to intricately branched objects. They have elongate cylindrical bodies and are sometimes called "worms" by fishermen and swimmers although upon close examination they are seen to

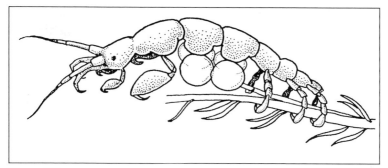

Figure 222

bear little resemblance to real worms. Most amphipods are laterally flattened and move with agility through the spaces in the habitat, but the cylindrical and elongate skeleton shrimps attach with their hind legs or move by creeping inchworm-fashion. There are three common species in our shallow coastal waters, and under appropriate conditions, they may be very common. They especially like hard bottoms with lush growths of bryozoans or hydroids and a strong flow of water. On pilings or jetties they may sometimes be present in staggering numbers. If dislodged from their attachments they cling to anything, including bathers, standing downstream.

We have three common species in shallow southeastern waters. Two members of the genus *Caprella, C. penantis* and *C. equilibra,* are fairly large (0.5″; 1.3 cm and 0.8″; 2 cm respectively) and have robust bodies and rows of long evenly spaced setae on the antennae. *Caprella penantis* has a small thornlike rostrum on the front of the head which *C. equilibra* lacks. Males of the latter have very long body segments. One form of *Caprella equilibra* is common on seawhips, especially during the winter months. *Paracaprella tenuis* is a small (0.4″; 1 cm), nondescript species that has no regularly arrayed setae on its antennae and has no rostrum.

Commercial Shrimps   *Color Plate C15*

Pink Shrimp *Penaeus duorarum*

Three species of large edible shrimps occur on the southeastern coast and all are found in shallow inshore waters. They are the pink shrimp, *Penaeus duorarum,* the brown shrimp, *P. aztecus,* and the white shrimp, *P. setiferus.* These are large shrimps that may reach 10″ (25 cm) in length, and they have antennae that are much longer than the body. They can be distinguished from most other shrimps by their three pairs of small pincers. With experience, the three species usually can be distinguished from each other on the basis of color and general appearance. Pink and brown shrimp have distinctive longitudinal grooves

239

that extend the entire length of the top of the carapace. The dorsal grooves of white shrimp are only about half as long as the carapace. Pink shrimp usually have a dark spot on either side of the abdomen between segments 3 and 4 that is usually lacking in our other two species. This spot is easily seen in Plate C15. In life the tail fan has a colored band across its outer edge. In pink shrimp this band is purple, in brown shrimp it is turquoise, and in white shrimp it is green. When all else fails, the width of the longitudinal grooves beside the dorsal median ridge of the last abdominal segment can be used to separate pink from brown shrimp: in pink shrimp these grooves are not wide enough to snag a human fingernail; in brown shrimp they are. White shrimp do not have these grooves.

The life cycles of these shrimps are similar although there are variations in detail depending on species and geographical location. In general, the shrimps spawn offshore as adults. The eggs hatch into planktonic larvae that make their way inshore into the upper regions of estuaries. Here they leave the plankton and begin to feed on small invertebrates, algae, and detritus on the bottom. For protection, they completely bury themselves, except for the eyes, in sand. They grow rapidly and gradually move down the estuary into increasingly saline water until they leave the estuary and move back offshore to spawn.

The closely related roughneck shrimp, *Trachypenaeus constrictus,* is similar but it never exceeds 4″ (10 cm) in length and is not commercially important. It has the three pairs of small pincers characteristic of the group, but it lacks teeth on the lower edge of the rostrum whereas all *Penaeus* species have teeth on both the upper and lower rostral margins.

Rock Shrimps

Brown Rock Shrimp *Sicyonia brevirostris*

The family Sicyoniidae includes the rock shrimps, none of which is common in shallow inshore waters. Juveniles are occasionally found on the rocks of jetties, among the rubble of tidal creek bottoms, or on the sand of protected beaches. Members of the family have very heavily calcified, stony exoskeletons and robust, stocky, shrimp-shaped bodies. As members of the penaeoid group of shrimps, the side plates of the abdominal segments each overlap that of the segment behind it. This contrasts with the caridean shrimps in which the side plate of the second abdominal segment overlaps the plates immediately in front of it as well as the one behind it. *Sicyonia brevirostris* is the largest of our rock shrimps, and mature specimens exceed 4″ (10 cm) in length, but individuals found in shallow water are usually less than 2″ (5 cm). This species is more common inshore than other species of *Sicyonia* but none is seen often.

Figure 223

Rock shrimps are carnivores that feed on a variety of benthic inverte-brates including bivalves, gastropods, polychaetes, crustaceans, and foraminiferans. They themselves are consumed by a variety of fishes and are harvested commercially in the Gulf of Mexico.

Caridean Shrimps   *Color Plate C16*

Grass Shrimp *Palaemonetes vulgaris*

There is a confusing assortment of small shrimps in our shallow coastal waters. Their identification is difficult, sometimes even for specialists, and is usually beyond the interest of amateurs. Of these small species, those most often noticed by casual observers are the grass shrimps, *Palaemonetes vulgaris* and *P. pugio,* often called "hardbacks" by fishermen. These two members of the family Palaemonidae are common in tidal creeks and salt marshes and around floating docks, oyster reefs, and pilings. They are less than 2″ (5 cm) long and are almost perfectly transparent and colorless except for a little orange *(P. vulgaris)* or yellow *(P. pugio)* pigment in the eyestalks. They are easily collected with a dipnet and can be maintained indefinitely in a saltwater aquar-ium on small pieces of frozen shrimp, lean raw beef, or hard-boiled egg yolk.

Species of *Palaemonetes* are often parasitized by a bopyrid isopod, *Probopyrus pandalicola,* which forms a conspicuous blister on one side of the carapace. This blister is inhabited by a large female isopod and a tiny male. The female is greatly modified and does not look like an

241

isopod but the male, which rides in a special seat on her posterior end, is obviously an isopod. The surface of the female is usually covered with masses of eggs.

Two commensal members of the family, *Neopontonides beaufortensis* (0.8"; 2 cm), the seawhip shrimp, and *Pontonia domestica* (1.2"; 3 cm), the pen clam shrimp, live with the seawhip, *Leptogorgia,* and pen clams in the genus *Atrina,* respectively. *Periclimenes longicaudatus* (0.8"; 2 cm) is a small, perfectly transparent shrimp that is common in submerged vegetation. *Periclimenes* is the host of a bopyrid isopod, *Schizobopyrina urocaridis.*

Small shrimps in the genus *Hippolyte* are also abundant in vegetation but belong to another family, the Hippolytidae. These shrimps, which belong to the species *H. pleuracanthus* and *H. zostericola,* are about 0.5" (1.3 cm) long and are usually brown, red, or bright green. They are very similar to each other and are sometimes considered to belong to the same species.

Snapping Shrimps *Color Plate C17*

Bigclaw Snapping Shrimp *Alpheus heterochaelis*

The snapping or pistol shrimps are recognized by their single, large, modified claw that is used to make a distinct popping or snapping sound. These noises are easily heard by human ears and are often noticed on exposed oyster reefs at low tide. In aquaria, the sound can be heard clearly across a large room and reportedly can break glass. The two fingers of the large pistol claw each bears a smooth flat disk at its base. When the movable finger is cocked, the two disks oppose each other with a thin film of water trapped between them. The cohesive force of the water holds the fingers open in opposition to the considerable force of the closing muscles of the pincer. When the cohesive forces between the disks are overcome, the disks separate, making a loud popping sound, and the fingers close. The concussion generated by the noise of the separating disks stuns small animals and is used by the shrimps to defend themselves and to capture prey.

There are many shallow-water snapping shrimps in the Southeast but only three are common. The bigclaw snapping shrimp, *Alpheus heterochaelis,* is the largest and most colorful, reaching about 2" (5 cm) in length. It is recognized by its color pattern, and its large claw has a notch in both the upper and lower margins at the base of the fingers. These notches are clearly visible on Plate C17 although one of them is partly hidden by the right antenna. This species is host of the bopyrid isopod, *Probopyria alphei.* A closely related species, the green snapping shrimp, *Alpheus normanni,* is smaller, reaching only about 1.2" (3 cm) in length, and has a notch and tooth on the upper edge of the large claw but not the lower. Its color is a drab brownish or greenish brown. It may also be infested by *P. alphei. Synalpheus fritzmuelleri,* the speckled snapping shrimp, is a smaller species. It reaches only about 0.8″ (2 cm) in length and has green claws. Under magnification, the body can be seen to be covered by numerous tiny red spots. *Synalpheus* is parasitized by the bopyrid isopod, *Hemiarthrus synalphei.*

Caridean Shrimps   *Color Plate C18*

Peppermint Shrimp *Lysmata wurdemanni*

The peppermint shrimp is one of the few easily identified small shrimps on our coast. Like many of our little shrimps, it has a transparent body but in this species the exoskeleton is attractively banded with bright red stripes that give the animal the appearance of a piece of peppermint candy. The eggs are bright green and a large female with a mass of eggs beneath the striped abdomen is a colorful sight. It reaches 2.8″ (7 cm) in length but is usually much smaller. It is common on rock jetties, but is rarely seen because it is mobile and fast. *Lysmata* is also found on tidal creek bottoms.

Peppermint shrimp belong to a group of crustaceans known as "cleaning shrimps" because of their practice of removing parasites and diseased tissue from the bodies of other animals, especially fishes and large crustaceans. This phenomenon is well known on tropical coral reefs, but our own shrimps are also reported to clean several species of local fishes including spiny boxfish and filefish. In aquaria they exhibit a characteristic and amusing side-to-side swaying motion and will move forward to approach an observer. They will settle on an arm or hand and move over it, presumably looking for parasites or loose skin.

The bushy, brown, arborescent bryozoan in Plate C18 is *Anguinella palmata.*

The long-eyed shrimps (family Ogyrididae), *Ogyrides hayi* (1″; 2.5 cm) and *O. alphaerostris* (0.6″; 1.5 cm), have very short rostrums and very long eyestalks. They are small transparent shrimps that live buried in sand. *Ogyrides hayi* has a single, tiny, movable spine just behind the rostrum and lives offshore or on silty sand beaches near inlets. It often has flecks of red and green pigment around the head and is parasitized by an undescribed bopyrid isopod. *Ogyrides alphaerostris* is smaller, has a row of many tiny immovable teeth behind the rostrum, and lives in muddy bottoms in estuaries.

Caridean Shrimps   *Color Plate C19*

Arrow Shrimp *Tozeuma carolinense*

These small, distinctively shaped shrimps are often found in grass beds in North Carolina and Florida but they are rare in South Carolina and Georgia. They are long and slender, achieving body lengths of about

2″ (5 cm). Each has a long sharp rostrum with smooth upper, and toothed lower, surface. The body is sharply bent at the third abdominal segment. A similar, but much less common, species, *T. serratum,* is larger, more robust, and has teeth on both upper and lower edges of its rostrum. It lives offshore on gorgonians. The little *Latreutes parvulus* (0.5″; 1.3 cm) belongs to the same family (Hippolytidae) and is sometimes common on bushy bryozoans. With a lens it can be seen to have a short, deep, toothy rostrum.

Two species of small shrimps belong to the gulfweed (*Sargassum*) community. One, *Latreutes fucorum,* is about 0.8″ (2 cm) long, pale transparent brown, yellow, or colorless, and often with bright blue spots. Its rostrum has no teeth on either the upper or lower edges. Like *Tozeuma* it belongs to the Hippolytidae. *Leander tenuicornis* resembles *Latreutes* and also lives on gulfweed, but it belongs to the Palaemonidae. It is usually about the size of *Latreutes,* but may reach almost 2″ (5 cm) in length. The body is brown or yellow and the rostrum has teeth on both the upper and lower edges.

The sand shrimp, *Crangon septemspinosa* (2.5″; 6 cm), is a common small shrimp of shallow water in the Northeast but it is rare in the South. It has a very short rostrum and subchelate claws which make it easily recognized. A subchelate claw has only one finger, which closes against a broad surface perpendicular to it, instead of the usual two fingers that close against each other. The body is slightly flattened from top to bottom and is transparent pale grey with small darker spots. In the North it may be found in large numbers in a variety of habitats, especially on sand, into which it burrows. The sand shrimp belongs to the family Crangonidae.

Ghost Shrimps

Ghost Shrimp *Callianassa biformis*

Among our shrimplike crustaceans are four species of mud and ghost shrimps that are actually more closely related to the hermit crabs than to the true shrimps. They have elongate bodies but tend to be flattened

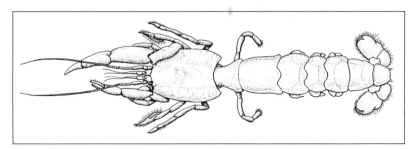

Figure 224

from top to bottom rather than from side to side. They belong to two genera, *Upogebia* (mud shrimps) and *Callianassa* (ghost shrimps). The former has one, the latter three, common species in the Southeast. All construct burrows in sand or mud and pump water through their burrow system with pistonlike abdominal appendages. Members of the genus *Callianassa* have a small smooth rostrum, and the two claws are usually unequal in size, often dramatically so. *Upogebia* has a fairly large, flat, spiny rostrum and claws of exactly the same size. *Callianassa* is more elongate and delicate than the robust *Upogebia*.

Callianassa major, the Carolinian ghost shrimp, is the largest of our ghost shrimps at about 4″ (10 cm) length. It lives on ocean beaches and is responsible for the profusion of small (0.2″; 5 mm) holes in the sand near the low tide line. These holes, often surrounded by a ring of small, brown fecal pellets, open into wider tunnels that may extend almost 6′ (2 m) into the sand. The animals move rapidly through their burrows, and it is very difficult to capture them by digging. One can often see a fountain of water welling out of these openings as the inhabitant ventilates the burrow or flushes unwanted sand and shell fragments from it. *Callianassa major* reportedly uses the hairy brushes on its anterior legs to sift sand for organic particles which it ingests. Little or no sand is consumed. Hermit crabs, and perhaps other beach animals, eat the fecal pellets of *Callianassa*. A small commensal crab, *Pinnixa cristata,* can usually be found in the burrow, where it takes advantage of the flow of oxygenated and food-rich water. A tiny orange copepod, *Clausidium caudatum,* is sometimes found in pairs on or under the carapace of *C. major* and other *Callianassa* species. Other species in the genus, *Callianassa atlantica* and *C. biformis,* are similar to but smaller than *C. major*. Both dig their burrows in the silty sand of protected beaches or bays. *Callianassa atlantica* occasionally reaches 2.8″ (7 cm) in length, but is usually smaller. It too is often accompanied by *Pinnixa cristata* or an undescribed species very much like it. *Callianassa biformis,* the smallest species at 1.2″ (3 cm) length, is the most common. Females of this species have equal claws, unlike other *Callianassa*.

Mud Shrimps

Coastal Mud Shrimp *Upogebia affinis*

Upogebia affinis (2.5″; 6 cm), the coastal mud shrimp, builds burrows and galleries in silty sand or mud. Glands in the abdomen secrete mucus that consolidates the sediment surrounding the burrows. *Upogebia* burrows often have many branches containing several individuals and have multiple openings to the surface. As is the case with *Callianassa major,* the burrow narrows markedly just before opening at the surface. The shrimps probably do not voluntarily leave their burrows and, if removed from them, do not seem to be capable of digging back into the

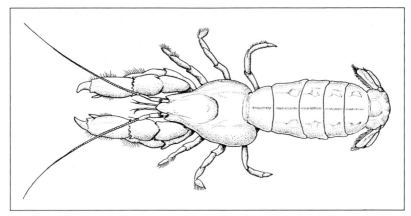

Figure 225

sediment. *Upogebia* ventilates the burrow by rhythmic motion of the circular flaplike abdominal appendages (pleopods). Mud shrimps are thought to be filter feeders which use the setae of the mouthparts to filter organic matter from the respiratory current. The equal claws and flat triangular rostrum distinguish this genus from *Callianassa.*

Several commensal animals live with *Upogebia,* including the flatworm, *Stylochus ellipticus,* the shrimp, *Leptalpheus forceps,* the copepod, *Hemicyclops adhaerens,* the crab, *Pinnixa sayana,* and the polychaete worm, *Parahesione luteola. Hemicyclops* has also been reported from the burrows of the mantis shrimp, *Squilla empusa.* Mud shrimp are sometimes parasitized by the bopyrid isopod, *Pseudione upogebiae,* which forms a large bulge on one side of the carapace. Either the right or left branchial chamber may be infested. The left branchial chamber of the individual in the drawing is infested. Bopyrid females are usually asymmetrical and may be curved either to the right or left depending on which side of the branchial cavity they inhabit. The two forms, dextral and sinistral, are mirror images of each other and both occur in most species of bopyrids.

Spiny Lobsters   *Color Plate C20*

Caribbean Spiny Lobster *Panulirus argus*

Spiny lobsters are the Southeast's gastronomic counterpart of the American lobster, *Homarus americanus* (2′; 61 cm), of commercial importance in the Northeast. Spiny lobsters (1.5′; 46 cm) range from North Carolina to Brazil and Bermuda, whereas American lobsters are rarely found south of Cape Hatteras. The American lobster resembles a giant crayfish with smooth carapace and large claws, but the spiny lobster lacks claws altogether and has a spiny carapace. Both have large, powerful, muscular abdomens. Spiny lobsters support a commercial fishery in the Florida Keys, the Caribbean, and northern Brazil.

Spiny lobsters undergo mass migrations in the fall. For unknown reasons, individuals march head to tail in queues including as many as 50 animals. They march continuously day and night and can cover up to 31 miles (50 km) in several days. *Panulirus* mates and spawns during the spring and summer once it reaches a length of about 8″ (20 cm) and a female can produce up to 4 million eggs in a season. The eggs hatch and become spidery phyllosoma larvae. This curious juvenile looks nothing like a lobster and is large, flat, and transparent. It rides about on jellyfishes, undergoing a series of molts, to become a young lobster of about 2″ (5 cm) in the first year. Spiny lobsters achieve full size in about 18 years. *Panulirus* eats a variety of prey, including hermit crabs.

Hermit Crabs   *Color Plate C21*

Striped Hermit Crab *Clibanarius vittatus*

We have three species of hermits common along the shoreline and several others in deeper water. The three common shallow-water species are the striped hermit, the long-wristed hermit, and the flat-clawed hermit. Most easily recognized is the fairly large, striped hermit, *Clibanarius vittatus,* which is often stranded on mud flats and oyster reefs by the ebbing tide. *Clibanarius* is more tolerant of desiccation than our other hermits and easily survives this exposure. It is dark brown with white stripes on the legs and claws. The two cylindrical claws are relatively small and are equal in size. The individual in Plate C21 is in a knobbed whelk shell about 4″ (10 cm) long. *Clibanarius* belongs to the family Diogenidae as do *Petrochirus* and *Dardanus.* Members of this family have more or less similarly sized chelae or, if unequal, the left is larger than the right.

All of our hermit crabs live in old snail shells, coiling their long, soft, asymmetrical bodies up into the shell for protection. As they grow they must find ever larger shells to accommodate their growing bodies, for without the protection of a shell they are easy targets for predators. A short supply of suitable snail shells often limits the size of hermit crab populations, and much interaction between individuals centers around disputes over shell ownership. Large crabs often evict smaller crabs if the small crab happens to inhabit a large shell. Individuals living in shells that are too small have decreased growth rates and females in this situation produce fewer eggs than females in roomier shells.

Hermit Crabs   *Color Plate C22*

Giant Red Hermit Crab *Petrochirus diogenes*

Among our several offshore hermits a few warrant brief mention. *Petrochirus diogenes* (7″; 18 cm) is our largest hermit and its juveniles

247

are sometimes found inshore. These crabs are red and have unequal, heavy, knobby pincers. Like the striped hermit, *Clibanarius,* they belong to the family Diogenidae. *Petrochirus* is often accompanied by the porcellanid crab, *Porcellana sayana,* a small, flat, pink and white species. The anemone, *Calliactis tricolor,* which also associates with the flat-clawed hermit, *Pagurus pollicaris,* is also found on shells inhabited by *Petrochirus.* The crab in Plate C22 has several of these anemones on its shell. Two individuals can be seen on the shoulder of the shell on the left of the photograph. One of these anemones is retracted, the other expanded. *Petrochirus* occurs in shallow water in south Florida.

Another offshore genus in this family is *Dardanus* of which we have two species. *Dardanus* also has unequal pincers, the left being much larger than the right. Our two species are difficult to distinguish but in *D. fucosus* the next to the last joint of the second left walking leg is very hairy and has a longitudinal ridge and groove on its outside surface. *Dardanus insignis* has none of these features. Members of this family have been observed killing and removing snails from their shells in order to provide themselves with a home.

Hermit Crabs

Flat-clawed Hermit Crab *Pagurus pollicaris*

Many of our shallow-water hermit crabs belong to the family Paguridae. Members of this family always have the right claw larger than the left. The flat-clawed hermit, *Pagurus pollicaris,* while the less

Figure 226

common of our two shallow-water pagurid species, is far from rare. It is about the same size as the striped hermit, *Clibanarius,* but is pale off-white and is not striped. The two broad flat claws are unequal in size and lock together neatly to form an operculum when the crab withdraws into its shell. These crabs are the hosts of a variety of commensal inverte-brates including the anemone *Calliactis tricolor,* the flatworm, *Styl-ochus zebra,* and the polychaete scaleworm, *Lepidonotus sublevis.* The slipper snails, *Crepidula fornicata* and *C. convexa,* often occur on the outside of the shell while another slipper snail, *Crepidula plana,* prefers the inside of the shell aperture.

Our most common hermit crab is the small long-wristed hermit, *Pagurus longicarpus,* which is usually less than 1″ (2.5 cm) in length. It is beige or off-white, without color pattern, and has two cylindrical claws of different sizes. This hermit is an omnivore that feeds primarily on detritus but can also turn on its back in shallow water and gather sea foam with its outstretched appendages. This foam, like beaten egg white, is protein. The hydroid, *Hydractinia echinata,* occasionally forms a low furry and spiny layer on the shell. This hermit may be seen in the photograph of *Hydractinia* (Fig. 94).

Two other small *Pagurus* species that are common in deeper water, especially offshore, may also be found in harbors and larger tidal creeks. They are about the size of *P. longicarpus* and like it, have claws of different sizes. Unlike it, they have distinctive color patterns that permit rapid identification. *Pagurus annulipes,* which is fairly common sub-tidally in estuaries, has broad, transverse, reddish bands on the claws and legs. *Pagurus carolinensis,* which is not often found inshore, has numerous thin, interrupted, longitudinal, brownish lines on the joints of the legs.

Pagurus longicarpus and *P. annulipes* are parasitized by the ento-niscid isopod, *Paguritherium alatum. Pagurus longicarpus* is also host to the bopyrid isopod *Asymmetrione desultor* and *Pagurus annulipes* to *Pseudasymmetrione markhami.*

Porcelain Crabs   *Color Plate C23*

Eroded Porcelain Crab *Megalobrachium soriatum*
Cherry-Striped Porcelain Crab *Petrolisthes galathinus*

Petrolisthes galathinus is an inhabitant of rock and coral in high salinity water. These small flat crabs are less than 0.8″ (2 cm) long and belong to the family Porcellanidae, which includes *Euceramus,* one of the "mole" crabs discussed elsewhere. The upper surface of the back and claws of *Petrolisthes* are ornamented with bright, cherry-red, transverse ridges. *Megalobrachium soriatum* (0.3″; 8 mm) is a small, flat por-cellanid that also lives on rocks and coral. It has a rough bumpy surface rather than the ridged surface of *Petrolisthes.* Our best known porcelain crab, *Polyonyx gibbesi* (0.6″; 1.5 cm), is one of the two species of crabs that live commensally with the parchment tube worm, *Chaetopterus variopedatus.* It is rarely found elsewhere and can be distinguished from the second species, *Pinnixa chaetopterana,* by the large fringed claws and long antennae. Still another porcellanid, *Porcellana sayana* (0.5″; 1.3 cm), has a reddish-brown or pinkish back with white spots. It lives commensally with some of the hermit crabs. All porcellanids are filter feeders. Many porcelain crabs, including *Petrolisthes galathinus* and *Porcellana sayana,* are parasitized by the bopyrid isopod, *Aporobopyrus curtatus,* which lives in the gill chamber.

Mole Crabs

**Square-Eyed Mole Crab *Lepidopa websteri*
Slender-Eyed Mole Crab *Albunea paretii***

The two most common mole crabs in the silty sand of inlets and quiet beaches are *Lepidopa websteri* and *Albunea paretii* (both about 1″; 2.5 cm in body length). They are similar, with antennae much longer than the short, wide body. The back is white with iridescent pinkish highlights. They differ in the shapes of their eyestalks. In both species the eyestalks are short, inconspicuous, flat, white plates at the front end of the animal. Those of *Lepidopa* are about as long as wide and are shaped like a lopsided square. The eyestalks of *Albunea,* while about as long as those of *Lepidopa,* are much narrower. The tiny black eyes are clearly

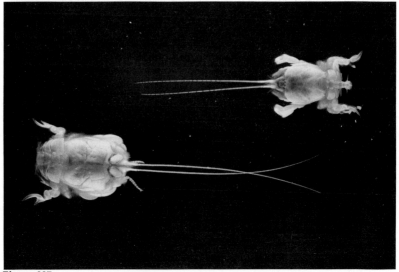

Figure 227

visible at the tip of the stalk. Both of these animals burrow backwards into silty sand, but little is known about their ecology and feeding. Another species, *A. gibbesii,* is not often found in shallow water.

Euceramus praelongus, in the family Porcellanidae, is the only other molelike crab occurring regularly in shallow quiet water but it is not frequently seen. It is greenish grey and more elongate than the above species. The front edge of the head is extended forward to form a broad three-toothed rostrum over the eyestalks. The antennae are shorter than the body and the last (5th) legs are very thin and spindly and are held above the back. *Euceramus* differs from all other molelike crabs in having chelate pincers. The common mole crab, *Emerita,* has no pincers, and both *Lepidopa* and *Albunea* have subchelate pincers.

Mole Crabs

Common Mole Crab *Emerita talpoida*

Mole crabs have no pincers and the shape of the body is modified for rapid digging in wet sand. There are several more or less similar species of uncrablike burrowing crustaceans that are known collectively as mole crabs but *Emerita* is by far the most familiar and is a characteristic inhabitant of the swash zone of ocean beaches. Other mole crab species are usually restricted to the silty sand of quieter waters.

Emerita talpoida is a football-shaped, beige or purplish crab less than 2″ (5 cm) in length. It has a fairly well-developed, pointed abdomen folded beneath the ovoid body. The antennae are short and fuzzy. The

Figure 228

animals burrow backwards into the sand in the swash zone, facing the sea, and hold the antennae above the sand surface. As the water of spent waves flows in thin sheets back to the sea it passes through these antennae which filter food particles from it. The crabs migrate continuously up and down the beach to maintain their position near the tide line. The animal in Figure 228 is beginning to burrow into the sand. Its posterior end is pointing down on the left and its head, with clearly visible antennae and eyestalks, is on the right.

A second species, *E. benedicti,* is less common and is reported from shelly bottoms in shallow water. The last segment of the first leg of *E. benedicti* is sharply pointed, that of *E. talpoida* bluntly pointed.

Sponge Crabs   *Color Plate C24*

Hairy Sponge Crab *Dromidia antillensis*

These remarkable crabs hide themselves by holding large pieces of sponge or colonial tunicate against the back. The hind legs, which can be seen on the crab in Plate C24, are modified for this purpose. This crab has a fuzzy, strongly arched back that fits into a recession in the sponge or tunicate but this covering is not permanently attached and does not grow to the crab. These crabs are fairly common on tidal creek bottoms and offshore in the southern part of the Carolinian Province but are rare in the Carolinas.

The crabs are about 1.2″ (3 cm) long (and wide) with variable color and thick bodies. The crab in the photograph is covered by the colonial tunicate, *Didemnum psammathodes.*

A related genus, *Hypoconcha* (the shellback crabs), contains three species in the southeastern United States. These crabs always carry a single clam valve over their back. The crab's soft and weakly arched back fits perfectly into the concavity of the shell, which is held firmly in place by the hind pair of legs. The crab holds to this shell so tightly that it cannot be removed without damaging the crab. These crabs are about 1″ (2.5 cm) or less in length and have thin bodies. They resemble hermit crabs in their habit of using a discarded mollusc shell for protection. They are not closely related to hermit crabs however and differ from them in many respects including the use of a clam valve instead of a snail shell. These subtidal animals are not often encountered in shallow water, especially in the Carolinas. *Hypoconcha arcuata* is probably the species most likely to occur in shallow water.

Box Crabs   *Color Plate C25*

Calico Box Crab *Hepatus epheliticus*
Flamed Box Crab *Calappa flammea*

The box crabs have thick bodies and wide flat claws that hide the face when they bury themselves in sand. When the claws are held against the face they enclose a respiratory antechamber that excludes sand. Water enters this antechamber, passes into the gill chamber under the carapace, flows over the gills, and then exits in strong jets via openings beside the mouth. These crabs are subtidal, mostly offshore, species that occasionally wash onto beaches. The most frequently seen box crab is the calico box crab, *Hepatus epheliticus* (3″; 7.5 cm), which lives on tidal creek bottoms as well as offshore. The calico crab has a smooth back decorated with distinctive, large, reddish-brown spots. The anemone, *Calliactis tricolor,* sometimes occurs on the carapace of *Hepatus.* A much less common species, *Hepatus pudibundus* (the flecked box crab), has a similar shape but its back is covered by small purplish spots. It is an offshore species not seen in shallow water.

Members of the genus *Calappa* are rarely seen alive near the shore but are fairly common offshore in deeper water. Their shape is similar to that of *Hepatus,* but the sides and hind margins of the body bear large jagged teeth which are lacking in *Hepatus.* The claws are large and, like those of *Hepatus,* are held in front of the face as if the crab is ashamed or bashful. They are sometimes called "shameface crabs." *Calappa flammea,* which reaches 5″ (13 cm) in width, is the most common species in this genus but there are others in our area. Juveniles of *C. flammea* are occasionally found in shallow water but specific identification of juveniles is difficult. Species of *Calappa* feed on clams, snails, and hermit crabs, which they expose by chipping away the shell margins. *Calappa* is an important host of the tiny stalked goose barnacle, *Octolasmis hoeki,* which lives externally on the shell as well as in the gill chamber. Sometimes both *O. hoeki* and the more common *O. muelleri* may be present on a single crab with the former outside and the latter in the gill chamber.

Purse Crabs

Mottled Purse Crab *Persephona mediterranea*

Mottled purse crabs, *Persephona mediterranea,* can achieve body lengths of about 2.5″ (6 cm) but are usually smaller. This species has a fat round body with a short, squared off, anterior end and three posterior points. The back has tiny bumps on its surface. The abdomen, which is folded forward under the body as in all true crabs, forms a large, deep, purselike pocket. The egg mass is brooded in this pocket and is protected from abrasion when the crab backs into the sand to bury itself. The body and legs are pale with diffuse reddish, brownish, or purple mottling, and the claws are long and slender. These crabs live in shallow water offshore and are often washed onto beaches after storms. When this happens they can be collected alive and maintained in sand-bottomed aquaria on a diet of frozen shrimp. Purse crabs bury them-

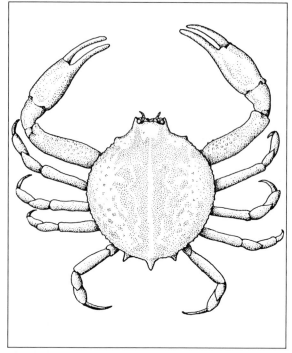

Figure 229

selves in sediment with only the tip of the rostrum extending above the sediment surface. *Persephona* does not reverse the direction of water flow through its gill chamber even though it burrows in sand. Water enters the gill chamber, as it does in most crabs, via an incurrent aperture at the base of the legs and exits through excurrent apertures beside the mouth. Some crabs, especially sand-dwelling species, reverse this flow to reduce the amount of sand entering the gill chamber.

Spider Crabs

Spider Crab *Libinia dubia*
Arrow Crab *Stenorhynchus seticornis*

There are two large species of spider crabs in the genus *Libinia* on this coast, and they are difficult to distinguish as juveniles. Both are common and are often found in shallow quiet water or washed ashore on beaches. They have more or less globose, spiny, brown bodies, with a prominent, often forked, rostrum. The long thin legs and fat body give them a spidery appearance. The legs end in curved points which collectively grip firmly onto irregular or flexible surfaces. *Libinia dubia* is a little smaller than its relative, *L. emarginata,* and reaches about 4″ (10

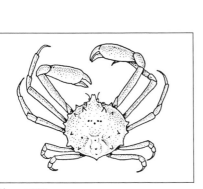

Figure 230   Figure 231

cm) in body length. Mature specimens of *L. dubia* have a longitudinal row of six bumps along the middle of the back, while those of *L. emarginata* have nine of these bumps. Juveniles of both species are often found riding on jellyfishes, especially cannonball jellies. The crabs apparently feed on the jellies. Juvenile crabs living on the bottom decorate themselves with some sponge or other material but they abandon this habit as they mature.

Pelia mutica, a small member of the spider crab family, is fairly common on rocky jetties and creek bottoms in high salinity water but it is not often noticed. It has a pear-shaped body less than 0.6″ (1.5 cm) long which is usually covered by red, orange, or yellow sponge. The crab attaches some living sponge to its back and legs and fastens it in place on special spines adapted for that purpose. The sponge remains alive and grows, eventually covering and camouflaging the entire body and legs.

There are several other species of crabs belonging to the group collectively known as spider crabs but none of them occurs commonly in shallow water in our area. One of many tropical species, the distinctive, yellow-lined arrow crab (2.5″; 6.5 cm), *Stenorhynchus seticornis,* has a smooth, triangular, striped, brown body with a long pointed rostrum. It does not decorate. The figures of *Libinia* and *Stenorhynchus* are not drawn to the same scale. Mature *Libinia* are much larger than *Stenorhynchus.*

255

Cancer Crabs   *Color Plate C26*

Rock Crab *Cancer irroratus*
Jonah Crab *Cancer borealis*

The rock crab, *Cancer irroratus* (5.5″; 14 cm) and the Jonah crab, *C. borealis* (4″; 10 cm), are northern species that occur on the continental shelf off the southeastern coast and occasionally stray into shallow southern waters. Juveniles and infrequent adults, especially of *C. irroratus,* appear on southern jetties and tidal creek bottoms in the cold winter months. As juveniles the two species are very difficult to distinguish. Both have roughly elliptical bodies and the front and sides have large blunt teeth or lobes. The hind margin is smooth, and the last pair of legs is not paddlelike. Adults of the two species are easily told apart by the large blunt teeth on the front and sides of the carapace. The edges of these teeth are saw-toothed in *C. borealis* and are smooth in *C. irroratus. Cancer irroratus* is more common than *C. borealis* in the Southeast. The animals in Plate C26 were collected in New England. Within their normal range, rock crabs are usually found on inshore rocky bottoms, whereas Jonah crabs tend to prefer sandy offshore bottoms.

Swimming Crabs   *Color Plate C27*

Blue Crab *Callinectes sapidus*

Blue crabs belong to the swimming crab family, Portunidae, whose members (with one exception) have a pair of flat oarlike hind legs. There are several members of this family on the southeastern coast of the United States and many of them are common. One species, the blue crab, *Callinectes sapidus* (8″; 20 cm), supports an important commercial fishery and is the largest of the group. The body of this crab is strongly flattened, wider than long, and has a long point or spike on each side. The front and side margins are saw-toothed whereas the hind margin is smooth. The back is usually olive green or greenish brown with tiny, obscure, light spots. The claws and legs are at least partially blue, but females have orange on the fingers. The undersurface is white. Adult blue crabs cannot be confused with any crabs except other members of the genus *Callinectes,* which they resemble closely. *Callinectes similis* (the lesser blue crab) and *Callinectes ornatus* also occur in the Southeast. Both of these species have six teeth between the eye sockets whereas the blue crab has only four. These two species are very difficult to tell apart, even for specialists. Neither exceeds 4.7″ (12 cm) in width, including spines. In the Carolinas the lesser blue crab is more common than *C. ornatus,* which increases in importance farther south.

Female blue crabs spawn in high salinity lower estuaries or the nearby ocean where the eggs hatch into planktonic larvae. These larvae begin development in the sea and then migrate into estuaries, settle to the bottom and continue growth and periodic molting to become mature adults. Mating occurs in the upper estuary in low salinity water. The females then migrate back to high salinity areas to spawn but the males usually do not leave the upper estuaries. Blue crabs have a varied diet and, as predators, will attack many species of animals, including fiddler crabs. Sometimes they lie barely submerged in the shallow edge of tidal creeks and ambush passing fiddler crabs. They will also eat dead or moribund animals.

Several commensals live with blue crabs and the photograph (Pl. C27) shows the crab barnacle, *Chelonibia patula,* which is found only on the backs of crabs and horseshoe crabs. Other species of barnacles, especially *Balanus amphitrite,* may also be found on crabs, but these occur elsewhere as well. A tiny goose barnacle, *Octolasmis muelleri,* lives on the gills of the crab. A small orange or white ribbon worm, *Carcinonemertes carcinophila,* also lives in the gills but preys on the egg mass. The large barnacle, *Loxothylacus texanus,* grows funguslike through the tissues of the crab and protrudes as a large soft mass beneath the abdomen. These parasites look like a crab egg mass and bear no resemblance to free-living barnacles.

Swimming Crabs   *Color Plate C28*

Lady Crabs
Ovalipes ocellatus
Ovalipes stephensoni

The two crabs in the photograph, often found on outer beaches, are swimming crabs belonging to the genus *Ovalipes.* Notice the presence of the distinctive swimming paddles on the hind legs which marks them as members of the Portunidae. These two *Ovalipes* species are the only swimming crabs on our coast that have bodies about as long as wide instead of wider than long. The ocellated lady crab, *Ovalipes ocellatus* (3.5″; 9 cm), is distinctively marked with purple spots on the back while the coarse-handed lady crab, *O. stephensoni* (3″; 7.6 cm), has no such spots. The former lives close inshore and is often washed onto beaches while the latter lives farther offshore and is less commonly seen. The young are more likely to be found on beaches than are the adults. *Ovalipes* buries itself shallowly in the sand by digging backwards. Most crabs ventilate the gills by pumping water in through openings at the bases of the legs and out through openings beside the mouth. Some sand-burrowing crabs, such as *Ovalipes,* reverse the direction of water flow to facilitate burrowing backwards in sand. The reversed flow reduces intake of sand into the gill chamber and the posterior outflow helps loosen the sand for burrowing backwards. Interestingly, the commensal barnacle, *Octolasmis muelleri,* lives on the opposite side of the gill chamber in *Ovalipes* than it does in crabs with normal flow direction.

Swimming Crabs

Speckled Crab *Arenaeus cribrarius*

The speckled crab, *Arenaeus cribrarius* (5.5″; 14 cm), is another member of the swimming crab family that is common in shallow water on outer ocean beaches. It spends much of its time in the sand, sometimes completely covered by it. It enters the sand backwards and almost vertically by flipping sand with its claws. Once hidden, a clear channel for exhalent water is maintained by the claws and a fringe of heavy setae beside the mouth parts. Speckled crabs live in or on the sand and are shaped, but not colored, like blue crabs. The body is much wider than long and has a sharp spike on either side. The back is tan or grey with numerous small distinct, white or pale tan, round spots of various sizes. Juveniles often have a large white area that is easily mistaken for a shell fragment when the animal is partially covered by sand. As swimming crabs, they have distinctive flat paddles on the last pair of legs but they are easily distinguished from *Ovalipes,* the other characteristic swimming crab of the outer beach, by body shape. It is easily told from blue crabs and other swimming crabs that may occur on outer beaches by its color pattern.

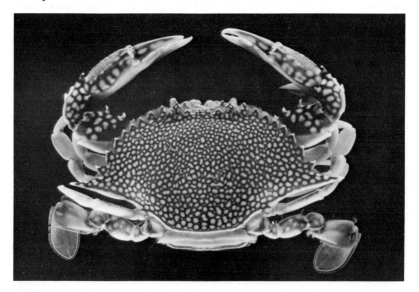

Figure 232

258

The green crab, *Carcinas maenas,* does not occur in the Southeast but is a common shallow-water and estuarine crab in the Northeast. It belongs to the swimming crab family but has no paddle on the hind leg. Its body is a little longer than wide (3″ × 2.5″; 7.6 cm × 6.4 cm) and it is shaped more like a lady crab than a blue crab. The back is usually greenish and has three blunt teeth between the eyes and five on each side. It is a common crab in Europe.

Swimming Crabs   *Color Plate C29*

Blotched Swimming Crab *Portunus spinimanus*

Two additional members of the family Portunidae, *Portunus spinimanus* (4.5″; 11 cm) and *P. gibbesii* (3″; 7.6 cm) occur commonly on our coast. They occur on creek bottoms and offshore but are not usually noticed because they live subtidally. They are occasionally seen in shallow water and are sometimes found on rock jetties. Like other swimming crabs, they have a pair of paddlelike hind legs. Their bodies are shaped more or less like those of blue crabs and speckled crabs, being wider than long and armed with a long spike on each side of the body. This shape prevents their being confused with the lady crabs (*Ovalipes*). They are best distinguished from blue crabs and speckled swimming crabs by their color as they lack the blue and red-orange of the former and the uniformly speckled back of the latter. These two *Portunus* species are often found together on tidal creek bottoms and are most easily distinguished from each other by the presence of a purple spot on the swimming paddle of *Portunus gibbesii* and the usually dark brown back and red-brown and white fingers of adult *P. spinimanus.* The tooth on the side of the body is small in *P. spinimanus* and long in *P. gibbesii.* A third species, *P. sayi* (2.5″; 6.4 cm), the sargassum swimming crab, is a member of the community associated with floating *Sargassum* (gulfweed). This pelagic species does not normally occur inshore unless washed in on *Sargassum.* Its yellow-brown color renders it inconspicuous on the weed and it is smaller than other species of *Portunus.*

Mud Crabs

Atlantic Mud Crab *Panopeus herbstii*
Hairy Crab *Pilumnus sayi*

The mud crabs, family Xanthidae, comprise a large and confusing group of mostly small crabs. Of the numerous species on the southeastern coast, only five or six are seen regularly but these can be very common. The saltmarsh mud crab, *Panopeus obesus,* and the broadbacked mud crab, *Eurytium limosum,* are restricted to salt marshes. They and the stone crab are discussed elsewhere.

Figure 233

Pilumnus sayi (1.2″; 3 cm), is easily recognized by its light brown and purplish, hairy, spiny body. There are several members of the genus *Pilumnus* but this is the most common. The Atlantic mud crab, *Panopeus herbstii,* is our largest mud crab with the exception of the Florida stone crab, and it reaches 2.5″ (6.4 cm) in width. It is common in the mud of oyster reefs but is found in other habitats also. It has black fingers on the claws and the movable finger of the larger claw bears a large conspicuous tooth at its base. *Panopeus herbstii* is parasitized by the entonioscid isopod, *Cancrion carolinus.*

The flatbacked mud crab, *Eurypanopeus depressus,* is also common on oysters (and elsewhere) but is a small species less than 1″ (2.5 cm) in width. Its back is nearly flat and the fingers of its small hand are scoop-shaped at the tips. Living specimens usually have flecks of bright blue pigment around the mouth. *Neopanope sayi* is common in a variety of habitats and is less than 1.2″ (3 cm) wide. The fingers are dark brown or black and do not have a large tooth at the base although they are slightly hooked at the tips. Another small species, *Rhithropanopeus harrisii* (0.8″; 2 cm), may be common on oysters in low salinity water. It has pale fingers that lack large teeth and the foward edge of the carapace between the eyes is double.

Mud Crabs   *Color Plate C30*

Florida Stone Crab *Menippe mercenaria*

Mud crabs of the family Xanthidae are well represented on the southeastern coast. Most members of the family are less than 1.5″ (3.8

cm) wide but the stone crab is much larger. Stone crabs are common along our coast and this is an important commercial species especially to the south. These are large robust crabs, reaching 5″ (13 cm) in body width, with massive claws. They are not pugnacious and are sluggish in comparison with blue crabs but should nevertheless be treated with respect as they can easily crush a finger with their powerful claws. Adults are brown or tan with a smooth oval back and the fingers of the claws are black. The juveniles also have smooth oval backs but they are a rich, deep, glossy purple (Pl. A29), often with one or two tiny white spots. The purple is gradually replaced by grey, then tan, as the crabs grow and mature. The individual in the photograph (Pl. C30) is losing the juvenile purple and will soon adopt the adult tan. Stone crabs feed on a variety of invertebrates including acorn barnacles and oysters of all sizes, which they crush and open with their claws. Stone crabs have a massive crusher claw and a smaller pincer claw. The inside surface of each palm bears numerous parallel ridges which are rubbed against the carapace to produce sound. Note the dense population of the barnacle, *Chthamalus fragilis,* on the rock in the photograph (Pl. C30).

Although stone crabs are common on rock jetties, most adults construct deep burrows in soft sediments. The mouth of the burrow is usually a broad conical depression in which the crab often sits. Many other invertebrates inhabit these burrows.

Mud Crabs   *Color Plate C31*

Broadbacked Mud Crab *Eurytium limosum*

In the grassy expanses of *Spartina* salt marsh along the southeastern coast there are four common species of small crabs in addition to the easily recognized fiddler crabs. Whereas other species live in the associated tidal creeks and oyster reefs, in the marsh itself there are only the wharf crab, *Sesarma cinereum,* the marsh crab, *Sesarma reticulatum,* the saltmarsh mud crab, *Panopeus obesus,* and the broadbacked mud crab, *Eurytium limosum.*

On the Atlantic coast, *Eurytium* is common only in Georgia and Florida although it is widespread along the Gulf of Mexico and in the Caribbean. It is rare or absent in the Carolinas. It belongs to the Xanthidae, a large family of mostly small crabs, known as the mud crabs, of which the best known member is the stone crab. Unlike most of the mud crabs, the broadbacked mud crab is colorful and easily recognized by its bright white fingers, orangish claws, and purple back. Like most of the mud crabs, it is shaped more or less like a small stone crab and has a smooth oval back. It does not exceed 1.6″ (4 cm) in width and has no large teeth on the fingers of the pincers. It digs burrows in the mud of the lower intertidal zone of *Spartina* salt marshes.

The saltmarsh mud crab, *Panopeus obesus,* also digs burrows in the mud of salt marshes and is similar in size and shape. *Panopeus obesus* has black or brown fingers, one of which has a conspicuous large tooth at its base. The other two saltmarsh crabs, which are both species of *Sesarma,* have square, not oval, backs, and are not likely to be confused with the mud crabs. They are discussed elsewhere.

Shore Crabs

Tidal Spray Crab *Plagusia depressa*

Two species of agile crabs are frequently found at the water's edge on wharves, floating docks, and jetties in high salinity water on or near outer coasts. Both have flat bodies and belong to the Grapsidae. The mottled shore crab, *Pachygrapsus transversus,* reaches 0.8″ (2 cm) in body width and has a more or less square or trapezoidal, dark green body with an untoothed front margin. The outer ends of the largest joints (meri) of the legs bear teeth on their *hind* margins. In the tropics, *Pachygrapsus transversus* is parasitized by the bopyrid isopod, *Leidya bimini.*

Plagusia depressa, which reaches 2.4″ (6.1 cm) in body width, is variously colored, reddish, greenish, or orangish. The body is nearly circular in outline with a toothed front margin. The largest segments (meri) of the walking legs have teeth on the *front* edge.

A third grapsid species, *Planes minutus,* the gulfweed crab, is found on floating objects, often *Sargassum* weed but also on turtles. It has a circular untoothed body. The joints of the legs do not bear obvious teeth. These crabs do not exceed 0.8″ (2 cm) in width and are variously

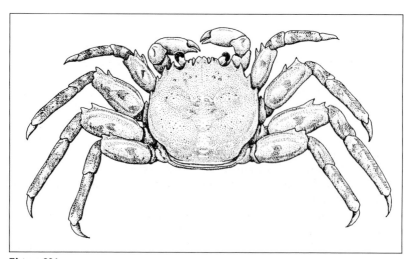

Figure 234

colored. They should not be confused with the small swimming crab, *Portunus sayi,* which also lives on *Sargassum* but has a paddle-shaped hind leg which is lacking in *Planes.*

Shore Crabs   *Color Plate C32*

Marsh Crab *Sesarma reticulatum*
Wharf Crab *Sesarma cinereum*

Two species of crabs in the genus *Sesarma* are common in southeastern salt marshes. These crabs subdivide the marsh habitat and each species is associated with a different and characteristic region of the marsh. *Sesarma cinereum,* variously known as the wharf crab, squareback marsh crab, or friendly crab, prefers the higher areas of the marsh, including the supralittoral fringe above the high tide mark. It is often seen scurrying over dry land or across docks or pilings. It prefers sandy sediments and salinities around 30 parts per thousand. It constructs burrows under boards and driftwood at the marsh edge. The body is less than 0.8″ (2 cm) in width, dark brown, thin, flat and square.

Sesarma reticulatum, the marsh crab, prefers lower, muddier areas of the marsh and is most common in areas with salinities around 20 parts per thousand. It is not terrestrial and does not venture above the high tide line. It constructs a burrow whose opening is surrounded by a mud chimney. Like *S. cinereum,* it has a square back but the body is thicker and heavier and is purplish-black or dark brown. These crabs are a little larger than the wharf crab, reaching 1.1″ (2.8 cm) in width and the last few joints of the middle legs are very fuzzy.

Commensal Crabs   *Color Plate C33*

Oyster Pea Crab *Pinnotheres ostreum*

Adult oyster pea crabs, *Pinnotheres ostreum* (0.4″; 1 cm), usually live on the gills of oysters where they steal food, but are occasionally found on other clams. Large adult crabs damage the oyster's gill tissue and interfere with growth. The crabs are specialized for this semiparasitic existence within the safety of the oyster shell and have thin spindly legs and a weak exoskeleton. These tiny crabs are well known to oyster fanciers, and their orange (when cooked) bodies are often encountered at table. It belongs to a family of crabs, the Pinnotheridae, whose members are adapted for living in close association (commensally) with other animals. Another species, *Pinnotheres maculatus,* is often found with mussels, scallops, and other hosts. The recently discovered *Pinnotheres chamae* lives with the jewel box, *Chama congregata.*

A related genus, *Pinnixa,* has many representatives on our coast, all of which live in the tubes or burrows of other invertebrates. A typical representative, *Pinnixa lunzi,* is a commensal with the spoon worm,

263

Thalassema hartmani, and is illustrated with its host in Figure 185. *Pinnixa chaetopterana,* which lives with the worms, *Chaetopterus variopedatus, Loimia viridis,* and *Amphitrite ornata,* is shown on Plate C7. *Pinnixa cylindrica* lives with the lugworm, *Arenicola cristata* (Fig. 207). *Pinnixa cristata* inhabits the burrows of the ghost shrimps, *Callianassa major* and *C. atlantica,* whereas *P. sayana* lives with their relative, the mud shrimp, *Upogebia affinis. Pinnixa retinens* is one of the many commensals that live with the capitellid worm, *Notomastus lobatus.* All *Pinnixa* species have bodies much wider than long and are similar to each other. *Dissodactylus mellitae* (Fig. 235), our smallest crab, lives on the disk of sand dollars and is also a pinnotherid.

Commensal Crabs

Sand Dollar Crab *Dissodactylus mellitae*

This, our smallest crab, is commensal with the sand dollar (or keyhole urchin), *Mellita quinquiesperforata.* It also lives with the sand dollars *Encope michelini* and *Echinarachnius parma* which do not occur in our area. Adults are only 0.2″ (5 mm) wide and are smaller than even the oyster pea crab. The individual in the photograph (Fig. 235) is an adult crab on a sand dollar. The spines of the dollar, which are small and inconspicuous when unmagnified, appear large in comparison with the crab. As many as eight crabs have been reported from a single sand dollar but there are usually less. There is evidence that males defend dollars on which there is a reproductive female and do not allow other

Figure 235

males or juveniles access to the dollar or the female. The crabs feed primarily on mucus and detritus but have also been reported to consume living host tissue as well. In a relationship on the Pacific coast, a similar crab lives near the anus of the dollar and feeds on feces. *Dissodactylus mellitae* is easily dislodged and, in spite of the thousands of sand dollars collected by tourists, it is rarely seen because it falls off before the sand dollar is removed from the water.

Another species, *Dissodactylus crinitichelis,* lives with the tropical sand dollars *Encope emarginata* and *E. michelini* and the sea biscuit, *Clypeaster subdepressus,* but do not occur in shallow water in the Carolinian province.

Ghost Crabs

Ghost Crab *Ocypode quadrata*

Visitors to southeastern swimming beaches always notice the large (1–2″; 2.5–5 cm) holes in the dry sand of the upper beach and sand dunes and wonder what made them. They are the openings of the burrows of the common ghost crab, *Ocypode quadrata.* These crabs are, sand-colored, terrestrial animals with thick square-backed bodies and large, stalked, black eyes. They reach about 2″ (5 cm) in body width and cannot be confused with any other crab in this region. They are nocturnal feeders and usually remain in the burrow during the day. At night they emerge to feed, mostly on coquina clams and mole crabs, which they unerringly locate, dig up, and crush with their claws. In the

Figure 236

morning they return to the burrow where they may undertake its repair or modification. Near midday they usually close the burrow opening with sand. Ghost crabs breathe air rather than water but use the usual crab gills for this purpose. The gills are protected inside the hard exoskeleton and air enters through narrow slitlike openings between the third and fourth legs. The gills must be kept moist in order to function. Most individuals rarely enter the water except to wet their gills in the swash zone, although they can accomplish this by wicking up water from damp sand if necessary. Females with eggs are an exception, for they must frequently enter the water to wet the egg mass. Ghost crabs do not swim but they sometimes turn upside down in the water to ventilate the eggs. Ghost crabs have lightweight exoskeletons and long legs which help them to run rapidly forwards, backwards, and sideways. The larvae begin life in the plankton and then become amphibious as they mature.

Fiddler Crabs   *Color Plate C34*

Redjointed Fiddler *Uca minax*
Sand Fiddler *Uca pugilator*
Mud Fiddler *Uca pugnax*

Fiddler crabs are easily recognized by the combination of semiterrestrial habitat, thick squarish body, herding tendency, and in males, possession of one greatly enlarged pincer. The three common species on the southeastern Atlantic coast are easy to distinguish on anatomical and ecological grounds. The sand fiddler, *Uca pugilator* (1″; 2.5 cm), lives on sandy areas of salt marshes and protected beaches. It is usually pinkish-purple and the inside of the palm of the large male pincer has no oblique row of small bumps or granules.

The mud fiddler, *Uca pugnax* (0.9″; 2.3 cm), is found in the same marshes as the sand fiddler but prefers muddier areas. The two species sometimes intermingle but often the boundary separating the two species is sharp. Mud fiddlers are usually brown or yellowish and the palm of the large male claw bears an oblique row of small granules about halfway between the base of the immovable finger and the wrist. Every species discussed here, except *U. pugilator,* has such a row of granules. Both species inhabit higher salinity marshes and they are similar to each other.

The redjointed fiddler, *Uca minax* (1.6″; 4 cm), prefers low salinity brackish marshes and is much larger than our other two species. Individuals are brownish and the large claw of the male has red joints. These three species are parasitized by the bopyrid isopod, *Leidya distorta,* which lives in the gill chamber.

The ranges of two Caribbean species extend into northeastern Florida. *Uca thayeri* is a large species, about the size of *Uca minax,* but it lacks red pigment on the joints of the large male cheliped and both fingers curve down at the tip. The immovable finger of our other *Uca* species curve upward or are straight at the tip. The eyestalks of *U. thayeri* are very long while those of *U. minax* are short. The part of the carapace which extends anteriorly between the bases of the eyestalks is very narrow in this species, very broad in *U. minax*. *Uca thayeri* lives in deep mud, often associated with mangroves. Ovigerous females build mud chimneys around the mouths of their burrows. *Uca rapax* (1″; 2.5 cm) is a tropical species found in northeastern Florida and the Gulf of Mexico. It lives in mud and sand, often with mangroves, its back is blue, and the carapace is narrow between the eyes.

Fiddler crabs live in marshes in dense aggregations, where they dig burrows into the sediment. They feed on organic material (bacteria, algae, detritus) in the surface sediments by using their small claws to transfer sand and mud to the mouthparts where desirable organic particles are separated form unwanted mineral particles. The food is swallowed but the sand and mud is rolled into little balls and placed back on the sediment surface, which may be covered by them before the tide returns. The crabs also form sand pellets when digging burrows but these are much larger than the feeding pellets. Females have two tiny claws which they use for feeding. Males have one small feeding claw and one enormous claw. The large claw is used for social interactions including signaling to females during courtship and for ritual combat with other males. Raccoons, blue crabs, clapper rails and other marsh birds prey on fiddler crabs.

Insects

Oyster Springtail *Anurida maritima*

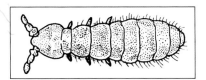

Figure 237

The oyster springtail is one of the insects associated with the interface between the sea and the land. These insects are restricted to the inter-tidal zone and are common on oysters, rocks and pilings. They are tiny, blue-black, wingless insects about 0.1″ (2 mm) long. The body is covered by a dense fuzz of short hairs and they have the three pairs of legs and single pair of antennae characteristic of insects. Like other spring-tails they have no wings, but unlike most species they lack a springing mechanism beneath the tail, and they do not jump. Because of the tiny size they are often overlooked, but they are common in the oyster zone of the intertidal hard-bottom community.

Insects are almost entirely terrestrial or freshwater animals and there are not many species that live in salt water. Those that do usually have waterproof bodies and breathe air at the water surface. *Anurida* is no exception and, even though it is immersed by the tide for much of the day, it does not rely on oxygen from seawater. As the incoming tide covers the animal, a layer of air is trapped in the body fuzz and the insect breathes from it while under water.

The greenish, wormlike larvae of the midge, *Telmatogeton japonicus,* live under oyster shells in the intertidal zone of our high salinity rock jetties. These larvae, which are about 0.4″ (1 cm) long, metamorphose into flying adult midges in the late spring. Midges are members of the family Chironomidae in the insect order Diptera, which includes the houseflies, mosquitoes, no-see-ums, and deer flies. Midges look superficially like mosquitoes but do not bite. The larvae of many species of biting flies (deer flies, mosquitoes, and no-see-ums) live in the water or mud of salt marshes.

Tiger beetles in the family Cicindelidae are found in several coastal habitats. The most noticeable are the pale, mottled grey *Cicindela dorsalis* and *C. gratiosa* of outer beaches. The former is strictly an outer beach species while the latter is a species of the maritime forest that also occurs on outer beaches. The two are difficult to tell apart. Tiger beetles are very fast and difficult to catch though they are a common feature of most beaches. They are predators and may bite a careless collector.

MAJOR GROUPS OF MARINE ANIMALS

MAJOR GROUPS OF MARINE ANIMALS

PHYLUM PORIFERA ("pore bearers")

There are approximately 40 species of sponges in shallow water in our area. They are sometimes large, branched, and brightly colored, such as *Microciona prolifera* (Fig. 238), small whitish tubes, such as *Clathrina coriacea,* or inconspicuous yellow bumps (Fig. 239) emerging from galleries in shells (*Cliona;* Pl. B12). Regardless of their size, shape, or color, all sponges are sessile filter-feeders. They feed by pumping water through their porous bodies. Flagellated cells, called collar cells, generate currents and trap and digest minute, suspended food particles. The openings for water entry, called ostia, are usually microscopic, numerous and scattered over the surface whereas openings for exit of the water (oscules) are often larger and elevated. The water flowing through the sponge is also used for gas exchange and release of gametes.

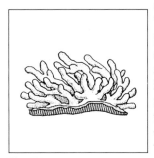

Fig. 238

Fig. 239

Sponges support their bodies with connective tissue that lies between their skin and the inner canals and chambers. The connective tissue framework is the familiar protein, collagen, which most sponges further stiffen by adding microscopic mineral spicules, additional protein fibers (spongin), or both. Sponges with a high density of interlocked spicules may be stiff and hard, whereas those with few spicules, or with spicules in a looser arrangement, tend to be soft and spongy. A few sponges have spongin fibers only and no spicules at all. These are members of a group that includes bath sponges, which are flexible and nonabrasive. There is one sponge (*Halisarca*) in our area that has neither spicules nor spongin and forms thin, slimy, encrusting sheets.

Sponges are classified partly on the basis of the composition of their skeletons. Those with spicules composed of calcium carbonate (lime) belong to the class Calcarea (Fig. 240). In our area those with skeletons of silicon dioxide (glass) or spongin or both belong to the class Demospongiae, a word meaning "most sponges." With the exception of a few members of the Calcarea, all of our sponges belong to the Demospongiae. Two other classes of sponges, the Hexactinellida and the Sclerospongiae, are not found in our region.

270

Fig. 240

The bright pigmentation of many sponges not only has visual appeal but also provides protection against sunburn—similar to that afforded to human skin by a healthy tan or naturally dark pigmentation. Many sponges produce and release antibiotics that help keep them from being eaten, encroached on by aggressive neighbors, or overgrown by fouling organisms. Many of these compounds are of interest to pharmaceutical companies who study sponges and other marine animals in the research field of "natural products chemistry."

Sedentary adult sponges are able to colonize new surfaces by releasing a tiny, ciliated, mouthless, swimming larva called a parenchymella (or sometimes an amphiblastula). When this larva finds a suitable surface, it attaches and metamorphoses to form a tiny sponge. Sponges usually are hermaphrodites with male and female reproductive cells scattered throughout the connective tissue of each individual. Spawning occurs when sperms are shed through the oscules and into the surrounding water. Neighboring sponges are fertilized internally by sperms which enter the sponge through the ostia. The fertilized eggs are retained internally until, as larvae, they escape through the oscules.

PHYLUM CNIDARIA ("like nettles")

The phylum Cnidaria is composed of four classes and includes the anemones, corals, sea whips (class Anthozoa), jellyfishes (classes Scyphozoa and Cubozoa), hydroids, and Portuguese men-o'-war (class Hydrozoa). Some cells in the skin of all cnidarians contain microscopic capsules (nematocysts) that eject stinging or sticky threads when stimulated. Fortunately, human skin is sensitive to the nematocysts of only a few species.

The cnidarian body is cylindrical and encloses a fluid-filled cavity, the coelenteron. The mouth opens into the coelenteron and is surrounded by tentacles. The coelenteron has multiple functions including digestion, absorption, and circulation, and in several species, it is also a fluid skeleton. The term, gastrovascular cavity, is often used instead of coelenteron. The body wall consists of two cellular layers separated by a thin or thick sheet of jellylike material, called mesoglea. The outer cellular layer is the skin, or epidermis, and this sometimes secretes a cuticle or exoskeleton as in hydroids and stony corals. The cellular lining of the coelenteron is secretory for digestion, ciliated for circulation, and often folded for absorption. Both cell layers may contain

271

muscles, nerves, nematocysts, and gonads. When muscles occur in both layers, the fiber orientation of the two layers is perpendicular and antagonistic.

Two body forms are common in cnidarians, the polyp and the medusa. The jellyfishlike medusa is solitary and usually free-swimming. Its mouth and tentacles are directed downwards and the mesoglea is thick. Jellyfishes are named for the thick, elastic, jellylike mesoglea, which is their skeleton. The coelenteron is often specialized into a central digestive cavity (stomach) and small, peripheral, circulatory canals, which radiate from it. The polyp is solitary or colonial, and usually attached by its base to some surface. The mouth and tentacles are oriented upward and the mesoglea is usually thin. Polyps may use a fluid skeleton or a calcareous or chitinous exo- or endoskeleton.

Cnidarians often reproduce by equal or unequal (asexual) division of the body followed by regrowth of the missing parts. A colony results when polyps divide but fail to separate completely. The sexual stage of the Anthozoa and some Hydrozoa is the polyp, whereas it is the medusa of the Scyphozoa and remaining Hydrozoa. The sexes are usually separate and fertilized eggs develop into a tiny, mouthless, ciliated, swimming larva, called a planula ("roamer"). The typical life cycle of scyphozoans and hydrozoans involves an alternation between polyp and medusa generations. The polyp asexually produces a medusa, then the medusa sexually produces a planula, and finally the planula becomes a polyp, thus completing the complex life cycle. The medusa stage is absent in the Anthozoa. There are approximately 9,000 species of cnidarians worldwide and about 60 shallow-water species in our area.

Class Scyphozoa ("cuplike animals")

This class includes the true jellyfishes such as moon jellies (*Aurelia*), sea nettles (*Chrysaora*), and jellyballs (*Stomolophus*). Scyphozoans are large medusae. The swimming bell, or umbrella, bears tentacles and sensory capsules (rhopalia) on the margin and a central mouth on the subumbrella, or lower surface. The lips of the mouth are typically greatly elongated into four oral arms that hang curtainlike from the subumbrella and help catch food. These should not be confused with the tentacles. Some jellyfishes, such as *Stomolophus,* have oral arms fused into a gristlelike clapper which bears many tiny secondary mouths. The coelenteron consists of a central stomach, four or more radial canals, and a marginal ring canal. The radial canals radiate from the central stomach to the ring canal which encircles the bell. The stomach is partially partitioned, as in anthozoans, by four mesenteries or septa. The septa enclose four gastric pockets from which most of the radial canals arise. The inner septal margins bear gastric filaments which, like anthozoan acontia, bear stinging cells to subdue swallowed prey. A gonad develops in each septum, or gastric pocket, and is underlain by a ciliated fingerlike indentation from the subumbrella. These "subgenital funnels" or "pits" circulate water and are gonad-associated gills. The radial and ring canals are the circulatory system of jellyfishes. Scyphozoan individuals are typically either male or female and each releases ripe gametes from the mouth. Fertilized eggs develop into planula larvae which settle on firm surfaces in quiet shaded places and become small polyps (scyphistomae) with long threadlike tentacles. These reproduce asexually to form other polyps and seasonally bud off tiny medusae by transverse fission (strobilation). Each young medusa is called an ephyra.

Jellyfishes are predators or suspension-feeders. One tropical species (the upside-down jellyfish, *Cassiopeia*) in the Florida Keys, West Indies, and Bermuda has symbiotic algae in its tissues and relies on them to supply its food. Only two of the four scyphozoan orders occur inshore in the Southeast, the Semaeostomeae and the Rhizostomeae, and only these are discussed. All scyphozoans are marine.

Order Semaeostomeae ("flag mouth")

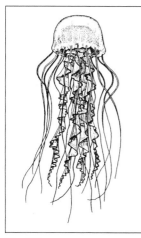

Semaeostomes are large jellyfishes (Fig. 241) with a central mouth flanked by four ruffled, flaglike oral arms, a scalloped bell margin, and 8 to 16 rhopalia. *Aurelia, Chrysaora,* and *Cyanea* are common semaeostomes in our area.

Order Rhizostomeae ("root mouth")

Root mouth jellyfishes are large and lack the usual central mouth of other jellies. Instead, the oral arms fuse over the original mouth and many secondary mouths open along these frilly, rootlike, fused arms. *Stomolophus,* the cannonball jellyfish, is our most common species (Pl. A8). This order also includes *Rhopilema* and, south of our range, *Cassiopeia.*

Fig. 241

Class Cubozoa ("cube animals")

The single order, Cubomedusae ("cube medusa"), includes jellyfishes with cubical transparent bodies which reach a height of about 10″ (25 cm). They are known as "box jellies" or "sea wasps" because of their shape and dangerous stings. The opening below the swimming bell is restricted to a central jet by a shelf of tissue (velarium) extending inward from the bell margin. Contraction of the bell forces water through the opening and generates thrust. Cubomedusae are common in tropical, subtropical, and warm temperate seas. Two species occur in our area, *Tamoya haplonema* and *Chiropsalmus quadrumanus.*

Major Groups of Marine Animals

Class Hydrozoa ("water animals")

The Hydrozoa is the most complicated class of Cnidaria, and identification of them is difficult for beginners. The life cycle often includes a polyp, medusa, and planula. The polyps usually form colonies, and the colonies may consist of many kinds of polyps, or polyps and medusae together. Individual hydrozoan polyps are usually less than 0.04″ (1 mm) and the medusae rarely exceed 1″ (2.5 cm). Because of the small size of individual polyps and medusae, large colonies are the most noticeable. Sessile colonies are composed of polyps of several types, whereas floating colonies are composed of polyps or polyps and modified medusae, also of different types. Hydrozoan medusae are similar to scyphozoan jellyfish but are much smaller and possess a shelf, the velum, under the margin of the bell which restricts the outlet of water to a small jet. The mouth is at the end of a long or short tube, the manubrium, which hangs clapperlike from below the center of the bell. Hydrozoan polyps are small, radially symmetrical, colonial, and arise from a rootlike stolon. The coelenteron is continuous throughout the colony and circulation is maintained by cilia. A chitinous exoskeleton may be present. Most hydroids are marine, but the familiar, albeit atypical, *Hydra* of biology classes is a hydrozoan that inhabits freshwater. *Hydra* is unusual in having no medusa generation, no chitinous exoskeleton, and in being solitary. Approximately 2,700 species of hydrozoans occupy all oceans of the world, and approximately 40 species occur in shallow southeastern waters.

Order Hydroida ("water serpentlike")

Most species of Hydrozoa in our area are hydroids. The hydroids form sessile colonies of polyps and are mistaken for seaweeds by many

Fig. 242

people (Fig. 242). They often produce microscopic, transparent, swimming medusae, but these usually escape notice, although sometimes they sting and cause mysterious skin rashes on swimmers in estuarine waters especially near docks. A few polyps such as *Velella* and *Porpita,* float freely at the surface of the sea. *Porpita* and *Velella* release thimble-shaped medusae like many other hydroids and are thought to be closely related to more typical sessile hydroids.

The hydroid life cycle of polyp-medusa-egg-planula-polyp is often modified in various ways. Some hydroid colonies, such as *Obelia, Halocordyle,* and *Bougainvillia,* release their medusae whereas others, such as *Eudendrium* and *Hydractinia* do not. Instead, the medusa, or a modified remnant of it, remains attached to the polyp and a planula is released by the attached, often reduced, medusa. *Tubularia* (Fig. 243)

274

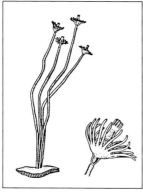

Fig. 243

goes a step further and releases a larva, called an actinula, that already has tentacles of the next polyp generation whereas its look-alike, *Ectopleura,* releases typical medusae.

Many hydroid colonies have polyps of different forms and functions which permit an efficient division of labor. Feeding polyps have mouths and tentacles and are known as gastrozooids; defensive or prey-capturing polyps have batteries of stinging capsules and are called nematophores or dactylozooids. Reproductive polyps, or gonozooids, produce medusa buds, called medusoids, or reduced gonophores.

Hydroid colonies are supported by a thin, often transparent, exoskeleton (perisarc) composed of chitin, a complex carbohydrate. In some hydroids, the exoskeleton extends up around the base of the polyps forming a cup (theca) into which the polyp can retract for protection. The detailed structure of the minute cup, visible only under a microscope, is often important in identifying species of hydroids.

Order Siphonophora ("siphon bearers")

The siphonophores are swimming or floating hydrozoan colonies composed of numerous polyps and medusae. The Portuguese man-o'-war is the best known representative (Fig. 244). The name si-

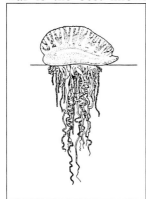

Fig. 244

phonophore derives from the appearance of feeding polyps (gastrozooids) each of which has a mouth and one very long, hollow, siphonlike tentacle with side branches. The dactylozooid polyps are long, hollow, unbranched tentacles resembling gastrozooids but lacking a mouth and side branches on their tentacles. In the siphonophores, the dactylozooids capture and kill prey and transfer it to the gastrozooid. Gonozooids resemble gastrozooids but lack the tentacle and bear clusters of gonophores. The float (pneumatophore) is a modified medusa. Many siphonophores, but not *Physalia,* have swimming bells which resemble typical medusae but lack a mouth, manubrium, tentacles, and sense organs. Siphonophores never release sexual medusae, and all species except *Physalia physalis* are hermaphrodites.

Siphonophores occupy all oceans of the world but are most common in warmer seas. The dangerous *Physalia* is the only conspicuous species in the Southeast but much smaller, transparent, harmless species occur commonly in the offshore plankton.

Major Groups of Marine Animals

Class Anthozoa ("flower animals")

The Anthozoa includes anemones, corals, sea whips, and sea pansies. The anthozoan polyp consists of a column, a flattened oral disk surrounding the mouth and bearing the tentacles, and a base. Some polyps, such as anemones, are solitary whereas others, such as most corals, are colonial. Anthozoan polyps are typically larger than those of other cnidarians. Hydrozoan polyps rarely exceed 0.04″ (1 mm) in diameter whereas some tropical anthozoan species may have diameters of 3′ (1 m). The coelenteron of anthozoans is partitioned by vanelike vertical sheets of tissue, called mesenteries, which help to regionalize functions, increase surface area, and circulate the coelenteric fluid. Feeding polyps always have eight or more mesenteries that radiate inward from the body wall. The unattached inner margin of each mesentery is often thickened by stinging cells which are used to subdue swallowed prey. In the base of some polyps, these thickened margins extend beyond the limit of the mesentery as long threads, called acontia. These can be expelled through the mouth or through special pores in the column (cinclides) and are used for defense and feeding. The anthozoan mouth does not open directly into the coelenteron, rather into a short flattened tube, the pharynx. One or two of the longitudinal creases of the pharynx usually have a specialized tract of cilia which pumps water into the coelenteron and inflates deflated polyps. These tracts, or siphonoglyphs, also maintain the fluid volume of inflated polyps. The pharynx is also a valve. When anthozoans bend or shorten, pressure in the coelenteron rises and collapses the flattened pharynx to prevent fluid loss through the mouth. When anthozoans retract, they release fluid through the mouth to decrease their volume. In this case, the pharynx and mouth are actively opened by contraction of radial muscles in mesenteries attached to their outer walls.

Fig. 245

Subclass Alcyonaria

The subclass Alcyonaria, or Octocorallia ("eight coral"), primarily includes colonial anthozoans whose polyps have eight pinnate tentacles. Pinnate tentacles have a row of short branches on opposite sides of each tentacle. Alcyonarians are sea whips (Fig. 245), sea fans, and sea pansies (Fig. 246). There are three species in shallow water in our area and many more in the tropics just south of us. In tropical areas, many alcyonarians harbor zooxanthellae.

Subclass Zoantharia

Subclass Zoantharia, or Hexacorallia ("six coral"), includes anemones, stony corals, zoanthinarians, and tube anemones. Zoantharians are solitary or colonial polyps with mesenteries in multiples of six.

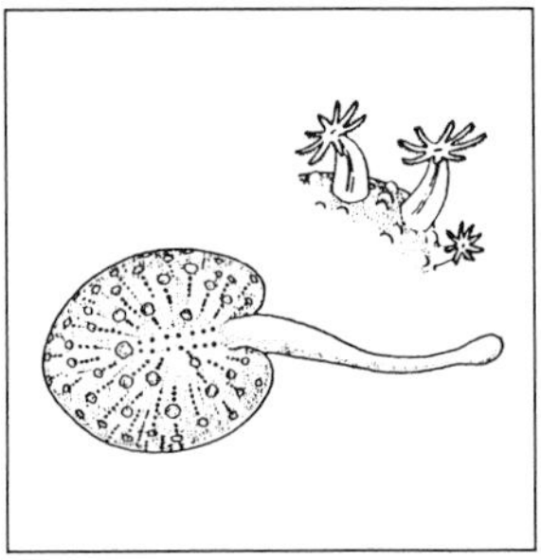

Order Actiniaria

Order Actiniaria ("raylike") contains the true anemones. Anemones are solitary and typically lack a rigid skeleton, instead they have a fluid skeleton (Fig. 247). The lower end of the column may be modified as a broad adherent pedal disk or a bulbous digging physa. The tissues of anemones may or may not contain symbiotic algae (zooxanthellae). There are about 800 species worldwide and 15 species in our waters.

Fig. 246

Order Scleractinia ("hard rays")

Stony corals are usually colonial and deposit a massive limestone exoskeleton. Each polyp inhabits a depression, or coral cup, in the exoskeleton (Fig. 248). The starlike radial partitions (sclerosepta) seen in individual coral cups result from the deposition of skeletal material in creases between the mesenteries at the base of the polyp. Their patterns are different for each species. Some coral species, the hermatypic corals, are reef-builders, are highly diversified in tropical seas, and invariably harbor zooxanthellae. Others are colonial but do not form reefs (ahermatypic corals), and a few are solitary polyps. These may or may not harbor zooxanthellae. There are 2,500 species worldwide and three species in the Southeast in shallow water.

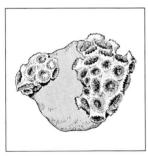

Fig. 247

Order Zoanthinaria ("animal flower")

The order Zoanthinaria, or Zoanthidea, includes the "colonial anemones." They are common in the tropics and are represented in the Southeast by one rare species, *Epizoanthus paguriphilus,* which is found on dredged mollusc shells. Tropical species typically harbor zooxanthellae. Approximately 225 species are known worldwide.

Fig. 248

Class Ceriantipatharia

The class Ceriantipatharia includes one order, the Ceriantharia ("horned flowers"), which is represented in the Southeast by one species. Known as "tube anemones," cerianthids are large, solitary, burrowing anthozoans that occupy tubes of interwoven discharged nematocysts. The tentacles are in two distinct whorls; short tentacles encircle the mouth and long slender tentacles radiate from the margin of the oral disk. They are hermaphrodites. Approximately 25 species occur worldwide.

·PHYLUM CTENOPHORA ("comb bearers")

The ctenophores are known as comb jellies, sea gooseberries, or sea walnuts (Fig. 249). They are delicate, transparent, non-stinging jellies

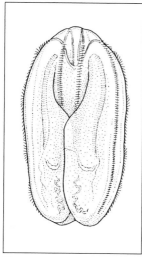

and, in our area, range in size from less than 0.5″ to 5″ (1.3–13 cm). In open waters, species of *Beroe* reach 16″ (41 cm) and *Cestum,* 7′ (2 m). The ctenophores are carnivores and most species are pelagic, but a few are benthic creepers. Planktonic ctenophores are often spherical, ovoid, or ribbonlike, whereas benthic forms are flattened disks. Ctenophores are found in all oceans and, except for a few species, are poorly studied because they are inaccessible and fragile.

The body surface of all ctenophores bears eight radially symmetrical rows of comblike paddles. Each paddle, known simply as a comb (ctene), consists of thousands of cilia bound together in a single plane. The combs beat like flippers and enable ctenophores to swim. Ctenophores change direction while swimming by altering the rate of beat in some rows with respect to others. All ctenophores are bioluminescent and light is produced beneath the comb rows. Most ctenophores have a pair of sticky retractile tentacles used to catch prey. These may be many times longer than the body, as in young *Mnemiopsis,* short and inconspicuous, as in adult *Mnemiopsis,* or absent, as in *Beroe.* Their stickiness is caused by special cells (colloblasts) which discharge an adhesive thread when touched. Many ctenophores feed on plankton but some, such as *Beroe,* swallow other ctenophores and cnidarian jellies that may be as large or larger than the predator. Prey that exceed the body size of *Beroe* are bitten into pieces by teeth composed of fused, stiff cilia which line the lips.

The gut extends through the jelly along the polar axis. The mouth is at the south pole (oral pole), and several anal pores surround the north pole (aboral pole). A gravity detector, or statocyst, which senses and controls the animal's orientation in the water, is also located at the aboral pole. The axial part of the gut consists of the mouth, pharynx, stomach, aboral canal, and anal pores and functions in ingestion and digestion of food. Vessel-like canals from the stomach pass through the thick jelly to the major structures, such as the comb rows, tentacle

Fig. 249

278

sheaths, and gonads to circulate and store nutrients. In the predator *Beroe,* these canals branch repeatedly, perhaps to increase storage capacity, and unite around the mouth as a ring canal reminiscent of that of some jellyfishes.

Ctenophores rapidly regenerate missing or damaged parts, but few reproduce by asexual division. Ctenophores are primarily hermaphrodites, and the gonads occur on the walls of the circulatory canals below the comb rows. Gametes are typically released into the sea where fertilization occurs. A developmental stage, called a cydippid larva, occurs in all ctenophores in our area, except *Beroe,* regardless of their adult form. The cydippid is globular or ovoid with well-developed comb rows and retractile tentacles. The phylum is divided into 7 orders of which 2 occur inshore in the Southeast.

Order Lobata ("lobes")

The lobates are species with the body compressed in the tentacular plane and expanded on each side of the mouth into two food-trapping lobes. During development, the flattened tentaculate cydippid develops lobes, and its tentacles migrate orally and lose their sheaths to persist as short tentacles around the mouth and on the lobes. Two genera, *Bolinopsis* and *Mnemiopsis,* occur in our area.

Order Beroida (after Beroe, a Greek sea nymph)

The order Beroida contains species which are strongly compressed in the tentacular plane. They have a large flexible mouth, a capacious pharynx, well-developed comb rows, highly branched gastrovascular canals, and no tentacles. One species, *Beroe ovata,* occurs in our area.

PHYLUM HEMICHORDATA ("half notochord")

The phylum Hemichordata has only one class, the Enteropneusta, or acorn worms, in our region. The only other class, the Pterobranchia ("winged gills"), consists of minute bryozoanlike colonies some of which are found on hard surfaces in Bermuda, the Gulf of Mexico, and elsewhere. The closely related phylum, Chordata, includes the sea squirts, lancelets, and our own group, the vertebrates. The term Enteropneusta ("breathing intestine") refers to the multiple gill pores on the front end of the tubular gutlike body. Although these burrowing animals are rarely or never seen on the surface, they are nevertheless large and abundant along our coast. The enteropneusts, like earthworms, burrow through and ingest sediment from which they digest what is of value and defecate the rest in little mounds at the surface. Acorn worms till the sand and mudflats of our creeks, sounds, and estuaries just as earthworms cultivate a backyard garden or a farmer's field (if the farmer does not use pesticides). Evidence of acorn worm activity is conspicuous indeed. The larger species leave fecal casts scattered about on intertidal mud flats where they sometimes number in the thousands. Each cast resembles a small briochelike sandcastle.

The soft, fragile, enteropneust body is divided into three regions, proboscis, collar, and trunk (Fig. 250). At the front is a muscular

extensible proboscis which is used to burrow and collect food. A slender stalk, which is supported by an internal cartilagelike skeleton, joins the proboscis to a short cylindrical collar. Together, the proboscis and collar were thought by early observers to resemble an acorn and its cap, hence the name "acorn worm." Behind the collar is a long trunk, and its front end bears many pairs (often hundreds) of small external gill pores through

Fig. 250

which water exits. The large mouth is located at the junction of the proboscis and collar. It leads directly into a long cylindrical pharynx perforated by several pairs of internal gill slits. Cartilagelike skeletal bars prevent collapse of the perforated pharyngeal wall and hoid the gill slits open. As cilia move water and food into the mouth and pharynx, water sweeps up through the gill slits and into an atrium (see Urochordata) before discharging through the gill pores at the body surface. The food, now with excess water removed, remains in the pharynx then passes into the intestine where organic material is digested. In some acorn worms, the front part of the intestine is specialized for nutrient storage and is called the liver, or hepatic, region. When present, it consists of numerous, fingerlike, dorsal gut outpockets which project from the upper body surface like sea slug cerata. The anus is at the hind end of the trunk.

Acorn worms are coelomate animals but the body cavity is reduced by the invasion of muscles. Only the proboscis, which produces peristaltic burrowing movements, relies on the coelom as a typical fluid skeleton. The proboscis also contains the heart and kidney, and these are supported by a short tubular outgrowth of the pharynx which projects forward into the proboscis. It is called the "stomochord" ("mouth notochord") and is the basis for the phylum name.

Enteropneusts produce copious amounts of mucus to line and stabilize their burrows. The mucus contains an antibiotic, called a bromophenol, which is responsible for their strong iodinelike odor.

The sexes are separate in acorn worms and the gonads occur in two longitudinal rows in the pharyngeal region. In *Balanoglossus* and *Ptychodera,* the gonadal rows are expanded into two long flaps ("genital wings") which fold over the back of the worm. Ovaries are usually grey and testes orange. Acorn worms release their gametes into the sea where fertilization occurs. Development leads either to a short-lived, nonfeeding, benthic larva (*e.g., Saccoglossus*) or a long-lived, feeding, planktonic larva, called a tornaria (all other genera in our area). One of the most remarkable attributes of the glass-clear tornaria larvae is their close resemblance to the larvae of sea stars and sea cucumbers, indicating a close evolutionary relationship between echinoderms and hemichordates.

Approximately 70 species of enteropneusts are described worldwide and 5 species occur in our area.

PHYLUM CHORDATA ("with a notochord")

The phylum Chordata includes the tunicates (sea squirts and their relatives), the lancelets, and the vertebrates. Members of this phylum have a rigid, dorsal, skeletal rod (notochord), gill slits, a dorsal hollow nerve cord, and a postanal tail during some part of the life cycle. During development, a temporary connection, the neurenteric canal, is formed between the gut and the hollow nerve cord. All chordates are fishlike at some time during their development. The non-vertebrate chordates are exclusively marine whereas the vertebrates occupy all major habitats.

Subphylum Tunicata ("with a tunic")

The Tunicata includes the class Ascidiacea, some of which are called sea squirts, and two pelagic classes, the Thaliacea and Appendicularia, which have no common names. The tunicate body is enclosed in a soft exoskeleton, or tunic, composed primarily of cellulose and has two external openings, called siphons. One opening, the oral siphon, leads into a large pharynx perforated by gill slits. The pharynx is used for food capture and respiration. Water is pumped into the pharynx by its cilia and suspended food particles are trapped in mucus on its lining. Water flows out the gill slits, enters an atrium that surrounds the pharynx, and is then discharged through the second external opening, the atrial siphon. The pharyngeal mucus is secreted by the endostyle, a ventral, ciliated, longitudinal groove in the wall of the pharynx. The food-laden mucus is rolled up and transported to the stomach by a specialized fold of ciliated tissue on the pharynx wall opposite the endostyle. The gut is U-shaped. After digestion in the stomach, feces are compacted into pellets, released into the atrium, and flushed out the atrial siphon. Tunicates are hermaphrodites. Sperm and eggs are released into the atrium and discharged from the atrial siphon. The larval stage is a near-microscopic, short-lived, nonfeeding, pelagic, fishlike, tadpole larva. Some species retain the larvae and brood them in the atrium.

Class Ascidiacea ("a leather bottle")

Class Ascidiacea contains the sessile tunicates, including both solitary and colonial species. Individual members of a colony are termed zooids. When colonial zooids are enclosed by a common tunic, as in *Eudistoma*

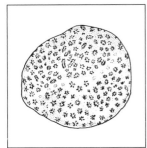

Fig. 251

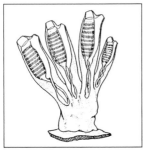

Fig. 252

Fig. 253

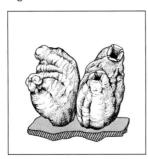

Fig. 254

or *Aplidium,* the colony is said to be compound (Fig. 251). Some compound ascidians grow more or less indefinitely and may cover a meter or more of substratum. These colonies are usually composed of microscopic zooids. Some colonial ascidians are united only at their bases, as in *Clavelina,* and the zooids are moderately large (Fig. 252). Others, such as *Perophora,* are small and linked only by a threadlike creeping stolon (Fig. 253). Such colonies are sometimes termed "social." Solitary ascidians, or sea squirts, are often large and a single individual of *Styela plicata* may be 4″ in length (Fig. 254).

The two siphons are usually close together and are never at opposite ends of the body. The oral siphon is anterior with the atrial siphon dorsal to it. All species of ascidians that have been studied concentrate heavy metals (vanadium, etc.) in specialized blood cells. These are believed to function in tunic synthesis and perhaps as antibiotics. Two unrelated deep-sea families, the Octonemidae and Hexacrobylidae, have abandoned filter-feeding and are predators. In these, the oral siphon is modified to form prey-seizing prehensile lobes. There are approximately 1,000 species of ascidians worldwide and about 25 species in our waters.

Order Aplousobranchia ("simple gill")

This order includes some of the most conspicuous and colorful ascidians, *e.g., Eudistoma hepaticum* (Pl. A23) and *Distaplia bermudensis* (Pl. A22). All aplousobranchs are colonial, and many are compound. Each tiny zooid is divided into two or three regions. The pharynx is always in the first region (thorax) and the gut, heart, and reproductive organs are in the second (abdomen) or second and third (postabdomen) regions. The zooids are usually small and, as a result, the pharyngeal area, number of gill slits, and blood supply are minimal. The pharyngeal lining is smooth, rows of gill slits do not usually exceed 12, and there are only transverse blood vessels. Gonads develop in the loop of the U-shaped gut.

Order Phlebobranchia ("veined gills")

Members of this order, such as *Perophora* (Pl. A24), *Ecteinascidia* (Pl. A25), and *Ascidia* (Pl. A21), are colonial or solitary and zooids may be moderately large (up to 6″ (15 cm) for species of *Ascidia*). The zooid body is composed of one or two regions and there is no postabdomen. The pharynx lining has transverse and longitudinal blood vessels. In addition, a second system of longitudinal blood vessels occurs internal to the first. These are elevated above the pharyngeal lining like swollen veins. They increase the blood supply to the pharynx and are responsible for the name of the order. The gonads develop in the loop of the U-shaped gut.

Order Stolidobranchia ("robed gills")

Members of this order, such as *Styela, Molgula, Symplegma* (Pl. A26), and *Botryllus* (Pl. A27), may be colonial, compound, or solitary. The viscera are entirely restricted to one body region (thorax). Solitary species may reach 4″ (10 cm) or more in length. The pharyngeal lining has pleatlike longitudinal folds which increase its area. Internal longitudinal vessels are present, as in phlebobranchs, particularly on the pleats. The gonads are situated beside the pharynx.

Classes Thaliacea and Appendicularia

The two remaining classes of the Tunicata are represented by motile planktonic species that are not covered in this guide although they are well-represented in the Southeast. Collection and observation of these animals requires a plankton net, microscope, and appropriate literature.

Subphylum Cephalochordata ("Head notochord")

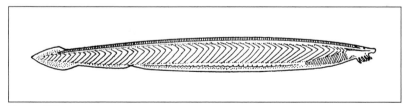

Figure 255

This group figures prominantly in discussions of vertebrate evolution. Cephalochordates are related to tunicates on one hand and vertebrates on the other. The fishlike body (Fig. 255) closely resembles the ammocoetes larva of a very primitive vertebrate, the lamprey eel. The common names for cephalochordates are "lancelet" or "amphioxus." Amphioxus, which means "pointed at both ends," correctly describes the body shape, as does lancelet, which means, "little lance."

Lancelets resemble small fish with a poorly developed head. There are no scales, eyes, skull, jaws, bones, or paired fins. Living animals are opalescent and have a fringe of feelers (cirri) around a large mouth. The notochord extends in front of the mouth into a knob (rostrum) which is used for burrowing. The notochord-containing rostrum is responsible for the name, Cephalochordata. In no other chordate does the notochord extend to the anterior end of the head. A tail and tail fin are located behind the anus. Conspicuous V-shaped body muscles (myomeres) extend the length of the body and are used for swimming and burrowing. Cephalochordates filter-feed by trapping particles in a specialized pharynx as in the tunicates, discussed above. Like them, an atrium surrounds the pharynx and opens at an exhalent atriopore. A dorsal, hollow, nerve cord with numerous light-sensitive eyespots is located dorsal to the notochord.

Lancelets burrow in coarse subtidal sands and feed with only the head exposed. There are approximately 20 species worldwide and species identification is difficult.

Subphylum Vertebrata

This important subphylum includes the fishes, amphibians, reptiles, birds, and mammals. The vertebrates are not covered by this field guide to invertebrate animals.

PHYLUM ECHINODERMATA ("spiny skin")

Echinoderms are represented in the Southeast by the sea stars, sea urchins, brittle stars, and sea cucumbers. The crinoids (sea lilies and feather stars) do not occur in our area and will not be discussed. Echinoderms are characterized by a water vascular system of fluid-filled spaces, channels, and tube feet arranged in five rows (ambulacra). They show five-part (pentaradial) symmetry and they have an internal skeleton composed of calcium carbonate. The name, Echinodermata, refers to the surface spines and bumps of many common species. Surprising as it may seem, echinoderms have internal skeletons, not external shells. The skeleton is very close to the surface but it is always covered by a thin living layer of soft tissue. Even the spines of sea urchins are covered with a thin layer of skin. Echinoderms are abundant and exclusively marine animals. They are bottom-dwellers as adults and are usually restricted to high salinity waters. They may be suspension-feeders, deposit-feeders, algal scrapers, scavengers, or predators.

Class Holothuroidea ("polyplike")

This class includes echinoderms known as sea cucumbers. The class contains over 1000 described species but only three occur commonly in our region. These are the large sea cucumber, *Sclerodactyla briareus,* a similar species, *Thyonella gemmata,* and the smaller wormlike, *Leptosynapta tenuis.* All three are burrowers in soft sediments.

Sea cucumbers are cylindrical animals with the mouth at one end and the anus at the other. A circle of retractile feeding tentacles surrounds the mouth. These are extended to collect suspended or deposited food particles and are then retracted, one at a time, into the mouth where the food is removed. The tentacles are modified tube feet. In many sea cucumbers, normal tube feet occur in five longitudinal rows (ambulacra) extending between the mouth and anus. In species with this arrangement, such as *Thyonella,* three of the rows are on the functional lower surface and two are on the upper. In *Sclerodactyla,* the tube feet are scattered over the surface of the body and in *Leptosynapta* they are absent.

Although most sea cucumbers are soft, compressible animals, they have a calcareous internal skeleton. The skeletal elements (ossicles) are microscopic but complex and variable in shape, like tiny snowflakes. They are embedded in the flexible body wall and contribute to its strength and stiffness. Species identifications are based partially on the size and shape of the ossicles. The holothuroid intestine opens into a rectum, or cloaca, before discharging to the outside. A pair of thin-walled, hollow, branched outgrowths of the cloacal wall, called respiratory trees, extends into the body cavity. The muscular cloaca pumps water in through the anus and into the respiratory trees. Contraction of the trees forces the water back out. Several inhalations precede each exhalation. Oxygen is absorbed from the water while it is in the trees.

Fig. 256

Leptosynapta, which lacks respiratory trees, pumps oxygenated water peristaltically into its burrow and over its thin skin.

Order Dendrochirotida ("treelike hands")

Dendrochirotes are suspension-feeders with ambulacral tube feet and ten or more highly branched tentacles. Two are usually short and used to wipe food off the eight larger tentacles. They are more or less sessile crevice-dwellers or burrowers with both ends exposed to the overlying water (Fig. 256).

Major Groups of Marine Animals

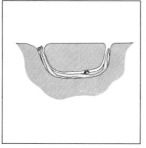

Fig. 257

Order Apodida ("lacking feet")

Apodans are represented by *Leptosynapta* (Fig. 257) and *Epitomapta* in our shallow waters. They are wormlike, fragile, lack tube feet and respiratory trees, burrow through sediments, and are subsurface deposit-feeders.

Order Aspidochirotida ("shieldlike hands")

The aspidochirotes include epibenthic species that occur south of our area, such as *Actinopyga, Isostichopus,* and *Holothuria.* They are large species (up to 7'; 2 m) with 15 or more unbranched tentacles ending in broad, flattened, shield-shaped disks used to shovel sediment into the mouth. They are nonselective deposit-feeders. The Aspidochirotida does not occur in the region covered by this guide.

Class Stelleroidea

Subclass Asteroidea ("starlike")

Members of this subclass are known as sea stars or starfish. They are echinoderms with wide arms that radiate horizontally, taper at their tips, and usually merge smoothly with the central disk (Fig. 258). The

Fig. 258

lower surface bears the mouth at its center and is known as the oral surface. The upper surface bears the anus, if there is one, and the madreporite and is known as the aboral surface. The oral surface of each arm has a single ambulacral groove flanked by tube feet and a double row of ossicles which close over the groove and protect the tube feet. The ambulacra radiate outward from the central mouth. The term ambulacrum means "a covered way" and refers to the groove and protective covering ossicles. There are about 1500 species of asteroids worldwide but only three common species in our area. *Asterias forbesi* (Pl. A29) is distributed intertidally, whereas *Luidia clathrata* and *Astropecten articulatus* (Pl. A28) are subtidal.

Sea star species in our area are exclusively pentaradial with five arms, although asteroids found elsewhere may have more. Paired tube feet originate from the ambulacral grooves on the oral side of each arm. They terminate in suckerlike disks in species found on hard surfaces and are pointed and suckerless in species living on soft sediments. They function in locomotion, feeding, nitrogen excretion, and gas exchange. Some predatory species (*A. forbesi*) use them to open large bivalves. Other predators (*Luidia, Astropecten*) use them to burrow in sand in pursuit of infaunal animals. *Asterias* everts its stomach onto the prey, secretes enzymes, and digests it externally. *Luidia* and *Astropecten* swallow the prey whole and digest it internally. Other species of asteroids are suspension-feeders, deposit-feeders, or omnivores. Most sea stars have specialized pincers (pedicellariae) situated on their upper surfaces. These remove fouling material and capture small food particles which are then passed to the mouth. (The pedicellariae may be greatly enlarged in some Northwest coast asteroids and in one species they are used like little traps to capture fish.) Specialized retractile gills, termed papulae, which resemble tube feet, project from the aboral body surface of some species. Asteroids regenerate well from fragments that include the disk. One tropical genus, *Linckia,* can regenerate from isolated arms.

Subclass Ophiuroidea ("snakelike")

Ophiuroids are known as brittle stars, serpent stars, or if the arms are branched, basket stars. There are approximately 2000 species worldwide but only nine common shallow-water species in our area. They have five or six slender snaky arms offset sharply from the disk (Fig.

259). The protective ambulacral ossicles of the asteroids are internalized and fused in the ophiuroids to form a backbonelike skeleton in each arm. The ambulacral groove is covered by tissue and protective plates. Although the tube feet are used in locomotion, ophiuroids move primarily by rowing movements of their arms. The tube feet are important as gills and as surfaces for collecting suspended food particles. Brittle stars have ten small, ciliated pockets (genital bursae), one on each

Fig. 259

side of the base of each arm, that open onto the oral surface. Water circulation through the bursae provides oxygen for the disk. Ophiuroids may burrow in soft sediments, or live at the surface under rocks, in crevices, or entangled in other organisms. They may be carnivores, suspension or deposit-feeders, or scavengers. Brittle stars regenerate well and one species in our area, *Ophiactis rubropoda,* reproduces asexually by disk division. *Axiognathus squamatus* is unusual because it is a viviparous hermaphrodite.

Class Echinoidea ("hedgehoglike")

This class includes the sea urchins, sand dollars, and heart urchins. There are approximately 950 species of echinoids worldwide and five species in this area. Two outstanding attributes of echinoids are numerous mobile spines and a rigid hollow skeleton, or test, composed of fused plates. All species have 20 rows of these plates, two for each of the five rows of tube feet (ambulacra) and two for each of the five intervening areas (interambulacra). The rows of plates and tube feet are meridional, running from aboral to oral pole. Pincers (pedicellariae) prevent

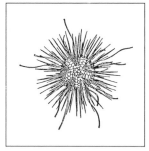

Fig. 260

fouling of the test and defend the organism. The echinoids are divided informally into two general groups, regular or irregular, based on their body shapes. Regular urchins are nearly spherical and radially symmetrical with the anus at the aboral pole (Fig. 260). Irregular urchins are non-spherical, variously depressed, and the anus is shifted away from the aboral pole thus establishing bilateral symmetry (Fig. 261).

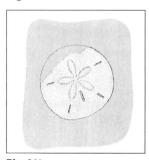

Fig. 261

Orders Cidaroida, Arbacioida, Temnopleuroida

Cidaroida includes the pencil urchins which are considered to be the most primitive of all living echinoids. They are regular urchins without specialized gills but with thick pencil-like spines. The skin wears off these spines and they are often overgrown with sessile organisms. This order is represented in our area only by *Eucidaris tribuloides*. The thick blunt spines sold for jewelry in shell and craft shops are not cidaroid spines, but spines belonging to reef-dwelling tropical slate pencil urchins (species of *Heterocentrotus* in the order Echinoida).

The remaining two regular urchins in our area, the purple urchin (*Arbacia*) and the short-spined urchin (*Lytechinus*), belong to the orders Arbacioida ("first king of Media") and Temnopleuroida ("cut sides") which are defined on the basis of technical characteristics.

Order Clypeasteroida ("shield stars")

This group includes irregular urchins known as sand dollars. Sand dollars are flattened urchins with a feltwork of numerous short spines. The anus is shifted from the center of the aboral surface to the oral surface, posterior to the mouth. Aboral tube feet are specialized as gills and are arranged in a flowerlike pattern. Sand dollars are primarily deposit-feeders in shallow sandy sediments, but one west coast species can stand on edge and filter-feed. Diatoms and other food particles are crushed with well-developed calcareous jaws, called "doves" by the beachcombing public.

Order Spatangoida ("a kind of sea urchin")

Spatangoids are irregular urchins known as heart urchins. Heart urchins exhibit conspicuous bilateral symmetry, the test is often ovoid, and spines and tube feet are regionally specialized for various functions. The anterior ambulacrum is a cleft which gives the test its heart shape. The mouth is shifted anteriorly and the anus is at the posterior margin of the test. In burrowing species, such as our *Moira atropos* (Pl. A32), the burrows are dug and maintained by highly extensible and specialized tube feet. Spatangoids lack jaws and are deposit-feeders.

PHYLUM CHAETOGNATHA

Chaetognaths, or arrow worms, are small, transparent, colorless, fishlike, planktonic predators. The arrowlike body is long, cylindrical,

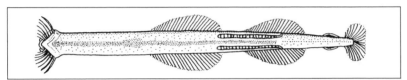

Figure 262

and stiff. It is divided into a head, trunk and tail. The head bears the mouth, which has rows of teeth, a pair of tiny eyes, and two groups of long, bristlelike, grasping spines (Fig. 262). The spines are responsible for the name of the phylum which means, "bristle-jawed." The head is separated from the trunk by a collarlike hood that extends forward while the animal swims to enclose the spines and streamline the head. The trunk contains the gut and female reproductive organs, whereas the tail contains the male structures of these hermaphroditic animals. Two conspicuous lateral bumps anterior to the tailfin are packets of sperms, called spermatophores. One or two pairs of lateral fins are situated on the trunk and tail and there is an unpaired horizontal tail fin. Microscopic stiff fans of vibration sensitive cilia are set at various angles along the length of the body.

Living chaetognaths are almost invisible in water. They suspend themselves head downward and sink slowly and motionlessly. When the prey, often a copepod, swims near an arrow worm, vibrations betray its presence and position. The arrow worm response is unhesitating and unerring. It darts forward to the prey, too rapidly to be followed by a human eye, sets the traplike head spines, and snaps them closed. The prey is swallowed whole even though it may be as large as the arrow worm.

Arrow worms are hermaphrodites that release their fertilized eggs into the plankton after mating. There is no larval stage and eggs develop directly into small arrow worms.

289

Myriads of arrow worms inhabit all the seas of the world but they are not found in freshwater. Species found near the surface are colorless whereas deeper forms may be pink or red. Eight unusual species are benthic, all members of the genus *Spadella*. Four species of *Sagitta* and one of *Krohnitta* occur commonly in our inshore plankton. *Sagitta tenuis* is likely to dominate the chaetognath fauna during the warm months of the year.

PHYLUM BRACHIOPODA ("arm-foot")

Brachiopods have a clamlike bivalved shell and range in size from 0.1″ to 3″ (2 mm to 7.6 cm). Because of their superficial similarity to clams, they were classified as molluscs by early biologists. Although they do resemble clams, they are not closely related to them, rather their relatives are phoronids, bryozoans, and hemichordates, and like them

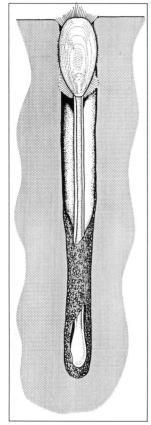

they have a lophophore. A lophophore is a crown of hollow, ciliated tentacles around the mouth. The brachiopod lophophore and body are completely enclosed by the shell except for a stalk (pedicle) which extends from it (Fig. 263). The pedicle usually functions as an anchor in sediment or as a holdfast on hard surfaces. Contraction of muscles in the pedicle allows withdrawal into the burrow or reorientation of the shell. The two valves are top and bottom (dorsal and ventral) in brachiopods instead of left and right (lateral) as in bivalves. In most brachiopods, the valves are unequal. The lower valve is usually larger, cup-shaped, and perforated at the hind end for outgrowth of the pedicle. This valve resembles an ancient oil lamp and, for this reason, brachiopods are called "lamp shells." The dorsal valve forms a cover over the ventral valve.

Fossil brachiopods date from 600 million years ago, and genera similar to our species, *Glottidia pyramidata,* have remained unchanged for at least 400 million years. The brachiopods, however, are a waning phylum and there are approximately 12,000 fossil species and only 335 living species. Brachiopods are not well-represented in shallow

Fig. 263

water in the Southeast. Only one species, the burrowing, *Glottidia pyramidata,* occurs here. The phylum is divided into two classes, the Inarticulata and the Articulata.

Class Inarticulata ("jointless")

Members of this class, which includes our species, have no shell hinge. Muscles and other soft tissues maintain the proper orientation of the two valves. *Glottidia* belongs to the order Lingulida ("tongue") which includes burrowing species with equal valves, a long pedicle which emerges between the valves, and the blood pigment hemerythrin. Lingulidans are characteristic of shallow sandy bottoms in warm temperate and tropical seas throughout the world.

Class Articulata ("jointed")

Articulate brachiopods have shells with a complex hinge consisting of teeth and sockets. No species of this class are reported from our area.

PHYLUM PHORONIDA

Members of this phylum are elongate, slender, unsegmented, coelomate worms with a funnel-like crown of tentacles (lophophore) at one

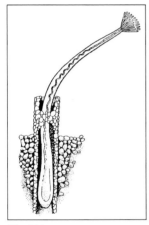

Fig. 264

end and a bulb (ampulla) at the other (Fig. 264). Phoronids are relatives of brachiopods, bryozoans, and hemichordates. They secrete and occupy membranous tubes and often cement sand or silt into them. Some species bore into limestone while others attach their tubes to hard surfaces or orient vertically in sediments. A few, such as *Phoronis australis,* are commensals in the tubes of cerianthids or the burrows of other animals. The ciliated lophophore is used for filter-feeding and as a gill and the ampulla anchors the body in the tube. The mouth, which leads into a U-shaped gut, is situated at the base of the circular, horseshoe-shaped, or spiraled lophophore. The anus opens near the mouth immediately outside the lophophore. A well-developed circulatory system contains red cells with the blood pigment hemoglobin. Phoronid individuals are usually males or females. Fertilized eggs are released through the excretory pores into the surrounding seawater or are brooded on the lophophore. Many species have a microscopic planktonic larva, called an actinotrocha. Phoronids range in length from 1″ to 6″ (2 mm to 15 cm). There are fewer that 20 decribed species worldwide in two genera, *Phoronis* and *Phoronopsis.* They are common to abundant in temperate seas worldwide.

PHYLUM BRYOZOA ("moss animals")

Bryozoan colonies are often large and conspicuous but are usually not recognized as animals by beginners. They are frequently assumed to be

291

seaweeds, but they are not. So plantlike are some bryozoans that one species, *Bugula turrita,* is dyed green and sold by gift shops under the name of "air fern." These are not ferns, or even plants, they are rather the dried skeletons of colonial animals.

Almost all bryozoans are colonies of tiny, nearly microscopic animals. Larger colonies may be soft and bushy (*Bugula*), leafy and crisp (*Thalamoporella*), moplike and rubbery (*Alcyonidium*), hard and crustose (*Membranipora* and *Schizoporella*), or flexible and noodlelike (*Zoobotryon*). Small colonies may adopt additional shapes and textures. Bryozoan colonies are composed of numerous nearly microscopic zooids which usually do not exceed 0.05″ (1 mm). Zooids are diversified for different functions. Feeding zooids resemble hydrozoan polyps and have a circle of ciliated suspension-feeding tentacles (lophophore) around the mouth. Nonfeeding zooids adopt various other shapes. Some form enclosures (ovicells) for developing eggs, others resemble birds' beaks (avicularia) and are used to pinch would-be fouling orga-

nisms and predators, still others form tubular stolons (kenozooids) that interconnect feeding zooids. Colonies grow by budding from a single founder larva, the ancestrula, and are always hermaphrodites. Moss animals secrete collagenous, chitinous, or calcareous exoskeletons that protect the zooids and help support the colonies. In many species, such as *Membranipora* and *Schizoporella,* each zooid is enclosed in a rigid, calcareous, boxlike exoskeleton (Fig. 265). Feeding zooids extend

Fig. 265

their soft unprotected lophophores from these boxes to feed. When disturbed, the lophophores are rapidly retracted and a protective operculum may be present to close the opening. Bryozoans are primarily marine but a few species live in freshwater.

The phylum Bryozoa is divided into three classes. The primitive class Phylactolaemata is found exclusively in freshwater and will not be discussed further. The class Stenolaemata is exclusively marine and the class Gymnolaemata is primarily so. The Bryozoa contains approximately 4000 species worldwide. This book illustrates and discusses only a few of our 30 or more species.

Class Stenolaemata ("narrow throat")

Members of this class are known as tubular bryozoans because individual zooids occupy long, narrow, calcified tubes. There is one common species (*Crisia eburnea*) in our area that forms brittle, white, bushy tufts and in the field can be confused with some white species of *Bugula*. All living species of Stenolaemata belong to the order Cyclostomata ("circular mouth").

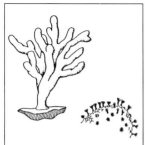

Fig. 266

Fig. 267

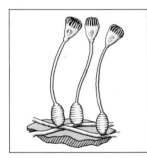

Fig. 268

Class Gymnolaemata ("naked throat")

The gymnolaemates are primarily marine and include the majority of bryozoan species. The mouth of each zooid lacks an upper lip, the lophophore is more or less circular, and the body wall lacks layers of muscle. The class is divided into two orders, the Ctenostomata and Cheilostomata.

The order Ctenostomata ("comb mouth") includes species with zooids lacking calcified exoskeletons, opercula, avicularia, and ovicells. The aperture of the zooid is closed by a sphincter muscle and embryos are brooded in the upper (distal) part of the feeding zooid. The common large ctenostomes in our area are *Anguinella palmata* (C18), *Alcyonidium hauffi* (Fig. 266), and *Zoobotryon verticillatum* (Pl. A34).

Members of the order Cheilostomata ("lip mouth") are diversified bryozoans with hard calcified exoskeletons. The zooids are often boxlike, and an operculum closes over the aperture when the lophophore is retracted. Ovicells and avicularia, as well as other specialized zooids, occur in many species. The cheilostomes are divided into three suborders, two of which are well-represented along our coast, the Anasca ("without a sac") and the Ascophora ("sac bearers"). Anascan zooids have rigid side walls but a flexible membranous upper wall. The upper wall can be bowed inward by attached muscles to cause the lophophore to pop out. Ascophoran zooids calcify the upper wall, presumably to resist predators, and have a small, internal, seawater-filled sac which opens to the outside at a pore. Muscles attached to one wall of the sac cause it to bow inward and extend the lophophore. Common anascan cheilostomes in our area are species of *Membranipora* and *Bugula* (Fig. 267). Ascophoran cheilostomes are represented by *Schizoporella unicornis*.

PHYLUM KAMPTOZOA

Kamptozoans are tiny tentaculate animals that attach to algae, rocks, shells, and animals. Each individual consists of a cuplike body atop a muscular attachment stalk (Fig. 268). The upper surface of the body bears a horseshoe-shaped row of short unbranched tentacles, a mouth, and an anus. The mouth and anus are connected by a U-shaped gut. The body also contains a minute brain, a pair of excretory organs, and one or two pairs of gonads.

Kamptozoans, which range in size from 0.1″–0.5″ (2 mm–1.3 cm), use the ciliated tentacles to produce water currents from which they trap suspended food particles. The larger species, such as *Barentsia laxa* or *Pedicellina cernua,* are colonial and individuals are interjoined by a creeping rootlike stolon. The larger kamptozoans are permanently attached but are capable of bending and twisting on their flexible stalks, a behavior that is responsible for the name kamptozoan, which means "flexible animal." Many of the smaller species are solitary, often motile, and commensal with other animals whose respiratory water currents are exploited to assist in feeding. Kamptozoans are also called entoprocts or calyssozoans. The name entoproct refers to the position of the anus within the ring of tentacles (in contrast to the bryozoans, or ectoprocts, in which the anus is outside of the ring). Calyssozoan means "cup animal" and refers to the shape of the body.

All kamptozoans are probably hermaphrodites although the sperms often mature before the eggs. Individuals may be found, therefore, that contain only sperms or eggs. Larvae may be released into the plankton or more commonly retained and brooded in a depression on the body inside the ring of tentacles. The tentacles curl, fingerlike, over the growing larvae to protect them.

There are approximately 150 species of kamptozoans described worldwide in three or four families and less than 10 described species from our region. Kamptozoans are common in our waters but because of their small size and cryptic habits they are frequently overlooked. Kamptozoans are primarily marine except for two species of *Urnatella* that occur in freshwater.

Fig. 269

PHYLUM SIPUNCULA ("a little siphon")

Sipunculans are unsegmented worms with a well-developed, fluid-filled body cavity (coelom). Adult sipunculans range in size from 0.5″ (1.3 cm) to more than 24″ (61 cm). The body consists of a wide bulbous or cylindrical trunk and a long, narrow, tubular introvert. The introvert terminates in a crown of hollow ciliated tentacles and can be retracted into the trunk (Fig. 269). The retracted introvert causes the trunk to swell and, in some species, resemble a shelled peanut, thus explaining the common name, "peanut worms." The skin of peanut worms is overlain with a thick, tough, flexible exoskeleton (cuticle). The cuticle on the trunk is usually bumpy but on the introvert it is smooth and often bears hooks and spines. The mouth and anus are both located anteriorly on the animal so that the alimentary canal is more or less U-shaped. The mouth is situated in the crown of tentacles on the anterior tip of the introvert. A long esophagus joins a long coiled intestine that extends posteriorly into the trunk. The intestine turns anteriorly, joins the rectum, and opens at a dorsal anus near the base of the introvert. The musculature is well-developed and two pairs of powerful retractor muscles pull the introvert into the body. Circular and longitudinal muscles compress the body and raise coelomic pressure to force the introvert out of the body. The coeloms of the trunk and tentacles are separate but both contain suspended cells that function in waste removal, internal defense, and gas exchange. Some of these cells are pink and contain the respiratory pigment hemerythrin. Sipunculans do not have blood vessels. Reproductive cells also undergo development in the fluid of the trunk coelom. They are collected and stored by a pair of excretory organs before being released to the sea. Sipunculans develop a larval stage, called a trochophore, that resembles larvae of annelids and molluscs. Some species pass through a second, long-lived, larval stage called a pelagosphera.

Sipunculans are entirely marine and are found at all depths in all oceans. They may be burrowers in sediments, nestlers in crevices or fouling material, occupants of abandoned shells, and borers in limestone. Burrowing species use the protraction-retraction cycle of the introvert to pull themselves through sediment. In other life styles, introvert retraction causes the trunk to swell and wedges it firmly in the substratum. Peanut worms are deposit or suspension feeders. There are over 300 species worldwide but only 3 common species in our area, *Sipunculus nudus* (Fig. 125), *Themiste alutacea* (Pl. B1), and *Phascolion strombus* (Fig. 124). The phylum is divided into four families.

PHYLUM NEMATODA ("threadlike")

Figure 270

Nematodes, or roundworms, are typically elongate worms that taper at both ends (Fig. 270). The mouth is at one end and the anus is near the other. Just behind the anus is a short tail which ends in a single adhesive toe. The body is covered with a tough flexible cuticle. It is molted four times but, unlike arthropods, growth continues between molts. The straight, cylindrical gut is divided into two parts, the pharynx and intestine. The pharynx is muscular and pumps fluid and small food particles from the mouth into the intestine. Often the cuticle lining the mouth is specialized as cutting teeth or a piercing stylet. Digestion occurs in the intestine. A pair of conspicuous anterior sense organs, called amphids, is typical of marine roundworms and useful in their classification. Nematode sexes are usually separate and, after mating and egg laying, the eggs develop directly into small roundworms. One common marine species, *Rhabditis marina,* gives birth to live young.

Roundworms are among the most numerous and diversified of all animals but are often overlooked because most are microscopic or internal parasites. Parasitic roundworms are familiar to most people. They cause damage and disease to crops, livestock, pets, and people. The dog heartworm is a parasitic roundworm (*Dirofilaria immitis*) as is the common human pinworm (*Enterobius vermicularis*). Hookworms, *Necator americanus,* were introduced from the Old World with the slave trade and still infect and debilitate nearly two million Americans, primarily in the Southeast. Those who eat raw or improperly cooked pork risk contracting trichinosis, a dangerous disease caused by another nematode, *Trichinella spiralis.* Not all terrestrial and freshwater nematodes are parasitic and many are free-living. Marine nematodes may also be parasites, as is the female of *Placentonema gigantissima,* which parasitizes the placenta of sperm whales and exceeds 27' (8 m) in length. At the other extreme, *Theristus polychaetophilus* is 0.1" (2 mm) long and is seen occasionally feeding with its head embedded in the skin of some of our polychaetes. Most marine nematodes are microscopic, free-living, and resemble the intestinal roundworms of cats and dogs. A few, however, are strikingly different. Members of the sand-dwelling family, Epsilonematidae, have a joint, like an ant's waist, in the middle of the body. They move like inchworms alternately attaching their front and hind ends to sand grains. Another atypical group, the fuzzy-looking Stilbonematinae, contains species which consume bacteria which they cultivate on their cuticles. The nematode, *Astomonema jenneri,* lives on the tube of the polychaete, *Kinbergonuphis jenneri,* and is mouthless but its reduced gut contains symbiotic bacteria. The bacteria apparently consume hydrogen sulfide in the sediment and release some of the energy to the host. Because of their minute size or parasitic habits, nematode identification is not considered in this guide.

PHYLUM MOLLUSCA ("soft")

The mollusc body includes a large muscular foot, a small head, and a soft unsegmented body covered by a hard, nonliving, calcareous shell. A fold of body wall, called the mantle, encloses a mantle cavity, in which the gills are usually located. The mantle secretes the shell and is often sensory. Many molluscs have a rasplike renewable ribbon of teeth, the radula, in the mouth cavity. Some have a renewable rod of crystallized digestive enzymes, the crystalline style, in the stomach. Enzymes are released as the style rotates against a hardened spot on the wall of the stomach. As it turns it winds a string of food and mucus into the stomach. There are eight classes of molluscs reflecting eight different ways of assembling the above components into a functional animal. Of

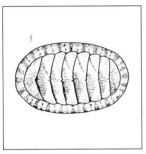

Fig. 271

the eight only five, the Polyplacophora, Gastropoda, Cephalopoda, Bivalvia, and Scaphopoda, are important in shallow water. The remaining three, the Caudofoveata, Solenogastres, and Monoplacophora occur in deeper water.

Class Polyplacophora ("bearer of many plates")

The class Polyplacophora consists of the chitons ("coat of mail"), which are unique in having shells composed of eight overlapping dorsal plates (Fig. 271). The chitons are elongate, oval, strongly flattened molluscs with a broad creeping foot and well-developed head. The

Fig. 272

mantle cavity with its many gills is on the two sides of the animal. The chitons as a class are adapted for life on turbulent rocky coasts where their low profile and broad foot help keep them from being swept away. They use the radula to scrape algae from the rocks. As might be expected in an area without rocky coasts, the Southeast has a poorly developed chiton fauna with only one common species. There are about 500 species worldwide.

Fig. 273

Class Gastropoda ("stomach foot")

The gastropods are the snails, slugs, and sea slugs. The ancestral gastropod body plan includes a broad creeping foot, a well-developed head with sensory tentacles and eyes, a spiraled one-piece shell, and an asymmetrical body twisted, or torted, 180° atop the foot (Figs. 272 and 273). The mantle cavity and gills are located anteriorly above the head. There is a radula but the style is usually absent. The shell is a calcareous cone that is usually coiled into a spiral (Fig. 274). A single opening, the aperture, is

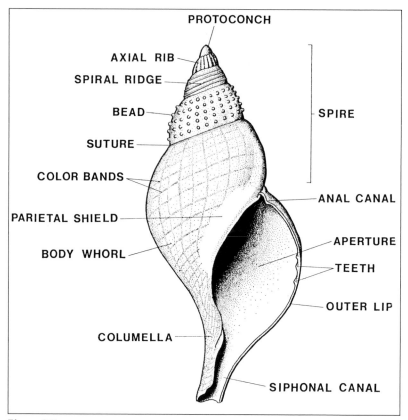

PROTOCONCH

AXIAL RIB

SPIRAL RIDGE

BEAD

SUTURE

COLOR BANDS

PARIETAL SHIELD

BODY WHORL

COLUMELLA

SPIRE

ANAL CANAL

APERTURE

TEETH

OUTER LIP

SIPHONAL CANAL

Figure 274

located at the base and permits the retraction of the head and foot into the shell. The coils wind around a central longitudinal axis, the columella, and each complete revolution is called a whorl. Because of twisting (torsion) and coiling, typical snails are asymmetrical. The animal begins life as a larva, called the veliger, in a tiny coiled shell, the protoconch. As the animal grows it adds calcareous material around the aperture to lengthen and enlarge the diameter of the shell. The oldest and smallest parts are at the apex of the shell with the youngest and largest at the base. Most of the body of the animal occupies the last whorl which is called the body whorl. The stack of whorls above the body whorl is the spire. The anterior end of the aperture often has a groove, the siphonal canal, beside the columella. Occasionally there is a second groove, the anal canal, at the opposite side of the aperture from the siphonal canal. Most gastropods have a doorlike operculum to close the aperture when the animal is withdrawn. Snail shells may be either dextral (right-handed) or sinistral (left-handed) and this handedness is sometimes important in identification. A shell viewed with the aperture facing the observer and the spire pointed up is dextral if the aperture is on the right of the shell, sinistral if on the left.

The slugs and sea slugs have altered many features of this basic plan. Notable changes are the reduction or complete loss of the shell and uncoiling and untwisting (detorsion) of the body to restore the original bilateral symmetry of the molluscs. There is also a tendency to modify the gills. Often the original gills are lost and replaced with new respiratory structures. The 35,000 species of living gastropods belong to three subclasses, the Prosobranchia, Opisthobranchia, and Pulmonata.

Subclass Prosobranchia ("front gill")

Almost all prosobranchs have coiled shells and torted (twisted) bodies. The mantle cavity is anterior and usually has one gill. A proteinaceous or calcareous operculum is usually present. The prosobranchs are primarily marine but there are some terrestrial and freshwater species. Members are typically dioecious, with separate sexes. There are three orders, the Archaeogastropoda ("ancient gastropoda"), Mesogastropoda ("intermediate gastropods"), and Neogastropoda ("new gastropods"). Most snails are either mesogastropods or neogastropods, but all three orders are represented on our coast. The archaeogastropods are thought to be the most primitive prosobranchs. They have two (primitive condition) or one (advanced condition) gills in an anterior mantle cavity. A shell is present but sometimes is not coiled. The body is torted although this may not always be apparent externally. The group includes the abalones, slit snails, top snails, keyhole limpets, true limpets, turban snails, nerites, and many others in six superfamilies. Only two of the superfamilies are represented in shallow water on our coast. One of these, the Fissurellacea ("little split"), includes the keyhole limpets. As adults these archaeogastropods have conical uncoiled shells that resemble volcanoes. There is a large opening at the base of the cone for the foot and a small opening at the apex for the exit of the respiratory water current. The mantle cavity is anterior and contains two gills, one right and one left. Externally the animal appears bilaterally symmetrical but the body is in fact torted beneath the shell. True limpets, in the superfamily Patellaceae ("dish"), are not present within the confines of the Carolinian faunal province. They resemble the keyhole limpets but have only one gill (the left) and lack the apical opening in the shell. The other Carolinean superfamily, the Trochaceae ("wheel"), includes among others, the top and turban snails in the families Trochidae (tops) and Turbanidae (turbans). These snails have well-developed, spiral, more or less conic shells. They have lost the right gill so that only the left is present.

Major Groups of Marine Animals

The orders Mesogastropoda and Neogastropoda include most marine snails. The differences between the two orders are technical and of little use in the field. They usually have strong, coiled shells, are usually dextral, and an operculum is usually present. The mantle cavity is anterior and only the left gill is present. The neogastropods are entirely marine but a few mesogastropods are found in freshwater or terrestrial situations. The southeastern families are discussed in the identification section.

Subclass Opisthobranchia ("rear gill")

Opisthobranchia is a varied group including the sea slugs, sea hares, bubble snails, and many others. Opisthobranchia is thought to be an advanced group derived from prosobranch-like ancestors. Primitively they are torted and asymmetrical with a spiral shell but there is a strong tendency within the subclass to detort the body, lose the shell, and readopt bilateral symmetry. Because of the variety that has resulted, the group is difficult to characterize. The body may be torted or detorted, the shell present or absent. If a shell is present it may be spiral or not. The mantle cavity may be present or absent. Gills may be present or absent and, if present, their morphology and position vary greatly. A radula is usually present. The foot is usually gastropodlike, *i.e.,* broad and flat for creeping, but in some groups it develops lateral wings, or parapodia, which are used for swimming. The head is usually well developed with sensory tentacles, eyes and in many species, sensory rhinophores. Part of the gut, the digestive gland, may be branched with the branches extending into fingerlike dorsal cerata projecting from the back of the animal. Opisthobranchs are hermaphrodites, with both sexes in each individual. There are nine orders of which four are important in our habitats.

Order Cephalaspidea ("head shield")

The cephalaspids are the bubble snails. Like most of the opistho-branch orders they exhibit much variability. A shell is present but tends to be reduced and may be internal. In our species it is external and may be coiled, well developed, and prosobranch-like or it may have a reduced spire and large open body whorl. The top of the head is often flattened to form a plowlike cephalic shield used in burrowing.

Order Sacoglossa ("sac tongue")

The sacoglossans resemble the nudibranchs but differ in some respects, including their adoption of an herbivorous diet of algae. They are usually more or less sluglike and the shell is absent in all of our species. They are detorted and the head bears a pair of tentaclelike sensory rhinophores. The radula bears a single file of teeth used to pierce the algal cells upon which they feed. Discarded teeth accumulate in a sac from which the order derives its name.

300

Order Anaspidea ("no shield")

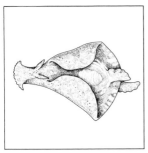

The sea hares are large swimming opisthobranchs that feed on seaweeds, especially green algae (Fig. 275). They have a long narrow foot, often with large, lateral, winglike parapodia which they use for swimming. The shell is reduced and, if present, is largely or entirely internal. The head is well developed with eyes, a pair of tentacles, and a pair of rhinophores. The latter resemble rabbit ears, hence the common name. The head has no flattened cephalic shield. A radula is present and many species are capable of releasing an inklike defensive substance.

Fig. 275

Order Nudibranchia ("naked gill")

This is the largest and most variable of the opisthobranch orders and we have many species on our coast. All nudibranchs, or sea slugs, are detorted, bilaterally symmetrical, and lack a shell. The head always bears a pair of rhinophores and may also have a pair of tentacles and eyes. Gills are variously located, occasionally absent. The foot is broad and flat. The back often bears numerous fingerlike processes called cerata which contain extensions of the digestive gland. Small capsules called cnidosacs, which contain undischarged stinging cells salvaged from cnidarian prey may be present at the tips of the cerata. The nudibranchs are carnivores, feeding mostly on sponges, cnidarians, or bryozoans. There are five suborders.

Suborder Doridoidea (Doris was a Greek sea goddess)

This is a diverse group which is difficult to characterize. The rhinophores are retractile but usually have no sheath surrounding them.

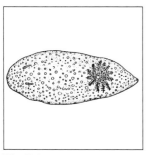

The head tentacles are small and often flattened. The anus is usually located mid-dorsally on the posterior end of the back where it is often surrounded by a ring of retractile gills. A radula is usually present. The body may be strongly flattened (Fig. 276) or sluglike. The back, or notum, may bear papillae, bumps, or ceratalike processes, but these never contain a lobe of the digestive gland or cnidosacs. The skin of the back may contain calcareous spicules similar to those of some sponges and there are often glands capable of releasing defensive substances. The doridoideans feed primarily on sponges but many species eat bryozoans, ascidians, hydroids, and other invertebrates.

Fig. 276

301

Major Groups of Marine Animals

Suborder Dendronotacea ("tree back")

The dendronotaceans mostly feed on cnidarians of various types (Pl. B16). The rhinophores are retractile and are surrounded by a sheath. The anus is on the right side. The notum has a longitudinal ridge on each side which bears branched treelike cerata. The cerata function as gills but may also contain lobes of the digestive gland and sometimes cnidosacs. Other gills are not present.

Suborder Arminoidea

Only one species of this suborder is present in the Southeast. The rhinophores of arminoideans lack sheaths and are usually not retractile. The anus is usually anterior on the right side and there are usually no tentacles on the head. Our only species, *Armina tigrina* (Pl. A13), belongs to the family Arminidae and is strongly flattened like a doridoid. *Armina* has no cerata. The notum overhangs the foot to form lateral mantle cavities into which the numerous gills protrude. Branches of the digestive gland extend into the gills.

Fig. 277

Suborder Aeolidoidea

This is a large suborder to which many of our nudibranchs belong. All aeolidoideans have depressed sluglike bodies with numerous smooth fingerlike cerata on the back (Fig. 277). The cerata contain outgrowths of the digestive gland and cnidosacs. The rhinophores are not retractile or sheathed. The head usually has a pair of tentacles and the anterior corners of the foot are often elongated to form an additional pair of tentaclelike processes. The anus is on the right. Most aeolidoideans feed on cnidarians and store their undigested nematocysts in cnidosacs for later use in their own defense. A radula is present. The aeolidoideans are often brightly colored.

Subclass Pulmonata ("having lungs")

Pulmonates are the terrestrial and freshwater snails and slugs. Very few are found in marine environments and those that are are mostly limited to the intertidal or supratidal fringe of the sea. Pulmonates may or may not have a shell but if one is present, it is usually coiled. Unlike most other snails, the pulmonates lack an operculum. Respiration is accomplished with a vascularized pouch in the mantle cavity which functions as a lung and breathes air. The lung opens to the exterior via an opening called the pneumostome. Some aquatic species have reinvented gills. The pulmonates have a radula and are hermaphrodites. Pulmonates are poorly represented in marine habitats and we have only three species of importance in our area. All are restricted to the intertidal fringe. They are the two marsh snails, *Melampus* and *Detracia,* and the false limpet, *Siphonaria.*

Class Cephalopoda ("head foot")

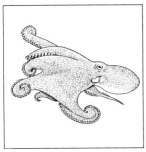

Fig. 278

The cephalopods consist of the chambered nautilus, paper nautilus, octopods (Fig. 278), and squids. The foot is closely associated with the head and is made of sucker-bearing arms and tentacles. The shell is usually reduced or absent and the head and nervous system are well developed. The mantle cavity contains the gills and is surrounded by powerful muscles which forcefully eject jets of water for use in swimming. The mouth has a pair of beaklike jaws and a radula. Sometimes there are poison glands derived from salivary glands. Cephalopods have vertebratelike eyes. The sexes are separate. Of the two cephalopod subclasses, Nautiloidea and Coleoidea, only the latter is represented on our coast. The nautiloids, reduced to only 5 living species of chambered nautilus, are restricted to the Indo-Pacific region. These animals have a well developed, spiral, external, chambered shell. The coleoids are the octopods and squids. Squids have eight arms and two longer tentacles,

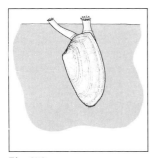

Fig. 279

are active swimmers, and have reduced internal, usually cartilagelike, shells. In one group the shell is a flat spiral but in most it is an elongate pen. Octopods have eight arms and no tentacles, are usually benthic, and have no shell, or at best, a vestigial internal one.

Class Bivalvia ("two doors")

The bivalves are the clams, oysters, mussels, shipworms, and their relatives (Fig. 279). The term clam is appropriate for any bivalve. Clams have a single shell composed of two parts, or valves, held together at the hinge by a protein ligament (Fig. 280). The hinge is dorsal and the valves are right and left. The bivalve head is reduced and poorly equipped with sense organs. The foot is well developed and is usually used for digging, but sometimes for creeping or other purposes. In many bivalve families the foot secretes protein strands which form a byssus for attachment to some object or surface. The mantle forms two large, thin, lateral lobes which secrete the shell and ligament and enclose a spacious mantle cavity on each side of the foot and body, or visceral mass, of the clam.

Major Groups of Marine Animals

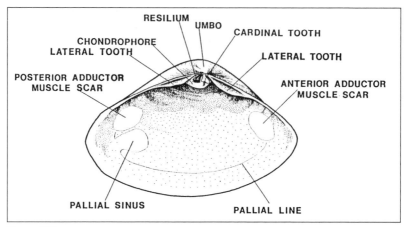

Figure 280

The gills are usually large and almost always function in filter feeding as well as respiration. The valves of a bivalve shell are held together by the hinge ligament, whose elastic protein fibers store the energy necessary to open the valves. Powerful adductor muscles inside the shell run from one valve to the other and are responsible for closing the valves. There are usually two adductor muscles, one anterior and one posterior. The attachment sites of these muscles, called adductor muscle scars, are usually easy to see on the inside surface of the valves. Some bivalves have only one adductor muscle. The mantle secretes and underlies the valves and is attached to them along the pallial line, which parallels the margin of the valve. Posteriorly, the mantle forms two tubes, the incurrent and excurrent siphons. The ventral incurrent siphon brings clean water into the mantle cavity, from which it will move upward through the gills and then out the dorsal excurrent siphon. In most bivalves, food and oxygen are removed from the water as it passes through the gills. Cilia on the surface of the gills move the food anteriorly to the mouth where it is mixed with mucus and then wound into the stomach by the twisting of the windlass-like crystalline style. The position of the siphons is marked on the valve by a concavity, the pallial sinus, in the posterior pallial line. When retracted, the siphons fit into this space.

Externally, the calcareous valves are covered by a proteinaceous periostracum, which may be thick, thin, eroded, or absent. The valves frequently bear sculpture, often in the form of radial or concentric ridges and grooves. The hinge contains teeth to maintain proper alignment between the two valves. In most molluscs the valves are symmetrical, or nearly so, but many species have asymmetrical valves. The oldest part of each valve is the umbo, or beak, which is a raised area beside the hinge.

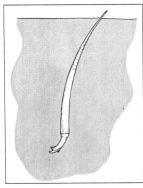

Fig. 281

There are over 20,000 species of bivalves living today arranged in 5 subclasses, 4 of which (Protobranchia, Pteriomorpha, Paleoheterodonta, and Anomalodesmata) are represented in our coastal marine waters. The fifth subclass (Heterodonta) comprises primarily freshwater species, which are often known as freshwater mussels.

Class Scaphopoda ("shovel foot")

The scaphopods are the tusk and tooth molluscs, so called because the shells resemble either an elongate tusk (Fig. 281) or a canine tooth. A shell is always present and is composed of a single piece in the form of a hollow cone, or tube, open at both ends. The mantle is well developed but the head is small. Long filamentous processes, called captacula, extend from the head and are used in feeding. Scaphopods inhabit the surface layer of sandy sediments where they use the captacula to capture foraminiferans and other small invertebrates. A foot is present and is used for digging. There are no gills and the sexes are separate. The scaphopods are poorly represented in our shallow waters.

PHYLUM NEMERTEA ("the unerring one")

The nemerteans are long, slender, soft, unsegmented worms with an eversible proboscis (Fig. 282). They range in body length from 0.1″ (2 mm) to over 40″ (1 m). The threadlike body of one European species,

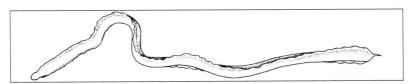

Figure 282

Lineus longissimus, is reported to reach 98′ (30 m) in length. Although southeastern species of nemerteans rarely exceed 8″ (20 cm), nemerteans in general are highly extensible animals that are capable of extending to 10 times their resting lengths. Many species can flatten their bodies like a ribbon and some, like *Cerebratulus lacteus,* can swim. For this reason, nemerteans are often referred to as "ribbon worms."

The nemertean proboscis may be as long or longer than the body and rests coiled in a fluid-filled reservoir, the rhynchocoel, above the gut. When muscles in the walls of this reservoir contract, the pressure increases and the proboscis is expelled rapidly through a small pore at the anterior tip of the worm. Nemerteans are predators and the proboscis is used primarily to capture prey although it is also used as a burrowing aid and in defense. It is long, threadlike, and coated with a sticky toxic mucus, or armed with a barb (stylet) which repeatedly stabs the prey. Nemerteans prey on annelids, small crustaceans, molluscs, and other animals. They are famous for the unerring accuracy of their proboscis attacks and are sometimes called "proboscis worms."

Nemerteans lack a cuticle or exoskeleton. The skin is densely ciliated and the action of the cilia circulates water for gas exchange and absorption of dissolved nutrients. Locomotion is primarily by muscular creeping. Conspicuous sensory organs occur on the head of many species. Reddish or blackish eyespots are often situated dorsally near the large brain and sometimes within the anterior ends of two lateral nerve cords. Ciliated grooves, which detect odors and tastes, are oriented laterally, transversely, or obliquely on the head. The circulatory system is well-developed but only rarely contains red blood cells. Often the brain and anterior ends of the nerve cords are pink or blood red with hemoglobin. The circulatory system is associated with the gut, gonads, muscles, excretory organs, and rhynchocoel. The mouth occurs at the anterior tip of the body or ventrally on the head. The gut is straight but often develops multiple side branches to increase the digestive surface area and to distribute nutrients. Food is digested rapidly in nemerteans, often within an hour after ingestion. The anus is at the hind end of the body. The sexes are usually separate and gonads develop as a series of small lateral sacs which interdigitate with branches of the gut in the trunk region. When ripe, each sac independently liberates gametes to the outside for fertilization. Nemertean development includes a short-lived larval stage (direct development) or a prolonged, planktonic, larval stage (indirect development) called a pilidium. A few species are viviparous. Nemerteans regenerate after damage or loss of body parts.

There are 900 species of nemerteans worldwide and approximately 25 species in our area. They may burrow actively in sediments, occupy crevices on hard surfaces, secrete and occupy membranous tubes on rocks and shells, creep among fouling organisms, live commensally on clams, or eat the eggs of crabs. There are some planktonic, freshwater, and even terrestrial species.

The phylum is divided into two classes, the Anopla and the Enopla. The Anopla ("unarmed") includes species without a proboscis stylet and with separate mouth and proboscis openings. The Enopla ("armed") includes species with a proboscis stylet and usually with a united mouth and proboscis pore.

PHYLUM PLATYHELMINTHES ("flat worms")

The Platyhelminthes is a large diverse phylum with approximately 13,000 species in three classes, the free-living, marine, freshwater, and terrestrial Turbellaria, the parasitic Trematoda, or flukes, and the parasitic Cestoda, or tapeworms. The three classes are discussed below but only turbellarians are identified in this guide.

Flatworms do not possess a circulatory system or coelom and rely instead on diffusion to deliver oxygen to their tissues. Because diffusion is not effective over distances greater than 0.04″ (1 mm), flatworms have small cylindrical or large flat bodies. Only the large flat species are noticeable without a microscope and these are responsible for the phylum name. The entire flatworm body surface functions as a gill and no tissue is more than one millimeter away from it. The gut, however, is a centrally-positioned tube or sac which may be more than one millimeter from the sides of the body in large flat species. In these species, blood vessel-like branches from the gut distribute nutrients to outlying tissues.

The mouth may be anterior and terminal or on the lower side of the body. It may be a simple ciliated pore in herbivores or at the end of an eversible muscular pharynx in many carnivores. Flatworms lack an anus. The flatworm skin lacks an exoskeleton and is ciliated and microscopically folded like a digestive tract lining. Consequently, the flatworm skin, like that of nemerteans, is well-suited for direct uptake of dissolved organic molecules and two of the three platyhelminth classes, the flukes and tapeworms, are parasites which take up nutrients from the host through their skin. The free-living turbellarians also may supplement their feeding by absorption of dissolved organics through the skin. A loose mass of cells called parenchyme ("an infusion") occupies the space between the skin and the gut. It surrounds the muscles, the excretory organs, and a complex hermaphroditic reproductive system. Most flatworms are hermaphrodites with internal fertilization. Eggs are laid singly or in masses and usually develop directly into juvenvile flatworms. A few turbellarians (polyclads), the flukes, and the tapeworms have larval stages.

Fig. 283

Class Turbellaria ("a disturbance")

There are approximately 2700 species of free-living flatworms but many are tiny and inconspicuous. The largest, which reach several centimeters in length, are very flat and belong to two of the 12 orders (Fig. 283). These are the primarily freshwater and terrestrial Tricladida ("three branches") whose gut is divided into three main branches which are themselves subdivided, and the primarily marine Polycladida ("many branches") whose gut gives rise to many, vessel-like, lateral branches. The triclads include the familiar "planaria" (*Dugesia*) of high school and college biology courses and the very long, sticky, terrestrial *Bipalium adventitium* which occasionally appears on damp porches and patios. All the flatworms illustrated in this book are polyclads. Polyclads are large, predatory, and often colorful. Most are benthic, many can swim, and a few are pelagic.

Class Trematoda ("perforated")

The trematodes, or flukes, are external or internal parasites of other animals and are not covered by this guide. They have more or less flattened, oval, superficially leechlike bodies with a sucker at each end. They have a gut and well-developed reproductive system. The life cycle is often complicated and many include up to four hosts and several different larval types. The intermediate hosts are inhabited by the larvae and are usually invertebrates, often snails. The final, or definitive, host is infested by the adult worm and is usually a vertebrate. Fluke larvae are freshwater or marine animals although the adult may inhabit terrestrial vertebrates, including humans. Most species infesting humans, such as liver flukes and those causing schistosomiasis, have freshwater intermediate hosts.

Order Monogenea ("one generation")

Monogenes are external parasities of fishes, or occasionally invertebrates, and they have only one host in the life cycle. Most are found on the skin or gills of fishes but some live in frogs, turtles or fishes whereas others live externally on crustaceans or squids. They tend to be very host specific.

Order Digenea ("two generations")

Digenes are internal parasites whose life cycle includes from one to three intermediate hosts. The adults parasitize vertebrates whereas the larvae are found in invertebrates and vertebrates. Many marine fishes serve as intermediate or definitive hosts. A condition known to fishermen as "black spot disease" is caused when fluke larvae (metacercariae) form small black cysts in the skin of fishes. The definitive host of these larvae is usually a fish-eating bird. Fishermen may also notice the very large stomach worms, *Hirundinella ventricosa,* in some pelagic billfish species such as wahoo and bonita. "Swimmer's itch" is caused by the larvae of a fluke, *Austrobilharzia variglandis,* which is discussed with its host, the mud snail, *Ilyanassa* (Fig. 139).

Class Cestoda ("a girdle")

The cestodes are the tapeworms. Members of this third class of flatworms are highly specialized for a parasitic life in the gut of vertebrates. They have entirely lost the gut and absorb all nutrients through the skin. They are very long and narrow, consisting of an anterior scolex, used to attach to the wall of the host's intestine, and a long chain of segments, or proglottids. All inhabit vertebrates as adults and all have at least one, sometimes two, intermediate hosts that may be arthropods or vertebrates. They are specialized for prodigious reproductive output and their segments consist of little more than efficient hermaphroditic reproductive systems. Segments at the posterior end are the oldest and contain ripe eggs ready for release with the host's feces.

Relatively few of our bony marine fishes serve as definitive hosts for adult worms but many are intermediate hosts for tapeworm larvae. The best known of these larvae are the spaghetti-like worms (*Poecilancistrium caryophyllum*) often seen in the flesh of sea trout, or occasionally redfish, drum, or croaker. These long white worms will develop into the adult tapeworm when ingested by the definitive host which is a shark. These worms are harmless to humans but most people find them unappetizing.

PHYLUM ECHIURA ("serpent tail")

Echiurans, or spoon worms, were formerly classified with the Sipuncula and Priapula in a phylum called the Gephyrea which means "a bridge" and refers to the idea that these groups were intermediate between annelids and echinoderms. Nowadays the three groups are maintained as separate phyla and, although their exact relationships are uncertain, echiurans are generally regarded as close annelid relatives whereas sipunculans share characteristics with both the annelids and molluscs. The tiny phylum Priapula, which is not covered in this book, is now thought to be only distantly related to the annelids. No priapulans are known from our coast.

The body of spoon worms is composed of an unsegmented sausage-shaped trunk and a ciliated, highly extensible, but not invertible, pros-

Fig. 284

tomium with a wide ventral groove or gutter (Fig. 284). The mouth is at the base of the prostomium and the anus opens at the hind end of the body. The shortened prostomium resembles an old-fashioned marrow spoon and is responsible for the common name, "spoon worm." It is also used for feeding and as a gill. Spoon worms range in trunk size from a few inches to about 20″ (50 cm). The extended prostomium can exceed 10′ (3 m) in some species of *Bonellia*. The often pink or green trunk is covered with a thin flexible cuticle and bumpy mucus glands. A pair of fanglike setae, which are used for burrowing, is located ventrally on the front end of the trunk. One or two rings of additional setae encircle the anus in *Urechis* and *Echiurus,* respectively. The trunk encloses a large coelom and the long looping gut. The coelom also

309

contains suspended cells, some of which contain hemoglobin. In addition, most species of spoon worms have blood vessels but the blood is not pigmented. Reproductive cells undergo development in the coelom and when mature are stored in one to many pairs of ducts (nephridia) before release. Two excretory sacs project into the coelom from the rectum. Species in the genus *Echiurus* and *Urechis* gulp water through the anus and use the hind part of the intestine as a gill. Development is similar to that of polychaetes. Although some embryonic tissues may be segmented, the adults show no signs of segmentation.

Echiurans occur in all seas from the intertidal zone to at least 5.5 miles (8.8 km) below the surface. They construct and occupy burrows in sediments, nestle in crevices, and colonize abandoned mollusc shells and echinoid tests. They deposit or filter feed using the ciliated prostomium. There are approximately 140 species worldwide and two common species in our area, *Thalassema hartmani* and *Lissomyema mellita.*

PHYLUM ANNELIDA ("ringed")

The Annelida, or segmented worms, are coelomate worms whose body is divided into segments that are usually visible externally as rings. They include the polychaetes, the earthworms and their relatives, and the leeches. Annelids range in size from about 10′ (3 m) for the giant Australian earthworm (*Megascolecides australis*) to less than one millimeter for many micro-polychaetes. Most conspicuous species are 4″ to 3′ (10 cm–1 m) in length. The phylum is large, containing over 10,000 species.

The annelid body, like that of other coelomates, is organized as a tube within a tube. The inner tube is the gut and the outer is the skin and body musculature. The tubes are separated by a fluid-filled cavity, the coelom, which, in most annelids, is partitioned transversely into segments by bulkheads (septa) and longitudinally into right and left halves by dorsal and ventral mesenteries. Dorsal and ventral blood vessels, which lie in the mesenteries, allow circulation through the septa. When septa are secondarily lost, the coelom circulates fluid through the body and blood vessels are reduced or absent. The red respiratory pigment hemoglobin is widely distributed in annelid blood vessels and coelomic cavities, as well as in muscle and nerve tissues. Another respiratory pigment, the pink or violet hemerythrin, is rare in the annelids and occurs only in the polychaete family Magelonidae.

The coelom is functionally important in annelids. In addition to its role in circulation, it stores and provides nutrients for gametes, and is a skeleton. The shape of many annelids, especially polychaetes and oligochaetes, is maintained by the pressurized coelomic fluid. Changes of body shape are caused by the displacement of coelomic fluid resulting from contraction of longitudinal or circular body wall muscles. Contraction of circular muscles causes a segment to become longer and thinner whereas longitudinal muscle contraction causes a segment to become shorter and wider. These shape changes are useful to burrowers, like earthworms, and many other annelids. Burrowing annelids often generate peristaltic waves of alternating longitudinal and circular muscle contractions along their bodies. As peristaltic waves propagate, the septal partitions isolate coelomic pressure changes within segments and some segments contract while others relax. In leeches, which do not burrow, septa are absent, the coelom functions primarily as a circulatory system, and specialized postural and swimming muscles are present. The skeleton of a leech, like that of a human tongue, is composed of connective and muscle tissues.

The segmental organization of annelids extends to most systems of the body. The nervous system, which controls segmental activity, consists of two ventral nerve cords (sometimes fused) with a pair of brainlike ganglia in each segment. These are joined by a transverse connection in each segment that integrates information from left and right sides. The brain consists of a pair of dorsal cerebral ganglia situated in the first body division (prostomium) and several pairs of fused segmental ganglia forming the subesophageal ganglion below the gut. The cerebral and subesophageal ganglia are joined by connectives encircling the foregut. The segmental nephridia regulate the body's fluid volume, aid in excretion, and often are gonoducts by which gametes reach the exterior. Two kinds of nephridia occur in annelids, metanephridia and protonephridia. Metanephridia are ciliated ducts that open directly into the coelom and discharge externally at small pores. They occur primarily in annelids with blood vessels. Protonephridia are ducts that open externally at pores but the internal openings are capped by special cells that filter body fluid before it enters the duct. Protonephridia occur primarily in annelid larvae and adults that lack blood vessels. Gonads are distributed segmentally in many annelids although regional restriction to special "genital segments" is a common trend. When appendages and setae are present on the body wall, they are arranged segmentally.

The skin of annelids secretes a flexible, tough, collagenous cuticle that protects the body from punctures, kinks and aneurisms as the animal moves. Chitinous setae project from the body wall of most polychaetes and oligochaetes. External gills are found in most polychaetes and some leeches but are rare in oligochaetes. When specialized gills are absent, gas exchange occurs across the general body surface.

Reproduction in annelids is diversified. Species have separate sexes (most polychaetes) or are hermaphrodites (oligochaetes, leeches). The gonads are segmental or regionally restricted. Fertilization is typically external but can be internal. Fertilized eggs may develop via a planktonic larval stage, known as a trochophore (many polychaetes), or directly in eggs masses or cocoons. Regeneration of missing parts and limited asexual reproduction by fragmentation occur only in polychaetes and oligochaetes.

The phylum is divided into three classes: the Polychaeta, Oligochaeta, and Hirudinoidea. Polychaetes are diversified in the sea but a few species occur in freshwater. Oligochaetes are common in marine, freshwater, and terrestrial habitats. Most marine oligochaetes, however, are nearly microscopic and escape notice by all except specialists. Leeches are marine, freshwater, and terrestrial.

Class Polychaeta ("many bristles")

With over 8000 species, the polychaetes are the largest class of annelids. Each body segment usually has a pair of fleshy legs, or parapodia, which bear chitinous bristles called setae (= chaetae). Parapodia usually function as crawling legs or swimming paddles but they are often modified for other tasks such as gas exchange or food capture. The parapodia are supported by an internal, chitinous, skeletal rod, the aciculum. Setae, like parapodia, occur in a variety of forms. They may be long and pointed to increase crawling traction, flattened as swimming paddles, hooklike to grip tube or burrow linings, rasplike to cut and modify tubes, or brittle and toxic for defense. Various other specialized structures may be associated with the parapodia. Ciliated, filamentous, dorsal cirri curl over the back of many species and generate a respiratory water current. Ventral cirri may also be present. In scaleworms, fishlike scales (elytra), supported on short stalks, occur on the back and enclose a respiratory space.

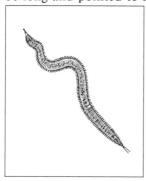

Fig. 285

Fig. 286

The polychaete body consists of an anterior preoral lobe (prostomium), a segment surrounding the mouth (peristomium), a variable number of segments, and a posterior lobe (pygidium), which bears the anus. The segments are usually numerous and similar to each other. Each one typically bears a pair of parapodia. The prostomium may be a simple rounded lobe or it may bear conspicuous sense organs and appendages such as eyes, ciliated chemoreceptive nuchal organs, antennae, tentacular crowns, and paired grooved palps. The polychaete head may consist solely of the prostomium and peristo-

312

mium but often one or more anterior body segments are incorporated into it. The parapodia and setae of segments included in the head are usually reduced but their cirri may persist as sensory head appendages called tentacular cirri. A pair of peristomial cirri may also be present.

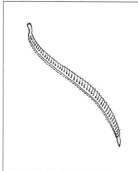

Fig. 287

Division of the body into numerous similar segments in polychaetes provides a basis for almost limitless variation (Figs. 285, 286, 287, 288, 289, 290). The number of segments varies from less than 10 to 800 or more. Regional specializations occur commonly, such as division of the body into a muscular burrowing thorax and a long digestive trunk as in capitellids. Similar functionally distinct regions occur in sabellariids and terebellids. Specialized gills may be absent (Arabellidae), restricted to the front of the body (Terebellidae), or present on each segment (Cirratulidae). Parapodia may be well-developed (Nereidae), regionally specialized (*Chaetopterus*), or virtually absent (Capitellidae).

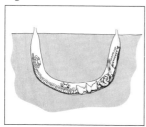

Fig. 288

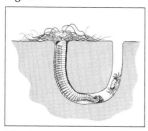

Fig. 289

The polychaete gut is straight and extends from the anterior ventral mouth on the peristomium to a terminal or dorsal anus on the pygidium. The gut is divided into two main regions, the pharynx and the intestine. The pharynx, or foregut, is specialized for food capture and may be ciliated, glandular, and muscular. Many polychaetes evert the pharynx through the mouth to catch prey, to defend themselves, or to aid in burrowing. The intestine is the site of digestion, absorption, and feces formation. One pair of excretory organs per segment is typical for most polychaetes although some, such as feather duster worms, have one giant pair per individual.

Fig. 290

Polychaete sexes are usually separate. The gonads may occur in all segments or only in specialized fertile segments. The gonad always develops just outside the coelomic lining and bulges into the coelomic cavity. As gametes form, they enter and often fill the coelom. During spawning, polychaetes with metanephridia release gametes through these ciliated ducts whereas those with protonephridia either develop a special gonoduct at maturity or the body wall simply bursts. Many reproductive polychaetes swim to the surface, *en masse,* at particular seasons to synchronize the release of gametes. Nightly reproductive swarms occur typically in spring and fall and often are triggered by moonlight. Because most polychaetes are benthic crawlers or burrowers, their bodies are not designed for swimming. Consequently, as the reproductive season approaches, many polychaetes undergo structural changes, such as enlargement of eyes and parapodia and replacement of setae, to sensitize them to light and improve their swimming performance. This metamorphosis is called "epitoky" and the reproductive individuals are known as "epitokes" ("on which young are brought forth"). In nereids, such as *Nereis succinea,* the entire adult transforms to an epitoke (or heteronereid), swims to the surface, and releases gametes through its nephridia. In other families (Syllidae, Eunicidae), the hind end of the adult becomes an epitoke, breaks free of the front end (atoke), and swims to the surface. These epitokal swarms of polychaetes can be spectacular. On our coast, myriads of pink, fishlike, fast swimming heteronereids of *N. succinea* are attracted to artificial lights in the spring and fall. In clear subtropical and tropical waters, species of syllid polychaetes time their swarms precisely to the lunar cycle and sunset and emit spectacular bioluminescent flashes.

Approximately 200 species of polychaetes occur in shallow southeastern waters and over 30 are illustrated in this book.

Class Oligochaeta ("few bristles")

The earthworms and the leeches share several features that distinguish them from polychaetes. Parapodia are absent, the prostomium is often reduced and lacks appendages, setae are simple or absent, all species are hermaphrodites, gonads are restricted to a few genital segments, and eggs are laid in cocoons produced by a glandular ring in the skin called the clitellum. The clitellum of many earthworms is a cream-colored, thickened, transverse band across a few front segments. In other oligochaetes and in leeches it is often inconspicuous.

The Oligochaeta includes the terrestrial earthworms and numerous small aquatic species, both freshwater and marine. Marine oligochaetes are earthwormlike in appearance but are rarely larger than 1″ (2.5 cm) and are very slender and threadlike, often being 30 to 60 times longer than wide. Most marine species are red because of the presence of hemoglobin. With the exception of the peristomium, each segment usually bears four bundles of setae, usually either long, slender, pointed hair setae or short, stout, curved sigmoid setae.

Identification of marine oligochaetes is exceedingly difficult and depends on microscopic examination of the internal reproductive apparatus of specially prepared specimens. The southeastern fauna is not yet well known and contains many undescribed species. They are sometimes confused with small capitellid polychaetes which are also red, threadlike, and without apparent parapodia. Oligochaetes are common

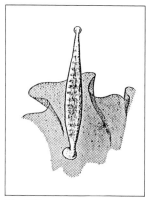

in marine, freshwater, and terrestrial sediments, particularly those with a high organic content. Marine oligochaetes feed on organic matter, like earthworms, in terrestrial soils, and are especially common in the surface sediments of salt marshes. Marine oligochaetes belong to the families Naididae, Tubificidae, and Enchytraeidae.

Class Hirudinoidea ("a leech")

Leeches are large, have a sucker at each end of the body, and lack setae and septa (Fig. 291). The body of one tropical South American species reaches 12″ (30 cm) in length but most of our marine species reach lengths of

Fig. 291

only 1–2″ (2.5–5 cm). Approximately three fourths of all leech species are blood-sucking parasites and the remaining one fourth are predators of other invertebrates. Unlike other annelids, leeches do not rely on a coelomic hydrostatic skeleton for locomotion and do not burrow. Instead, they move inchwormlike by alternate attachment of front and rear suckers or they flatten, undulate, and swim. Complex sets of antagonistic muscles accomplish these movements without the aid of a typical fluid skeleton. The usually voluminous annelid coelom is subdivided in leeches to form a dense network of capillarylike vessels joining two lateral, contractile, circulatory channels. The cells lining the coelomic vessels store nutrients and release them during the periods of starvation between feedings. The large capacity of this storage system permits leeches to gorge themselves while feeding and survive long intervening periods of starvation. While feeding, species of blood-sucking leeches may increase their body weight 2 to 10 times and afterwards survive without eating for over one year.

When feeding, leeches secrete an anticoagulant, hirudinin, into the host to prevent clotting of the blood as they drink. Recent studies have revealed a second substance, hementin, in some leeches. Unlike hirudinin, which prevents the formation of clots, hementin is an enzyme that destroys existing clots by breaking down the clot-forming protein, fibrin. This newly discovered anticoagulant may have important medical applications, perhaps in the removal of clots in human coronary arteries.

There are about 14 species of marine leeches on the east coast of the United States, most of them in the family Piscicolidae with the remainder in the Ozobranchidae. The piscicolids are the fish leeches and most are parasites of marine fishes, including sharks and rays. Members of the family Ozobranchidae parasitize marine turtles. Of our two ozobranchid species, *Ozobranchus branchiatus* is apparently restricted to the green turtle, *Chelonia mydas,* whereas *O. margoi* is found on several species of marine turtles and also on the porpoise, *Stenella longirostris.* Some members of the family parasitize crocodiles, but not in the Carolinean province, where there are no crocodiles.

PHYLUM ARTHROPODA ("jointed feet")

The phylum Arthropoda includes the crustaceans, insects, and chelicerates. Members of this phylum typically have a rigid exoskeleton that is molted periodically to allow the animal to grow. Arthropods have segmented bodies and some or all the segments bear paired jointed appendages. These appendages are specialized for a variety of functions including chemoreception, food manipulation, locomotion, and respiration. Adults of one group, the insects, usually have wings. The insects and chelicerates (*e.g.,* spiders, scorpions, ticks) are primarily terrestrial or freshwater animals with few representatives in the sea. The crustaceans, on the other hand, are abundant in the sea, common in freshwater, but nearly absent from the land.

Subphylum Chelicerata ("having pincers")

This subphylum is composed almost entirely of terrestrial and freshwater animals with few marine representatives. The group includes the terrestrial spiders, ticks, mites, and scorpions as well as the marine horseshoe crabs, sea spiders, and mites.

The chelicerate body is usually divided into two parts, the cephalothorax and abdomen. The cephalothorax is the combined head and

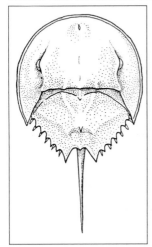

thorax and it has six pairs of appendages. The first pair is chelicerae, the second is pedipalps, and the remaining four are walking legs. The chelicerae and pedipalps usually function as mouthparts. There are no antennae or mandibles. The abdomen usually does not have appendages.

There are three classes in the Chelicerata, all of which are represented in the sea. The horseshoe crabs (Fig. 292) belong to the class Merostomata. The cephalothorax of a horseshoe crab is covered dorsally by a large, unjointed, horseshoe-shaped carapace. Ventrally it bears an anterior pair of chelicerae and five pairs of walking legs. In males, the second pair of appendages is modified to form pedipalps. A vestige of a seventh pair of

Fig. 292

appendages, the chilaria, remains behind the walking legs. The abdomen is covered by its own unjointed exoskeleton which fits neatly into the posterior concavity of the cephalothorax. Laterally it bears six pairs of spines and posteriorly there is a long spikelike telson. Ventrally,

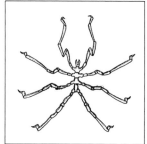

the abdomen bears six pairs of broad flaplike appendages. The first of these is an operculum and the remaining five are book gills. The horseshoe crabs, of which there are only four living species in the world, are exclusively marine.

The class Pycnogonida is composed of the sea spiders (Fig. 293), of which there are several species on our coast. A few of our species are very common. These unusual animals are spiderlike in appearance but are not closely

Fig. 293

related to true spiders. While their relationships are not clearly understood, they are usually included in the Chelicerata. They are common among hydroids and bryozoans in epibenthic communities in shallow water. They usually have long, narrow, segmented bodies with chelicerae, pedipalps, and four pairs of walking legs, although the body shape is variable, chelicerae or pedipalps may be absent, and the number of legs may vary. The abdomen is vestigial. All species are marine.

Mites, in the class Arachnida and order Acarina, are often found in epibenthic communities. They are tiny (less than 0.1″; 2 mm) and usually escape notice in spite of their often brilliant coloring. They have no readily apparent body subdivisions. There is no abdominal segmentation and the division between the cephalothorax and abdomen is obscured. They have chelicerae, pedipalps, and four pairs of legs. Mites are present in terrestrial, freshwater, and marine habitats and one species attaches to beachhoppers.

Subphylum Crustacea ("having a shell")

The subphylum Crustacea is one of the most important groups of marine animals. Because of the relatively large size and commercial importance of many species, they are well known. The group includes the crabs, shrimps, lobsters, and barnacles as well as many less familiar animals. There is much variability within the group but most species are readily recognizable as crustaceans.

The crustacean body is segmented although the divisions between segments are not always visible, especially anteriorly. The segments are usually arranged into a head, thorax, and abdomen. In many crustaceans the head and thorax grow together to form a cephalothorax. The anterior part of the body, including the head and all or part of the thorax, is often covered by a large unsegmented fold of exoskeleton called the carapace. The crustacean head consists of five segments fused tightly together so that there is no external indication of the original segmentation. These five segments bear five pairs of appendages typical of the crustacean head. These are two pairs of antennae, a pair of mandibles, and two pairs of maxillae. The thorax is composed of a variable number of segments which usually remain separate and distinct. It may, however, be wholly or partly covered by a dorsal carapace, in which case the segments may not be visible from above. The appendages of the thorax are often specialized for locomotion, respiration or, in the case of the most anterior segments, food handling. The abdominal segments are usually separate and readily apparent. The abdomen may or may not have appendages. The most posterior abdominal appendages are often called uropods.

Most crustaceans begin life as a planktonic larva and mature through a series of molts and successive larval types to become an adult. The basic crustacean larva is the nauplius but there are many other types and stages.

Within the subphylum there are ten classes, only three of which are important in our benthic habitats. Members of the remaining classes either do not occur in our area in appreciable numbers or they are too small to be noticed by most users of this guide. Our three important classes are the Cirripedia (barnacles), Copepoda (copepods), and Malacostraca (crabs, shrimps, lobsters) and, of them, only the Cirripedia and Malacostraca are covered by this guide. All ten classes are briefly discussed below.

Class Remipedia ("oar foot")

This recently discovered class (not illustrated) is known from a few species that inhabit marine caves. Remipedians are elongate polychaete-like crustaceans with similar, biramous, swimming appendages on most of the body segments. Of all living crustaceans, the remipedians are thought to be most like the ancestor of modern crustaceans. No remipedians are known from the Southeast.

Class Cephalocarida ("head shrimp")

The cephalocarids (not illustrated) are tiny crustaceans inhabiting soft sediments. They are primitive crustaceans similar to the ancestors of modern crustaceans. All are less than 0.2" (5 mm) in length and only about 10 species have been described since their discovery in 1955. They are very rarely encountered, especially in the Southeast.

The head is large and bears five pairs of appendages but unlike that of other crustaceans, the last pair is unspecialized and identical to the thoracic appendages. There is no carapace. The thorax has eight segments, none of which are fused with the head so there is no cephalothorax. All thoracic segments bear a pair of appendages. The abdomen has 11 segments, the first of which bears a pair of rudimentary appendages. The remaining segments lack appendages although there is a pair of long whiplike caudal rami on the last segment.

Class Branchiopoda ("gill foot")

This class (not illustrated) consists of an assortment of dissimilar crustaceans, none of which is found in marine benthic habitats. The group is most important in inland waters, including salt lakes and temporary waters, although there are some planktonic marine species. Included in the Branchiopoda are the fairy shrimps and brine shrimps (Anostraca), tadpole shrimps (Notostraca), clam shrimps (Conchostraca), and water fleas (Cladocera). Cladocera is the largest group and it has some representatives in the marine zooplankton.

Class Ostracoda ("shelled")

The ostracods (not illustrated), whose small size excludes them from consideration in this guide, are the seed shrimps and are common in marine and freshwater habitats. They are small, usually microscopic, and the largest of the 2000 known species is a little less than 1″ (2.5 cm) in length. The body is reduced in length through loss of segments and they never have more than 7 pairs of appendages. They are easily recognized by their distinctive bivalved carapace which encloses all of the animal save the antennae and tips of some of the appendages. They look like tiny swimming seeds.

Class Mystacocarida ("mustache shrimp")

The mystacocarids (not illustrated) are small elongate crustaceans that live in the interstices between sand grains on sandy beaches. The class is small with only about a dozen species, all in the genera *Derocheilocaris* and *Ctenocheilocaris.* Mystacocarids are less than 0.1″ (2

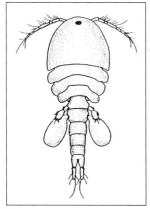

mm) in length and have the long wormlike bodies characteristic of interstitial animals. There is a head, subdivided into two parts and a five-segmented thorax, both with appendages. The ten-segmented abdomen lacks appendages but has a pair of caudal rami on its last segment. While they occur in the Southeast (the common intertidal species is *D. typica*), the mystacocarids are not covered in this guide because of their near microscopic size.

Fig. 294

Class Copepoda ("oar foot")

The class Copepoda (Fig. 294) includes nearly 10,000 species of marine and freshwater crustaceans. They are abundant in most marine habitats, especially the planktonic, meiofaunal, and epibenthic communities, but are usually very small and escape notice. Copepods are usually less than 0.1″ (2 mm) in length and have a head with five fused segments, a thorax of six segments and an abdomen with 1–5 segments. The head bears the usual appendages and the thoracic segments each bear a pair of appendages. Abdominal segments do not have appendages but the last abdominal segment bears a pair of tail-like caudal rami. There are six copepod orders, three of them free-living and three parasitic or commensal. Members of the free-living orders Cyclopoida and Calanoida are mostly planktonic while the Harpacticoida are mostly benthic. The parasitic groups tend to be highly modified for their specialized lives and often look nothing like the copepods in the free-living orders. The only species of copepod included in this guide, *Lernaeenicus radiatus,* is one of the parasitic species and is by no means representative of the class. The cursory treatment of copepods in this guide is a reflection of their small size and not their numerical or ecological importance.

Class Branchiura ("gill tail")

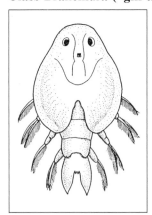

Fig. 295

This is a small class of about 75 species of parasites known as fish lice (Fig. 295). They are external parasites found on the skin or in the gill chambers of freshwater and marine fishes. They are usually less than 1″ (2.5 cm) in length and are strongly flattened dorsoventrally. There is a large oval or circular carapace over the head and part of the thorax. They have two large compound eyes and the first pair of maxillae is a pair of suckers for attaching to the host. There are four thoracic segments, each with a pair of legs. The abdomen is reduced, flattened, unsegmented, and bilobed. Fish lice attach to the host with the suckers and feed on mucus or blood. They retain their mobility through life and can change position on the host or leave one host for another. Most species, including the nine reported from the Southeast (including the Gulf of Mexico), belong to the genus *Argulus.* These nine species together parasitize at least 25 species of fishes.

Class Tantulocarida

This small class consists entirely of deep-water species that parasitize other crustaceans. It is not represented in our area.

Class Cirripedia ("curled feet")

The cirripedes are the barnacles, an exclusively marine group of very specialized and atypical crustaceans. As adults they bear little resemblance to other crustaceans and were thought to be molluscs by early naturalists. Their larval stages, however, are unmistakably crustacean and on close inspection the anatomy of most adults can be seen to be

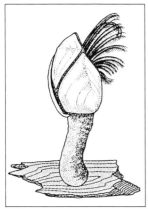

Fig. 296

crustacean. Most of the barnacles are enclosed in a vaguely mollusclike calcareous shell which is responsible for the early mistakes in classification. The typical barnacle has a reduced head, a six-segmented thorax, and a five segmented abdomen. The thorax bears six pairs of appendages while the abdomen has only the caudal furca at the posterior end. The group includes a few primitive members that bear a reasonably close resemblance to other crustaceans, some parasitic members with virtually no adult resemblance to crustaceans, and a large group of typical barnacles with a discernible, albeit obscure, resemblance to the other crustaceans.

Order Thoracica ("breast plate")

Fig. 297

The order Thoracica is the largest group of barnacles and contains the sort of animals that usually come to mind when the word barnacle is mentioned. It includes the familiar goose barnacles (suborder Lepadomorpha = "limpet-shaped," Fig. 296) and the acorn barnacles (suborder Balanomorpha = "acorn-shaped" (Fig. 297). The goose barnacles live attached to the substratum by a fleshy stalk while the acorn barnacles are attached directly to the substratum without a stalk. Both types are protected by an armor of calcareous plates. These barnacles are mostly filter feeders that use their six pairs of featherlike thoracic appendages to remove plankton from the water. The opening to the calcareous case is closed by four movable calcareous plates consisting of a pair of anterior scuta and a pair of posterior terga. These plates are controlled by muscles and are opened to allow extension of the thoracic appendages. The barnacle itself never leaves its shell.

Order Rhizocephala ("root head")

Some barnacles are specialized for parasitizing other crustaceans, especially the decapods. As adults these barnacles resemble a fungus and look nothing like other crustaceans. They send rootlike processes into the tissue of the host while a saclike reproductive structure extends outward from the body of the host. They have no appendages, mouth, gut, or segmented body as adults. They are known to be crustaceans only by their nauplius larva. Blue crabs are often parasitized by one of these rhizocephalan barnacles, *Loxothylacus texanus*. This parasite forms a large, amorphous, reproductive mass beneath the crab's abdomen where it looks superficially like the egg mass of the crab. Another species, *Loxothylacus panopaei*, parasitizes species of mud crabs including *Eurypanopeus, Neopanope*, and *Pilumnus*. The northern green crab, *Carcinus*, is attacked by *Sacculina carcini*.

The two other barnacle orders are small and contain small animals. One of them (Acrothoracica) includes small filter feeders that bore into calcareous substrata. The other order (Ascothoracica) consists of cnidarian and echinoderm parasites.

Class Malacostraca ("soft shell")

This large and important class contains all the large and familiar marine, freshwater, and terrestrial crustaceans, as well as many that are not so large or familiar. The crabs, shrimps, krill, crayfish, pill bugs, lobsters, mantis shrimps, and beachhoppers all belong to this class. The malacostracan body plan consists of the usual crustacean head of five fused segments, a thorax of eight segments, and an abdomen of six (seven in some primitive species). The head is usually fused with some of the anterior thoracic segments to form a cephalothorax and there is usually a carapace covering the head and part or all of the thorax. The head bears two pairs of biramous antennae, a pair of mandibles, and two pairs of maxillae. The thorax has eight pairs of appendages specialized for food manipulation, walking, swimming, or grasping. The appendages of those thoracic segments fused with the head are specialized to function as mouthparts and are called maxillipeds. The appendages of the remaining free thoracic segments are usually called legs, or pereopods, The malacostracan abdomen bears paired appendages of two types. In most malacostracans, the first five pairs of abdominal appendages are called pleopods, whereas the last pair are uropods. The uropods are usually stiff, flat, and leaflike and are used for swimming. The flexible pleopods are used for swimming, respiration, carrying eggs, or for generating water currents. The last, or sixth, abdominal segment bears the telson in addition to the uropods. The telson is a final, median, unpaired, segmentlike, posterior process. There are five superorders of malacostracans of which three, the Hoplocarida, Peracarida, and Eucarida, are important in our waters. The remaining two, the Leptostraca and the Syncarida, are not discussed here. Syncarida is a freshwater group and the Leptostraca have not been reported from the Carolinian faunal province although there is no apparent reason why they should not be here since they occur north and south of us. Leptostracans are tiny, primitive, shrimplike malacostracans with an enormous carapace and seven abdominal segments. *Nebalia bipes* occurs in the Northeast.

Superorder Hoplocarida ("weapon shrimp")

Fig. 298

Stomatopoda ("mouth foot") is the only order in this group. These are the mantis shrimps (Fig. 298) which are represented by a few common species in shallow southeastern waters. This is an homogenous group with all 350 or so species conforming closely to a common body plan and any stomatopod is quickly and easily recognized as such. The body is long, relatively narrow, and flattened from top to bottom (depressed). There is a carapace. The first antennae are triramous with three whiplike branches. The second antennae are biramous with one whiplike branch and one that is flat and leaflike. The eyes are large and stalked. The first five pairs of thoracic appendages are pincers and the second is spectacularly developed to form two large raptorial claws. These are folded beneath the body like those of a praying mantis and are extended rapidly to capture prey. The last three pairs of thoracic appendages are slender walking legs. The first five pairs of abdominal appendages are pleopods with gills. The last pair is two large, flat, biramous uropods. The two uropods and the flat telson make up a tail fan. The telson is often spiny.

Superorder Peracarida ("pouch shrimp")

This group, with over 11,000 species, is the largest of the malacostracan superorders. Its members, however, are almost all small and few of them come to the attention of most visitors to the coast. The abundant and ecologically important amphipods and isopods belong to this group as do several other crustaceans such as the mysids, cumaceans, and tanaids. Most people have some experience with peracarids through encounters with the terrestrial woodlice, or pillbugs, that inhabit most backyard gardens and woodpiles. The woodlice are isopods and are the only really successful terrestrial crustaceans.

The peracarids as a group are characterized by the presence of a thoracic brood chamber, or marsupium. Some of the thoracic legs of females bear large, flexible plates that together form a basket beneath the body of the animal. Eggs are released into this brood pouch where they are incubated until they hatch. After hatching the young may linger awhile in the pouch before setting out on their own.

Order Mysidacea

Our mysids (Fig. 299) are small shrimplike crustaceans less than 1″ (2.5 cm) long. They are common but are not usually encountered except in plankton or in benthic collections made with fine nets. None is discussed in this guide. They have a large carapace that covers most of

Fig. 299

the thorax and the eyes are stalked. The thoracic appendages are biramous. The inner branch of the uropod usually contains a statocyst for the detection of gravity. This sense organ is clearly visible, with a microscope, as a sphere in the base of the ramus. True shrimps have no statocyst in the uropod and no brood pouch. The abdominal appendages of the mysids are reduced and may be absent but a telson and uropods are present.

Order Cumacea

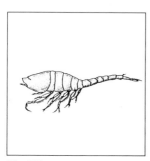

Fig. 300

These small bizarre crustaceans (Fig. 300) are represented by a handful of species on our coast. They are found on or in soft sediments and are best collected with fine nets or a fine 0.04″ (1 mm) sieve. They are usually less than 0.1″ (2 mm) in length and the head and anterior thorax are covered by a carapace to form a large swollen cephalothorax from which extends a long skinny abdomen. The anterior abdominal appendages are reduced, or absent, but a pair of uropods is present. These are biramous and are long and slender. The telson may be well developed or vestigial but there is no tail fan. Although several species are present on our coast they are too small to warrant coverage by this manual.

Order Isopoda ("similar feet")

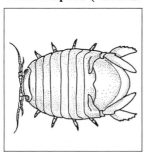

Fig. 301

This important peracarid group has many representatives on our coast but most are less than 1″ (2.5 cm) in length and are frequently overlooked. They are often confused with the amphipods to which they are closely related and which they sometimes resemble. Isopods (Fig. 301) are typically dorsoventrally flattened (depressed) whereas amphipods are usually, but not always, laterally flattened (compressed). Like amphipods, the isopods have unstalked (sessile) eyes and the head is fused with the first thoracic segment to form a small cephalothorax. There is no carapace and the remaining seven thoracic segments are visible dorsally. The usual crustacean head appendages are present and the first pair of thoracic appendages is a maxilliped. The remaining seven pairs of thoracic appendages are legs of various types usually modified for walking, clinging, swimming, or digging. The anterior legs may bear pincers. Females in breeding condition have a brood pouch. Unlike the amphipods, the abdominal appendages consist of five pairs of biramous pleopods which are the respiratory organs. They also generate a water current used in swimming. The last pair of abdominal appendages are uropods. These may contribute to a tail fan, may bear sensory setae, or may form a pair of doors to protect the delicate pleopods. The telson is fused with the sixth abdominal segment to form a pleotelson.

There is much diversity among the isopods and they have become adapted to many ecological situations, some of them unusual for crustaceans. Most are aquatic in either freshwater or marine habitats but one suborder is terrestrial and two suborders have parasitic members. They are not well represented in planktonic habitats. There are nine suborders, several of which are important in our waters, and many are represented by illustrations in this guide. Only the suborders important on our coast are discussed below.

Suborder Anthuridea

These isopods are usually small, elongate, and cylindrical so that they resemble jointed sticks or rods. The uropods, or parts of them, arch dorsally over the pleotelson. They are often sexually dimorphic. They are benthic and live in burrows in soft sediments.

Suborder Flabellifera

This large group has many members in the Southeast. They are usually dorsoventrally depressed with wide, often oval, bodies. Some are fish parasites and have asymmetrical bodies but most are free-living in epibenthic habitats and have symmetrical bodies. Some resemble the terrestrial pillbugs and like them can roll themselves into balls. A few species bore into wood, causing extensive damage.

Suborder Oniscoidea

This is the terrestrial suborder and it contains the woodlice (pillbugs, sowbugs, or ballup bugs) that are common near human habitations. It is represented in marine habitats by the wharf roaches (*Ligia*) which live in the supralittoral fringe just above the high tide line.

Suborder Valvifera

The valviferans are usually more or less elongate, with slightly depressed bodies. They have unique uropods that form a set of doors to protect the delicate respiratory pleopods.

Suborder Asellota

Most asellotes are freshwater or deep water marine animals but a few are found in shallow water. Most, or all, of the abdominal segments are fused together and one or more pairs of pleopods form a cover to protect the remaining respiratory pleopods.

Major Groups of Marine Animals

Suborder Epicaridea

The epicarideans are all parasitic on crustaceans and feed on blood. There are four families of which the Bopyridae is most likely to be encountered in our waters. The bopyrids are parasites of decapod crustaceans. The females are modified for parasitism but retain external segmentation. Sexual dimorphism is pronounced and the females are much larger than the males, are usually asymmetrical, have a very large brood pouch, and do not greatly resemble typical isopods. They usually inhabit the host's gill chamber, which in decapods is located under the carapace. Males are much smaller than females and are recognizable as small isopods. They live on the body of the female. Most infested shrimp are easily recognized by the large blister on one side of the body but infected crabs cannot be recognized without dissection.

Members of the epicaridean family Entoniscidae are internal parasites of decapod crustaceans. They are sexually dimorphic, segmentation is obscured, and females are shapeless and deformed. Parasites in the family Cryptoniscidae infest many crustacean groups, including other isopods, ostracods, barnacles, mysids, amphipods, and cumaceans. All traces of segmentation are lost and the male is a tiny dwarf living in the brood pouch of the female. Cryptoniscids are protandric hermaphrodites that begin life as tiny males that later become females. The final epicaridean family, the Dajiidae, are parasites of mysids and eucarideans.

Order Tanaidacea

Fig. 302

The tanaids (Fig. 302) resemble isopods and were formerly included in the order Isopoda. They are occasionally encountered in our benthic habitats and one species, *Hargeria rapax* (0.2″; 5 mm), may be common in salt marshes, where it builds small soft tubes of detritus. The tanaids have elongate cylindrical or depressed bodies. The first two thoracic segments are fused with the head and are covered by a short carapace which encloses the respiratory chamber. The first thoracic appendage is a maxilliped and the second is a pincer, or chela. There is a single pair of uropods with slender filamentous rami. The tanaids are not covered by this guide.

Order Amphipoda ("different feet")

We have almost 100 species of amphipods in shallow benthic habitats on our coast. Most communities have many species, of which some are likely to be abundant. All our species are small (usually less than 0.5″; 1.3 cm) and superficially similar to each other.

The amphipods are usually laterally compressed (flattened side to side) but some are cylindrical and some are depressed like their relatives, the isopods. They have two pairs of antennae, the eyes are sessile, and only one thoracic segment is fused with the head. There is no carapace. The seven pairs of thoracic legs are usually of two types, a condition reflected in the name Amphipoda. The first two pairs typically end in pincers and are called gnathopods. These are often different in males and females (sexually dimorphic). The remaining five pairs of legs do not have pincers and are used for locomotion. Females, of course, have a brood pouch when in breeding condition. The gills are located on the thoracic legs. The abdomen, in sharp contrast with that of isopods, has three pairs of pleopods and three pairs of uropods. The pleopods are delicate and feathery and are used to generate a swimming and respiratory current, whereas the uropods are robust. The telson is not fused to the abdomen.

The amphipods have not undergone extensive radiation in terrestrial and parasitic habitats as have the isopods but they do have an important planktonic suborder, the Hyperiidea, which has no equivalent in the Isopoda. There are a few terrestrial and a few parasitic amphipods but most are free-living marine or freshwater animals. There are four suborders, only two of which are represented in shallow benthic habitats.

Fig. 303

Suborder Gammaridea

This is the largest and most important group of amphipods (Fig. 303) and we have scores of species, a few of which are considered in this guide. Gammaridea is a diverse group with members specialized for life in almost all inshore habitats especially epibenthic and infaunal. Their characteristics are those of the order Amphipoda.

Fig. 304

Suborder Caprellidea

This is a relatively small group of unusual amphipods (Fig. 304) that are highly modified for a life spent clinging to various substrata. They are usually elongate, cylindrical, and sticklike. They have two pairs of gnathopods but thoracic legs 3-4 are usually reduced or absent. Legs 5-7 are well developed and are used to hold tightly to the substratum. The abdomen is vestigial and abdominal appendages are absent. We have three important species in our area. Whale lice (Cyamidae), which are found only on the skin of whales and other cetaceans, also belong to this suborder.

Suborder Hyperiidea

The hyperiid amphipods are some of nature's most bizarre animals. They are all pelagic and are an important component of the offshore zooplankton and do not occur in benthic communities. A few species are parasitic on jellyfish and these may sometimes be seen when their hosts wash ashore. Hyperiids have large heads almost completely covered by enormous compound eyes. Hyperiids do not occur in the habitats covered by this guide and are not included.

Superorder Eucarida ("true shrimps")

This malacostracan superorder includes the euphausids and the decapods. The euphausids are entirely planktonic open ocean animals known as krill. They are an important food of baleen whales but do not occur in benthic or inshore habitats and are not treated by this guide. The decapods, on the other hand, include our most familiar inshore crustaceans such as the crabs, shrimps, and lobsters, and are some of the most common and conspicuous invertebrates in coastal habitats. The eucarids are a diverse group whose members have stalked eyes and a well developed carapace covering the thorax.

Order Decapoda ("ten feet")

The decapods have a large carapace covering the dorsal and lateral surfaces of the thorax so that the segments of the thorax are visible only from the ventral surface. The carapace encloses the gill chamber and the gills are feathery processes on the thoracic legs. There is the usual complement of eight thoracic segments typical of the malacostracans but the first three are always fused with the head to form a cephalothorax and their appendages are maxillipeds. The remaining five free thoracic segments each bears a pair of legs. There is thus a total of 10 thoracic legs, hence the name "decapod" for the order. All crabs, shrimps, and lobsters have a total of 10 legs and can be distinguished from other crustaceans by that characteristic. The abdomen has six segments as expected of malacostracans, and primitively it is well developed and bears the usual five pairs of pleopods and a single pair of uropods. In decapod evolution there has been a strong tendency to reduce the importance of the abdomen and its appendages. Consequently, the primitive shrimps and lobsters have well developed abdomens while the evolutionarily more advanced crabs have small abdomens.

The classification of the decapods is complicated and many of the higher categories are based on characteristics, such as the branching pattern of the gills, that most laymen would consider obscure and difficult to employ. Consequently, the classification used below is simplified and condensed from the more technical modern arrangement as presented in the classification chapter. Here we will divide the decapods into the shrimps, lobsters, anomuran crabs, and brachyuran crabs. The shrimps and lobsters are not natural groups as you will see, but they are convenient and reflect the way most people perceive these animals.

Shrimps

The shrimps are elongate, cylindrical, or slightly compressed crustaceans with a well developed muscular abdomen. They are active and efficient swimmers. The abdominal appendages (pleopods) are well developed and provide the primary locomotory force for swimming. The uropods and telson form a broad tail fan that can be used for locomotion also. Technically, there are two quite distinct suborders of decapods with some shrimps belonging to one, and some, along with all other decapods, to the other. The first group is the suborder Dendrobranchiata which includes the large, often commercially important, shrimps in the families Penaeidae and Sicyoniidae. The remaining shrimps are known as caridean shrimps (infraorder Caridea) and belong to the suborder Pleocyemata.

Fig. 305

The family Penaeidae (Fig. 305) includes the pink, white, and brown shrimps that are caught in tremendous numbers along the southeastern coast by commercial and sports fishmermen.The family Sicyoniidae includes the commercially important rock shrimps that are fished from deeper waters. All these shrimps have pincers on the first three thoracic legs and the sideplate of the second abdominal segment overlaps the sideplate of the third segment but is itself overlapped by that of the first. Penaeid shrimps have relatively thin and flexible exoskeletons and very long antennae. The sicyoniids have heavily calcified rocklike exoskeletons and short antennae.

The caridean shrimps are usually small and have pincers on only the first two, never the third, pair of legs. The second abdominal sideplate overlaps those of segments 1 and 3.

Lobsters and Burrowing Shrimps

The lobsters, American and spiny, belong to two different infraorders of decapods and are not closely related. Both are large animals reaching 1.5–2′ (46–61 cm) in length. They are slightly flattened dorsoventrally. The abdomen is large, muscular and equipped with a well developed tail fan. American lobsters, which are rarely encountered in the Southeast,

329

resemble gigantic freshwater crayfish and have a smooth carapace. They

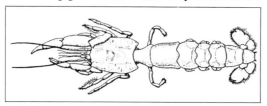

are closely related to the mud and ghost shrimps with which they share the infraorder Astacidea. The first three pairs of legs have pincers. The pincers of the first legs are massive and

Fig. 306

powerful while those of the second and third legs are small and inconspicuous. The ghost shrimps (Fig. 306) and mud shrimps have well developed abdomens that extend straight back from the thorax. The abdomen is symmetrical and bears paired appendages on most segments. The tail fan is well developed. These "shrimps" all burrow in soft substrata.

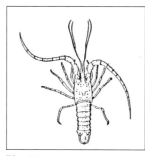

Spiny lobsters (Fig. 307), which are in an infraorder by themselves, do occur in the Southeast but they are most abundant in the Caribbean province to the south of us. They have a spiny carapace and none of the legs has pincers, large or small.

Anomuran Crabs

Fig. 307

The Anomura ("irregular tail") includes the hermit crabs, the porcelain crabs, and the mole crabs. This is a heterogeneous group of diverse decapods whose exact composition is disputed by specialists. They are mostly crablike animals and within the group the size of the abdomen decreases.

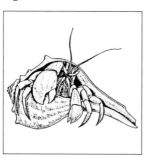

There are two families of hermit crabs in the Anomura (Fig. 308). These decapods usually inhabit snail shells and their bodies are appropriately modified. They have large abdomens that extend posteriorly from the thorax. The abdomen is soft and asymmetrical with reduced appendages. It is usu-

Fig. 308

ally coiled to fit into a gastropod shell and the abdominal appendages are reduced or absent. They have two pincers. Most of the body is soft and the animal relies on the snail shell for protection.

The porcelain crabs, family Porcellanidae, belong to another group of anomurans. They are usually the most crablike of the anomurans with strongly depressed bodies and a symmetrical abdomen that is moderately reduced and flexed beneath the thorax. They have a pair of large

Fig. 309

crablike pincers, or chelae. The antennae are long and the telson is made of several calcareous plates.

Our remaining anomurans are mole crabs (Fig. 309). They have reduced symmetrical abdomens that are flexed beneath the thorax. They tend to have thick, ovoid, uncrablike bodies adapted for burrowing into soft sediments. They may or may not have a pair of pincers.

Fig. 309

Brachyuran Crabs

The brachyurans ("short tail") are the true crabs. They have a greatly reduced, inconspicuous, symmetrical abdomen that is flexed to lie in a recess beneath the thorax. The cephalothorax is usually dorsoventrally flattened and the antennae are usually short. They have a pair of pincers. The infraorder is a large one and we have numerous representatives in our waters.

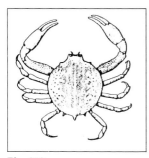

Fig. 310

The sponge and shellback crabs (section Dromioidea; Pl. C24) cover themselves with sponges, colonial tunicates, or a bivalve valve. They are common only in the southern part of our range. They are reminiscent of the anomuran crabs with their thick bodies, weak fifth legs, and long antennae.

The box and purse crabs (section Oxystomata; Fig. 310) also have thick bodies but the antennae are short like those of most other brachyurans. The fifth legs are not especially reduced.

Fig. 311

The spider crabs (section Oxyrhyncha) have relatively small usually teardrop-shaped bodies with very long thin legs (Fig. 311). The fifth legs are not unusually reduced. The pincers are usually long and thin and relatively weak. We have many species of spider crabs, of which a few are common.

The cancer crabs (section Cancridea; Pl. C26) are typically crablike in appearance with flattened, transversely oval bodies. The fifth legs are normal in size and are not modified for swimming. They are not found regularly in shallow waters in the Southeast.

The portunid crabs (section Brachyrhyncha, family Portunidae, Fig. 312; Pls. C27–C29) are our best known brachyurans. These are the swimming crabs of which the blue crab is the best known example. We

Fig. 312

have several other species, many of which are common. All our species have well developed fifth legs which are flat and oarlike. No other crabs have legs like these. Swimming crabs are active and often pugnacious. They frequently have a strong pointed tooth or spike on each side of the body at the widest point.

The xanthid crabs (family Xanthidae) are the mud crabs. We have many species of this family and they can be difficult to distinguish from each other. Our best known representative is the stone crab. Most xanthid species are shaped like stone crabs although none approach it in size. The xanthids usually have smooth transversely oval bodies with strong pincers. They never have a swimming paddle or a strong lateral spike like those of the portunids.

Fig. 313

The grapsids, or shore crabs (family Grapsidae), are often found associated with habitats at the water's edge, sometimes supratidally (Fig. 313). They are usually strongly depressed and have oral or square bodies. They are agile and fast on land. Their scurrying gait and low leggy profile are reminiscent of spiders.

The pinnotherids (family Pinnotheridae; Pl. C33) are a family of commensal or semiparasitic crabs. We have many species, all of which live with other invertebrates.

The fiddler and ghost crabs (family Ocypodidae; Pl. C34) are semiterrestrial and have thick squarish bodies. We have four common species of these crabs.

Subphylum Uniramia ("one branch")

This recently established arthropod subphylum contains the insects, centipedes ("100 legs"), and millipedes ("1,000 legs") and is roughly equivalent to the old group Mandibulata with the crustaceans excluded. Uniramians have uniramous appendages, a single pair of antennae, and a pair of mandibles. They are almost entirely restricted to terrestrial or freshwater habitats. Of them, only the insects are found in marine environments. The insects, which are so overwhelmingly successful on land, are represented in the sea by only a few species, most of which live on or near the water surface and respire in air, not water. Insect bodies are divided into a head, thorax, and abdomen. The head of adults bears a single pair of antennae, a pair of mandibles, and other mouthparts. The thorax is composed of three segments, each of which bears a pair of legs. Adults of most insects also have one or two pairs of wings on the thorax. The abdomen is composed of about ten segments, none of which bears paired jointed appendages. Many groups, such as the flies and butterflies, exhibit distinctly different shapes and habits as juveniles and undergo a major reorganization, or metamorphosis, when they become adults. Other insects, such as the true bugs, begin life looking like miniature adults and undergo no drastic metamorphosis.

The most familiar marine insects are undoubtedly the all too abundant biting flies in the order Diptera ("two wings"). These inhabitants of coastal salt marshes include the mosquitos, sand flies (no-see-ums), greenhead flies, and deerflies. The adults of these species are aerial while the larvae are aquatic.

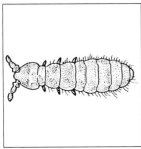

Fig. 314

The primitive order Collembola is represented by the oyster springtail, (*Anurida maritima*), which lives intertidally (Fig. 314). The Collembola, or springtails, differ from most other insects in being wingless as adults. Most species have a tail that folds beneath the body which is used for hopping. It happens that *Anurida* lacks this springing mechanism and does not hop, but is nevertheless a springtail.

Insects and other uniramians are very common in terrestrial habitats close to the waterline. There are, for example, over 400 species of insects in the saltmarsh but they live in the grass or air above the water and are not aquatic animals.

WATER, CURRENTS, WAVES AND TIDES

Water

Three fourths of the surface of the earth is covered with water. Marine organisms are approximately 85% water and some species are more than 95% water. Marine organisms are bathed, nourished, and transported by water and the chemical reactions that sustain life occur in intracellular water. Water is a unique substance whose many unusual properties are essential to life.

Water absorbs and stores more of the sun's heat with less change in temperature than any naturally occurring liquid or solid except ammonia. The amount of heat necessary to raise a unit of water 1.8°F (1°C) will raise the temperature of the same weight of iron 18°F (10°C). Consequently, the oceans can store and release vast amounts of heat with little change in temperature. Temperatures in the sea rarely fluctuate more than 1.8°F (1°C) per day or 18°F (10°C) per season as contrasted with daily fluctuations of about 18°F (10°C) per day and 99°F (55°C) per season on the land. As a result, marine animals are usually not subjected to temperature extremes and rapid temperature fluctuations. Heat absorbed by the ocean at the equator is distributed to higher latitudes by the great ocean currents, such as the Gulf Stream. These warm currents moderate air and ocean temperatures and promote stable conditions conducive to life. For example, palm trees grow on the Isles of Scilly in southwestern England at the latitude of Labrador because the climate of southern England is moderated by the Gulf Stream.

The buoyancy of water is noticeable because its density is close to that of living tissue. Any body immersed in a fluid, such as air or water, is buoyed up by a force equal to the weight of the displaced fluid. Seawater is 792 times more dense than air and thus weighs more and exerts more upward force than an equivalent volume of displaced air. As a result, water contributes to the support of tissues and the skeletons of marine organisms are rarely as well-developed as those of terrestrial animals. Many marine animals, spider crabs for example, have rigid skeletons and long spindly legs. In water, the legs support the nearly weightless body but they are awkward and ineffective on land. Some marine animals, such as jellyfishes and comb jellies, whose bodies are almost pure seawater, are naturally buoyant and drift weightlessly. Others have gas-filled spaces in their bodies, thereby achieving a positive bouyancy that allows them to float. For example, the by-the-wind sailor (*Velella*), and blue button (*Porpita*), have air bubbles trapped in a chitinous framework resembling styrofoam. The gulfweed, *Sargassum,* has air-filled bladders and the Portuguese man-o'-war (*Physalia*), has an air-filled float.

334

Water develops surface tension where it comes into contact with air and its surface behaves like a stretched membrane or skin. As a child, you may have floated a magnetized steel needle on the surface of a glass of water to make a simple compass. If positioned carefully, the needle rests on the surface "skin" and does not sink although the density of the steel is greater than that of water. Animals such as the pelagic marine bug, *Halobates,* glide or rest on the surface tension and are aided in this by water repellent exoskeletons. The purple snail, *Janthina,* the sea slug, *Glaucus,* and the leech, *Calliobdella,* attach in various ways to the underside of the surface and hang down into the water. People with aquaria may have watched small snails crawl across the underside of the water surface supported by the surface tension.

Water also adheres strongly to surfaces such as glass and it creeps up the walls of containers. This effect is noticeable in small diameter glass tubes where the attraction of water to glass and surface tension cause water to rise. This phenomenon is called capillarity and is familiar to those who have seen a drop of blood enter a capillary tube in a physician's office, kerosene move up a wick, or water soak upward, against gravity, into a household sponge. Ghost crabs (*Ocypode*) take advantage of capillarity when they press tufts of fine exoskeletal hairs against moist sand and "wick" ground water up to moisten their gills.

Water is often called the "universal solvent" because it dissolves more substances than any other common liquid. Seawater contains a large quantity of dissolved materials, especially salts, and is said to be saline.The salinity of seawater is a measure of the amount of dissolved solids it contains. All dissolved materials in the sea contribute to its salinity but the dominant substances are the salts, sodium chloride (=table salt: 77.5%), magnesium chloride (10.9%), magnesium sulfate (=Epsom salts: 4.7%), calcium sulfate (=gypsum: 3.6%), potassium sulfate (2.5%), calcium carbonate (=limestone: 0.34%), and magnesium bromide (0.22%). The salts occur as electrically charged ions rather than neutral molecules. In addition to the salts, about 64 elements occur in seawater. Four of these, chlorine, sodium, magnesium, and bromine, are recovered commercially. Salinity is expressed in parts per thousand (‰) and the open ocean ranges from 34 to 37 ‰. This is the same as 3.4 to 3.7 parts per hundred (percent or %). In laboratories or on oceanographic vessels salinity is usually measured with a salinometer or an electrical resistance meter but this equipment is expensive and marine aquariists usually use an inexpensive hydrometer purchased at a pet shop. Hydrometers measure the specific gravity of liquids and, since specific gravity is directly dependent on the amount of dissolved solids, the measurement can be converted to salinity using the graph in Figure 315.

Near the coast, ocean water is often diluted with freshwater runoff and the salinity is decreased by it. This less saline water is said to be brackish. Estuaries are coastal areas where rivers or creeks enter the sea.

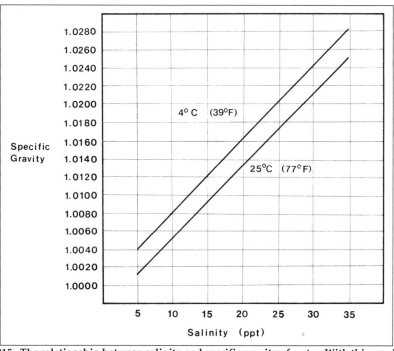

315 The relationship between salinity and specific gravity of water. With this graph the salinity of seawater in parts per thousand ($^o/^{oo}$) can be determined from its specific gravity as measured with a hydrometer.

They are characterized by mixing of fresh and salt water, high turbidity, fluctuations in salinity, high ecological stress, and relatively low species diversity.

The dissolved solids in sea water are important for maintenance of water balance in marine organisms. All particles in solution, including water molecules and salt ions, tend to move from areas of high concentration to areas of lower concentration by a process called diffusion. For example, when a cucumber is placed in a strong brine solution, it dehydrates because water moves from the cucumber, where the water concentration is high and the salt concentration is low, to the brine, where there is less water and more salt. If the water should cross a cell membrane then the process is called osmosis, which is a special type of diffusion. Similarly, organisms placed in water with a salt concentration greater than in their tissues lose water, gain salts, and shrink while those in water with a salt concentration less than that in their tissues will gain water, lose salts, and swell. In either case, a stress results which may cause death or impairment if not countered by physiological mechanisms. The tissues of freshwater fishes and invertebrates contain more salt and less water than the surrounding fresh water. Consequently, large amounts of water constantly flood into their bodies across the gill

336

membranes. They have kidneys or nephridia that produce a copious, dilute urine, that is little more than water, to get rid of the excess water as fast as it accumulates. Like freshwater animals, most marine organisms, except bony fishes, have tissues slightly saltier than their environment (seawater) and therefore tend to gain water by osmosis unless they actively eliminate water. They too often have kidneys or nephridia. The tissues of marine bony fishes, on the other hand, have more water and less salt than the surrounding sea and they are faced with the problem of losing water by osmosis and gaining salts. Their kidneys produce a very scant and concentrated urine in an attempt to conserve water and get rid of salts. Invertebrate animals remove excess water from their bodies by urination through ducts called nephridia.

The problem of water balance becomes acute if marine animals enter brackish water. Here the surrounding water concentration is higher than in the open sea and more water enters the animal and must be pumped out. The diversity of animals in estuaries is limited by the fluctuations in salinity that must be tolerated there. In general, diversity is high in the sea, decreases in brackish water, and then rises again in freshwater. Animals that tolerate a wide variation of salinities are termed euryhaline whereas intolerant species are stenohaline. Some organisms, including many marine invertebrates, allow the salinity of their tissue fluid to fluctuate, within limits, to match that of the surrounding water. Such animals are called osmoconformers and they spend relatively little energy pumping water or combating water loss. Other animals, including fishes and many marine invertebrates, are osmoregulators that spend large amounts of energy maintaining a constant internal salinity regardless of conditions outside their bodies.

Seawater is salty because it contains dissolved salts but it also contains other important dissolved substances. Of these, dissolved carbon dioxide and oxygen are the most important to life because plant photosynthesis uses carbon dioxide and microbial, plant, and animal respiration require oxygen. Photosynthetic plankton, or phytoplankton, use light energy, water, and carbon dioxide to synthesize carbohydrates and release oxygen as a byproduct. Photosynthesis, of course, is the source of almost all the world's food energy and is fundamental to life. The phytoplankton accounts for about 40% of the world's photosynthesis with the rest coming primarily from land plants. The productivity (amount of carbohydrate produced) of the phytoplankton is lower than that of land plants, even though more sunlight falls on the oceans, because of the scarcity of nutrients (fertilizer), especially nitrogen. To compound the problem, most of the nutrients in the sea tend to accumulate near the bottom in water too deep for photosynthesis. As dead organisms sink to the ocean floor, nitrogen and other nutrients are lost to the phytoplankton except in places where deep water mixes with surface water by a process called upwelling. Nitrogen levels and productivity are low in tropical and subtropical seas because warm, lightweight, nutrient-poor surface water does not mix easily with cold, dense, nutrient-rich, deep water except in these distinct zones of upwelling. In these zones, various combinations of air and water currents, water temperatures, and local geography may cause nutrient-rich bottom water to move to the surface where the nutrients become available to the phytoplankton. In these areas, as for example on the coast of Peru and around Antarctica, the waters are very productive and support important fisheries. Elsewhere, the productivity of tropical waters is very low. The clarity and transparency of the tropical ocean results partly from the scarcity of phytoplankton. In temperate and polar seas, mixing occurs more readily because surface and deep water temperatures, and hence densities, are similar. Nutrient levels remain high throughout the year in polar seas where surface and deep water temperatures are constant but high productivity is restricted to summer months by the low light levels of other seasons.

Compared to soil water on land, the nutrients in seawater are very dilute. The dilution of nutrients partly explains why open water plants are small single cells. Small objects have more surface area relative to their volume than do large objects. By remaining small, each phytoplankter maximizes its surface for absorption in the dilute medium. With the exception of the floating gulfweed, *Sargassum,* there are no large plants in the open ocean. All dissolved materials, including oxygen, carbon dioxide, organic molecules, and nutrients, must cross the surface of any organism in order to be used by the cytoplasm or tissues within. The amount of these substances that can enter or leave is determined by the amount of surface area surrounding the organism. Consequently, most large organisms have contrived to increase their surface areas to facilitate the uptake of sufficient quantities of materials to support their relatively large volumes. Gills and lungs are examples of surfaces areas that have been expanded for the uptake of gases while the folds, villi, and microvilli of the intestine are examples of surface area elaborations to facilitate the absorption of food molecules. On the other hand, a very small organism, such as a phytoplankter, has a large surface area in relation to its volume and its surface need not be enlarged further for absorption.

Light is absorbed, or "diluted," much more rapidly in water than in air and its intensity diminishes quickly as it penetrates the sea. Because of the rapid absorption of light by surface water, photosynthesis is restricted to the upper layer of the sea. In clear ocean water about 60% of the radiation is absorbed by the first yard (1 m). Red, infrared, and ultraviolet rays are absorbed first whereas blue penetrates the deepest. In very clear water, such as that of the Sargasso Sea, there may be enough blue light at 300′ (100 m) to support the growth of phytoplankton. The presence of any suspended particles including phytoplankton, zooplankton, silt, or detritus decreases the penetration of sunlight into water. Coastal waters characteristically have more particulate matter than oceanic waters and almost all radiation is absorbed in the first 30′ (10 m). Another reason for the small size of plankton is that small particles sink less fast than larger particles. Very small plants, therefore, will remain in the upper lighted waters longer than larger plants, unless of course, the large plants have floats to make themselves buoyant.

Seawater contains dissolved organic matter in the form of amino acids (the building blocks of proteins) and sugars in amounts estimated at 20,000 times the world's annual wheat harvest. The solutes are very dilute (20–50 mg/ml) in seawater but they may be 30 times more concentrated in marine sediments. Dilute as they are, dissolved organics are 10 times more concentrated than suspended particulate organic material, which is the food of a large percentage of marine animals. It has recently been discovered that many marine invertebrates absorb dissolved organic molecules to supplement their normal intake of solid food.

The availability of oxygen for cellular respiration depends on its concentration immediately outside the organism. Although the only source of dissolved oxygen in the sea is near the surface, either from the air or from photosynthesis in the lighted regions, oxygen is present from the surface to the bottom of the sea. It is not transported effectively by diffusion, however, and water currents are necessary to distribute it at a rate useful to the organisms that need it. For example, if the oxygen in water were removed to a depth of 1 yd. (1 m), replacement by diffusion from the surface would take over 3 years. Water must be in motion in order to transport gases and nutrients rapidly to organisms and also carry away their wastes.

Currents

Major ocean currents, such as the Gulf Stream and Florida current, are caused by winds which result from uneven heating of the atmosphere. Several important ocean currents affect marine life in the Southeast (Fig. 316). The west-flowing South Equatorial Current enters the Caribbean Sea, passes through the Yucatan Channel, and flows at a speed of 3.5 knots through the Straits of Florida as the Florida Current. The Florida Current continues northward along the east coast of Florida where it is approximately 95 miles (153 km) wide and 2 miles (3.2 km) deep. It is joined off southern Florida by a branch of the west-flowing North Equatorial Current and together these form the Gulf Stream. The Gulf Stream flows north at about 1 mile per hour (1.6 km/hr) over the continental shelf until it reaches Cape Hatteras. There it veers east in a long arc that eventually carries its warm water, as the North Atlantic Drift, to Great Britain and Europe. Some of this water moves northeast

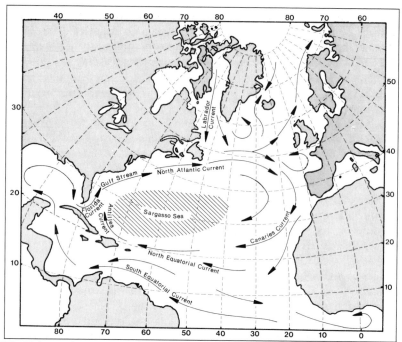

316 Major surface currents in the North Atlantic Ocean. The hatched area is the approximate distribution of the gulfweed, *Sargassum*, in the Sargasso Sea.

as the Norway Current while the remainder flows south along the coast of Spain and the bulge of Africa as the Canary Current. It then turns westward and moves across the Atlantic as the Equatorial Current. These several currents in the north Atlantic combine to form a large clockwise-rotating gyre around a central eddy called the Sargasso Sea. The Sargasso Sea is characterized by high salinity (38 %), very low nutrient content, clear blue water, and an abundance of floating gulfweed. Because it is an isolated eddy with no important source of nutrients, it is one of the least productive areas in the sea.

Currents, such as the Florida Current and Gulf Stream, are major avenues of larval transport. The dispersal of many tropical species into the Carolinean province probably occurs along these routes.

Waves

To shallow-water organisms, waves, and the local currents generated by them, are among the most important types of water movements. Depending on the inclination and exposure of the coast and the angle of wave attack, coastal areas may be eroded or deposited and sand may be coarse and clean or fine and muddy. As waves approach a coast they curve towards headlands and concentrate their energy on them but in bays they spread and disperse energy over a wider area. Exposed areas,

340

such as Cape Hatteras, receive high wave energy and have clean coarse sand. Beaches in Onslow Bay along the coasts of South Carolina and Georgia are medium energy beaches with fine and sometimes muddy sand. Low-energy beaches occur in areas protected from waves and strong currents.

Tides

Tides are another important form of water movement. Surprisingly, tides are also waves but waves with a very long distance (wavelength) between crests. The wavelength of wind-driven waves is usually a few inches to many hundreds of feet but tidal wavelengths are hundreds of miles. Tides are produced by gravitational and centrifugal forces between the earth, moon, and sun which cause the sea to bulge upward on the side of the earth facing the moon and on the side of the earth opposite the moon. Thus at any time, there are two bulges, or high tides, on opposite sides of the earth. Similarly, halfway between these crests there are two troughs, which are low tides. As the earth rotates once each 24 hours, most coastal areas experience two high tides and two low tides as the earth passes beneath these two bulges and troughs. Such twice daily, or semidiurnal, tides are characteristic of the southeastern Atlantic coast. In this area the tidal amplitude, or difference between the height of high and low tides, varies between 3-9 vertical feet (1–3 m) with most exposed sites having an amplitude of about 6 feet (2 m). The number of tides daily and the tidal amplitude varies over the world. Tidal amplitude in the Bay of Fundy, for example, is about 45 feet (15 m), an impressive range that makes it difficult to tie a boat to the shore. The Gulf of Mexico has a complex tidal regime. Many areas of the Gulf have only one daily tidal cycle (diurnal tide) with one high and one low tide in a 24 hour period. Other parts have two highs and two lows daily but they are unequal in amplitude (mixed tide). Semidiurnal tides also occur. The Gulf of Mexico has a reduced tidal amplitude of less than 3 feet (1 m).

The moon's orbit around the earth requires 24 hours 50 minutes while the earth itself makes a complete rotation in only 24 hours. Consequently, the tides are 50 minutes later on each successive day. Because there are two tidal cycles daily, the time between successive high or successive low tides is 12 hours 25 minutes and the time from any given high to the next low is 6 hours 12 minutes. An incoming tide is said to be flooding whereas a receding tide is ebbing. The interval at full high or full low when the direction of flow is changing is called "slack water."

The sun also affects the tides. Despite the enormous mass of the sun, about 27 million times greater than that of the moon, its gravitational influence on the earth and tides is a little less than half of the moon's effect because of its far greater distance from the earth. It nevertheless has an important effect on the height of the tides and can either increase or decrease tidal height. During new and full moons the sun aids the moon in producing tides whereas it hinders it during quarter moons. When the moon is new or full, the sun and moon are aligned and their gravitational forces add together and exceed that of the moon alone. Under these conditions, the high tides are higher and the low tides lower than average. These tides are known as spring tides (regardless of season) and they are characterized by high tidal amplitudes. There are two periods of spring tides each lunar month that are separated by about 15 days and they occur throughout the year. When the moon is in the first or third quarter, the sun and moon are at right angles to each other in relation to the earth and their gravitational pulls tend to cancel each other so that the net effect is less than that of the moon alone. These tides are known as neap tides and they have a low amplitude. Neap high tides are lower than average and neap low tides higher than average. There are two periods of neap tides each month separated by about 15 days. During each lunar month of 29½ days we experience four successive tidal regimes of 7.5 days each progressing from spring to neap to spring to neap as the moon moves from full to quarter to new to quarter (Fig. 317).

Where the sea meets the coast, the rhythmic flood and ebb of the tides successively inundates and exposes a strip of land called the intertidal zone (The term littoral is sometimes used in reference to this zone but is

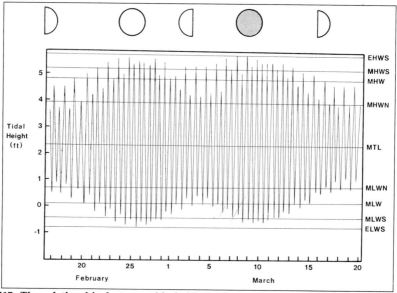

317 The relationship between tide height and phase of the moon in Charleston, South Carolina for February and March of 1986.

preferably used to mean the entire continental shelf to a depth of about 600′ (200 m)). This zone is defined as lying between the highest and lowest tide lines. It is convenient for purposes of description to divide this zone according to tide levels. The three principal levels are marked by the average height of the water at low, mid, and high tides and these are termed mean low water (MLW), mean tide level (MTL), and mean high water (MHW), respectively. During spring tides, the average high water level is designated "mean high water springs" (MHWS), and the average low water level, "mean low water springs" (MLWS). Similarly, the tide levels of neap tides are abbreviated by addition of the suffix, "N," to the low and high water designations. From the low water mark to the bottom of the deep sea is the subtidal zone, an area which, by definition, is never exposed by the tide. The subtidal zone just below low water is termed the infralittoral fringe and the splash and spray zone above the high water mark is called the supralittoral fringe. The intertidal is the most accessible region of the sea for people interested in marine life. Most of the animals in this guide occur in the intertidal or high subtidal.

MARINE ECOLOGY

Marine Communities and Habitats

An ecological community is an interacting and interdependent group of species that is relatively isolated and independent of other communities. The community of living organisms together with its physical environment is an ecosystem. Ecosystems are the basic functional units of ecology and each type of physical environment supports a characteristic type of community.

The two most fundamental types of marine environments, or habitats, are the water itself and sea bottom beneath it and these are reflected by the division of marine habitats into pelagic and benthic, respectively. Pelagic communities occupy the water whereas benthic communities are on or in the bottom. This guide is concerned with benthic communities along the southeastern coast and little attention is devoted to pelagic communities. Nevertheless, benthic communities are everywhere in contact with the pelagic communities of the overlying water so that it is impossible to consider one without reference to the other.

Pelagic Communities

There are several different pelagic communities in the waters of the sea. The plankton community consists of suspended organisms, plants and animals, that lack the power to control their motion through the water. Although many plankters are capable of limited mobility they cannot oppose the drift of the current and are carried with it. These are usually small, often microscopic, organisms but their ecological importance should not be underestimated. The phytoplankton is composed of tiny unicellular or colonial marine algae. These photosynthetic plant cells provide most of the energy for marine food webs and generate much of the world's oxygen. Their position and importance in marine ecosystems is equivalent to that of grass, shrubs, and trees in terrestrial ecosystems. The zooplankton consists of small animals in many phyla which drift with the phytoplankton and feed on it, on other zooplankters, or on inanimate organic matter (detritus) suspended or dissolved in the water. The most important animal groups in the zooplankton are the copepods, arrowworms, hydromedusae, krill, tunicates, and the larvae of many kinds of benthic (bottom-dwelling) organisms.

The neuston is another subdivision of the pelagic realm. Neustonic organisms are associated with the boundary between the sea and the overlying air. A limited but well developed and integrated community of animals, and sometimes plants, is associated with this region. The

344

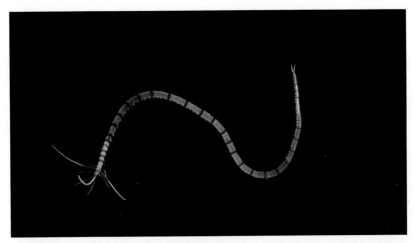

C1. Red white and blue worm, *Proceraea fasciata*

C2. Caterpillar fireworm, *Amphinome rostrata*

C3. Orange fringed worm, *Cirriformia grandis*

C4. Sandpaper worm, *Piromis eruca*

C5. Maitre d' worm, *Notomastus lobatus,* with attached commensal clam, *Entovalva* sp. B

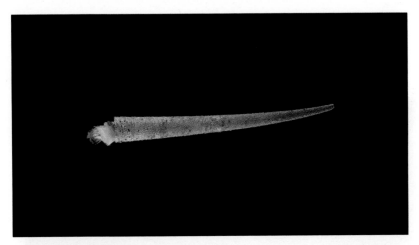

C6. Ice cream cone worm, *Cistenides gouldii*

C7. Spaghetti worm, *Amphitrite ornata*, and worm pea crab, *Pinnixa chaetopterana*

C8. Feather duster worm, *Sabella melanostigma*

C9. Black sea spider, *Anoplodactylus lentus,* on the hydroid, *Eudendrium carneum*

C10. Parasitic copepod, *Lernaeenicus radiatus,* on an anchovy

C11. Goose barnacle, *Lepas anatifera*

C12. Seawhip barnacle, *Conopea galeata,* on the seawhip, *Leptogorgia virgulata*

C13. **Mantis shrimp,** *Squilla empusa*

C14. **Wharf roach isopod,** *Ligia exotica*

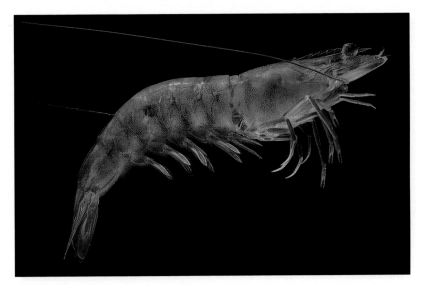

C15. Pink shrimp, *Penaeus duorarum*

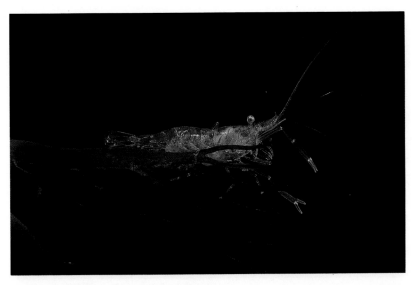

C16. Grass shrimp, *Palaemonetes vulgaris*

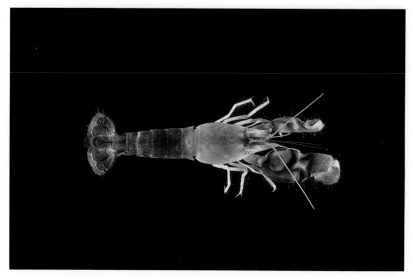

C17. Bigclaw snapping shrimp, *Alpheus heterochaelis*

C18. Peppermint shrimp, *Lysmata wurdemanni*

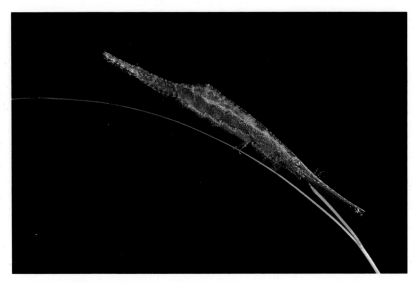

C19. Arrow shrimp, *Tozeuma carolinense*

C20. Caribbean spiny lobster, *Panulirus argus*

C21. Striped hermit crab, *Clibanarius vittatus,* in shell of the knobbed whelk, *Busycon carica*

C22. Giant red hermit crab, *Petrochirus diogenes,* in shell of the channeled whelk, *Busycon canaliculatum*

C23. Eroded porcelain crab, *Megalobrachium soriatum* (left), cherry-striped porcelain crab, *Petrolisthes galathinus* (right)

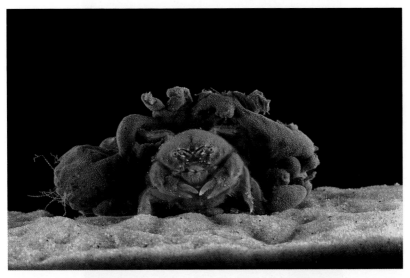

C24. Hairy sponge crab, *Dromidia antillensis,* covered with the chocolate tunicate, *Didemnum psammathodes*

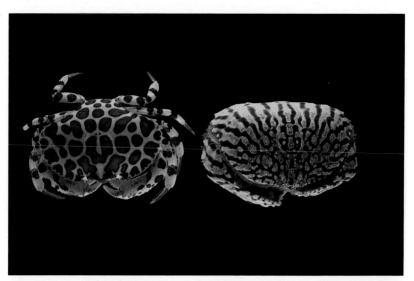

C25. Calico box crab, *Hepatus epheliticus* (left), flamed box crab, *Calappa flammea* (right)

C26. Rock crab, *Cancer irroratus* (top), Jonah crab, *Cancer borealis* (bottom)

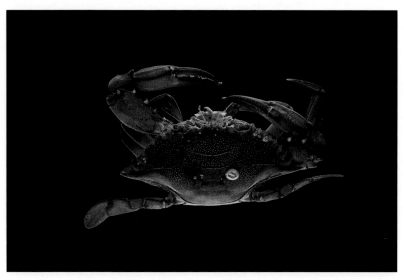

C27. Blue crab, *Callinectes sapidus*, with commensal barnacle, *Chelonibia patula*

C28. Lady crabs, *Ovalipes ocellatus* (left) and *O. stephensoni* (right)

C29. Blotched swimming crab, *Portunus spinimanus*

C30. Florida stone crab, *Menippe mercenaria*

C31. Broadbacked mud crab, *Eurytium limosum*

C32. Marsh crab, *Sesarma reticulatum* (left), wharf crab, *S. cinereum* (right)

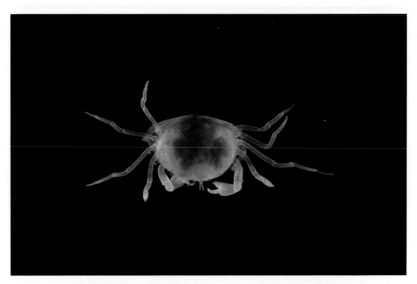

C33. Oyster pea crab, *Pinnotheres ostreum*

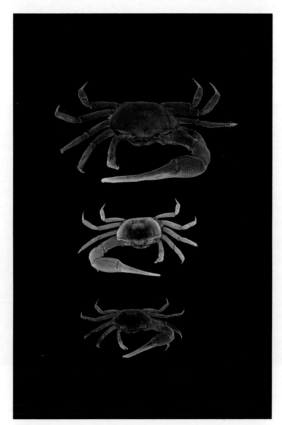

C34. Redjointed fiddler crab, *Uca minax* (top), Sand
fiddler crab, *U. pugilator* (middle), Mud fiddler crab,
U. pugnax (bottom)

Portuguese man-o'-war, the by-the-wind sailor, and the snail, *Janthina,* are neustonic organisms. The best known marine insect, *Halobates,* is a bug that skates on the surface of the water up to hundreds of miles from land. Some of these organisms occur in inshore waters, especially after storms or favorable winds, and may then be seen by land-based observers. Many are included in this guide even though they are not really shallow water organisms.

Larger pelagic animals, those that move under their own power in any direction they choose, belong to the nekton, a third subdivision of the pelagic region. The fishes, squids, and marine mammals are nektonic.

Benthic Communities

The benthos includes all organisms living on or in the floor of the ocean from the water's edge to the deepest trenches. This guide is devoted to benthic communities in shallow water, particularly those in the intertidal zone. In the Southeast, there are seven major shallow-water benthic communities although there are physical and ecological intergradations between them. Benthic communities may be on hard or soft bottoms although in the Southeast most natural communities are on soft bottoms since natural hard surfaces are rare. Animals living within the bottom are said to be infaunal, whereas those living on its surface are said to be epifaunal or epibenthic. The word sessile refers to attached, immobile, benthic organisms whereas the term free-living describes mobile organisms that can move on, in, or above the bottom.

Soft-bottom Communities

The southeastern coast is, with trivial exceptions, a sedimentary coast of sand and mud. Most of our natural shallow-water communities occur on sediments of some type, and not on hard bottoms. Organisms in these communities may live on the surface of the sediments (epifaunal) but more often than not they burrow into the sediment to live beneath its surface (infaunal). This strategy tends to protect the animal from predation while exposing it to problems of food and oxygen supply, which are usually solved by pumping water into the burrow from above.

Our four major soft-bottom communities intergrade physically and ecologically with each other and many species occur in more than one community.

Outer Beach: The beaches on the outer coast are exposed to the full force of onshore winds, waves, and currents, receiving little or no protection from their onslaught. They are called "high energy" or "medium energy" beaches in reference to the energy level of these waves. Our highest energy beaches are mostly in North Carolina and Florida, with the energy being less in South Carolina and Georgia. The nature of the beach, its sediment type, and the animal community it supports depend on its energy level. High energy beaches are composed of pure well-sorted sand. With decreasing wave energy, the size of the sediment particles decreases, sorting is less effective, and beaches become mixtures of sand, silt, and clay.

High energy beaches are harsh environments with constantly shifting unstable sands and little food. Few animals and no rooted plants can tolerate these conditions and the diversity of outer beach communities is low. As usual in highly stressed communities, a few species have solved the problems associated with life in the stressful habitat and those species are abundant. The outer beach community is dominated by ghost crabs, mole crabs, coquina clams, spionid worms, and burrowing haustoriid amphipods. At best only about 20-30 species of invertebrates are likely to be found on our high energy outer beaches. The community does not include rooted plants and consequently most organic material (food) must be imported from other nearby communities where plants are present.

Protected Beaches and Subtidal Bottoms: Wave energy is reduced or absent in areas where the coastline is protected by headlands, offshore bars, or islands from onshore winds. Beaches in these areas are said to be "low-energy." Still water has no power to transport sediment and all particles, including the very fine silt and clay, are deposited to form bottoms of mixed sand, silt, and clay. With decreasing energy the percentage of sand decreases while that of silts and clays increases. Protected beaches are located inside inlets and beside sounds, bays, and estuaries. Here the physical environment is much more stable and benign than that of outer beaches and the animal community may include up to 300 species of invertebrates, more than 10 times the number on high energy beaches. Protected beach communities may lack rooted vegetation so most food energy must be imported from other ecosystems. Most protected beaches support large populations of unicellular algae (diatoms), forming a golden or greenish brown film over the sediment surface. These photosynthetic organisms produce food for some members of the community, notably the fiddler crabs. Protected intertidal beaches are the edges of the more extensive subtidal bottoms of tidal creeks, sounds, and other estuarine waters. The community of these subtidal bottoms is continuous with that of the adjacent beaches.

Salt Marsh: Two quite different southeastern marine habitats are dominated by rooted vegetation and both are restricted to protected, low energy, sedimentary coasts. The most extensive of these is the tidal salt marsh, a characteristic feature of the entire southeastern coastline. Submerged grass beds, the second vegetated habitat, are restricted in the Southeast to North Carolina and Florida.

The salt marsh is an intertidal community which establishes itself in very low energy situations beside tidal creeks, lagoons, sounds and estuaries. It is dominated by two species of rooted plants and its sediment is usually soft sticky mud although some salt marshes are established on sand. The community is intertidal, lying between the low and high tide lines, and is alternately flooded and exposed twice daily by the tide. It may be up to several miles wide. This frequent flooding with salt water places great stress on the plants in the community and results in a distinct zonation in the vegetation.

The lowest areas of the marsh, around mid tide level, are flooded by every tide and are occupied by pure stands of a tall form of the grass, *Spartina alterniflora* (smooth cordgrass). Landward, on slightly higher ground, the *Spartina* is shorter and is often mixed with two other species, *Limonium carolinianum* (sea lavender), a small plant with tiny lavender flowers, and *Salicornia virginica* (glasswort), a low-growing fleshy species. The highest areas of the intertidal marsh are flooded only by spring tides and are occupied by dense stands of the large rush, *Juncus roemerianus* (black needlerush). *Juncus* has long cylindrical leaves with sharp points. The *Juncus* zone may be narrow, even absent, or it may be very wide. The color of its vegetation (dark grey-green) contrasts with the bright green of the adjacent *Spartina alterniflora* and it is taller than the short *S. alterniflora* which is usually adjacent to it. The supratidal region immediately above the high tide line is technically not a marine habitat but it supports a characteristic group of organisms associated with the salt marsh. Here are found two grasses, *Distichlis spicata* (salt grass) and *Spartina patens* (saltmeadow cordgrass), and the composites, *Borrichia frutescens* (sea oxeye) and *Aster tenuifolia* (saltmarsh aster), and the woody shrub, *Iva frutescens* (marsh elder), which is also a composite. The region below the high tide line is usually called the low, or intertidal, marsh whereas that above the line is the high, or supratidal, marsh. There is often a drift line of broken, decaying *Spartina* stems stranded at the line between the high and low marsh. The high marsh typically grades quickly into the low pine flatwoods community of poorly drained wet soils or the maritime forest or sand dune community on well drained soils.

Because of its twice daily flooding and drying, fluctuating temperatures, and soft sediments with high organic matter and low oxygen content, the salt marsh is another highly stressed environment. The plants, which are derived from freshwater origins, are stressed by the frequent flooding with seawater whereas the animals, with their marine origins, are stressed by the frequent exposure to air. Like the outer beaches, saltmarshes support a few common species. The characteristic animals are fiddler crabs (*Uca*), shore crabs (*Sesarma*), blue crabs (*Callinectes*), mud crabs (*Panopeus* and *Eurytium*), mussels (*Geukensia*), periwinkles (*Littorina*), mud snails (*Ilyanassa*), and a few species of worms living in the sediment (*Amphitrite, Haploscoloplos,* and others). Large populations of tiny hydrobiid snails may occupy the sediment surface and oligochaete worms are common infaunally. The tanaid crustacean, *Hargeria rapax,* constructs little tubes of detritus at the sediment surface. The blades and stems of *Spartina* usually support populations of the small intertidal barnacle, *Chthamalus fragilis.* The small amphipods, *Gammarus palustris* and *Uhlorchestia spartinophila* are characteristically found with *Spartina.* At flood tide the shrimp, *Palaemonetes pugio,* is abundant among the plants. The landward edge of the marsh supports populations of the wharf crab, *Sesarma cinereum,* the small snail, *Melampus,* and the beachhopper, *Orchestia grillus.* In low salinity marshes the last two species tend to be replaced by the snail, *Detracia,* and the amphipod, *Uhlorchestia uhleri,* respectively.

Despite the harshness of this environment and the resulting paucity of species in the community, the salt marsh is the site of production of much of the food that supports surrounding shallow-water communities, such as the outer and protected beaches, which have no vegetation of their own. *Spartina* stems and leaves are broken apart and ground into finely divided organic particles, called detritus, by the action of waves, tides, and microorganisms. The lightweight detritus is suspended in the water and transported throughout coastal waters where it provides food for animals in other communities.

Grass Beds: In North Carolina and Florida many shallow, protected, sandy bottoms support growths of rooted plants of several species. Unlike the salt marsh, which is intertidal and supports emergent vegetation the grass beds are located in the high subtidal and the plants are usually not exposed at low tide. The most extensive and ecologically important grass beds are formed either by *Zostera marina* (eelgrass) or *Thalassia testudinum* (turtlegrass). These two plants are similar in appearance as both have long, wide, flat, straplike leaves arising in clusters from a horizontal runner. *Zostera,* a northern species, has narrower blades (0.2″; 5 mm wide) and does not occur in Florida. *Thalassia,* with leaves about 0.5″; 1.3 cm wide, is a southern species that does not occur in North Carolina. Georgia and South Carolina lack grass beds. A few other species of lesser importance also form submerged beds in the Southeast. *Halodule wrightii* resembles *Zostera* and *Thalassia* but has much smaller, flat, straplike leaves only about 0.1″ (2 mm) wide. *Syringodium filiforme* (manatee grass) resembles *Halodule* in size but has narrow leaves that are round in cross section. Both propagate from runners. All the above species are restricted to high salinity water. *Ruppia maritima* (widgeon grass), another small species, is found in low salinity water. Its leaves arise from an erect stem rather than horizontal runners. Grass beds support a distinctive association of animals and are a source of exportable organic food for other ecosystems.

Hard-bottom Communities

As already noted, the southeastern coast has few naturally occurring hard substrata and most of our hard-bottom communities occupy artificial surfaces such as rock jetties, pilings, floating docks, and sea-walls. There are limited outcrops of coquina rock at Ft. Fisher, North Carolina, and Marineland, Florida, but the remainder of the coast lacks natural rocks. The bodies and products of many organisms, however, provide important natural hard substrata. Most important among these are oyster shells (and mangrove roots in Florida), but the shells, egg cases, and exoskeletons of various molluscs, arthropods, and other invertebrates also provide attachment sites for sessile species and their free-living associates.

Oyster Reef: The only extensive naturally occurring hard bottom community in the Southeast exists in association with the oyster, *Crassostrea virginica.* These molluscs colonize vast areas of soft bottoms substituting their hard shells for soft mud and sand. Numerous other organisms live on and between the oyster shells to form a distinct community. Oyster reefs are largely restricted to the mid and low intertidal zone by several subtidal predators and competitors. Characteristic members of the oyster community include the worms *Phyllodoce fragilis, Hydroides dianthus, Nereis succinea,* and *Notaulax nudicollis;* the crabs, *Panopeus herbstii, Eurypanopeus depressus, Clibanarius vittatus,* and *Pinnotheres ostreum,* the snails; *Urosalpinx cinerea, Diodora cayenensis,* and *Boonea impressa,* the sponges; *Cliona celata* and *Hymeniacidon heliophila,* the shrimp; *Palaemonetes vulgaris,* and the anemone, *Aiptasia pallida.*

Rocks, Jetties, Pilings, Groins, and Seawalls: These hard substrata are artificial and the communities they support resemble each other in species composition. The makeup of these communities depends more on local salinity, turbidity, and water currents than on the nature of the substratum and the fauna resembles that of oyster reefs under similar circumstances.

These artificial substrata often extend across the entire intertidal zone into the subtidal, something that oyster reefs and floating docks do not do. Hard surfaces in the intertidal region support communities arranged in distinct zones which are determined by the length of exposure at low tide. The high intertidal is exposed to air during most of the tidal cycle. Any marine organism living here would be exposed to long periods of high temperatures in summer and low in winter. In addition, such organisms would be subject to desiccation, would not be able to feed, and might not be able to respire during low tide. Consequently, the upper portion of the intertidal zone is not inhabited by marine animals. This part of rocks and pilings is usually bare and does not support attached animal life, although the large, fast, isopod, *Ligia,* may be common here. The highest permanently occupied zone supports pure stands of the small intertidal barnacle, *Chthamalus fragilis,* (and *C. stellatus* in Florida). This highly stressed region experiences lengthy daily exposure to dry air and extremes of temperature. *Chthamalus* is the only animal in our area that can withstand these conditions and it is abundant here. It occupies a similar position on the stems and leaves of *Spartina* in salt marshes. Slightly lower in the intertidal, the period of exposure is not as long and oysters find conditions appropriate for their existence. This zone is dominated by the eastern oyster, *Crassostrea virginica,* but a few other invertebrate species may be present in the moist interstices between oyster shells. Between the oyster zone and the mean low water line, especially in clean high salinity water, there is often, but not always, a mussel zone comprised of dense mats of the small mussel, *Brachidontes exustus.* This zone is exposed for relatively little time during low tide and consequently physical conditions are less harsh and several species live in association with the mussels. The area between mean low water and mean low water springs is not exposed at all by most tides and exposed only briefly by spring tides. It is the most hospitable of the intertidal zones and supports the most diverse community. A bushy bryozoan usually dominates this zone, often *Bugula neritina* in clean water or *Anguinella palmata* in silty water. In clean high salinity water the large warty anemone, *Bunodosoma cavernata,* is common in this zone. Near and below the low water line the community becomes progressively more diverse and complex with the addition of scores of species. This area, and below, is physically dominated by sessile hydroids, sponges, encrusting bryozoans, and ascidians.

Floating Docks: These artificial substrata are common at marinas and residences in tidal coastal waters. Boat hulls floats, bell buoys and channel markers are other forms of the same habitat. These habitats differ from the other hard substrata in being exclusively restricted to the high subtidal. Subtidal organisms on floating docks live at the water surface and in the sunlight without being exposed to air at low tide, a situation that is not duplicated in any other major habitat. Obviously there is no tidal zonation. In this less stressful environment, where there is no exposure to air, surfaces often support rich and diverse communities whose composition varies depending on salinity, current strength, exposure to sunlight, and the amount of silt and particulate food in the water. In high salinity areas they usually support sponges, tunicates, bryozoans, and hydroids along with associated mobile species, especially worms and amphipods. Community composition varies within a floating dock complex, sometimes dramatically, depending on differences in sunlight, currents, and particulate food and silt. Exposure to sunlight often results in luxuriant growths of seaweeds which may eliminate most of the attached animal community.

Other Communities

In addition to the conspicuous and widespread communities discussed above there are several other southeastern associations that deserve mention.

Live Bottom Community: The bottoms of tidal creeks often support associations known as "live bottoms" which consist of sponges and sea whips growing on oyster or other shells. An extensive and diverse community of animals lives in association with these living substrata. They are subtidal and sometimes lie below the level of light penetration in turbid water.

Leptogorgia *Association:* The sea whip, *Leptogorgia virgulata,* lives attached to oyster or other shells in the subtidal region of tidal creeks. Associated with it are several species of symbionts and predators adapted for life on the whip and found nowhere else. The predators are *Simnialena uniplicata* (snail), *Tritonia wellsi* (sea slug), and *Neopontonides beaufortensis* (shrimp). Most of the commensal species simply use the whip as a surface for attachment. These are *Conopea galeata* (barnacle), *Pteria colymbus* (pearl oyster), and *Alyconidium hauffi* (bryozoan). A special variant of the skeleton shrimp, *Caprella equilibra,* lives only on *Leptogorgia.* The dead brown skeletal rod of the sea whip is sometimes overgrown by the calcareous, white, encrusting bryozoan, *Membranipora arborescens.*

Sargassum *Community:* The Sargasso Sea, located between Bermuda and the West Indies, is so named because of the large amounts of the seaweed, *Sargassum,* floating at its surface. *Sargassum,* or gulfweed, is a brown alga which, in or from the Sargasso Sea, belongs to the species *S. natans* and *S. fluitans.* Other species grow attached to the bottom in shallow coastal waters in the South. The weed in the Sargasso Sea seems to be independent of coastal populations and reproduces vegetatively at sea. *Sargassum* is yellow-brown and equipped with a stem, leaflike processes, and small, spherical, berrylike air bladders, or vesicles, which keep it afloat. Storms and winds blow floating *Sargassum* from the Sargasso Sea into coastal waters where it may become stranded on outer beaches. The floating weed supports a diverse and well adapted community that is relatively independent of other communities. Most members of the community are yellow-brown and difficult to see against a background of gulfweed. They depend on it to keep them at the surface, for food, cover, or attachment surface. About 70 species belong to this community and many of them are still present when the weed appears in coastal waters. Most of the mobile species, however, abandon ship before the weed is stranded on the beach. The community includes several species of fishes, including the sargassum fish, a seahorse, a pipefish, and a triggerfish, a swimming crab, a shore crab, shrimps, a goose barnacle, an anemone, a sea spider, a sea slug, several polychaetes, hydroids, bryozoans, and amphipods.

Interstitial Community: The tiny spaces between sand grains on outer beaches support a diverse community whose variety and importance was unsuspected a few decades ago. The animals occupying this habitat are said to be meiofaunal, or intermediate in size between the microfaunal Protozoa and macrofaunal animals, which are more than 0.04″ (1 mm) in length. Members of the interstitial community are shorter than 0.04″ (1 mm) and are usually elongate and wormlike in order to slip between sand grains without dislodging them. These animals are not burrowers and do not dig through the sand, rather they move easily through the water in the spaces (interstices) between sand grains. This fauna is dominated by harpacticoid copepods, nematodes, and flat-worms but every major phylum of animals except the poriferans has at least one representative in the interstitial fauna and several, such as the gastrotrichs and kinorhynchs, are best represented here. This is a wide-spread and important community present on all sandy beaches but it is not covered in this guide because it requires special collection tech-niques and microscopes for its study.

Energy Flow in Marine Communities

With few exceptions, energy enters ecosystems as sunlight and is converted to chemical energy by green plants. Photosynthesis, which occurs only in green plants and some bacteria, uses solar energy to convert carbon dioxide and water to carbohydrates, releasing oxygen in the process. The solar energy is trapped in the resulting carbohydrate molecule as chemical energy (= food energy). This carbohydrate, which can be converted to other organic molecules such as proteins, fats, and nucleic acids, is the food of almost all the living world. Every ecosystem must have a source of these energy-rich organic molecules, either manufactured by photosynthetic organisms within the ecosystem or imported from other ecosystems. The photosynthetic organisms are called autotrophs (= self feeders), or producers, and they are the base, or starting point, of almost all food chains and webs. A less common and much less well known type of autotrophic organism uses energy from inorganic chemicals, such as hydrogen sulfide, methane, or ammonia, rather than sunlight, as a source of energy. These organisms are also self feeding autotrophs, but are said to be chemosynthetic, rather than photosynthetic, and are important in a few restricted ecosystems.

Food manufactured by autotrophs is consumed by other members of the community, collectively known as heterotrophs (= other feeding), or consumers. The heterotrophs include the familiar feeding types known as herbivores (which feed directly on the autotrophs), carnivores (which feed on other heterotrophs), and the decomposers (which feed on dead organisms).

The organisms in a community belong to different trophic (feeding) levels with energy flowing from one level to the next. The producers, or autotrophs, are the first level, the herbivores the second level, and the carnivores the next two or three levels. Decomposers can be at any level except the first. Transfer of food energy from one trophic level to the next is called feeding and it involves the consumption of the organic material of one level by members of the next level. This transfer of energy is exceedingly inefficient and approximately 80-90% of the chemical energy of one level is irretrievably lost as heat with every transfer of energy from one level to the next. Consequently, only about 20%, at best, of the energy at one level can be passed to the next. This rapid loss of energy severely limits the length of any food chain to about five or fewer trophic levels.

There are many ways for heterotrophs to gather and consume their food. Consumption of living plants is herbivory and consumption of living animals is carnivory, but there are many ways to be a carnivore or an herbivore. Raptors are carnivores that hunt and kill living individual prey. Browsers and grazers are herbivores or carnivores that consume parts of living prey, often leaving the remaining parts alive to regenerate. Their prey is often sessile and immobile and reproduces vegetatively so that it is not killed by the grazing process. It is not necessary to consume living or even intact organisms to gain a supply of organic molecules and their energy. The decomposers are heterotrophs that consume dead organisms. Often the dead organic material is in the form of small particles which in the sea are called detritus. Organisms that eat detritus are called detritivores.

Marine waters usually carry loads of lightweight, suspended organic particles, either alive or dead, that form the food of a number of consumers. Suspension feeders collect and consume this suspended material. The most common means of separating suspended matter from the water is by filtering. Filter feeders, which may be benthic or pelagic, pass the water and its suspended material through a sieve to collect the particles and eliminate the water. Filter feeding is very common in marine habitats and the particles may be large shrimplike krill, small zooplankters, or tiny individual algal cells, bacteria, or detritus. The major groups of filter feeders are the sponges, bryozoans, sea squirts, bivalves, barnacles, and baleen whales.

The inorganic clay, sand, and silt particles in marine sediments are mixed with varying amounts of deposited organic material that was formerly suspended in the water. Some organisms, called deposit feeders, rely on this deposited organic material for food. Deposit feeders are of two types, selective and nonselective. Selective deposit feeders carefully choose organic particles, rejecting the surrounding inorganic sand or clay particles which have no food value. Nonselective deposit feeders indiscriminately ingest sediment, with organic and inorganic deposits combined. As the sediment moves through the animal's gut the organic material is digested and absorbed while the inorganic mineral particles remain unchanged and are eventually defecated.

Marine Ecology

In addition to the particulate organic matter in sea water there are also large quantities of organic molecules in solution, called dissolved organic material, or DOM, and there is increasing evidence that many, perhaps most, marine invertebrates absorb these molecules across the skin directly from the seawater and use them for food.

It is usually thought that photosynthesis in shallow water and at the surface of the sea provides the energy to sustain all life in the ocean but chemosynthetic bacteria rely on the energy of inorganic chemicals rather than solar energy for food. The chemicals are usually simple energy-rich compounds such as hydrogen sulfide, methane, or ammonia that exist in anaerobic environments. These molecules are absorbed by chemosynthetic bacteria and oxidized to release energy, just as heterotrophs oxidize organic molecules to produce energy. The bacteria can apparently use the energy from oxidation of inorganic compounds to manufacture organic molecules using some of the same metabolic pathways that green plants use. An increasing number of instances are being documented in which bacteria of this type live symbiotically in the tissues of animals and provide their host with organic compounds (food) whose energy is ultimately derived from the oxidation of inorganic compounds such as hydrogen sulfide. The best known example in the Southeast is *Solemya velum,* the awning clam, which has a small vestigial gut and relies completely on a diet of dissolved energy-rich hydrogen sulfide, which is processed for it by symbiotic chemosynthetic bacteria on its gills. Recent studies have shown that other bivalves, including some lucinids and mussels, rely on symbiotic chemosynthetic bacteria for their energy needs and it appears that chemosynthesis is a more important source of ecological energy than was formerly thought. Hydrogen sulfide is abundant in anaerobic, or oxygen-free, muds and is responsible for their characteristic rotten-egg odor and for their black color. Hydrogen sulfide reacts with iron to form iron sulfides which color the sediment grey-black and anaerobic sediments are often black. Oxidized, or aerobic, sediments have no hydrogen sulfide and are light colored. Hydrogen sulfide is toxic to most animals. Several shallow-water species in the Southeast rely on chemosynthetic bacteria in their tissues to provide them with energy derived chemosynthetically from stinky black sediments. Included in this group are a nematode, an oligochaete, and a flatworm which have no gut at all. Entire communities supported by chemosynthesis have recently been discovered associated with hot springs on the floor of many deep parts of the ocean.

Species Interactions

The members of biological communities can interact with each other in three basic ways, *viz.* through competition, predation, or symbiosis.

Competition is the attempt by two species to use simultaneously some vital resource that is in short supply. The resource may be space, food, oxygen, water, attachment sites, or any other commodity that is necessary for the survival of each species but is not present in quantities sufficient for both. For example, the many species of fishes in the sea do not compete for water, even though it is a vital resource, because there is no shortage of it. Trees in a forest, on the other hand, often compete intensely for water which, in this situation, is both vital and limited. The species that successfully garners most of the resource for itself will tend to eliminate potentially competitive species from the community. Competition does not necessarily involve physical contact.

Predation is the consumption of one living organism by another and obviously must involve physical contact. Predation is the transfer of energy from one trophic level to the next higher one. The definition includes consumption of both plants and animals so that both herbivory and carnivory are forms of predation. Parasitism is also a form of predation because one organism eats another and energy is passed from one level to another. Parasites are predators that are usually smaller than their prey, that take small "bites" of the prey over long periods of time, and usually do not kill the prey, at least not immediately.

Symbiosis is two species living in intimate physical contact with each other. If both members benefit from the association, as for example is the case with humans and the bacteria in our colons, the relationship is said to be mutualism. If one partner benefits without harming or helping the other, as with the tiny mites that live in human hair follicles, the association is commensalism. Parasitism also fits the defnition and can be considered a type of symbiosis in which one partner benefits at the expense of the other. The relationships between humans and ticks, tapeworms, and pathogenic bacteria are examples of parasitism.

Faunal Provinces

The coasts of continents are physically subdivided by capes and headlands into more or less distinct hydrologic regions with characteristic physical conditions and with reduced interchange of water and organisms between adjacent regions. This physical subdivision of coasts is reflected by the organisms inhabiting them. The coasts of continents are divided into faunal provinces which support characteristic assemblages of species more or less distinct from those of neighboring geographic regions. The provinces are separated from each other by geographic features that in some way limit the flow of water and the spread of organisms, usually through the maintenance of independent and discrete water masses.

The Atlantic coast of North America is divided into several provinces or subprovinces. The boundaries between the provinces are usually capes but are not definite and vary depending on the group of organisms being considered. The Boreal province extends from the Arctic to Newfoundland. The Acadian province occupies the coast from Newfoundland to Cape Cod, whereas the Virginian province extends from Cape Code to Cape Hatteras. Almost all of the southeastern United States lies in the Carolinian faunal province but this province has two discontinuous parts. An Atlantic portion extends from Cape Hatteras to Cape Canaveral and is the subject of this book, whereas the coast of the Gulf of Mexico from Florida to west Texas forms the second part. Since the southern tip of Florida belongs to the Caribbean province, the Carolinian fauna of the Atlantic is not in physical contact with the Carolinian fauna of the Gulf of Mexico, although it was in the recent geologic past when northern Florida was under water. Florida between Cape Canaveral and Miami is a transition zone between the Carolinian and the Caribbean provinces. The Caribbean province includes Florida south of Miami, the West Indies and the east coast of Central America and northern South America. This book deals specifically with the shallow-water fauna of the Atlantic portion of the Carolinian province but will be useful in the Gulf of Mexico, the Florida transition zone, and in the Virginian province.

GLOSSARY

abdomen In general, the posterior region of the body of an animal; more specifically, the posteriormost of the three major body regions of head, thorax, and abdomen.

aboral surface in jellyfishes, echinoderms, and other radially symmetrical animals, the side of the body opposite the mouth.

accessory plate one of a series of median calcareous plates that cover the dorsal hinge and gape of clams in the family Pholadidae. One of these, the mesoplax, is directly above the hinge and the metaplax lies over the posterior dorsal midline.

acontium (pl. acontia) threadlike cnidocyte-bearing internal filament of some anemones. They are ejected through the mouth and openings in the body wall (cinclides) when the animal is disturbed. Sometimes they are visible through the body wall.

acrorhagus one of several hollow, distensible, hemispherical bumps below the outer whorl of tentacles in some anemones. Acrorhagi bear a high density of cnidocytes and are used in territorial defense against other anemones.

actinula A polyplike pelagic larval stage in the hydrozoan family Tubulariidae which resembles a short stemless hydranth with two whorls of tentacles.

acute sharp or pointed at the end.

adductor muscle a powerful muscle running transversely between the two valves of a bivalve shell. When contracted it draws the valves together and closes the shell.

aerobic with oxygen.

ambulacrum In echinoderms, a radial canal and the structures associated with it. Usually manifest externally as a groove, ridge, or band with tube feet.

anaerobic without oxygen.

anterior the forwardmost, or head, end of a bilaterally symmetrical animal. It is usually associated with a concentration of sense organs, the brain, and the mouth.

aperture an opening 1. Gastropoda: the opening in the shell through which the head and foot protrude. 2. Bryozoa: the opening in the zooecium through which the lophophore is extended.

apex the tip, point, or narrow end of an object. Also used in reference to the free, or unattached, end.

apical pertaining to the apex.

apophysis A shelly process below the hinge of some bivalve molluscs (*viz.* Pholadidae) for the attachment of foot muscles.

arborescent branching in a treelike or bushlike fashion.

articulate to unite with joints.

atoke in nereid polychaetes, the unmodified benthic individuals before they become specialized for reproduction. See epitoke.

atrium In the tunicates, a seawater chamber into which open the gill slits, the anus, and the gonoducts. It discharges water, wastes, and gametes to the exterior through the atrial siphon.

atrial siphon the exhalent, or exhaust, opening from the atrium of tunicates and their relatives.

Glossary

autotomy   self amputation. Deliberate loss of appendages by an animal, usually at special joints or planes.

autotroph   An organism that produces metabolically useful energy independently of other organisms. Of the two types of autotrophy, photosynthesis utilizes the energy of the sun whereas chemosynthesis depends on the energy of simple inorganic compounds.

avicularium   a specialized, presumably defensive, bryozoan zooid resembling a raptorial bird's head with bulbous cranium and large, movable, hooked jaw. The lower jaw is typically held open.

axial rib   ridges or elevations parallel to the long axis of a gastropod shell.

axial rod   the proteinaceous central supporting rod found in many of the Alcyonaria, or Octocorallia.

basal   pertaining to the base.

base   the broad, supporting, or attached end of an object or organism.

beachhopper   a common name applied to the semiterrestrial amphipods in the family Talitridae. Beachhoppers live above the high tide line on beaches and leap vigorously using the abdomen and their appendages.

bead row   in gastropods, a spiral or axial row of small bumps which gives the appearance of a row of beads.

bell   in scyphozoan and hydrozoan medusae, the hemispherical, cuplike or saucerlike jelly mass which encloses the coelenteron and bears the tentacles and manubrium. Also called the umbrella.

benthic   pertaining to the bottom of a body of water.

benthos   the community of organisms living on or in the bottom.

bifid   divided in two, having two points.

bilateral symmetry   a body organization with right and left mirror images. There is only one plane that divides the animal into two equal (right and left) halves. *e.g.,* flatworms, segmented worms, crabs, cats, clams, fishes, and fishermen.

bioluminescence   biologically generated light such as that of fireflies and numerous marine animals.

biramous   referring to the division of arthropod and polychaete appendages into two branches, or rami.

body whorl   the lowermost, or basal, whorl of a gastropod shell. It is the largest and most spacious whorl and as such houses the head, foot, and much of the body.

bore   to drill or otherwise penetrate hard objects or bottoms such as wood, shell, or rock.

branchial sac   1. Protochordata. The expanded pharynx of the tunicates and cephalochordates. It is perforated by the gill slits, secretes mucus, and is a filter for filter feeding. Also known as pharyngeal basket, branchial basket, or pharyngeal sac. 2. Enteropneusta. A cavity between the internal pharyngeal gill slits and the external gill pores.

brood   to retain eggs in or on the body until they hatch and begin or complete development.

byssus   a holdfast of protein threads secreted by some bivalves to attach themselves to the substratum.

358

calcareous   made of calcium carbonate or limestone, limy.

callus   a calcareous deposit, often in the umbilicus or near the aperture of gastropods.

cancellate   bearing a gridwork of lines or ridges.

captaculum   a filamentous feeding appendage on the head of scaphopod molluscs.

carapace   a plate of exoskeleton extending posteriorly from the crustacean head and covering all or part of the thorax.

cardinal,   cardinal tooth   the teeth located in the central region of the bivalve hinge, usually beneath the umbo.

carnivore   an organism that eats animals.

Carolinian Faunal Province   The continental shelf from Cape Hatteras to Cape Canaveral and the northern Gulf of Mexico. The marine animals of this area form a natural biological unit more or less distinct from units to the north (Virginian Province) and south (Caribbean Province).

Carolinian   belonging to the Carolinian Faunal Province.

caudal cirrus   a small, slender, short "tail" at the posterior end of some heteronemerteans.

ceras (pl. cerata)   dorsal, unbranched, fingerlike process on the back of some nudibranch molluscs. Each contains a branch of the gut and a distal cnidosac for the storage of stinging cells.

chela, cheliped (pl. chelae)   a pincerlike grasping mechanism formed by the last two joints of an arthropod appendage.

chelate   bearing chelae, or pincers, composed of two opposing fingers.

chemosensory   capable of detecting chemicals (taste or odor) in the environment.

chemosynthesis   the extraction of metabolically usable energy from simple inorganic substances.

cephalothorax   the combined head and thorax.

chitin   a polysaccharide commonly used for structural purposes, especially exoskeletons, in many invertebrates.

chloroplast   an intracellular structure where photosynthesis occurs.

chondrophore   a spoonlike projection or pitlike depression on the hinge of some bivalves. It holds a padlike resilium of protein.

chromatophore   special pigment-containing cells in the skin which can be expanded or contracted to alter the color of an animal.

cinclide   opening in the column of some anemones through which the acontia are ejected.

cirrophore   a basal process supporting a cirrus.

cirrus (pl. cirri)   1. Polychaeta: a sensory process, usually slender and tentaclelike. a. tentacular cirrus: a cirrus arising from the peristome or a modified anterior (tentacular) body segment. b. dorsal cirrus: a cirrus arising from the upper part of the parapodium. c. ventral cirrus: a cirrus arising from the lower part of the parapodium. d. anal cirrus: a cirrus arising from the pygidium. 2. Nemertea: a short median tentacle arising from the posterior end of the animal, see caudal cirrus.

clam   any bivalve mollusc.

Glossary

cloaca a chamber associated with the posterior gut which receives wastes from the intestine and excretory organs as well as sperm or eggs. The cloaca opens to the exterior by an opening called the vent. In some compound tunicates, the cloaca is a common chamber into which open the atrial siphons of more than one zooid. Cloaca is the Latin word for sewer.

cnidocyte a cnidarian cell specialized for stinging. Contains an explosive capsule, the nematocyst.

cnidosac an ovoid sac at the distal end of a nudibranch ceras. It contains undischarged nematocysts from the cnidarian prey of the nudibranch.

coelenteron another name for the gastrovascular cavity of cnidarians. The body cavity and gut of cnidarians.

coelom any body cavity completely enclosed in mesoderm and surrounded by a peritoneum.

coenenchyme epidermis, mesoglea, and deposited calcareous spicules of the Alcyonaria.

collagen a fibrous protein in connective tissue throughout the animal kingdom.

columella the central, internal, longitudinal pillar of a gastropod shell around which the whorls are coiled.

column the cylindrical, elongated, central portion of an anemone. It bears the oral disk, mouth, and tentacles at one end and sometimes a basal attachment disk at the other. The column is sometimes divisible into a basal scaphus and an apical scapulus (thick-walled) or capitulum (thin walled) or both.

commensal any organism that lives in intimate association with another organism to its own advantage but without benefit or harm to host.

community a group of interacting and interdependent species in a restricted area.

compressed flattened laterally with the principal plane of the animal oriented vertically.

crenulate with a scalloped margin.

dactylozooid specialized, non-feeding, stinging, defensive polyps of some Hydrozoa.

denticle a small tooth.

denticulate bearing denticles, or tiny teeth.

deposit feeder an animal that feeds on organic particles that have settled from the water onto the bottom.

depressed flattened dorsoventrally. The principal plane of the animal is oriented horizontally.

derived having changed, or evolved, from the ancestral condition.

dermal pertaining to the dermis, or inner layer of the skin.

desiccate to dry out, dehydrate.

detritus fine particulate organic matter.

detritivore an animal that feeds on detritus.

dextral right handed. When a snail is viewed with the spire up and the aperture pointed towards the observer, the aperture is on the right side if the animal is dextral.

dimorphism   having two appearances, usually as sexual dimorphism in which males and females have recognizably different appearances independent of the structure of the gonads and genitalia.

dioecious   male and female sexes in different individuals.

dorsal   the back of a bilaterally symmetrical animal.

ecosystem   a biological community plus its abiotic (nonliving) environment.

ectosymbiont   a symbiont that lives on the outer surface of its partner.

ectoparasite   a parasite that lives on the outside of its host.

endoparasite   a parasite that lives inside its host.

endopod   the inner, or medial, ramus of a biramous crustacean limb.

endostyle   the ventral, ciliated, longitudinal groove in the branchial sac of tunicates and their relatives. It secretes the mucus feeding net which lines the pharynx.

endosymbiosis   symbiotic association in which one partner lives inside the other.

epibenthic   any organism living on or just above any substratum, including the sea bottom.

epifauna   animals living on or just above any substratum, especially the sea bottom.

epitoke   in the Polychaeta, an individual which is structurally modified for increased mobility for purposes of reproduction. See atoke.

escutcheon   an elongate or heart-shaped depression or surface posterior to the umbos of a bivalve mollusc shell.

estuary   the region of reduced and fluctuating salinity where a river enters the sea. Used loosely to indicate any coastal body of water with salinity intermediate between that of fresh water and ocean water.

eukaryote   any organism whose cell or cells contain a membrane-surrounded nucleus, mitochondria, chloroplasts (if appropriate), and Golgi bodies. Plants, animals, fungi, protozoa, and algae are all eukaryotic whereas bacteria and bluegreen bacteria are not.

eversible   capable of being everted.

evert   to extend by turning inside out.

excurrent siphon   the dorsalmost of the two bivalve mollusc siphons. It conducts water out of the mantle cavity after it passes over the gills and openings of the gonads, kidney, and gut.

exopod   the outer, or lateral, ramus of the biramous crustacean appendage.

exoskeleton   a firm, non-living, external covering secreted by an animal for structural support, protection, and muscle attachment.

fan   the combined array of feeding tentacles of polychaete worms belonging to the Sabellidae, Serpulidae, and Spirorbidae.

filter feeder   a suspension feeder that concentrates suspended organic particles by filtration.

finger   either of the two opposing processes of the crustacean chela, or pincer. The movable finger is the dactyl, or last joint of the leg, and the immovable finger is a distal process on the propodus, or penultimate joint.

foliose, foliaceous   leaflike.

Glossary

foot corners   the anterior-lateral margins of the nudibranch foot. These corners may be elaborated to form tentaclelike processes or they may be smoothly rounded.

fossorial   adapted for digging.

fouling community   a casual term used in reference to the epibenthic community of hard surfaces. Includes barnacles, bryozoans, hydroids, tunicates, oysters, seaweeds, and their associates.

free living   1. living unattached on the substratum and free to move over its surface. 2. non-parasitic.

frontal wall, frontal   the free or unattached face of the zooid of an encrusting bryozoan. It bears the aperture and other features such as avicularia, tubercles, ovicells, and pores.

furca   in crustaceans, a pair of processes on the last region of the abdomen.

gallery   underground chambers and connecting passageways.

ganglion   a concentration of nerve cell bodies.

gape   the opening between the ventral margins of the valves of a bivalve mollusc.

gastrozooid   in the Hydrozoa, a feeding polyp with mouth and tentacles.

gastrovascular cavity   the gut cavity of cnidarians and platyhelminths. So called because it is responsible for the distribution of food as well as its digestion.

genital bursa   in brittle stars, one of ten ciliated sacs located in the disk at the bases of the arms. They communicate with the exterior via a slit and function as gills and sometimes as brood chambers.

girdle   in the Polyplacophora this is the name applied to the mantle. It is most evident as a band encircling the body just below the edges of the eight shell plates and above the foot. It overgrows the shell to greater or lesser extent.

globose   globular or globelike.

gnathopod   one of the first pairs of free thoracic appendages of amphipod crustaceans. Gnathopods usually have pincers and are used for grasping.

gonangium   in the thecate hydroids, the gonozooid and its enclosing gonotheca.

gonophore   a reduced medusa that is retained on a hydrozoan polyp. The medusa may be little more than a gonad, as in *Hydractinia* or *Eudendrium.* In hydroids that liberate a medusa, *e.g., Obelia* or *Bougainvillia,* it arises from a bud, or medusoid.

gonotheca   the perisarc, or exoskeleton, surrounding a gonozooid.

gonozooid   a hydrozoan polyp specialized for reproduction.

habitat   the environment of an organism.

herbivore   an animal that consumes plants.

hermaphrodite   having both sexes in a single individual either simultaneously or consecutively.

hermit, hermit crab   Any of the paguridean crabs. These animals typically inhabit discarded gastropod shells.

heteronereid   an epitoke in the polychaete family Nereidae.

heterotrophic   an organism that depends on other organisms for food energy.

hinge the dorsal area of a bivalve shell where the two valves are held together. Usually, but not always, with teeth and a proteinaceous ligament and/or resilium.

horny composed of a tough, hard, proteinaceous material.

hydranth a typical feeding hydrozoan polyp with tentacles and gut.

hydrocaulus the main stem of a hydroid colony.

hydrotheca the chitinous exoskeleton surrounding and protecting the hydranth of some hydroids.

hypostome the hollow elevation surrounding the mouth and itself surrounded by the tentacles in the center of a hydrozoan polyp.

incurrent siphon the ventral siphon of a bivalve mollusc. It conducts water into the mantle cavity.

infauna collective term referring to animals living within the substratum underlying a body of water.

inflated fat, obese, or swollen, with cross section broadly ellipitical, circular, or ovoid.

inner beach beaches bordering quiet protected waters where there is little or no sustained wave action.

interstice space between adjacent objects or particles.

intertidal the region of the coast between the extreme high tide line and the extreme low tide line.

jetty used here in reference to a long barrier of jumbled rock extending from the shore into the water and used to alter or direct water currents.

introvert the retractile anterior portion of the sipunculan body.

lamella (pl. lamellae) a flattened sheetlike or platelike structure. In the Opisthobranchia, the rhinophores often bear flat ringlike or bladelike lamellae perpendicular, parallel, or oblique to the long axis.

lamellate having lamellae.

lateral pertaining to the sides of the body and away from the midline.

laterally compressed see compressed.

ligament a proteinaceous pad located dorsal to the hinge between two valves of a bivalve shell. It is under tension when the valves are closed and pulls the valves open when the adductor muscles are relaxed.

lime calcium carbonate, or limestone.

limy pertaining to lime.

longitudinal parallel to the anterior-posterior axis of the body.

Lophophorata an unofficial superphyletic group including the phyla Brachiopoda, Phoronida, and Bryozoa, all of whose members bear lophophores.

lophophore a crown of ciliated feeding tentacles surrounding the mouth of phoronids, bryozoans, and brachiopods.

lunule a heart-shaped depression or flattened area anterior to the umbo of some bivalve molluscs. Also an opening through the test of a sand dollar.

madreporite the opening of the echinoderm water vascular system. It is a perforated external plate in asteroids, ophiuroids, and echinoids, whereas in holothuroids it is usually internal.

Glossary

mantle   1. Mollusca: the fleshy body wall exclusive of the head and foot or their derivatives. It typically encloses the animal and secretes the shell. 2. Ascidiacea: the thin saclike membrane lying under the much thicker and tougher tunic. The mantle is the body wall of the animal whereas the tunic is largely a product of the mantle.

manubrium   a structure surrounding the mouth of hydromedusae, cubomedusae, and scyphomedusae. Often bears oral arms in the scyphomedusae.

medial, median   on or toward the midline of the body.

medusa   jellyfishlike stage in the life cycle of hydrozoans, scyphozoans, and cubozoans. Medusae are typically free-swimming, solitary, sexual stages with a thick mesoglea and a downward-oriented mouth.

merus (pl. meri)   the fourth article of a crustacean leg (counting from either direction). It lies between the ischium and the carpus.

mesoglea   the middle of the three layers of the cnidarian body. It is thin in polyps but thick and jellylike in medusae.

metanephridium   a type of excretory organ consisting of a ciliated funnel extending from the body cavity to the exterior.

mussel   In marine waters, any clam in the family Mytilidae. In freshwater, any clam in the family Unionidae.

mutualism   an intimate association between individuals of two species in which both benefit.

nacreous   referring to the smooth, glossy, pearly or iridescent inner lining of some bivalve shells; mother-of-pearl.

neap tide   any one of the tides that occurs when the gravitational pull of sun and moon partially cancel each other. Neap tides have the smallest amplitude between high and low.

nekton   pelagic animals that move independently of water currents. Includes the fishes and marine mammals.

nematocyst   microscopic capsule in special cnidarian cells (cnidocytes) which discharges a stinging or sticky thread when stimulated.

nephridium   an invertebrate excretory organ; responsible for maintenance of water balance and/or nitrogen excretion.

nestler   an organism that inhabits the spaces between other organisms of the same or different species.

neuston   ecological assemblage of organisms associated with the surface film of a body of water.

notochord   a stiff, flexible, longitudinal rod in the back of chordate animals. It functions much like the vertebral column which it preceded evolutionarily.

notum   the dorsal surface, or back, of an animal.

nuchal organ   a ciliated groove, ridge, or eversible sac on, and sometimes extending posteriorly from, the prostomium.

obese   fat, swollen. Circular or nearly so in cross section.

oblique   slanting, at an angle.

octocoral   any member of the anthozoan subclass Alcyonaria (=Octocorallia) in the phylum Cnidaria. Including the sea pens, sea whips, soft corals, sea fans, and sea pansies.

omnivore   on organism that eats both animals and plants.

operculum 1. Mollusca: a thin, flat, proteinaceous or calcareous, closing plate for the aperture of gastropods. 2. Polychaeta: a modified pluglike head appendage used to close the tube. 3. Cirripedia: the four movable calcareous plates that close the aperture. It consists of two posterior terga and two anterior scuta.

oral arm one of four processes flanking the mouth of many scyphozoans. These hang beneath the animal and are often long and frilly.

oral disk 1. Cnidaria: the mouth- and tentacle-bearing apical surface of the column of an anemone. 2. Echinoderms: the mouth-bearing oral surface of the central part of the body of sea stars and brittle stars.

oral siphon the incurrent, or intake, opening in sea squirts and their relatives. It opens into the branchial sac. Also called buccal siphon.

oral surface the surface of a radially symmetrical animal that bears the mouth.

osculum (pl. oscula, oscules) the excurrent opening or openings of sponges. They are usually relatively large in comparison with the incurrent openings.

ossicle literally, a "tiny bone"; small calcareous skeletal elements of the echinoderms, some bivalves, and other animals.

ostium (pl. ostia) small incurrent pores on the surface of sponges through which water enters.

outer beach beach bordering the open ocean; unprotected and subjected to sustained wave action.

pallet one member of a pair of plumelike or paddlelike processes found at the siphonal end of shipworms and used to close the gallery opening.

pallial line a line paralleling the anterior and ventral internal borders of a bivalve valve. It marks the line of attachment of the mantle muscles to the valve.

pallial sinus a posterior invagination of the pallial line marking the position of the siphons.

palp sensory or feeding structures arising from the lateral, ventral or dorsal prostomium or peristomium of polychaete annelids.

parapodium 1. Polychaeta: the fleshy lateral limb or foot of a polychaete. Primitively it has two major branches, the dorsal notopodium and the ventral neuropodium. 2. Mollusca: winglike, muscular, lateral lobes of the foot used for swimming.

parietal shield a flat area beside the inner lip of the aperture of a gastropod shell.

paxilla raised, spinous, dermal ossicles characteristic of the surface of some asteroids.

pedal disk the flattened basal end of the anemone column, it is used to attach to the substratum.

pedicel 1. Hydrozoa: a short stemlike branch supporting each hydranth. These may originate from the stolon, hydrocaulus, or branches of the hydrocaulus. Sessile hydranths lack a pedicel and attach directly to the stolon, hydrocaulus, or one of its branches. 2. Kamptozoa: the stalklike attachment organ of the Kamptozoa. Sometimes called a peduncle.

pedicellaria small pincerlike dermal appendage of some asteroids and echinoids.

pellucid translucent and colorless.

Glossary

periopod, pereopod one of the free thoracic appendages of peracarid crustaceans.

periostracum the outermost, organic layer of the mollusc shell.

perisarc the chitinous cuticular covering of hydroid colonies.

peristomium the anterior body segment surrounding the annelid mouth, it is immediately posterior to the prostomium.

pharynx the anterior region of the gut just posterior to the mouth cavity, it is often muscular and eversible and may be used for feeding or burrowing.

photosynthesis the production of carbohydrates and oxygen from carbon dioxide, water, and light energy by plants and bacteria.

physa a pedal disk specialized for digging or floating.

piling, pile a wooden or concrete post used to support a dock, bridge, wharf, or other marine structure.

pillbug a common name applied to some terrestrial isopod crustaceans capable of rolling into a ball.

pinnate with branches extending symmetrically from two sides of a long axis. Featherlike.

plankton the ecological community of mostly microscopic organisms suspended in the water and involuntarily subject to transport by its currents. Including the photosynthetic phytoplankton and the heterotrophic zooplankton.

planula the microscopic, ciliated, non-feeding larval stage of cnidarians.

pleon the anterior abdominal segments of malacostracans. The number varies, there being 3 in amphipods and 5 in isopods, cumaceans and decapods. Sometimes used to refer to the entire abdomen.

pleopod the anterior appendages of the crustacean abdomen.

pleotelson the combined pleon and telson of isopods.

podium (pl. podia) an echinoderm tube foot.

polyp one of two major body forms in the Cnidaria. A polyp consists of an elongate cylinder, an attached base, and an upper whorl of tentacles surrounding the mouth. Polyps are usually colonial, asexual, and attached to a substratum.

posterior the hind, or trailing, end of a bilaterally symmetrical animal. The end opposite the anterior, or head, end.

prehensile modified for grasping.

proboscis In the sea spiders, an anterior process which bears the mouth.

process an extension or projection.

prokaryote primitive cells, such as those of bacteria and blue-green bacteria, which lack nuclei, mitochondria, and chloroplasts.

prostomium the anteriormost part of an annelid. Anterior and dorsal to the mouth, this is usually the site of the brain and a concentration of external sensory structures.

proteinaceous made of protein.

protonephridium an invertebrate structure important in maintaining water balance and sometimes in nitrogen excretion. It consists of a simple tubular duct, blind at one end, with a single cilium or tuft of cilia at the blind end.

proventricle an ovoid muscularized region of the anterior gut of some polychaetes, especially the syllids.

ptychocyst   non-stinging nematocysts of cerianthid cnidarians which, when discharged, interweave to form a tube around the animal.

pulmonate   a member of the gastropod subclass Pulmonata in the phylum Mollusca. These snails and slugs have a lung and breathe air and are usually found in terrestrial or freshwater habitats.

pygidium   the posteriormost portion of an annelid. The pygidium bears the anus and the anal cirri.

pyriform   pear-shaped.

quadrate   square.

radius (pl. radii)   1. Echinodermata: the body axes through the rays, or arms. 2. Cirripedia: a flangelike process on one side of each lateral plate. The radii overlie similar flangelike processes, the alae, of adjacent plates.

radula   a rasplike ribbon of tiny teeth in the mouth of most molluscs (except clams).

radial symmetry   the organization of a body around a central axis so that any of several planes passed through the axis will divide the body into equal (mirror image) halves. *e.g.,* jellyfishes, sea stars.

ramus   a branch.

raptorial   predatory; adapted for hunting, killing, and dismembering prey.

resilium   a proteinaceous pad ventral to the hinge of bivalve molluscs. It is compressed when the valves are closed and pushes them open when the adductor muscle relaxes.

respiratory pigment   a biological pigment, such as hemoglobin, hemerythrin, or hemocyanin that transports or stores oxygen in blood or tissues. They occur frequently in animals in oxygen-poor environments and in animals with high activity levels.

reticulation   a network.

rhinophore   anterior, dorsal, paired, fingerlike sensory tentacle of opisthobranch molluscs. Rhinophores are sometimes retractile and are often provided with lamellae, sheaths, papillae, or other surface features.

rhopalium   a marginal sensory organ on the swimming bell of scyphozoan medusae. Each rhopalium consists of separate structures for the detection of light, orientation, and tastes.

rib, riblet   1. Bivalvia: a ridge extending radially from the umbonal region of the valve. 2. Gastropoda: a ridge oriented parallel to the long axis of the shell.

rostrum   a dorsal, median, anterior projection of the head of a crustacean.

Sargassum   a genus of attached or floating brown alga, or seaweed, whose members are composed of leafy yellow-brown stalks with small pea-size spherical floats.

scaleworm   any of the polychaete worms belonging to the Polynoidae, Polyodontidae or Sigalionidae and characterized by possession of dorsal scales, or elytra.

scud   a common name for an amphipod crustacean.

sculpture   the relieved surface ornamentation of a mollusc shell consisting of ribs, grooves, bumps, beads, lines, cords, spines, teeth, and ridges.

Glossary

scutum one of the two anterior opercular plates that close the aperture of a barnacle. A single scutum is roughly triangular in shape and is easily distinguished from the posterior tergal plates by the absence of a projecting spur.

sea whip some of the members of the anthozoan order Gorgonacea. The sea whips are slender branching cylinders of colored tissue overlying a tough proteinaceous axial rod. *e.g., Leptogorgia.*

sediment the material deposited at the bottom of a body of water. Including clay, silt, sand, and gravel.

sessile 1. attached to the substratum. 2. without a stalk

seta (pl. setae) a chitinous bristle.

setiger a polychaete segment which bears setae.

shoulder usually the region of greatest width of a whorl of a gastropod shell.

siliceous composed of silicon.

sinistral referring to left-handed gastropod shells. With the snail held with the spire up and the aperture facing the observer, the aperture is on the left if the shell is sinistral.

siphon 1. Mollusca: one of a pair of tubular or tubelike extensions of the posterior bivalve mantle. 2. Urochordata: one of two tubes or passageways leading into or out of the tunicate body.

social living in loose aggregations of individuals.

spadix fingerlike branch or branches of the sporosac coelenteron extending around the developing embryo in the hydroid genus *Eudendrium.*

spicule 1. Porifera: microscopic or nearly microscopic, calcareous or siliceous, skeletal parts. 2. Alcyonaria: microscopic, calcareous, often pigmented, skeletal parts.

spiralzooid elongate, coiled, extensible, tentacle-less polyps of the hydroid, *Hydractinia.*

spire the upper or apical end of a gastropod shell consisting of all the whorls except the body whorl.

spongin flexible fibrous protein comprising the skeletal fibers of sponges.

sporosac a sac that forms a chamber in which the sex cells of some hydroids mature. In species with sporosacs, the medusoid generation is suppressed and gametes are produced by reduced medusa tissue in the sporosacs. In some species the ova may be retained in the female sporosacs until they become planulae.

spring tides tides that occur when the gravitational pull of sun and moon combine. Spring tides have especially large amplitudes with exceptionally high high tides and low low tides.

stolon 1. Hydrozoa, Bryozoa, and tunicates. A creeping stem that gives rise to zooids. 2. Polychaeta. An asexually produced miniature worm formed in chains at the posterior end of the larger adult worm.

striate bearing a series of parallel lines, grooves, or ridges.

subchelate a pincer in which there is only one finger. The finger closes against the palm of the preceding joint rather than against another finger.

subequal similar, or nearly equal.

substratum (pl. substrata) a firm surface on or in which an organism lives.

subtidal below the extreme low tide line.

subumbrella Below the bell, or umbrella, of a medusa. The oral surface of a medusa.

suctorial producing suction.

supratidal above the extreme high tide line.

surf the breaking waves at the edge of the sea.

suspension feeder an animal that feeds on organic particles suspended in the water.

swash zone the area of a beach above the surf zone where the water from the waves rushes back and forth.

tadpole larva the characteristic larva of the tunicates.

taxodont having numerous similar teeth.

telson the posteriormost region of the crustacean body, it bears the anus.

tentacular cirrus a cirrus arising from the peristomium or a specialized anterior segment incorporated into the head.

tergum one of the two posterior opercular plates that close the aperture of a barnacle. Bears a process, the tergal spur, on one edge.

terminal at the end.

theca short for hydrotheca.

transverse at right angles to the anterior-posterior axis, crossing the longitudinal axis.

trophic level The position of an organism in its food chain.

truncate Ending abruptly, not tapering.

tubicole An animal that dwells in a tube.

tunic the tough outer cellulose covering of a tunicate.

umbilicus a hole, hollow, or concavity at the base of the shell of some gastropods, it extends into the central axis, or columella.

umbo the raised area above the hinge of a bivalve valve, it is the oldest part of the shell.

umbrella The bell, or body, of a medusa.

uniramous a polychaete or arthropod appendage composed of a single branch, or ramus.

univalve a shell composed of a single piece, or valve.

uropod 1. Amphipoda: any of the last three of the six pairs of abdominal appendages. 2. Decapoda and Isopoda: the last of six pairs of abdominal appendages.

valve one of the right or left halves of a bivalve shell.

varix, varices an axial rib or raised ridge formed near the aperture of a snail shell during a period when the shell was not growing.

ventral the belly, or surface opposite the back, of a bilaterally symmetrical animal.

vermiform worm-shaped.

verrucae adhesive warts on the column of some anemones.

viscera collective term for the internal organs of an animal, especially the gut tube and associated structures.

viviparous referring to species in which the female gives birth to active juveniles rather than eggs.

Glossary

whorl   a single turn or coil of the tentacles of cnidarian polyps or the gastropod shell.

wrack   seaweeds or other vegetation cast up and stranded on the shore.

zooecium (pl. zooecia)   the external skeleton of a bryozoan zooid.

zooxanthellae   unicellular, mutualistic, dinoflagellate algae living in the cells or tissues of other organisms.

zooid   an individual member of colonial species such as bryozoans and tunicates.

SELECTED REFERENCES

This reference list includes the most important taxonomic works for use in identifying shallow-water macroinvertebrates on the southeastern coast. At least one or two of the most useful works for each major taxonomic group have been included except for those groups for which there are no references. More extensive access to the regional literature is provided by Dowds (1979) and Zingmark (1978).

General Works

Coker, R. E. 1954. This great and wide sea. An introduction to oceanography and marine biology. Harper Torchbooks. New York. 325 p.

Dowds, R. E. 1979. References for the identification of marine invertebrates on the southern Atlantic coast of the United States. NOAA Tech. Rept. NMFS SSRF-729:1–37.

Fox, R. S. & E. E. Ruppert. 1985. Shallow-water marine benthic macroinvertebrates of South Carolina. Univ. of South Carolina Press, Columbia. 330 p.

Gosner, K. L. 1978. A field guide to the Atlantic shore. Houghton Mifflin, Boston. 329 p.

Heard, R. W. 1982. Guide to the common tidal marsh invertebrates of the northeastern Gulf of Mexico. Mississippi Alabama Sea Grant Consortium MASGP-79-004:1–82.

Kaplan, E. H. 1982. A field guide to coral reefs of the Caribbean and Florida. Houghton Mifflin, Boston. 289 p.

Meinkoth, N. A. 1981. The Audubon Society field guide to North American seashore creatures. Knopf, New York. 799 p.

Miner, R. W. 1950. Field book of seashore life. Putnam, New York. 888 p.

Overstreet, R. 1978. Marine maladies. Worms, germs, and other symbionts from the northern Gulf of Mexico. Mississippi-Alabama Sea Grant Consortium MASGP-78-021. 140 p.

Parker, S. P. (ed) 1982. Synopsis and classification of living organisms. Volumes 1,2. McGraw-Hill, New York. 2398 p.

Smith, R. I. 1964. Keys to marine invertebrates of the Woods Hole region. Syst-Ecol. Prog. Mar. Biol. Lab. Contr. II:1–208.

Spotte, S. 1973. Marine aquarium keeping, the science, the animals, and the art. Wiley-Interscience, New York.

Sterrer, W. 1986. Marine fauna and flora of Bermuda. Wiley. New York. 742 p.

Voss, G. L. 1976. Seashore life of Florida and the Caribbean. Banyan Books, Miami. 199 p.

Wilson, W. H. 1979. An annotated checklist of the shallow-water marine invertebrates of the Morehead City-Beaufort region of North Carolina. C. H. Peterson (ed.). Univ. North Carolina Inst. Mar. Sci. Publ., 42 p.

Zeiller, W. 1974. Tropical marine invertebrates of southern Florida and the Bahama Islands. Wiley-Interscience, New York. 132 p.

Zingmark, R. G. 1978. An annotated checklist of the biota of the coastal zone of South Carolina. Univ. South Carolina Press, Columbia. 364 p.

Selected References

Zinn, D. 1985. The handbook for beach strollers. Globe Pequot Press. Chester, Connecticut. 246 p.

Porifera

Hartman, W. D. 1958. Natural history of the marine sponges of southern New England. Bull. Yale Peabody Mus. Nat. Hist. 12:1–155.

Hopkins, S. H. 1956. The boring sponges which attack South Carolina oysters, with notes on some associated organisms. Contr. Bears Bluff Lab 23:1–30.

Old, M. C. 1941. The taxonomy and distribution of the boring sponges (Clionidae) along the Atlantic coast of North America. Chesapeake Biol. Lab. Publ. 44:1-30.

Wells, H. W., M. J. Wells & I. E. Gray. 1960. Marine sponges of North Carolina. J. Elisha Mitchell Sci. Soc. 76:200–245.

Cnidaria

Bayer, F. M. 1961. The shallow-water Octocorallia of the West Indian region. Nijhoff, The Hague. 373 p, 27 pl.

Calder, D. R. 1977. Guide to common jellyfishes of South Carolina. South Carolina Sea Grant Marine Advisory Bull. 11:1–12.

Calder, D. R. 1971. Hydroids and hydromedusae of southern Chesapeake Bay. Virginia Inst. Mar. Sci. Spec. Pub. 1:1–125.

Carlgren, O. 1949. A survey of the Ptychodactiaria, Corallimorpharia and Actiniaria. Kungl. Svenska Vet. Handl. 1(1):3–121, 4 pl.

Fraser, C. M. 1944. Hydroids of the Atlantic coast of North America. Univ. Toronto Press, Toronto. 451 p, 94 pl.

Larson, R. J. 1976. Marine flora and fauna of the northeastern United States. Cnidaria: Scyphozoa. NOAA Tech. Rept. NMFS Circ. 397:1–17.

Kramp, P. L. 1959. Hydromedusae of the Atlantic Ocean and adjacent waters. Dana Repts. 46:1–283.

Schwartz, F. J. 1979. Common jellyfish and comb jellies of North Carolina. Privately published.

Ctenophora

Bishop, J. W. 1972. Ctenophores of the Chesapeake Bay. Chesapeake Sci. 13 Suppl. :S98–S100.

Mayer, A. G. 1912. Ctenophores of the Atlantic coast of North America. Carnegie Inst. Washington Publ. 162:1–58.

Chordata

Monniot, C. & F. Monniot. 1972. Clé mondial des genres d'Ascidies. Arch. Zool. Éxp. Gén. 113:311–367.

Plough, H. H. 1978. Sea squirts of the Atlantic continental shelf from Maine to Texas. Johns Hopkins Univ. Press, Baltimore. 118 p.

Van Name, W. G. 1945. The North and South American Ascidians. Bull. American Mus. Nat. Hist. 84:1–476, 31 pl.

Selected References

Echinodermata

Deichmann, E. 1930. The holothurians of the western part of the Atlantic Ocean. Bull. Mus. Comp. Zool. 71:43–226.

Deichmann, E. 1954. The holothurians of the Gulf of Mexico. *in:* Galtsoff, P. S. (ed.), Gulf of Mexico: Its origin, waters and marine life. Fish. Bull. 55:381–410.

Downey, M. E. 1973. Starfishes from the Caribbean and the Gulf of Mexico. Smithson. Contr. Zool. 126:1–158.

Gray, I. E., M. E. Downey & M. J. Cerame-Vivas. 1968. Sea-stars of North Carolina. Fish. Bull. 67:127–163.

Pawson, D. L. 1977. Marine flora and fauna of the northeastern United States: Holothuroidea. NOAA Tech. Rept. NMFS Circ. 405:1–15.

Thomas, L. P. 1962. The shallow-water amphiurid brittle stars (Echinodermata, Ophiuroidea) of Florida. Bull. Mar. Sci. Gulf Carib. 12:623–694.

Lophophorata

Emig, C-C. 1971. Taxonomie et systematique des Phoronidiens. Bull. Mus. Nat. Hist. Natur. 3:473–568.

Maturo, F. J. S. 1957. A study of the Bryozoa of Beaufort, North Carolina, and vicinity. J. Elisha Mitchell Sci. Soc. 73:11–68.

Maturo, F. J. S. 1966. Bryozoa of the Southeast coast of the United States: Bugulidae and Beaniidae (Cheilostomata: Anasca). Bull. Mar. Sci. 16:556–583.

Stancyk, S. E., F. J. S. Maturo & R. W. Heard. 1976. Phoronids from the east coast of the United States. Bull. Mar. sci. 26:576–584.

Winston, J. E. 1982. Marine bryozoans (Ectoprocta) of the Indian River area (Florida). Bull. American Mus. Nat. Hist. 173:100–176.

Kamptozoa

Maturo, F. J. S. 1957. A study of the Bryozoa of Beaufort, North Carolina, and vicinity. J. Elisha Mitchell Sci. Soc. 73:11–68.

Nielsen, C. 1966. Some Loxosomatidae (Entoprocta) from the Atlantic coast of the United States. Ophelia 3:249–275.

Sipuncula

Cutler, E. B. 1973. Sipuncula of the western North Atlantic. Bull. American Mus. Nat. Hist. 152:103–204.

Cutler, E. B. 1977. Marine Flora and fauna of the northeastern United States. Sipuncula. NOAA Tech. Rept. NMFS Circ 403:1–6.

Stephen, A. C. & J. J. Edmonds. 1972. The phyla Sipuncula and Echiura. British Mus. (Nat. Hist) Publ. 517:1–528.

Mollusca

Abbott, R. T. 1968. Seashells of North America. Golden Press, New York. 280 p.

Abbott, R. T. 1974. American Seashells. Van Nostrand, 2nd edition, New York. 367 p.

Selected References

Arnold, W. H. 1965. A glossary of 1001 terms used in conchology. The Veliger 75 (supplement):iii–50.

Boss, K. J. 1966. The subfamily Tellininae in the western Atlantic. The genus *Tellina* (Part I). Johnsonia 4:217–272.

Boss, K. J. 1968. The subfamily Tellininae in the western Atlantic. The genera *Tellina* (Part II) and *Tellidora*. Johnsonia 4:273–344.

Emerson, W. K. and M. K. Jacobson. 1976. The American Museum of Natural History guide to shells. Knopf, New York. 482 p.

Eyster, L. M. 1977. Shell-less opisthobranchs of North Inlet estuary, South Carolina, with emphasis on *Doriopsilla pharpa* Marcus (Nudibranchia: Doridacea: Dendrodorididae). M.S. thesis, University of South Carolina, Columbia. 157 p.

Fox, T. H. 1979. Reproductive adaptations and life histories of the commensal leptonacean bivalves. Ph.D. dissertation, University of North Carolina, Chapel Hill. 207 p.

Porter, H. J. 1974. The North Carolina marine and estuarine Mollusca. University of North Carolina Institute of Marine Sciences, Morehead City. 351 p.

Stanley, S. M. 1970. Relation of shell form to life habits of the Bivalvia (Mollusca). Geol. Soc. America, Mem. 125:1–296.

Thompson, F. G. The Aquatic Snails of the Family Hydrobiidae of Peninsular Florida. Univ. Florida Press. Gainesville. 268 p.

Turner, R. D. 1966. A survey and illustrated catalog of the Teredinidae (Mollusca: Bivalvia). Mus. Comp. Zool. Harvard. 265 p.

Turner, R. D. 1971. Identification of marine wood-boring molluscs. *In* Marine borers, fungi, and fouling organisms of wood. *Ed by* E. B. G. Jones & S. K. Eltringham. Organization for Economic Cooperation and Development, Paris. (Reprint available from the Museum of Comparative Zoology, Harvard University.)

Nemertea

Coe, W. R. 1943. Biology of the nemerteans of the Atlantic coast of North America. Trans. Connecticut Acad. Arts Sci. 35:129–328.

Coe, W. R. 1951. The nemertean faunas of the Gulf of Mexico and southern Florida. Bull. Mar. Sci. Gulf Carib. 1:149–186.

Corrêa, D. D. 1961. Nemerteans from Florida and Virgin Islands. Bull. Mar. Sci. Gulf Carib. 11:1–44.

McCaul, W. E. 1963. Rhynchocoela: nemerteans from marine and estuarine waters of Virginia. J. Elisha Mitchell Sci. Soc. 79:111–124.

Platyhelminthes

Hyman, L. H. 1941. The polyclad flatworms of the Atlantic coast of the United States and Canada. Proc. U. S. Nat. Mus. 89:449–495.

Hyman, L. H. 1944. Marine Turbellaria from the Atlantic coast of North America. American Mus. Nov. 1266:1–15.

Hyman, L. H. 1952. Further notes on the turbellarian fauna of the Atlantic coast of North America. Biol. Bull. 103:195–200.

Selected References

Pearse, A. S. 1938. Polyclads of the east coast of North America. Proc. U. S. Nat. Mus. 86:67–98.

Pearse, A. S. & J. W. Littler. 1938. Polyclads of Beaufort, North Carolina. J. Elisha Mitchell Sci. Soc. 54:235–244.

Echiura

Stephen, A. C. & J. J. Edmonds. 1972. The phyla Sipuncula and Echiura. British Mus. (Nat. Hist.) Pub. 517:1–528.

Annelida

Blake, J. A. 1971. Revision of the genus *Polydora* from the east coast of North America (Polychaeta: Spionidae). Smithson. Cont. Zool. 75:1–32.

Brinkhurst, R. O. & B. G. M. Jamieson. 1971. Aquatic Oligochaeta of the world. Oliver & Boyd, Edinburg. 860 p.

Cook, D. G. & R. O. Brinkhurst. 1973. Marine flora and fauna of the northeastern coast of the United States: Oligochaeta. NOAA Tech Rept. NMFS Circ. 374:1–22.

Day, J. H. 1973. New Polychaeta from Beaufort, with a key to all species recorded from North Carolina. NOAA Tech. Rept. NMFS Circ. 375:1–140.

Fauchald, K. 1977. The Polychaete worms. Los Angeles County Mus. Sci. Ser. 38:1–188.

Gardiner, S. L. 1975. Errant polychaete annelids from North Carolina. J. Elisha Mitchell Sci. Soc. 91:77–220.

Hartman, O. 1945. The marine annelids of North Carolina. Duke Univ. Press, Durham. 53 p.

Hartman, O. 1951. The littoral marine annelids of the Gulf of Mexico. Inst. Mar. Sci. (Texas) Publ. 2:7–124.

Mikkelsen, P. S. & R. W. Virnstein. 1982. An illustrated glossary of polychaete terms. Harbor Branch Fnd. Tech. Rept. 46:1–92.

Pettibone, M. 1963. Marine polychaete worms of the New England region. Bull. U. S. Mus. Nat. Hist. 227:1–356.

Sawyer, R. T., A. R. Lawler & R. M. Overstreet. 1975. Marine leeches of the eastern United States and the Gulf of Mexico with a key to species. J. Nat. Hist. 9:633–667.

Arthropoda

Pycnogonida

Child, C. A. 1979. Shallow-water Pycnogonida of the Isthmus of Panama and the coasts of Middle America. Smithson. Contr. Zool. 293:1–86.

Hedgpeth, J. W. 1948. The Pycnogonida of the western north Atlantic and the Caribbean. Proc. U. S. Nat. Mus. 97:157–343.

McCloskey, L. R. 1967. New and little-known benthic pycnogonids from North Carolina. J. Nat. Hist. 1:119–134.

McCloskey, L. R. 1973. Marine flora and fauna of the northeastern United States: Pycnogonida. NOAA Tech. Rept. NMSF CIRC-386:1–11.

Stock, J. H. 1974. Pycnogonida from the continental shelf, slope, and deep sea of the tropical Atlantic and east Pacific. Bull. Mar. Sci. 24:957–1092.

Selected References

Crustacea: Cirripedia

Newman, W. A. & A. Ross. 1976. Revision of the balanomorph barnacles; including a catalog of the species. San Diego Soc. Nat. Hist. Mem. 9:1–108.

Tomlinson, J. T. 1969. The burrowing barnacles (Cirripedia: Order Acrothoracica). Bull. U. S. Nat. Mus. 296:1–162.

Zullo, V. A. 1979. Marine flora and fauna of the northeastern United States. Arthropoda: Cirripedia. NOAA Tech. Rept. NMFS Circ. 425:1–29.

Crustacea: Stomatopoda

Manning, R. B. 1969. Stomatopod Crustacea of the western Atlantic. Univ. Miami Inst. Mar. Sci. Stud. Trop. Oceanogr. 8:1–380.

Crustacea: Decapoda

Williams, A. B. 1984. Shrimps, lobsters, and crabs of the Atlantic coast of the eastern United States, Maine to Florida. Smithsonian Inst. Press, Washington. 550 p.

Crustacea: Mysidacea

Stucks, K. C., H. M. Perry, & R. W. Heard. 1979. An annotated key to the Mysidacea of the north central Gulf of Mexico. Gulf Res. Repts. 6:225–238.

Wigley, R. W. & B. R. Burns. 1971. Distribution and biology of mysids (Crustacea: Mysidacea) from the Atlantic coast of the United States in the NMFS Woods Hole collections. Fish. Bull. 69:717–745.

Crustacea: Tanaidacea

Sieg, J. & R. Winn. 1978. Keys to suborders and families of Tanaidacea (Crustacea). Proc. Biol. Soc. Washington 91:840–846.

Sieg, J. & R. N. Winn. 1981. The Tanaidae (Crustacea: Tanaidacea) of California, with a key to the world genera. Proc. Biol. Soc. Washington 94:315–343.

Crustacea: Cumacea

Calman, W. T. 1912. The Crustacea of the order Cumacea in the collections of the United States National Museum. Proc. U. S. Nat. Mus. 41:603–676.

Watling, L. 1979. Marine flora and fauna of the northeastern United States. Cumacea. NOAA Tech Rept. NMFS Circ. 423:1–23.

Zimmer, C. 1980. Cumaceans of the American Atlantic boreal coast region (Crustacea: Peracarida). Smithson. Contr. Zool. 302:1–29.

Crustacea: Isopoda

Markham, J. C. 1985. A review of the bopyrid isopods infesting caridean shrimps in the northwestern Atlantic Ocean, with special reference to those collected during the Hourglass Cruises in the Gulf of Mexico. Mem. Hourglass Cruises 7:1–156.

Menzies, R. J. & D. Frankenberg. 1966. Handbook on the common marine isopod Crustacea of Georgia. Univ. Georgia Press, Athens. 93 p.

Menzies, R. J. & P. W. Glynn. 1968. The common marine isopod crustaceans of Puerto Rico. Stud. Fauna Curacao Carib. Is. 27:1–133.

Menzies, R. J. & W. L. Kruczynski. 1983. Isopod Crustacea. Mem. Hourglass Cruises 6:1–126.

Selected References

Richardson, H. 1905. A monograph of the isopods of North America. Bull. U. S. Nat. Mus. 54:1–727.

Schultz, G. A. 1969. How to know the marine isopod crustaceans. Brown, Dubuque. 359 p.

Crustacea: Amphipoda

Bousfield, E. L. 1973. Shallow-water gammaridean Amphipoda of New England. Cornell Univ. Press, Ithaca. 312 p.

Fox, R. S. & K. H. Bynum. 1975. The amphipod crustaceans of North Carolina estuarine waters. Chesapeake Sci. 16:223–237.

McCain, J. C. 1968. The Caprellidae of the western north Atlantic. Bull. U. S. Nat. Mus. 278:1–147.

Insecta

Borror, D. J., D. M. Delong, & C. A. Triplehorn. 1981. An introduction to the study of insects. Saunders, Philadelphia. 827 p.

ANIMAL CLASSIFICATION

The modern biological classification of organisms reflects current understanding of the evolutionary relationships between species. The system is organized around seven basic categories, *viz.,* kingdom, phylum, class, order, family, genus, and species. The kingdom is the most inclusive and least restrictive category in that it contains a large number of organisms that may have relatively little in common. On the other hand, the species is the most restrictive and least inclusive category. Membership in a species is restricted to a single kind of organism whose members are capable of interbreeding with each other. The degree of relationship between any two organisms is indicated by their relative positions in the classification. For example, organisms assigned to the same species, *e.g.,* all housecats, are very closely related and share a recent common ancestor. At the other extreme, organisms that have nothing in common save membership in the same kingdom, as for example lions and jellyfishes, may be only distantly related and share a remote common ancestor but are more closely related than organisms in different kingdoms, such as lions and dandelions.

Field guides and species lists are, by convention, arranged in phylogenetic order, with more primitive groups toward the front and more advanced groups near the end. In this guide the phyla are arranged in a phylogenetic order that reflects the evolutionary relationships of the invertebrates as perceived by the authors. The evolution of the invertebrate phyla is currently an area of intense study and controversy and other zoologists may see things differently and will order the phyla differently. The organization within each phylum is also phylogenetic but is adapted from the scheme in *Synopsis and Classification of Living Organisms* (Parker, 1982). Within each family, the genera and species are arranged in alphabetical, rather than phylogenetic, order.

The classification below includes all Carolinian species that are figured or discussed in the guide, but is not an exhaustive list of Carolinian species. An asterisk (*) is used to indicate species that are mentioned in the text but are not illustrated. Species without an asterisk are illustrated. Species and higher taxa that have not been reported from the Carolinian Province are not included in the list even though they may be discussed in the text. Those desiring a more complete list should refer to Zingmark (1978) and Fox and Ruppert (1985) for a list of all species known from shallow waters in South Carolina. At present there is no published list of all southeastern species.

The name following the scientific name is that of the author who first described and named the species. The date of the description of each animal species is indicated also. If the author's name is in parentheses it means that the generic name has been changed since the orginal description. In some cases in which scientific names have been changed recently, the former name is indicated in parentheses following the author's name.

**SUPERKINGDOM
EUKARYOTAE**
Kingdom Plantae
Subkingdom Thallobionta
 Division
 CHROMOPHYCOTA
  Class Dinophyceae
  Subclass Dinophycidea
   Order Gymnodiniales
    Family Gymnodiniaceae
     Amphidinium chattoni
     (Hovasse, 1922)
     *Symbiodinium
     microadriaticum*
     (Freudenthal, 1962)
  Class Phaeophyceae
   Order Fucales
    Family Sargassaceae
     Sargassum fluitans Borg.
     Sargassum natans Meyen
Subkingdom Embryobionta
 Division
 MAGNOLIOPHYTA
  Class Magnoliopsida
  (=Dicotyledoneae)
  Subclass Caryophyllidae
   Order Caryophyllales
    Family Chenopodiaceae
     Salicornia virginica
     Linné
   Order Plumbaginales
    Family Plumbaginaceae
     Limonium carolinianum
     (Walter)
  Class Liliopsida
  (=Monocotyledoneae)
  Subclass Alismatidae
   Order Hydrocharitales
    Family Hydrocharitaceae

     Thalassia testudinum
     Koenig & Sims
   Order Najadales
    Family Ruppiaceae
     Ruppia maritima Linné
    Family Zosteraceae
     Zostera marina Linné
    Family Cymodoceaceae
     Halodule wrightii
     Ascherson
     Syringodium filiforme
     Kutzing
  Subclass Commelinidae
   Order Juncales
    Family Juncaceae
     Juncus roemerianus
     Scheele
   Order Cyperales
    Family Poaceae
     Spartina alterniflora
     Loisel
Kingdom Animalia
Subkingdom Parazoa
 Phylum PORIFERA
  Class Demospongiae
  Subclass Tetractinomorpha
   Order Spirophorida
    Family Tetillidae
     Craniella laminaris
     (George & Wilson, 1919)
   Order Hadromerida
    Family Clionidae
     Cliona celata Grant, 1826
   Order Axinellida
    Family Euryponidae
     Cyamon vickersi
     (Bowerbank, 1893)
  Subclass Ceractinomorpha
   Order Dendroceratida

Family Halisarcidae
Halisarca purpura Little,
1963
Family Aplysillidae
Aplysilla longispina
(George & Wilson, 1919)
Order Haplosclerida
Family Haliclonidae
Adocia tubifera (George &
Wilson, 1919)
Haliclona loosanoffi
Hartman, 1958
Haliclona permollis
(Bowerbank, 1866)
Order Petrosiida
Family Petrosiidae
Xestospongia
halichondrioides (Wilson,
1902)
Order Poecilosclerida
Family Amphilectidae
Tenaciella obliqua
(George & Wilson, 1919)
Family Mycalidae
Mycale americana van
Soest, 1984
Family Tedaniidae
Lissodendoryx isodictyalis
(Carter, 1882)
Family Clathriidae
Microciona prolifera (Ellis
& Solander, 1786)
Order Halichondrida
Family Halichondridae
Halichondria bowerbanki
Burton, 1830
Family Hymeniacidonidae
Hymeniacidon heliophila
(Parker, 1910)
Class Calcarea
Subclass Calcinia
Order Clathrinida
Family Clathrinidae

Clathrina coriacea
(Montagu, 1818)
Order Leucettida
Family Leucettidae
Leucetta imberbis
(Duchassaing &
Michelotti, 1864)
Subclass Calcaronia
Order Sycettida
Family Sycettidae
Scypha barbadensis
(Schuffner, 1877)
Subkingdom Eumetazoa
Phylum CNIDARIA
Class Scyphozoa
Order Semaeostomeae
Family Cyaneidae
Cyanea capillata (Linné,
1758)
Family Pelagiidae
Chrysaora quinquecirrha
(Desor, 1848)
Pelagia noctiluca
(Forskal, 1775)
Family Ulmariidae
Aurelia aurita (Linné,
1758)
Order Rhizostomeae
Family Rhizostomatidae
Rhopilema verrilli
(Fewkes, 1887)
Family Stomolophidae
Stomolophus meleagris L.
Agassiz, 1862
Class Cubozoa
Order Cubomedusae
Family Carybdeidae
Tamoya haplonema
Müller, 1859
Family Chirodropidae
Chiropsalmus
quadrumanus (Müller,
1859)

Class Hydrozoa
 Order Hydroida
 Suborder Anthomedusae
 (=Gymnoblastea, Athecata)
  Family Bougainvilliidae
   Bougainvillia rugosa
   Clarke, 1882
  Family Clavidae
   Turritopsis nutricula
   (McCrady, 1856)
  Family Eudendriidae
   Eudendrium carneum
   Clarke, 1882
   Eudendrium ramosum
   Linné, 1758)
   Eudendrium tenellum
   Allman, 1887
  Family Halocordylidae
   Halocordyle disticha
   (Goldfuss, 1820)
   (=*Pennaria tiarella*)
  Family Hydractiniidae
   Hydractinia echinata
   Fleming, 1828
   Stylactis hooperi
   Sigerfoos, 1899
  Family Tubulariidae
   Ectopleura dumortieri
   (van Beneden, 1844)
   Tubularia crocea (L.
   Agassiz, 1862)
  Family Porpitidae
   Porpita porpita Linné,
   1758
  Family Velellidae
   Velella velella (Linné,
   1758)
 Suborder Leptomedusae
 (=Calyptoblastea, Thecata)
  Family Campanulariidae
   Obelia bidentata Clarke,
   1875

   Obelia dichotoma (Linné,
   1758)
   Obelia geniculata (Linné,
   1758)
  Family Lovenellidae
   Lovenella gracilis Clarke,
   1882
  Family Plumulariidae
   Plumularia floridana
   Nutting, 1900
  Family Sertulariidae
   Sertularia marginata
   (Kirchenpauer, 1864)
 Order Siphonophora
 Suborder Cystonectae
  Family Physaliidae
   Physalia physalis (Linné,
   1759)
Class Anthozoa
Subclass Alcyonaria
 Order Gorgonacea
 Suborder Holaxonia
  Family Gorgoniidae
   Leptogorgia setacea
   (Pallas, 1766)
   Leptogorgia virgulata
   (Lamarck, 1815)
 Order Pennatulacea
 Suborder Sessileflorae
  Family Renillidae
   Renilla reniformis (Pallas,
   1766)
Subclass Zoantharia
 Order Actiniaria
  Family Actiniidae
   Actinia bermudensis
   (McMurrich, 1889)
   Anemonia sargassensis
   Hargitt, 1908
   Anthopleura carneola
   (Verrill, 1907)
   Bunodosoma cavernata
   (Bosc, 1802)

Family Actinoscyphiidae
Paranthus rapiformis
(LeSueur, 1817)
Family Aiptasiidae
*Aiptasiogeton
eruptaurantia* (Field,
1949)
Aiptasia pallida (Verrill,
1864)
Family Diadumenidae
Diadumene leucolena
(Verrill, 1866)
Family Edwardsiidae
Edwardsia elegans Verrill,
1869
*Nematostella vectensis
Stephenson, 1935
Family Haliplanellidae
Haliplanella luciae
(Verrill, 1898)
Family Haloclavidae
Haloclava producta
(Stimpson, 1856)
Family Hormathiidae
Calliactis tricolor
(LeSueur, 1817)
Order Scleractinia
Suborder Faviina
Family Oculinidae
Oculina arbuscula Verrill,
1864
Family Rhizangiidae
Astrangia danae L.
Agassiz, 1847
Suborder Fungiina
Family Siderastreidae
*Siderastrea radians
(Pallas, 1766)
Order Zoanthinaria
Family Epizoanthidae
*Epizoanthus paguriphilus
Verrill, 1882
Subclass Ceriantipatharia

Order Ceriantharia
Family Cerianthidae
*Ceriantheopsis
americanus* (Verrill, 1874)
Phylum CTENOPHORA
Order Lobata
Family Bolinopsidae
*Bolinopsis vitrea (L.
Agassiz, 1860)
*Mnemiopsis gardeni L.
Agassiz, 1860
*Mnemiopsis leidyi A.
Agassiz, 1865
Mnemiopsis mccradyi
Mayer, 1900
Order Beroida
Family Beroidae
*Beroe ovata Chamisso &
Eysenhardt, 1821
Phylum CHAETOGNATHA
Class Sagittoidea
Order Aphragmophora
Suborder Ctenodontina
Family Sagittidae
*Sagitta tenuis Conant,
1896
Phylum HEMICHORDATA
Class Enteropneusta
Family Harrimaniidae
Saccoglossus kowalevskii
(A. Agassiz, 1873)
Family Spengelidae
Schizocardium brasiliense
Spengel, 1893
Family Ptychoderidae
Balanoglossus aurantiacus
A. Agassiz, 1873
*Balanoglossus gigas
Müller, 1893
Ptychodera jamaicensis
Willey, 1899
Phylum CHORDATA

Subphylum Tunicata
(=Urochordata)
Class Ascidiacea
Order Aplousobranchia
Family Polyclinidae
Aplidium constellatum
(Verrill, 1871)
(=*Amaroucium*)
*Aplidium exile (van
Name, 1902)
(=*Amaroucium*)
*Aplidium stellatum
(Verrill, 1871)
(=*Amaroucium*)
Family Didemnidae
Didemnum duplicatum F.
Monniot, 1983
*Didemnum
psammathodes* Sluiter,
1895
Diplosoma listerianum
(Milne-Edwards, 1841)
Family Polycitoridae
Clavelina oblonga
Herdman, 1880
*Clavelina picta (Verrill,
1900)
Distaplia bermudensis
van Name, 1902
Eudistoma carolinense
van Name, 1902
Eudistoma hepaticum
(van Name, 1921)
Order Phlebobranchia
Family Perophoridae
Ecteinascidia turbinata
Herdman, 1880
*Perophora formosana
Oka, 1983 (=*P.
bermudensis*)
Perophora viridis Verrill,
1871
Family Ascidiidae

Ascidia interrupta Heller,
1878
Order Stolidobranchia
Family Styelidae
Botryllus planus (van
Name, 1902)
*Polyandrocarpa
zorritensis* (van Name,
1931)
*Styela partita (Stimpson,
1852)
Styela plicata (LeSueur,
1823)
Symplegma rubra C.
Monniot, 1972
*Symplegma viride
Herdman, 1866
Family Molgulidae
Molgula manhattensis
(DeKay, 1843)
*Molgula occidentalis
Traustedt, 1883
Subphylum Cephalochordata
Family Branchiostomidae
Branchiostoma caribaeum
Sundevall, 1853
Subphylum Vertebrata
Class Osteichthyes
Subclass Actinopterygii
Order Clupeiformes
Suborder Clupeoidei
Family Clupeidae
*Brevoortia tyrannus
(Latrobe, 1802)
Order Perciformes
Suborder Stromateoidei
Family Stromateidae
*Nomeus gronovii
(Gmelin, 1789)
*Peprilus alepidotus
(Linné, 1766)
*Poronotus burti (Fowler,
1944) (=*Peprilus burti*)

Animal Classification

Phylum ECHINODERMATA
Subphylum Asterozoa
Class Stelleroidea
Subclass Asteroidea
 Order Platyasterida
 Family Luidiidae
 Luidia clathrata (Say, 1825)
 Order Paxillosida
 Family Astropectenidae
 Astropecten articulatus (Say, 1825)
 Order Forcipulata
 Family Asteriidae
 Asterias forbesi (Desor, 1848)
Subclass Ophiuroidea
 Order Ophiurida
 Suborder Chilophiurina
 Family Ophiodermatidae
 Ophioderma brevispinum (Say, 1825)
 Suborder Gnathophiurina
 Family Ophiactidae
 Ophiactis rubropoda Singletary, 1974
 Family Amphiuridae
 Amphioplus abditus (Verrill, 1871)
 Axiognathus squamatus (delle Chiaje, 1829) (=*Amphipholis squamata*)
 Hemipholis elongata (Say, 1825)
 Microphiopholis atra (Stimpson, 1852) (=*Micropholis, Amphipholis*)
 Microphiopholis gracillima (Stimpson, 1852) (=*Micropholis, Amphipholis*)

Ophiophragmus filograneus (Lyman, 1875)
 Ophiophragmus wurdemani (Lyman, 1860)
 Ophiophragmus septus (Lutken, 1859)
 Family Ophiothricidae
 Ophiothrix angulata (Say, 1825)
Subphylum Echinozoa
Class Echinoidea
Subclass Perischoechinoidea
 Order Cidaroida
 Family Cidaridae
 Eucidaris tribuloides (Lamarck, 1816)
Subclass Euechinoidea
 Superorder Echinacea
 Order Arbacioida
 Family Arbaciidae
 Arbacia punctulata (Lamarck, 1816)
 Order Temnopleuroida
 Family Toxopneustidae
 Lytechinus variegatus (Leske, 1778)
 Superorder Gnathostomata
 Order Clypeasteroida
 Suborder Scutellina
 Family Mellitidae
 Mellita quinquiesperforata (Leske, 1778)
 Superorder Atelostomata
 Order Spatangoida
 Suborder Amphisternata
 Family Schizasteridae
 Moira atropos (Lamarck, 1816)
Class Holothuroidea
Subclass Dendrochirotacea
 Order Dendrochirotida
 Family Sclerodactylidae

Sclerodactyla briareus
(LeSueur, 1824)
Family Cucumariidae
Thyonella gemmata
(Pourtales, 1851)
Subclass Apodacea
Order Apodida
Family Synaptidae
*Epitomapta roseola
(Verrill, 1874)
(=*Leptosynapta roseola*)
Leptosynapta tenuis
(Ayres, 1851)
Phylum PHORONIDA
Phoronis architecta
Andrews, 1890
*Phoronis australis
Haswell, 1883
*Phoronis muelleri Selys-
Longschamps, 1903
*Phoronis ovalis Wright,
1856
*Phoronis psammophila
Cori, 1889
*Phoronopsis harmeri
Pixell, 1912
Phylum BRACHIOPODA
Class Inarticulata
Order Lingulida
Superfamily Lingulacea
Family Lingulidae
Glottidia pyramidata
(Stimpson, 1860)
Phylum BRYOZOA
(=ECTOPROCTA)
Class Gymnolaemata
Order Ctenostomata
Suborder Carnosa
Superfamily
Alcyonidioidea
Family Alcyonidiidae
Alcyonidium hauffi
Marcus, 1939

*Alcyonidium
mammillatum Alder,
1857
*Alcyonidium polyoum
(Hassall, 1841)
Superfamily
Paludicelloidea
Family Nolellidae
Anguinella palmata van
Beneden, 1845
Suborder Stolonifera
Superfamily
Vesicularioidea
Family Vesiculariidae
*Amathia convoluta
Lamouroux, 1816
Amathia distans Busk,
1866
*Amathia vidovici Heller,
1867
Zoobotryon verticillatum
(delle Chiaje, 1828)
Order Cheilostomata
Suborder Anasca
Family Membraniporidae
*Conopeum seurati
(Canu, 1908)
*Membranipora
arborescens (Canu &
Bassler, 1928)
Membranipora tenuis
Desor, 1848
*Membranipora
tuberculata (Bosc, 1802)
Family Thalamoporellidae
Thalamoporella floridana
Osburn, 1940
Family Bugulidae
*Bugula fulva Ryland,
1960
Bugula neritina (Linné,
1758)

Bugula stolonifera
Ryland, 1960
Suborder Ascophora
Family Smittinidae
Parasmittina nitida
Maturo & Schopf, 1968
Family Schizoporellidae
Schizoporella unicornis
(Johnston, 1847)
Phylum KAMPTOZOA
(=ENTOPROCTA)
Family Loxosomatidae
Loxosoma spathula
Nielsen, 1966
Loxosomella bilocata
Nielson, 1966
Loxosomella cricketae
Nielsen, 1966
Loxosomella minuta
(Oxburn, 1912)
Loxosomella tethyae
(Salensky, 1877)
Loxosomella worki
Nielson, 1966
Family Pedicellinidae
Pedicellina cernua
(Pallas, 1771)
Family Barentsiidae
Barentsia laxa
Kirkpatrick, 1890
Phylum SIPUNCULA
Family Golfingiidae
Phascolion strombus
(Montague, 1804)
Themiste alutacea
(Grube, 1859)
(=*Dendrostoma*
alutaceum)
Family Sipunculidae
Sipunculus nudus Linné,
1766
Phylum NEMATODA
(=NEMATA)

Class Adenophorea
Subclass Chromadoria
Order Monhysterida
Suborder Monhysterina
Superfamily
Monhysteroidea
Family Monhysteridae
Theristus
polychaetophilus Hopper,
1966
Superfamily
Siphonolaimoidea
Family Siphonolaimidae
Astomonema jenneri Ott,
Rieger, Rieger, &
Enderes, 1982
Class Secernentea
Subclass Rhabditia
Order Rhabditida
Suborder Rhabditina
Superfamily Rhabditoidea
Family Rhabditidae
Rhabditis marina
Bastian, 1865
Phylum ROTIFERA
Class Bdelloidea
Order Bdelloida
Family Philodinidae
Zelinkiella synaptae
Zelinka, 1888)
Phylum MOLLUSCA
Class Polyplacophora
Subclass Neoloricata
Order Ischnochitonida
Family Ischnochitonidae
Ischnochiton striolatus
(Gray, 1828)
Family Chaetopleuridae
Chaetopleura apiculata
(Say, 1830)
Class Gastropoda
Subclass Prosobranchia
Order Archaeogastropoda

Superfamily Fissurellacea
Family Fissurellidae
Diodora cayenensis
(Lamarck, 1822)
Superfamily Trochacea
Family Trochidae
Calliostoma euglyptum
A. Adams, 1854
Calliostoma pulchrum
(C. B. Adams, 1850)
Family Turbinidae
Astraea phoebia Roding,
1798
Turbo castanea Gmelin,
1791
Superfamily Neritacea
Family Neritidae
Neritina reclivata (Say,
1822) (=*Neritina usnea*)
Order Mesogastropoda
Superfamily Littorinacea
Family Littorinidae
Littorina irrorata (Say,
1822)
Littorina saxatilis (Olivi,
1792)
Littorina ziczac (Gmelin,
1791)
Superfamily Rissoacea
Family Hydrobiidae
Family Assimineidae
Assiminea succinea
(Pfeiffer, 1840)
Family Caecidae
Caecum carolinianum
Dall, 1892
Caecum cycloferum
Folin, 1867
Caecum floridanum
Stimpson, 1851
Caecum pulchellum
Stimpson, 1851
Family Vitrinellidae

Cyclostremiscus
pentagonus (Gabb, 1873)
Family Tornidae
Cochliolepis parasitica
Stimpson, 1858
Superfamily Cerithiacea
Family Cerithiidae
Cerithium atratum (Born,
1778) (=*Cerithium*
floridanum)
Litiopa melanostoma
Rang, 1829
Family Diastomatidae
Bittium varium (Pfeiffer,
1840) (=*Diastoma*
varium)
Family Potamididae
Cerithidea scalariformis
(Say, 1825)
Family Cerithiopsidae
Cerithiopsis emersoni
(C. B. Adams, 1838)
Cerithiopsis greeni (C. B.
Adams, 1839)
Seila adamsi (Lea, 1845)
Family Siliquariidae
Siliquaria squamata
Blainville, 1827
Family Turritellidae
Turritella exoleta (Linné,
1758)
Vermicularia knorrii
(Deshayes, 1843)
Superfamily
Heterogastropoda
Family Pyramidellidae
Boonea impressa (Say,
1822) (=*Odostomia*
impressa)
Boonea seminuda (C. B.
Adams, 1839)
(=*Odostomia seminuda*)
Superfamily Epitoniacea

Family Epitoniidae
Epitonium angulatum
(Say, 1830)
Epitonium humphreysi
(Kiener, 1838)
Epitonium krebsii
(Morch, 1874)
Epitonium multistriatum
(Say, 1826)
Epitonium rupicola
(Kurtz, 1860)
Family Janthinidae
Janthina globosa
Swainson, 1822
Janthina janthina (Linné,
1758)
Janthina pallida
(Thompson, 1840)
Superfamily Calyptraeacea
Family Calyptraeidae
Crepidula aculeata
(Gmelin, 1791)
Crepidula convexa Say,
1822
Crepidula fornicata
(Linné, 1758)
Crepidula plana Say, 1822
(=*Crepidula unguiformis*)
Superfamily Cypraeacea
Family Cypraeidae
*Cypraea spurca
acicularis* Gmelin, 1791
Family Ovulidae
Cymbula acicularis
(Lamarck, 1810)
(=*Simnia acicularis*)
Cyphoma gibbosum
(Linné, 1758)
Simnialena uniplicata
(Sowerby, 1848)
(=*Simnia, Neosimnia*)
Family Eratoidae
(=Triviidae)

Erato maugeriae Gray,
1832
Trivia candidula
Gaskoin, 1835
Superfamily Naticacea
Family Naticidae
Polinices duplicatus (Say,
1822)
Sinum perspectivum (Say,
1831)
Sinum maculatum Say,
1831)
Superfamily Tonnacea
Family Cassidae
Cassis madagascariensis
Lamarck, 1822
Cassis tuberosa (Linné,
1758)
Phalium granulatum
(Born, 1778)
Family Cymatiidae
Cymatium pileare
(Linné, 1758)
Order Neogastropoda
Superfamily Muricacea
Family Muricidae
Eupleura caudata (Say,
1922)
*Thais haemastoma
floridana* (Conrad, 1837)
Urosalpinx cinerea (Say,
1822)
Family Buccinidae
Cantharus multangulus
(Philippi, 1848)
Pisania tincta (Conrad,
1846) (=*Cantharus
tinctus*)
Family Columbellidae
Astyris lunata (Say, 1826)
(=*Mitrella lunata*)
Astyris raveneli (Dall,
1889)

Costoanachis avara (Say, 1822) (=*Anachis avara*)
Costoanachis lafresnayi (Fischer & Bernardi, 1856) (=*Anachis translirata*)
*Parvanachis obesa (C. B. Adams, 1845)
Family Nassariidae
Ilyanassa obsoleta (Say, 1822) (=*Nassarius obsoletus*)
*Nassarius albus Say, 1826
Nassarius trivittatus (Say, 1822)
Nassarius vibex (Say, 1822)
Family Melongenidae
Busycon canaliculatum (Linné, 1758)
Busycon carica (Gmelin, 1791)
*Busycon contrarium (Conrad, 1840)
*Busycon spiratum (Say, 1822)
Melongena corona (Gmelin, 1791)
Family Fasciolariidae
Fasciolaria hunteria Perry, 1811
Fasciolaria tulipa (Linné, 1758)
Pleuroploca gigantea (Kiener, 1840)
Family Olividae
Oliva sayana Ravenel, 1834
*Olivella floralia (Duclos, 1853)
Olivella mutica (Say, 1822)

*Olivella nivea (Gmelin, 1971)
Family Marginellidae
*Granulina ovuliformis (Orbigny, 1841)
*Hyalina avena (Kiener, 1834) (=*Volvarina avena*)
*Marginella apicina Mencke, 1828 (=*Prunum apicinum*)
*Marginella aureocincta (Stearns, 1872) (=*Dentimargo aureocincta*)
Marginella roscida Redfield, 1860 (=*Prunum roscidum*)
Superfamily Cancellariacea
Family Cancellariidae
*Cancellaria reticulata (Linné, 1758)
Superfamily Conacea
Family Conidae
Conus delessertii Recluz, 1843 (=*Conus sozoni*)
Family Terebridae
*Terebra concava Say, 1827
Terebra dislocata (Say, 1822)
Subclass Pulmonata
Order Archaeopulmonata
Superfamily Melampidacea
Family Melampidae
Detracia floridana (Pfeiffer, 1856)
Melampus bidentatus Say, 1822
Order Basommatophora
Superfamily Siphonariacea
Family Siphonariidae
Siphonaria pectinata Linné, 1758

Animal Classification

Subclass Opisthobranchia
Order Cephalaspidea
Family Scaphandridae
Acteocina canaliculata
(Say, 1822)
Family Bullidae
*Bulla striata Bruguiere,
1792
Family Atyidae
Haminoea solitaria (Say,
1822)
Order Sacoglossa
Family Stiligeridae
Placida dendritica (Alder
& Hancock, 1843)
(=*Hermaea dendritica*)
Family Elysiidae
*Elysia chlorotica (Gould,
1870)
Order Anaspidea
Family Aplysiidae
Aplysia brasiliana Rang,
1828 (=*Aplysia willcoxi*)
Family Notarchidae
*Bursatella leachii Rang,
1828
Order Nudibranchia
Suborder Doridoidea
Superfamily Anadoridacea
Family Corambidae
*Doridella obscura Verrill,
1870
Family Goniodorididae
*Ancula evelinae Marcus,
1961
*Okenia impexa Marcus,
1957
Okenia sapelona Marcus
& Marcus, 1967
Family Polyceratidae
Polycera chilluna Marcus,
1961

*Polycera hummi Abbott,
1952
*Polycerella emertoni
Verrill, 1881
Superfamily Eudoridacea
Family Dorididae
Doris verrucosa Linné,
1758
Family Discodorididae
*Anisodoris prea Marcus
& Marcus, 1967
Superfamily Porodoridacea
Family Dendrodorididae
Doriopsilla pharpa
Marcus, 1961
Suborder Dendronotoidea
Family Tritoniidae
*Tritonia bayeri Marcus,
1967
Tritonia wellsi Marcus,
1961
Family Scyllaeidae
Scyllaea pelagica Linné,
1758
Family Dotoidae
*Doto chica Marcus, 1960
*Miesea evelinae (Marcus,
1957)
Suborder Arminoidea
Superfamily Euarminiacea
Family Arminidae
Armina tigrina
Rafinesque, 1814
Suborder Aeolidoidea
Superfamily Acleioprocta
Family Fionidae
*Fiona pinnata
(Eschscholtz, 1831)
Superfamily Cleioprocta
Family Glaucidae
*Cratena pilata (Gould,
1870)

Dondice occidentalis
(Engel, 1925)
Glaucus atlanticus
Forster, 1777
Learchis poica Marcus &
Marcus, 1960
Family Aeolidiidae
Berghia benteva (Marcus,
1958)
Berghia coerulescens
(Laurillard, 1830)
Spurilla neapolitana
(delle Chiaje, 1823)
Class Cephalopoda
Subclass Coleoidea
Order Sepioidea
Family Spirulidae
Spirula spirula Linné,
1758
Order Teuthoidea
Suborder Myopsida
Family Loliginidae
Loligo pealeii LeSueur,
1821
Lolliguncula brevis
(Blainville, 1823)
Suborder Oegopsida
Family Ommastrephidae
Illex illecebrosus
(LeSueur, 1821)
Order Octopoda
Suborder Incirrata
Family Octopodidae
Octopus briareus
Robson, 1929
Octopus vulgaris Cuvier,
1797
Family Argonautidae
Argonauta argo Linné,
1758
Class Bivalvia
Subclass Protobranchia
Order Nuculoida

Superfamily Nuculacea
Family Nuculidae
Nucula proxima Say,
1822
Nuculana acuta (Conrad,
1831)
Order Solemyoida
Superfamily Solemyacea
Family Solemyidae
Solemya velum Say, 1822
Subclass Pteriomorphia
Superorder Isofilibranchia
Order Mytiloida
Superfamily Mytilacea
Family Mytilidae
Brachidontes exustus
Linné, 1758)
Geukensia demissa
(Dillwyn, 1817)
(=*Modiolus demissus*)
Ischadium recurvum
(Rafinesque, 1820)
Lithophaga aristata
(Dillwyn, 1817)
Lithophaga bisculcata
(Orbigny, 1842)
Modiolus americanus
(Leach, 1815)
*Modiolus modiolus
squamosus* Beauperthuy,
1967
Musculus lateralis (Say,
1822)
Mytilus edulis Linné,
1758
Superorder Prionodonta
Order Arcoida
Superfamily Arcacea
Family Arcidae
Anadara brasiliana
(Lamarck, 1819)
Anadara floridana
(Conrad, 1869)

Anadara ovalis (Bruguiere, 1789)
Anadara transversa (Say, 1822)
*Arca imbricata Bruguiere, 1789
Arca zebra (Swainson, 1833)
Family Noetiidae
Noetia ponderosa (Say, 1822)
Superorder Eupteriomorphia
Order Pterioida
Suborder Pteriina
Superfamily Pteriacea
Family Pteriidae
Pteria colymbus (Roding, 1798)
*Pinctada imbricata Roding, 1798
Suborder Pinnina
Superfamily Pinnacea
Family Pinnidae
*Atrina rigida (Lightfoot, 1786)
*Atrina seminuda (Lamarck, 1819)
Atrina serrata (Sowerby, 1825)
Order Limoida
Superfamily Limacea
Family Limidae
Lima pellucida C. B. Adams, 1846
*Lima scabra (Born, 1778)
Order Ostreoida
Suborder Ostreina
Superfamily Ostreacea
Family Ostreidae
Crassostrea virginica (Gmelin, 1791)

*Ostrea equestris Say, 1834
*Ostrea permollis Sowerby, 1841
Suborder Pectinina
Superfamily Pectinacea
Family Pectinidae
*Aequipecten muscosus (Wood, 1828)
*Argopecten gibbus (Linné, 1758)
Argopecten irradians (Lamarck, 1819)
*Chlamys sentis (Reeve, 1853)
*Lyropecten nodosus (Linné, 1758)
Family Spondylidae
*Spondylus americanus Hermann, 1781
Superfamily Anomiacea
Family Anomiidae
Anomia simplex Orbigny, 1842
*Pododesmus rudis (Broderip, 1834)
Subclass Heterodonta
Order Hippuritoida
Superfamily Chamacea
Family Chamidae
Chama congregata Conrad, 1833
*Chama macerophylla (Gmelin, 1791)
Order Veneroida
Superfamily Lucinacea
Family Lucinidae
*Anodontia alba Link, 1807
Divaricella quadrisulcata (Orbigny, 1842)
Lucina multilineata (Tuomey & Holmes, 1857)

Family Ungulinidae
(=Diplodontidae)
Diplodonta punctata (Say,
1822)
*Diplodonta semiaspera
(Philippi, 1836)
Superfamily Leptonacea
Family Leptonidae
Lepton sp.
*Lepton longipes
Stimpson, 1855
Family Lasaeidae
(Montacutidae)
Aligena elevata
(Stimpson, 1851)
Entovalva sp. A
Entovalva sp. B
*Montacuta floridana
Dall, 1899
Montacuta percompressa
Dall, 1899
*montacutid sp. A
*Mysella sp. A
Mysella sp. B
Mysella sp. C
*Mysella sp. D
Mysella cuneata (Verrill
& Bush, 1898)
Superfamily Cardiacea
Family Cardiidae
Dinocardium robustum
(Lightfoot, 1786)
*Laevicardium laevigatum
(Linné, 1758)
**Trachycardium
egmontianum*
(Shuttleworth, 1856)
**Trachycardium
muricatum* (Linné, 1758)
Superfamily Mactracea
Family Mactridae
*Anatina anatina
(Spengler, 1802)

Mactra fragilis Gmelin,
1791
Mulinia lateralis (Say,
1822)
Raeta plicatella
(Lamarck, 1818)
Rangia cuneata (Sowerby,
1831)
*Spisula raveneli (Conrad,
1831)
Spisula solidissima
(Dillwyn, 1817)
Superfamily Solenacea
Family Solenidae
Solen viridis Say, 1821
Family Cultellidae
Ensis directus Conrad,
1843
Superfamily Tellinacea
Family Tellinidae
Macoma balthica (Linné,
1758)
Macoma tenta (Say, 1834)
Tellina aequistriata Say,
1824
*Tellina agilis Stimpson,
1857
Tellina alternata Say,
1822
*Tellina iris Say, 1822
Tellina texana Dall, 1900
Tellina versicolor Dekay,
1843
Family Solecurtidae
Tagelus divisus (Spengler,
1794)
Tagelus plebeius
(Lightfoot, 1796)
Family Semelidae
Abra aequalis (Say, 1822)
Cumingia tellinoides
(Conrad, 1831)

Semele proficua
(Pulteney, 1799)
Semele purpurascens
(Gmelin, 1791)
Family Donacidae
Donax variabilis Say,
1822
Donax parvulus Philippi,
1849
Superfamily Corbiculacea
Family Corbiculidae
Polymesoda caroliniana
(Bosc, 1801)
Superfamily Veneracea
Family Veneridae
Chione cancellata (Linné,
1767)
Chione grus (Holmes,
1858)
Cyclinella tenuis (Recluz,
1852)
Dosinia discus (Reeve,
1850)
Dosinia elegans (Conrad,
1846)
Gemma gemma (Totten,
1834)
Macrocallista nimbosa
(Lightfoot, 1786)
Macrocallista maculata
(Linné, 1758)
*Mercenaria
campechiensis* (Gmelin,
1791)
Mercenaria mercenaria
(Linné, 1758)
Pitar fulminatus (Menke,
1828)
Family Petricolidae
Petricola pholadiformis
(Lamarck, 1818)
Rupellaria typica (Jonas,
1844)

Order Myoida
Superfamily Myacea
Family Myidae
Mya arenaria Linné,
1758
Paramya subovata
(Conrad, 1845)
Sphenia antillensis Dall &
Simpson, 1901
Family Corbulidae
Corbula swiftiana C. B.
Adams, 1852
Superfamily
Gastrochaenacea
Family Gastrochaenidae
Gastrochaena hians
(Gmelin, 1791)
Gastrochaena ovata
Sowerby, 1834
Superfamily Pholadacea
Family Pholadidae
Barnea truncata (Say,
1822)
Cyrtopleura costata
(Linné, 1758)
Diplothyra smithii Tryon,
1862
Martesia cuneiformis
(Say, 1822)
Martesia fragilis Verrill
& Bush, 1890
Martesia striata (Linné,
1758)
Pholas campechiensis
Gmelin, 1791
Family Teredinidae
Bankia gouldi Bartsch,
1908
Nototeredo knoxi
Bartsch, 1917
Subclass Anomalodesmata
Superfamily Pandoracea
Family Periplomatidae

Periploma margaritaceum (Lamarck, 1801) (=*Periploma inequale*)
Family Lyonsiidae
Lyonsia beana (Orbigny, 1842)
Lyonsia hyalina Conrad, 1831
Family Pandoridae
Pandora trilineata Say, 1822
Class Scaphopoda
Order Dentalida
Family Dentaliidae
Dentalium eboreum Conrad, 1846
Dentalium laqueatum Verrill, 1885
Dentalium meridionale Pilsbry & Sharp, 1897
Dentalium texasianum Philippi, 1848
Order Gadilida
Family Gadilidae
Cadulus carolinensis Bush, 1885
Cadulus quadridentatus (Dall, 1881)
Phylum NEMERTEA
Class Anopla
Order Paleonemertea
Family Carinomidae
Carinoma tremaphoros Thompson, 1900
Family Tubulanidae
Tubulanus pellucidus (Coe, 1895)
Tubulanus rhabdotus Corrêa, 1954
Order Heteronemertea
Family Lineidae

Cerebratulus lacteus (Leidy, 1851)
Evelineus tigrillus Corrêa, 1954
Lineus bicolor Verrill, 1892
Lineus socialis (Leidy, 1855)
Micrura leidyi (Verrill, 1892)
Family Valenciniidae
Zygeupolia rubens (Coe, 1895)
Class Enopla
Order Hoplonemertea
Suborder Monostilifera
Family Amphiporidae
Amphiporus cruentatus Verrill, 1879
Amphiporus ochraceus Verrill, 1873
Zygonemertes virescens (Verrill, 1879)
Family Emplectonematidae
Paranemertes biocellatus Coe, 1944
Nemertopsis bivittata (delle Chiaje, 1841)
Family Carcinonemertidae
Carcinonemertes carcinophila (Kölliker, 1845)
Family Prosorhochmidae
Prosorhochmus americanus Gibson, Moore, Ruppert, & Turbeville, 1986
Phylum PLATYHELMINTHES
Class Turbellaria
Order Catenulida
Family Retronectidae

Paracatenula urania
Sterrer & Rieger, 1974
Order Tricladida
Suborder Maricola
 Family Bdellouridae
 Bdelloura candida
 (Girard, 1850)
 Syncoelidium pellucidum
 Wheeler, 1894
Order Polycladida
Suborder Acotylea
 Family Discocelidae
 Coronadena mutabilis
 (Verrill, 1873)
 Family Stylochidae
 Stylochus ellipticus
 (Girard, 1850)
 Stylochus zebra (Verrill,
 1882)
Suborder Cotylea
 Family Pseudoceridae
 Pseudoceros crozieri
 Hyman, 1939
 Thysanozoon nigrum
 Girard, 1851
 Family Euryleptidae
 Oligoclado floridanus
 Pearse, 1938
Class Trematoda
Subclass Digenea
 Order Strigeidida
 Suborder Strigeata
 Superfamily
 Schistosomatoidea
 Family Schistosomatidae
 Austrobilharzia
 variglandis Miller &
 Northup, 1926
Class Cestoda
Subclass Eucestoda
 Order Trypanorhyncha
 Suborder Cystidea
 Family Otobothriidae

Peocilancistrium
caryophyllum (Diesing,
1850)
Phylum ECHIURA
 Order Echiuroinea
 Family Echiuridae
 Lissomyema mellita
 (Conn, 1886)
 (= *Thalassema mellita*)
 Thalassema hartmani
 Fisher, 1947
Phylum ANNELIDA
 Class Polychaeta
 Order Phyllodocida
 Superfamily
 Phyllodocidacea
 Family Phyllodocidae
 Phyllodoce fragilis
 Webster, 1879
 Superfamily Glyceracea
 Family Glyceridae
 Glycera americana
 Leidy, 1855
 Glycera dibranchiata
 Ehlers, 1868
 Superfamily Nereididacea
 Family Pilargidae
 Ancistrosyllis
 commensalis Gardiner,
 1975
 Family Hesionidae
 Gyptis vittata Webster &
 Benedict, 1887
 Parahesione luteola
 (Webster, 1880)
 Podarke obscura Verrill,
 1873
 Podarkeopsis levifuscina
 Perkins, 1984 (= *Gyptis*
 brevipalpa in part)
 Family Syllidae
 Exogone dispar
 (Webster, 1879)

Proceraea fasciata (Bosc, 1902) (=*Autolytus ornatus*)
*Syllis spongicola Grube, 1855
Family Nereididae
*Ceratonereis irritabilis (Webster, 1879)
*Laeonereis culveri (Webster, 1880)
*Nereis falsa Quatrefages, 1865
Nereis succinea Frey & Leuckart, 1847
*Platynereis dumerilii (Audouin & Milne-Edwards, 1833)
Superfamily Nephtyidacea
Family Nephtyidae
*Aglaophamus verrilli (McIntosh, 1885)
Nephtys bucera Ehlers, 1868
*Nephtys picta Ehlers, 1868
Superfamily Aphroditacea
Family Polynoidae
Harmothoe aculeata Andrews, 1891
*Lepidametria commensalis Webster, 1879
Lepidasthenia varia Treadwell, 1917
*Lepidonotus inquilinus Treadwell, 1917
*Lepidonotus sublevis Verrill, 1873
*Malmgrenia lunulata (delle Chiaje, 1841)
Family Polyodontidae
Polyodontes lupinus (Stimpson, 1856)

Family Sigalionidae
Sthenelais boa (Johnston, 1833)
Order Amphinomida
Family Amphinomidae
Amphinome rostrata (Pallas, 1766)
*Hipponoe gaudichaudi Audouin & Milne Edwards, 1830
*Pseudeurythoe ambigua (Monro, 1933)
Order Eunicida
Superfamily Eunicacea
Family Onuphidae
*Americonuphis magna (Andrews, 1891) (=*Onuphis magna*)
Diopatra cuprea (Bosc, 1802)
Kinbergonuphis jenneri (Gardiner, 1975) (=*Onuphis jenneri*)
*Mooreonuphis nebulosa (Moore, 1911)
*Onuphis eremita Audouin & Milne-Edwards, 1833
Family Eunicidae
Eunice antennata (Savigny, 1820) (=*Eunice rubra*)
Marphysa sanguinea (Montagu, 1815)
Family Lumbrineridae
*Lumbrineris coccinea (Renier, 1804)
*Lumbrineris impatiens (Claparède, 1868)
Family Arabellidae
Arabella iricolor (Montagu, 1804)

Drilonereis magna
Webster & Benedict, 1887
*Notocirrus spiniferus
(Moore, 1906)
Family Dorvilleidae
Dorvillea sociabilis
(Webster, 1879)
*Ophryotrocha puerilis
Claparede & Mecznikow,
1869
Schistomeringos rudolphi
(delle Chiaje, 1828)
Order Orbiniida
Family Orbiniidae
*Haploscoloplos fragilis
(Verrill, 1873)
*Haploscoloplos robustus
(Verrill, 1873)
Orbinia ornata (Verrill,
1873)
*Orbinia riseri (Pettibone,
1957)
*Scoloplos rubra
(Webster, 1879)
Order Spionida
Family Spionidae
*Polydora colonia Moore,
1907
*Polydora websteri
Hartman, 1943
Scolelepis squamata
(Müller, 1806)
Order Chaetopterida
Family Chaetopteridae
Chaetopterus variopedatus
(Renier, 1804)
*Mesochaetopterus taylori
Potts, 1914
Spiochaetopterus oculatus
Webster, 1879
Order Magelonida
Family Magelonidae

Magelona phyllisae Jones,
1963
Order Cirratulida
Family Paraonidae
Aricidea fragilis Webster,
1879
Family Cirratulidae
*Cirriformia filigera (delle
Chiaje, 1828)
Cirriformia grandis
(Verrill, 1873)
*Dodecaceria concharum
Hartman, 1951
*Tharyx marioni (Saint-
Joseph, 1894)
Order Flabelligerida
Family Flabelligeridae
Piromis eruca (Claparède,
1869)
Order Opheliida
Family Opheliidae
Armandia agilis
(Andrews, 1891)
*Armandia maculata
(Webster, 1884)
Order Capitellida
Family Capitellidae
*Capitella capitata
(Fabricius, 1780)
*Heteromastus filiformis
(Claparède, 1864)
Notomastus lobatus
Hartman, 1947
Family Maldanidae
*Axiothella mucosa
(Andrews, 1891)
Clymenella torquata
(Leidy, 1855)
*Petaloproctus socialis
Andrews, 1891
Family Arenicolidae
*Arenicola brasiliensis
Nonato, 1958

Arenicola cristata
Stimpson, 1856
Order Oweniida
Family Oweniidae
Owenia fusiformis delle
Chiaje, 1844
Order Terebellida
Family Amphictenidae
Cistenides gouldii (Verrill,
1873) (=*Pectinaria
gouldii*)
Family Sabellariidae
Sabellaria floridensis
Hartman, 1944
Sabellaria vulgaris
Verrill, 1873
Family Ampharetidae
Melinna maculata
Webster, 1879
Family Terebellidae
Amphitrite ornata (Leidy,
1855)
Loimia viridis Moore,
1903
Order Sabellida
Family Sabellidae
*Demonax
microphthalmus* (Verrill,
1873) (=*Sabella
microphthalma*)
Fabricia sabella
(Ehrenberg, 1837)
Notaulax nudicollis
(Kroyer, 1856)
(=*Hypsicomus
phaeotaenia*)
Sabella melanostigma
Schmarda, 1861
Family Serpulidae
Filograna implexa
Berkeley, 1835
(=*Salmacina dysteri*)

Hydroides dianthus
(Verrill, 1873)
Order Dinophilida
Family Dinophilidae
Dinophilus jagersteni
Jones & Ferguson, 1974
Class Hirudinoidea
Subclass Hirudinea
Order Rhynchobdellae
Family Ozobranchidae
Ozobranchus branchiatus
(Menzies, 1791)
Ozobranchus margoi
(Apathy, 1890)
Family Piscicolidae
Branchellion torpedinis
Savigny, 1822
Branchellion ravenelii
(Girard, 1850)
Calliobdella vivida
(Verrill, 1872)
Myzobdella lugubris
Leidy, 1851
Stibarobdella macrothela
(Schmarda, 1861)
Class Oligochaeta
Order Haplotaxida
Suborder Tubificina
Superfamily Tubificoidea
Family Tubificidae
Olavius tenuissimus
(Erséus, 1979)
Phylum ARTHROPODA
Subphylum Chelicerata
Class Merostomata
Order Xiphosura
Suborder Xiphosurida
Family Limulidae
Limulus polyphemus
(Linné, 1758)
Class Pycnogonida
Family Callipallenidae

Callipallene brevirostrum
(Johnston, 1837)
Family Phoxichilidiidae
Anoplodactylus lentus
Wilson, 1878
Family Ammothoeidae
Achelia sawayai Marcus,
1940
Family Tanystylidae
Tanystylum orbiculare
Wilson, 1878
Family Pycnogonidae
Pycnogonum cessaci
Bouvier, 1911
Subphylum Crustacea
Class Copepoda
Order Calanoida
Suborder Heterarthrandria
Family Pontellidae
Anomalocera ornata
Sutcliff, 1949
Order Cyclopoida
Family Clausidiidae
Clausidium caudatum
(Say, 1818)
Hemicyclops adhaerens
(Williams, 1907)
Order Notodelphyoida
Family Botryllophilidae
Botryllophilus brevipes
Sars, 1921
Order Caligoida
Family Lernaeidae
Lernaeenicus radiatus
(LeSueur, 1824)
Class Cirripedia
Order Acrothoracica
Suborder Pygophora
Family Lithoglyptidae
Kochlorine floridana
Wells & Tomlinson, 1966
Order Thoracica
Suborder Lepadomorpha

Family Lepadidae
Lepas anatifera Linné,
1758
Lepas pectinata Spengler,
1793
Family Poecilasmatidae
Octolasmis hoeki
(Stebbing, 1895)
Octolasmis muelleri
(Coker, 1902)
Suborder Balanomorpha
Superfamily
Chthamaloidea
Family Chthamalidae
Chthamalus fragilis
Darwin, 1854
Chthamalus stellatus
(Poli, 1791)
Superfamily Coronuloidea
Family Coronulidae
Chelonibia caretta
(Spengler, 1790)
Chelonibia patula
(Ranzani, 1818)
Chelonibia testudinaria
(Linné, 1758)
Family Tetraclitidae
Tetraclita stalactifera
(Lamarck, 1818)
Superfamily Balanoidea
Family Archaeobalanidae
Conopea galeata (Linné,
1771) (=*Balanus
galeatus*)
Family Balanidae
Balanus amphitrite
Darwin, 1854
Balanus eburneus Gould,
1841
Balanus improvisus
Darwin, 1854
Balanus subalbidus
Henry, 1973

Balanus trigonus
Darwin, 1854
Balanus venustus
Darwin, 1854
Megabalanus antillensis
(Pilsbry, 1916)
Order Rhizocephala
Suborder Kentrogonida
Family Sacculinidae
Loxothylacus panopaei
(Gissler, 1884)
Loxothylacus texanus
Boschma, 1933
Class Malacostraca
Superorder Hoplocarida
Order Stomatopoda
Suborder Unipeltata
Superfamily
Lysiosquilloidea
Family Coronididae
Coronis excavatrix
Brooks, 1886
(= *Lysiosquilla*
excavatrix)
Superfamily Squilloidea
Family Squillidae
Chloridopsis dubia (H.
Milne-Edwards, 1837)
Squilla empusa Say, 1818
Squilla neglecta Gibbes,
1850
Superorder Peracarida
Order Tanaidacea
Suborder Dikonophora
Family Paratanaidae
Hargeria rapax (Harger,
1879)
Order Isopoda
Suborder Flabellifera
Family Limnoriidae
Limnoria lignorum
(Rathke, 1799)

Limnoria tripunctata
Menzies, 1951
Family Sphaeromatidae
Ancinus depressus (Say,
1818)
Cassidinidea ovalis (Say,
1818)
Exosphaeroma diminuta
Menzies & Frankenberg,
1966
Paracerceis caudata (Say,
1818)
Sphaeroma quadridentata
Say, 1818
Sphaeroma destructor
Richardson, 1897
Sphaeroma walkeri
Stebbing, 1905
Family Cymothoidae
Aegathoa oculata (Say,
1818)
Lironeca ovalis (Say,
1818)
Olencira praegustator
(Latrobe, 1802)
Suborder Oniscoidea
Family Ligiidae
Ligia exotica Roux, 1828)
Suborder Valvifera
Family Idoteidae
Chiridotea caeca (Say,
1818)
Cleantis planicauda
Benedict, 1899
Edotea triloba (Say,
1818)
Erichsonella attenuata
(Harger, 1873)
Erichsonella filiformis
(Say, 1818)
Idotea baltica (Pallas,
1772)
Suborder Anthuridea

Family Anthuridae
Apanthura magnifica
Menzies & Frankenberg,
1966
Cyathura burbancki
Frankenberg, 1965
Cyathura polita
(Stimpson, 1855)
Suborder Epicaridea
Family Bopyridae
Aporobopyrus curtatus
(Richardson, 1904)
Asymmetrione desultor
Markham, 1975
Hemiarthrus synalphei
(Pearse, 1950)
Leidya bimini Pearse,
1951
Leidya distorta (Leidy,
1855)
Probopyria alphei
(Richardson, 1900)
Probopyrus pandalicola
(Packard, 1879)
*Pseudasymmetrione
markhami* Adkison &
Heard, 1978
Pseudione upogebiae
(Hay, 1917)
*Schizobopyrina
urocaridis* (Richardson,
1904)
Synsynella deformans
Hay, 1917
Family Entoniscidae
Cancrion carolinus
Pearse & Walker, 1939
Paguritherium alatum
Reinhard, 1945
Order Amphipoda
Suborder Gammaridea
Superfamily Gammaroidea
Family Gammaridae

Gammarus palustris
Bousfield, 1969
Superfamily
Pontoporeioidea
Family Haustoriidae
Haustorius canadensis
Bousfield, 1962
Superfamily Leucothoidea
Family Leucothoidae
Leucothoe spinicarpa
(Abildgaard, 1789)
Family Colomastigidae
*Colomastix
halichondriae* Bousfield,
1973
Superfamily Talitroidea
Family Talitridae
Orchestia grillus Bosc,
1802
Talitroides alluaudi
(Chevreux, 1901)
Talitroides topitotum
(Burt, 1934)
Talorchestia longicornis
(Say, 1818)
*Talorchestia
megalophthalma* (Bate,
1862)
*Uhlorchestia
spartinophila* Bousfield &
Heard, 1986
Uhlorchestia uhleri
(Shoemaker, 1930)
Superfamily
Liljeborgioidea
Family Liljeborgiidae
Listriella clymenellae
Mills, 1962
Superfamily Ampeliscoidea
Family Ampeliscidae
Ampelisca verrilli Mills,
1967
Superfamily Melitoidea

Family Melitidae
Dulichiella appendiculata
(Say, 1818) (=*Melita*
appendiculata)
Suborder Hyperiidea
Infraorder Physocephalata
Superfamily Phronimoidea
Family Hyperiidae
*Hyperia galba (Montagu,
1813)
Suborder Caprellidea
Family Caprellidae
*Caprella equilibra Say,
1818
Caprella penantis Leach,
1814
*Paracaprella tenuis
Mayer, 1903
Superorder Eucarida
Order Decapoda
Suborder Dendrobranchiata
Superfamily Penaeoidea
Family Penaeidae
*Penaeus aztecus Ives,
1891
Penaeus duorarum
Burkenroad, 1939
*Penaeus setiferus (Linné,
1767)
*Trachypenaeus
constrictus (Stimpson,
1871)
Family Sicyoniidae
Sicyonia brevirostris
Stimpson, 1871
Suborder Pleocyemata
Infraorder Caridea
Superfamily
Palaemonoidea
Family Palaemonidae
*Leander tenuicornis (Say,
1818)

*Neopontonides
beaufortensis (Borradaile,
1920)
*Palaemonetes pugio
Holthuis, 1949
Palaemonetes vulgaris
Say, 1818
Periclimenes
longicaudatus (Stimpson,
1860)
Pontonia domestica
Gibbes, 1850
Superfamily Alpheoidea
Family Alpheidae
Alpheus heterochaelis Say,
1818
*Alpheus normanni
Kingsley, 1878
*Leptalpheus forceps
Williams, 1965
*Synalpheus fritzmuelleri
Coutiere, 1909
*Synalpheus longicarpus
(Herrick, 1892)
Family Hippolytidae
*Hippolyte pleuracanthus
Stimpson, 1871
*Hippolyte zostericola
(Smith, 1873)
*Latreutes fucorum
(Fabricius, 1798)
*Latreutes parvulus
(Stimpson, 1866)
Lysmata wurdemanni
(Gibbes, 1850)
Tozeuma carolinense
Kingsley, 1878
*Tozeuma serratum A.
Milne Edwards, 1881
Family Ogyrididae
*Ogyrides alphaerostris
(Kingsley, 1880)

Ogyrides hayi Williams,
1981
Superfamily Crangonoidea
Family Crangonidae
Crangon septemspinosa
Say, 1818
Infraorder Astacidea
Superfamily Nephropoidea
Family Nephropidae
Homarus americanus H.
Milne-Edwards, 1837
Superfamily
Thalassinoidea
Family Callianassidae
Callianassa atlantica
Rathbun, 1926
Callianassa biformis
Biffar, 1971
Callianassa major Say,
1818
Family Upogebiidae
Upogebia affinis (Say,
1818)
Infraorder Palinura
Superfamily Palinuroidea
Family Palinuridae
Panulirus argus (Latreille,
1804)
Infraorder Anomura
Superfamily Coenobitoidea
Family Diogenidae
Clibanarius vittatus (Bosc,
1802)
Dardanus fucosus Biffar
& Provanzano, 1972
Dardanus insignis
(Saussure, 1858)
Petrochirus diogenes
(Linné, 1758)
Superfamily Paguroidea
Family Paguridae
Pagurus annulipes
(Stimpson, 1860)

Pagurus carolinensis
McLaughlin, 1975
Pagurus longicarpus Say,
1817
Pagurus pollicaris Say,
1817
Superfamily Galatheoidea
Family Porcellanidae
Euceramus praelongus
Stimpson, 1860
Megalobrachium soriatum
(Say, 1818)
Petrolisthes galathinus
(Bosc, 1802)
Polyonyx gibbesi Haig,
1956
Porcellana sayana
(Leach, 1820)
Superfamily Hippoidea
Family Albuneidae
Albunea gibbesii
Stimpson, 1859
Albunea paretii Guérin-
Méneville, 1853
Lepidopa websteri
Benedict, 1903
Family Hippidae
Emerita benedicti
Schmitt, 1935
Emerita talpoida (Say,
1817)
Infraorder Brachyura
Section Dromiacea
Superfamily Dromioidea
Family Dromiidae
Dromidia antillensis
Stimpson, 1859
Hypoconcha arcuata
Stimpson, 1858
Section Oxystomata
Superfamily Leucosioidea
Family Calappidae

Calappa flammea
(Herbst, 1794)
Hepatus epheliticus
(Linné, 1763)
*Hepatus pudibundus
(Herbst, 1785)
Family Leucosiidae
Persephona mediterranea
(Herbst, 1794)
(= *Persephona punctata*)
Section Oxyrhyncha
Superfamily Majoidea
Family Majidae
Libinia dubia H. Milne-
Edwards, 1834
*Libinia emarginata
Leach, 1815
*Pelia mutica (Gibbes,
1850)
Stenorhynchus seticornis
(Herbst, 1788)
Section Cancridea
Superfamily Cancroidea
Family Cancridae
Cancer borealis Stimpson,
1859
Cancer irroratus Say,
1817
Section Brachyrhyncha
Superfamily Portunoidea
Family Portunidae
Arenaeus cribrarius
(Lamarck, 1818)
*Callinectes ornatus
Ordway, 1863
Callinectes sapidus
Rathbun, 1896
*Callinectes similis
Williams, 1966
Ovalipes ocellatus
(Herbst, 1799)
Ovalipes stephensoni
Williams, 1976

Portunus gibbesii
(Stimpson, 1859)
*Portunus sayi (Gibbes,
1850)
Portunus spinimanus
Latreille, 1819
Superfamily Xanthoidea
Family Xanthidae
*Eurypanopeus depressus
(Smith, 1869)
Eurytium limosum (Say,
1818)
Menippe mercenaria (Say,
1818)
*Neopanope sayi (Smith,
1869)
Panopeus herbstii H.
Milne-Edwards, 1834
*Panopeus obesus Smith,
1869
Pilumnus sayi Rathbun,
1897
*Rhithropanopeus harrisii
(Gould, 1841)
Superfamily Grapsidoidea
Family Grapsidae
Plagusia depressa
(Fabricius, 1775)
*Planes minutus (Linné,
1758)
*Pachygrapsus transversus
(Gibbes, 1850)
Sesarma cinereum (Bosc,
1802)
Sesarma reticulatum (Say,
1817)
Superfamily
Pinnotheroidea
Family Pinnotheridae
Dissodactylus mellitae
(Rathbun, 1900)
Pinnixa chaetopterana
(Stimpson, 1860)

Pinnixa cristata
Rathbun, 1900
Pinnixa cylindrica (Say,
1818)
Pinnixa lunzi Glasswell,
1937
Pinnixa retinens
Rathbun, 1918
Pinnixa sayana
Stimpson, 1860
Pinnotheres chamae
Roberts, 1975
Pinnotheres maculatus
Say, 1818
Pinnotheres ostreum Say,
1817
Superfamily Ocypodoidea
Family Ocypodidae
Ocypode quadrata
(Fabricius, 1787)
Uca minax (LeConte,
1855)
Uca pugilator (Bosc,
1802)
Uca pugnax (Smith, 1870)

Uca rapax (Smith, 1870)
Uca thayeri Rathbun,
1900
Subphylum Uniramia
Class Insecta
Subclass Apterygota
Order Collembola
Family Poduridae
Anurida maritima
Guérin, 1836
Subclass Pterygota
Order Coleoptera
Suborder Adephaga
Family Cicindelidae
Cicindela dorsalis Say,
1817
Cicindela gratiosa
Guérin-Méneville, 1840
Order Diptera
Suborder Nematocera
Superfamily Culicoidea
Family Chironomidae
Telmatogeton japonicus
Tokunaga, 1933

INDEX TO COMMON AND SCIENTIFIC NAMES

Pages with illustrations are indicated by italics. Pages with the primary description of a taxon are printed in bold type.

Index

408

Index

Index

Index

Index

416

Index

Index

Index

Index

424

Index

Index